THE THIRD TEMPTATION

Rethinking the Role of the Church in Politics

Austin Rogers

THE THIRD TEMPTATION

Copyright 2020 – Austin Rogers

Austin's writing can be found on the Libertarian Christian Institute blog as well as the finance website, Seeking Alpha, under the pseudonym, "Cashflow Capitalist."

Cover design by Bespoke Book Covers.

Formatting by Rik – Wild Seas Formatting
(http://WildSeasFormatting.com)

http://www.austinrogers.net

TABLE OF CONTENTS

A NARRATIVE PREFACE

Temptation in the Wilderness

His tongue catches against his dry gums like fish scales on fabric. Every hot breath further saps the moisture from his mouth and warms the inside of his chest. The sunlight cooks his already-burnt and craggy skin. His rib cage bulges as he sucks air into his tight throat. Weak groans escape him as even the act of inhaling and exhaling becomes a struggle.

At least the hunger pangs have passed. Four Sabbath days have gone by since the hunger wracked his body and threatened him with insanity. Forty times the sun has risen and set since the Spirit of God led him into the wilderness. How fresh his faith was then, in the beginning of this testing. How unwavering were his prayers. And now, even with faith unbroken, his body has decayed. His mind has slowed. His prayers have simplified to, *Abba, Abba*. The Father knows the feelings of his heart, the yearnings of his spirit. He remembers this truth with a small burst of hope and clings to it.

Blinking away soreness in his eyes from the sun's constant barrage, Yeshua lifts his heavy head to look up. In the distance, a figure as small as the jot of a pen wriggles amidst undulating waves of heat. It is a strange sight—movement. Yeshua has seen nothing move in this barren, sun-beaten landscape for as long as he can remember. The figure approaches, passing a few of the scarce shrubs and gnarled olive trees that grow in the Judean wilderness. A man takes shape, his arms, shoulders, and head shaded in a thin cloak. His torso leans to one side from the weight of a bucket which he carries in that hand. A cloth covers the top of it, draped between the handles.

Yeshua drops his eyes and whispers a prayer in his remaining moments of solitude.

"Abba, give me strength."

The traveler's sandals kick up small clouds of dust as he stops beside Yeshua, catches his breath for a moment, then sets the bucket down. Its contents slosh enticingly. A hand reaches down and swipes the cloth away, revealing many handfuls of shimmering, beautiful water. Yeshua's stomach quakes with thirst at the sight of it. He tells himself that faith is better, but his body rebels.

In the corner of his vision, Yeshua sees the traveler's feet shift one way and then the other as the man looks for a place to sit. A scraggly bush nearby offers some speckled shade.

"Still you have not found a tree to sit under," the traveler observes between breaths. His voice is familiar, the only voice Yeshua has heard since coming into the wilderness.

"I am not here to be comfortable," Yeshua replies weakly.

"Why *are* you here, then?" the traveler asks as he squats down to sit.

Yeshua presses his dry, cracked lips together. "You have always been curious, Lucifer. But it is not for you to know. Nor me. It is for the Father to know, the Spirit to guide, and the Son to obey."

Lucifer tilts his head back and laughs. He laughs like a man with full belly and lips still moist from his last drink.

"Even after this long in the wilderness," Lucifer says, "sermons drip from your tongue like spittle from a possessed man."

"You would know something about possessed men, wouldn't you?"

Yeshua lifts his eyes to look at the traveler sitting in the meager shade nearby. The hood darkens the man's face, but he can still see smooth-shaven skin, a prominent jawline, and a gleaming, lopsided smile. The haunting glints of his eyes hint at the terrible strength he possesses. The prince of this world senses no threat from a Galilean carpenter's son, feels no fear in his presence.

"There is much I know about men," Lucifer says with unfazed confidence. "I could teach you something, if you would like to hear it."

"Speak, then," Yeshua replies. "Teach the Son of Man a lesson about these creatures you know so well."

Lucifer leans forward and hooks his elbows over his knees, locking his hands together in front of them. His face takes on a new gravity.

"For as much as they fear my legions, they would rather be possessed and powerful than free and weak." Lucifer stares brazenly at the frail man before him. "I know something about you, too, Son of Man."

"You know only what you are permitted to know," Yeshua says.

"Oh, yes," Lucifer replies quickly. "I am permitted to know man. And I am permitted to know the Father. And I am permitted to know you. I have known you since this world was only a thought in the Father's mind."

Yeshua's nostrils whistle as he takes in a breath. "Say what you've come to say, Lucifer."

The hooded traveler stares a while longer, observing Yeshua, examining him. The Son has never seemed so vulnerable. So powerless. Lucifer waits and watches like a vulture contemplating whether to cut short its prey's misery. Yeshua has no doubt that Lucifer would do just that if given the chance.

Then, abruptly, Lucifer pushes off the ground, dusts off his hands, and steps to the bucket. A long ladle reaches up to the brim. He takes it and lifts a scoop of clear water, offering it to Yeshua.

"Drink."

The water ripples seductively in the ladle. Drops spill off the side and fall back into the bucket. Yeshua's parched tongue cries out for it, but he doesn't take it.

"Is it a sin to drink water?"

Yeshua turns his eyes away from the bucket. "I don't thirst for what you would give me."

"It's only water." Lucifer brings the ladle to his lips and sips off the side. He uses his cloak to wipe the excess off his chin and drops the ladle back into the bucket with a splash. "But you yearn for something greater than water, don't you?"

Yeshua closes his eyes and lets his head hang in front of his chest, resting. "What is it that I yearn for, Lucifer?"

The prince of this world paces in front of Yeshua, letting his cloak shield him from the sun. "You were born of a woman, were you not? You are flesh and blood, no different than any other man."

Yeshua does not waste his breath with an answer.

"They were made in your image," Lucifer says. "Their deepest desires are a reflection of their maker's deepest desires. Why else create them but for the joy of ruling over them, just as they enjoy their rule over creation? You yearn for power just as they do. But your beloved creatures have found a new master to serve, a master with many names, many faces. Like sheep, they have gone astray. You look upon your creation with jealousy. This isn't the way you wanted it, is it? That's why you have come. That's why you walk my world as one of them."

Yeshua stirs. "Your world?"

"Yes, *my* world," Lucifer insists. "The very same world that the Son of David now comes to reclaim. But he will have some trouble, for I have been quite busy since your creatures left Eden."

"You don't know the plans the Father has for this world," Yeshua says.

"No, not precisely," Lucifer replies, "but I know they will fail. Will the Lion of Judah try to rally his faithful zealots to retake Zion and sit on the throne of David? His armies will be like waves dashed against the rocks when my servant Tiberius Caesar hears of it. Will he rise to challenge Herod Antipas for reign over his homeland? Perhaps a reminder of Herod's commitment to his reign will dissuade him. Will he join the priesthood and try to reform the religion of Moses? Not after I whisper his subversive plans in the ear of Caiaphas."

Lucifer stops pacing. His shadow is cast on the sitting Galilean.

"You see, Yeshua, you cannot win. You cannot wrest this world from my hands. Its people have already chosen their master, and they didn't choose you."

The words grieve Yeshua in his heart. Even the Father of Lies can speak truth when it suits him. Yet Yeshua's mission remains the same. No words of Lucifer can weaken his resolve.

"But there is another way you can rule them," Lucifer says knowingly.

Yeshua's empty stomach writhes inside him as he ruminates on Lucifer's words.

"Open your eyes, Yeshua."

Yeshua cracks his eyelids and sees new colors around him. Gone is the sun-cracked soil of the wilderness. Now he sits in cold, hard-packed snow. The wind whips and flurries of snowflakes brush his skin. Lucifer stands before him, cloak fluttering, offering his hand. Yeshua takes it and, for the first time in days, rises shakily to his feet.

Once standing, the sight of Yeshua's surroundings startles him. He and Lucifer stand at the narrow peak of a high mountain. Its slopes curve down at treacherously steep angles. Beyond the mountain's foothills, in every direction, lie great cities and palaces and temples. To the west, buildings of white stone, bolstered by pristine Corinthian columns, sit upon seven hills. Statues of the caesars, adorned in carved armor and wearing laurels in their hair, rise in the city squares. To the east, the vast Han Dynasty sprawls across valleys and pastures. To the north and south, tribal chieftains squabble for power and prestige in forests, on plains, and across deserts.

"Behold, the kingdoms of the world in all their glory," Lucifer says. "Every tribe, nation, and tongue, every majestic empire and band of hunters . . . These are the people you have come to take back under your rulership, are they not?"

Yeshua says nothing, only marvels at this panoramic vision of the world of men.

"They can be your people," Lucifer says in a soft voice. "Every kingdom and nation and tribe can be yours to rule however you wish. Tiberius and Herod can be your regents, if you wish, or you can replace them with others. You can be king of kings, or you can get rid of them all and be the world's only sovereign."

Yeshua studies Lucifer as the prince of this world weaves his web. Lucifer flashes a brief smile before turning to pace around their platform of even ground on the mountain peak.

He stretches out his arm and points to a bowl-shaped structure embedded in a vast city. "Look upon the amphitheater, where, daily, men are sliced to pieces as crowds cheer. You could stop the bloodshed immediately and put an end to the gladiatorial games forever. Imagine standing in the center of the theater with an audience of thousands listening to your words."

Lucifer's gaze shifts to a tall, sturdy temple atop one of the seven hills. "And there, in the Temple of Venus, young girls are taught how to please men and the gods with their bodies. They do not choose that life, of course. You could declare an edict against temple prostitution and spare the girls 'innocence, once and for all."

Lucifer turns back to Yeshua's homeland, the land between the Mediterranean Sea and the Jordan River. "Look at your people as they languish under Roman rule. The land that was promised to Abraham and his descendants is trampled upon by foreign soldiers in service to their foreign king. Your people live in the territory of their forefathers but they might as well be back in Egypt, enslaved to the pharaoh, doing his bidding. You could free them. You could restore the land to them as your prophets promised."

Yeshua feels a warmth in his heart for his people, a pain for their oppression. But the pain only worsens when his eyes sweep past the rest of creation. Warlords and generals plot wars that would claim the lives of millions. Slavers bind his image-bearers into lifelong servitude. Infants are thrown into the fire to appease demons dressed in divine garb. Kings amass vaults of grain and gold while their people starve. Widows and orphans eat scraps and drink filthy water to survive.

"And think of what the future holds," Lucifer says with wonder. "Horrors the people of this world cannot yet imagine. Weapons that kill hundreds or thousands of men with one blow. Cruel princes who turn the sword on their own people. Perhaps some of them will turn the sword on *your* people, Yeshua." Lucifer smiles as he gazes into the distance. "My imagination is rich."

Yeshua sees the untamed cruelty in Lucifer's heart, and also his cunning. "You would give this up of your own will?"

"Yes," Lucifer says without hesitation. "I would hand you the crowns of every kingdom of the world and they would be yours to do with as you please."

"What do you want, Lucifer?" Yeshua asks.

Lucifer sobers. His eyes do not waver in their distant stare.

"I want what I have always wanted but can now rightfully claim. Every ruler and authority demands submission. Every prince commands his people's worship." Lucifer faces Yeshua and shamelessly meets his eyes. "I am the ruler of this world. Its kings are my captains. Its warriors, my servants. And yet they don't know me. They don't offer me praise because they don't know I am there. But you know me, Yeshua. You know what power and authority I possess. You know I am free to roam this world and enslave its people."

Lucifer straightens his back and stands tall. "Just as I am the only one who can give you what you want, you are the only one who can give me what I want."

"I ask again," Yeshua says. "What *do* you want?"

"When you took on human flesh, you entered my domain," Lucifer says with fire in his eyes. "So bow to me. Worship me as king of all the kingdoms of the earth. And then . . . I will give them to you. All of their glory and power will be yours forever."

Yeshua steps away and lets his gaze fall back down to the kingdoms of the world. His mind swarms with thoughts. He could sit on the Throne of David and rule the world with justice and love. His people could walk freely up to the mountain of the Lord, to the house of the God of Jacob. Yeshua could teach all men his ways so that they would walk in his paths. From out of Zion could come righteous laws, and the word of the Lord could be heard from Jerusalem. Yeshua could judge among the nations and rebuke those who rebel against his perfect law. He could command all the people in all the lands to beat their swords into plowshares and their spears into pruning hooks so that nation would never again rise up against nation, and neither would men learn war anymore.

And all of this he could have *now*. Not many thousands of years in the future. Now. He could have it painlessly. He could have it without struggle or strife.

Yeshua's eyes cloud and a tear breaks down his cheek. How desperately he longs for such a world! But it is not the Father's plan to make it so. Not yet. Not like this.

"You know the Scriptures." Yeshua closes his eyes to squeeze off the flow of tears.

"Yes," Lucifer says impatiently. "What of them?"

"It is written," Yeshua says, "'You shall worship the Lord your God, and him only shall you serve.'"

Lucifer growls in frustration. "*Think*, Yeshua! You know what I'm capable of. You know what I can do to you."

Yeshua rubs the skin of his wrist with his thumb. His legs weaken with the thought of what his future holds. But his faith does not break.

In a small but firm voice, Yeshua says, "Begone, Satan."

In an instant, the snowy wind ceases. The cold disappears. The dry air scorches Yeshua's throat again. He opens his eyes and finds himself back in the wilderness. The sun hovers above the horizon, casting long shadows past the bushes and olive trees. The cicadas croon their evening song. Figures approach swiftly from behind bushes and boulders—angels sent by the Father. One of them drops to his knee beside Yeshua and pulls the cork from a waterskin.

"Drink, Yeshua."

Yeshua takes it gladly and gulps huge helpings of water. The cool stream floods his mouth, flows down his throat, fills his aching belly. In his heart he feels a twinge of sadness and fear about his fate. But he clings to the knowledge that the Father's plan is greater—*infinitely* greater—than all the kingdoms of this world.

INTRODUCTION

The Wilderness Battlefield

Sometimes the most familiar things in life hold some of the most surprising insights. Subtle but powerful truths get overlooked as our acquaintance with the subject matter grows deeper and more entrenched. Things that would stand out to a newcomer are lost on us because our minds naturally focus on the same old points they always have. Familiarity breeds a selective blindness.

As a lifelong Christian raised in a Christian home, I have experienced such "familiarity blindness" on numerous occasions when reading Scripture. I think of John 3:16, probably the most famous Bible verse today, which reads (everyone say it with me), "For God so loved the world, that he gave his only Son, that whoever believes in him should not perish but have eternal life." For someone who has had that verse memorized since he first learned to read, the words sound flat and trite. Only after intentionally setting out to mine their riches can the verse come alive again.

Something similar happened recently with a different passage of Scripture, only this time the words struck a new chord. The passage came alive and called out to me like a voice in the wilderness. What was previously opaque and seemingly inapplicable to today's world became illuminated and timelessly applicable.

The narrative comes from the period just before the beginning of Christ's earthly ministry, recorded in Matthew 4 (and Luke 4). After being baptized by John the Baptist, Jesus is led by the Holy Spirit into the wilderness to be tempted (a word in the Greek that can also mean "tested") by Satan. The text says that Jesus spent forty days and nights in the wilderness during this time of testing, an obvious harkening back to the Israelites' forty-year period of testing in the wilderness outside of the Promised Land (Deut. 8:2-3). Because of their disobedience, they were not allowed to partake in the land and blessings that God had promised them. Jesus, a representative of the Jewish people, goes into the wilderness to redeem his people's disobedience through his own act of obedience.

After forty days and nights of going without food, naturally, Jesus is hungry. He must also be incredibly weak and frail. The human body isn't meant to go that long without sustenance. Enter Satan, the tempter, when Jesus is in the most vulnerable state of his life thus far. First, Satan tempts Jesus with the obvious: food. You're hungry, Jesus. Command these stones to become loaves of bread. How could anyone resist such a temptation? It is within Jesus's power to miraculously provide himself with desert manna, and surely he wanted it. Carbohydrates are the body's primary source of energy, and bread tastes wonderful when you're starving.

Lacking any physical strength of his own, Jesus relies on the truth of Scripture: "Man shall not live by bread alone, but by every word that comes from the mouth of God."

If Jesus is able to resist such a base, imminently human lure as food, Satan realizes he needs to be more clever. Jesus has grown up soaked in Scripture, devouring it daily, even debating it with the rabbis. Satan sees where Jesus's confidence lies, so he takes Jesus to the highest peak of the temple's rooftop to tempt him right at the source of his confidence. In essence, he says to Jesus, quoting Psalm 91, "If you really are the Son of God, jump off. The angels will catch you. Surely they wouldn't let any harm come upon the Son of God!"

Satan thinks he has Jesus trapped. If Jesus jumps, he will have done so for a vain reason—to prove himself. If Jesus doesn't jump, Satan will be proven right that Jesus is not the

Son of God and has no authority over the angels.

Again, Jesus destroys this false dilemma and resists temptation by quoting Scripture: "You shall not put the Lord your God to the test."

After two false starts, Satan is desperate. He realizes Jesus is more formidable than he looks in his current frail state. He needs to pull out all the stops. He needs to tempt Jesus with something that will be absolutely irresistible to him. So Satan thinks about why Jesus is here, walking the earth as a human being. Why would God lower himself to take on flesh? It must be in order to attain greater glory on earth. The Jewish Messiah, after all, was predicted to be a warrior king, breaking nations and bringing the world under his rulership. Yes, Jesus must be here to become that Warrior Messiah and conquer all the kingdoms of the world. Here, Satan believes he has the upper hand, because the whole world and its kingdoms lie in his power (1 Jn 5:19).

Satan thinks that if he offers Jesus the very thing for which Jesus came to Earth, the Messiah will have to give in, and Satan will be able to ask for whatever he wants in return.

So what does Satan offer? All the kingdoms of the world and their glory.

"All these I will give you," Satan says, "if you will fall down and worship me" (Matt. 4:9). Satan, whose name in Hebrew means "enemy" or "adversary," cares less about controlling earthly kingdoms and governments than he does about thwarting the plans of God. Whether or not Satan knew or had any inkling that Jesus's actual purpose on Earth was the saving cross rather than the conquering sword, he figured that if he could corrupt it, the entire plan would collapse. Just the slightest compromise—a momentary act of worship—would be victory enough for Satan and, presumably, enough to defeat God.

From Jesus's perspective, this offer is the greatest of all of Satan's temptations, for it presents a way that Jesus might reassert rule over creation *without* having to suffer the painful self-sacrifice of the cross. We know that Jesus will feel tremendous fear and anguish about his sacrificial death some years later (Lk 22:44), but that event must loom in the back of his mind even during the wilderness temptations. Moreover, the idea of gaining power over *all* earthly nations, as well as the glory of being their king, in exchange for such a seemingly innocuous act as briefly bending the knee to Satan, bears a strong allure.

Of course, in retrospect, we know that in the wilderness Satan displayed a fundamental misunderstanding of God and His plan for the world through His Son. Rather than retaking the nation of Israel for God, re-instituting a complex code of laws, and crushing all earthly forces that oppose them, Jesus came to change the world in a radically different way. He came to conquer the earthly kingdoms and overthrow Satan's reign not by shedding the blood of his enemies and thereby forcing them into submission, but by shedding *his own* blood and thereby swaying them to his cause from the inside out. "I will give them one heart, and a new spirit I will put within them," God promised in Ezekiel 11:19 (and 36:26). "I will remove the heart of stone from their flesh and give them a heart of flesh." God's plan is to take over the world through changing hearts so that all of His subjects are willing and joyful.

There are no dissidents in the Kingdom of God. There is no opposition party. That is what Satan misunderstands. He believes he can give Jesus what Jesus wants (the kingdoms of the earth and their glory), Jesus can give Satan what Satan wants (worship and recognition from his divine nemesis), and they can both happily go their separate ways. But notice that while Satan offered to give up his rule over mankind's kingdoms, he never offered to release his grasp on human hearts. Satan's political power would be turned over to Christ, but his subtler and more entrenched influence over humanity would remain without constraints. What good would it be for Jesus to gain the whole world and yet forfeit the soul of his mission there? The answer is none. That would be putting the cart before the horse—politics before the gospel.

So why does Jesus turn down Satan's offer? He turns it down because *means* matter just as much as *ends*. The importance of the goal is matched by how that goal is achieved, and thus doing evil so that good may result is just as condemnable as doing evil so that evil may result (Rom. 3:8). It wouldn't suit God's character to be glorified and to become the name at which every knee should bow just by any means necessary. Jesus has a specific plan and purpose through which he will be glorified and become the name at which every knee should bow (see Phil. 2:4-11).

Therefore, Jesus responds to Satan's third temptation in the wilderness by quoting Scripture yet again—"You shall worship the Lord your God, and him only shall you serve"—and affirming that God's plan is indeed greater than all the kingdoms of the world.

* * *

The purpose of this book, in short, is to explore the political implications of Christ's denial of earthly power in the third temptation. More broadly, the book will attempt to construct a biblical view of earthly power and human governments, how God's people ought to relate to those institutions, and some principles of good governance that the church ought to encourage.

Of course, in order to more fully understand God's intention for government, we must understand God's overarching plan for creation. Why did God create humans to begin with? What kind of relationship did God intend to have with humans? Was government part of God's plan from the beginning? These questions will be discussed in chapter one, before anything else, because our answers will lay the groundwork for the rest of the book. God is not arbitrary about what He does; when He acts, He acts with intention. Knowing how God arranged things in a sinless world may not tell us exactly how to arrange things in a world stained by sin, but it will help us understand God's ideals and the ultimate goals we should aim for in our imperfect world.

The presence of sin in the world tainted all human endeavors, but some were corrupted faster than others. Working and childbearing immediately became painful and difficult, but governmental structures took some time to develop, and some of their early forms (which wouldn't even be considered governments the way we use the word now) were not objectionable to God. Only when they formed kingdoms did their governments threaten God's desired relationship with humanity. Chapter two will cover the form of social organization that God found acceptable as well as the slide toward a powerful and centralized government that went against God's wishes. Interestingly, God accommodated His people despite their rejection of Him as their sole King.

In chapter three, we will examine the Kingdom of God which Christ inaugurated as well as the *manner* in which he inaugurated it. The church lives in an age when the Kingdom has *already* broken in, and believers can and should shape our lives to reflect this reality. And yet, we must acknowledge that the Kingdom of which we are citizens has *not yet* fully manifested in creation (only God can make it so), and thus we must temper our expectations of earthly governments. Instead, we must see ourselves as ambassadors living in a foreign land and put on the uniquely Christlike character traits of the Kingdom of God.

In chapter four, we tackle the God-given role of earthly governments (the state) in the church age. For this task, we will construct a definition of the state from several biblical passages that deal with it directly, then we will extrapolate the few functions that governments have explicitly been assigned by God to play. In the process, it will be necessary to deal with the thorny issue of how Satan's earthly authority fits with God's sovereignty. If no authority exists except as granted by God, how can Satan claim that all earthly authority "has been delivered to me, and I give it to whom I will" (Lk 4:6)? How can Satan gift powers that aren't really his? Is he simply lying to Jesus about this ability? Or might there be some nuanced explanation of the spiritual balance of power?

Chapter five will deal with how the New Testament authors approach the church's relationship to the state. The church and the state have unique roles to play in the world. As we will see from Scripture, the two institutions 'roles are compatible and complementary but also distinct and non-overlapping. This concept is of utmost importance. Nearly every misuse of government power encouraged or carried out by Christians, from the crusades to the Inquisition to the Salem witch trials, is at least partially attributable to a misunderstanding of this relationship. God designed church and state to function independently from each other, and that is how each works best. The church cannot fulfill the gospel by means of the sword, and the state cannot restrain and punish evil by means of the cross. This nifty formula may seem trite, but it has profound consequences for the Christian political philosophy that are sometimes difficult to accept.

Consistency in this historically unprecedented New Testament principle (separation of church and state) is rare among contemporary American Christians, and, as we will see in chapter six, it has been rare in Western Christianity since the era of Emperor Constantine. In the first few centuries after Christ, however, alliances with the state were scarcely an option, and thus not a temptation, for the early church. It will be insightful, then, to trace the widespread view of the relationship between church and state among the early church fathers up to the conversion of Emperor Constantine in 313 AD.

During the reign of Constantine, the Roman Empire's population was split between adherents to the traditional Roman panoply of gods—and the various sects stemming from it—and followers of the small but rapidly growing monotheistic religion called Christianity. This decentralized Christian religion had become well known throughout the empire and swung back and forth through periods of relative peace and persecution. Another emperor in this era, Diocletian, had in 303 AD declared the most widespread and organized persecution of Christians the world had seen to date. It lasted until 311 AD, when the empire issued an official edict of toleration toward the Christians, followed two years later by the Edict of Milan, which made freedom of religion an empire-wide policy. In two years the church witnessed a shift from the worst persecution of their 300-year history to open and official acceptance by their former persecutors.

After Emperor Constantine saw a vision of a cross in the sky (which he believed helped him win the Battle of Milvian Bridge) in 312 AD, Constantine's government began operating with a friendliness to, and eventually a preference for, Christians. By 324, the emperor began generously patronizing the church. Roman temples were converted into churches. Great shrines were built in the newly declared capital, Constantinople (named, of course, after Constantine). Bibles were copied and distributed. The practice of crucifixion was banned. Christianity intermixed with paganism to shape the character of Rome. But, as we will see in chapter six, this intermingling also changed the character of the church. What was once decentralized and focused on practicing the gospel with purity of heart became centralized in a hierarchical authority structure and preoccupied with defining doctrines and dominating thought. In 380 AD, the highest authorities of the Roman Empire issued the Edict of Thessalonica, making Christianity—specifically, *Trinitarian* Christianity—the official state religion of the empire. The state went even further when, in 391, under the influence of the Bishop of Milan, Emperor Theodosius issued his "Theodosian Decrees" eliminating freedom of religion in the Roman Empire. With the approval of their governing authorities, Christians pillaged and destroyed many pagan temples, shrines, and tombs, and even killed pagan priests. Adherents of the traditional Roman religion were driven underground and often feigned belief in

Christianity so as not to be oppressed.

In less than a hundred years, Christians had gone from the *persecuted* to the *persecutors*.

In chapter seven, we will sum up the political principles we have garnered from our study of Scripture and history thus far. A general framework of two compatible but non-overlapping kingdoms will emerge. Church and state, as we will see, are complementary yet distinct bodies in the world, each with unique roles to play. The two-pronged thesis of this book, in short, is that (1) *The ideal political state is one in which God exercises direct authority over His human creatures*, and also that (2) *Christ denied using earthly power and government to accomplish his mission, and since Christians are called to imitate Christ, we should do the same.*

This does not mean that Christians cannot engage in politics, only that they should not do so in an attempt to fulfill the church's specific, God-given mission. Likewise, we ought to encourage the government to remain within its limited, God-given role of restraining evil and fairly dispensing retribution. As stated previously, the church cannot fulfill the gospel by means of the sword, and the state cannot restrain and punish evil by means of the cross. It is impossible to make disciples and to teach them to obey all that Christ commanded through force, and it is equally impossible to restrain and punish evil by turning the other cheek.

Thereafter, at long last, will come the section of the book applying these biblical principles to our contemporary political context. As we will see in these chapters, the biblical principles we have gathered as well as specific Bible passages speak to a broad range of topics, although they often do not provide answers that would fit on a bumper sticker. Some issues are simply more complicated, and require a more nuanced approach, than many Christians on the political Right or Left would prefer.

On other contemporary political issues, such as immigration, global trade, climate change, or the right to possess firearms, the Bible is silent. While biblical teachings provide guidance for Christians in all areas of life, there are not unambiguous instructions on how (or if) the governing authorities ought to handle certain issues. On those subjects, we ought to take the advice that God gave to His exiled people in Jeremiah 29:7: "Seek the welfare [Hebrew: *shalom*] of the city where I have sent you into exile, and pray to the Lord on its behalf, for in its welfare you will find your welfare." In other words: Do what is best for society as a whole rather than merely what would benefit you individually or as a group. Chapter thirteen will address these silent issues and seek to disprove those who twist Scripture in an attempt to justify their preconceived political stances on these topics.

The book will close with some final comments tying together the various strands of thought woven through our study and attempt to connect our political theology with the situation we find ourselves in today as we enter into the third decade of the twenty-first century.

My sincere hope and prayer for this book is that it would be a conduit through which Christians of all political persuasions and national contexts (not just American!) learn more about the role of the church in the political realm. I hope and pray that whatever biblical truths *The Third Temptation* imparts would remain with you, the reader, and that any mistaken ideas or ways of thinking — anything contrary to the Word of God — would blow away like chaff in the wind.

Also, I readily acknowledge that I am an imperfect vessel through which to impart these ideas, but I have yet to find another book that makes the particular case made here. While my ideas and arguments are by no means wholly original, I believe they need to be presented clearly and comprehensively in today's turbulent political context.

* * *

A Note on Personal Bias

In the book *The Righteous Mind*, Jonathan Haidt argues with unsettling persuasion that our reasoning about political and religious subjects operates roughly the opposite of the way most of us assume it does. While most of us believe that our political views and religious beliefs are the product of evidence- and logic-based reasoning, Haidt says that we tend to hold these convictions without reasoning or evidence *until* they are required.

He gives an illustration of an elephant and a rider. The rider attempts to exert control over the elephant, but the elephant is powerful and stubborn and more often than not controls the direction both of them go. In this illustration, Haidt labels the rider as the "reasoning-why" function of our brain that uses cold, hard logic. The elephant is the "seeing-that" function of our brains—emotion, instinct, gut reactions.

Most of us think of ourselves as logical creatures, whose emotions and intuitions are subservient to our reasoning abilities. Not so, says Haidt. He says that "thinking is the rider; affect is the elephant. The thinking system is not equipped to lead—it simply doesn't have the power to make things happen—but it can be a useful advisor."[1] Why is this? Because, the way our brains work, "intuitions come first, strategic reasoning second." First we have hunches, gut reactions, or snap judgements about ideas, then we evaluate them based on those intuitive responses, *and then* we use strategic reasoning to prove that our intuitive responses are truthful. In other words, we instinctively believe certain things, due to upbringing or education or for whatever reasons, and we use our rational abilities when necessary to defend *why* we believe those things or when trying to persuade others of our instinctive beliefs. As Haidt puts it, "[w]e do moral reasoning not to reconstruct the actual reasons why *we ourselves* came to a judgement; we reason

---

[1] Haidt, Jonathan. *The Righteous Mind*, 66.

to find the best possible reasons why *somebody else ought to join us* in our judgement."[2]

In essence, Haidt is echoing an observation made by the ancient Greek philosopher Demosthenes: "Nothing is easier than self-deceit. For what every man wishes, that he also believes to be true." Consciously or unconsciously (typically the latter), we believe what we *want* to believe, what we are *predisposed* to believe. That bias shapes the direction we go in our thinking and the sources of information we trust.

Haidt demonstrates how our moral intuitions are often formed by groupthink—identification with those whom we are familiar and comfortable, along with a desire to fit in. We learn from a young age that it feels good to be commended by family and community members for behaving in certain ways or professing certain beliefs. This unconscious desire for social acceptance heavily informs the intuitive elephant on which our logical selves ride. As children, teenagers, and young adults, "fitting in" and being accepted and admired by our tribe—whether it be family, peers, or respected authority figures—is one of the weightiest factors in the formation of self-esteem. It's also one of the most significant factors in the formation of one's moral intuitions and worldview.

Haidt's conclusion about politics is that each one of us views it somewhat like we would an inkblot picture. Psychologists use inkblot pictures—seemingly random blotches of black or variously colored ink on a white background—in what's called a Rorschach Test to discern the innermost aspects of their subject's mind and thinking. The blotches of ink on paper form no actual patterns or depictions, but by asking the subject what they see in them, psychologists believe that one's core, instinctive ways of thinking can be extracted. Politics, in Haidt's view, is less about rational disagreements than it is about differing instincts—seeing different pictures from the same blotches of ink. Some feel a

---

[2] Haidt, Jonathan. *The Righteous Mind*, 52

stronger instinct about patriotism, for instance, while others feel a stronger instinct about equality.

Regardless how much of a role our instincts play in the formation of our political views, it would be arrogant to doubt that they play *any* role. None of us arrived at our political stances in a vacuum. Someone or another, whether it be our parents, teachers, friends, coworkers, or favorite late-night talk show hosts, have influenced us to lean toward certain values. You, the reader, probably approach this book with preconceived notions about political rights and wrongs, truths and falsehoods. Some of your political views just seem intuitively and inevitably true. I can sympathize.

I come from a loving, evangelical Christian family, and as I grew up I yearned for their approval (and still do). I attended a private Christian high school and got my bachelor's degree from Biola University. The word "Biola" is an acronym for the "**B**ible **I**nstitute **o**f **L**os **A**ngeles." My family, both immediate and extended, is thoroughly conservative—culturally, politically, and theologically. So was my high school, as well as most of my friends there. My college experience boasted slightly more diversity of political opinion, but not that much. Biola prides itself on its theological conservatism, and that often translates into political conservatism. In graduate school at Western State Colorado University, in which I studied creative writing, I was hit with a major culture shock, being immersed in a close-knit cohort of politically and religiously disparate individuals with whom I remain friends today. And finally, it shouldn't be left out that I come from several generations of successful businessmen, who I admire and would certainly like to emulate.

I admit these things neither to disparage nor to celebrate my heritage. While I'm immensely grateful for the family in which I grew up and the schools at which I've studied, I want to be careful not to let them inform my reading of Scripture or the principles derived from it. This book will not seek to defend a progressive or conservative point of view. It will not presume the basic goodness of one political party and the ignorance or wickedness of the other. It will search the scriptures for a framework to understand and deal with our contemporary political context, and *then and only then* will it draw applicable conclusions. Some of those conclusions may seem closer to progressive ways of thinking, while others may resemble conservative ways of thinking. We should not expect any or all of the political principles we might draw from the various writings of the Bible, completed two millennia ago, to neatly fit our twenty-first century Left-Right dichotomy. If they do, praise God! Voting will be easy. But we shouldn't expect it.

Perhaps I am too ambitious in my presumption of neutrality. Perhaps my personal political instincts will creep back in and inform my interpretation of Scripture or my reasoning about the principles derived from it. I will leave it to the reader to determine if I fall prey to that temptation. But I hope that, through careful interpretation and reasoning, we might arrive at whatever truth about this subject God has made available to us.

With that said, let us humbly and prayerfully begin our task of rethinking the church's role in politics.

CHAPTER ONE

Walking in the Garden: Why God Created Humans

When I was a kid, I played a computer game called *The Sims*. Maybe you've heard of it or played it yourself. The basic idea is that you have the godlike power to create characters, plop them into an open world, and control them as they live their lives. Characters can go to work, go out to eat, enjoy a variety of potential hobbies, woo a mate, or cook delectable meals. Of course, Sims characters are also annoyingly needy; they regularly require food, water, trips to the bathroom, and eight hour periods of sleep.

But after a while of playing *The Sims*, the game began to feel empty and shallow. My characters felt like hollow vessels. The game felt pointless. After a while of controlling characters who get up, go to work, come home to play their guitar or cook dinner, then go to sleep only to wake up and repeat the process again, the experience felt vacuous to me. I felt no connection to my character-creatures, and there was no overarching story to latch onto. Why did I choose to immerse myself in this game to begin with?

Compare this to the God of the Bible's creation and creatures. Orthodox Christian theology holds that God created *ex nihilo*—out of nothing. If God has the power to create *something* from *nothing*, then it is reasonable to assume He could have created any kind of world He wanted. If God can create any kind of world He wants and He chose to create *this one* with *these* creatures inhabiting it, clearly He did so for a reason. When God acts, He does so with a purpose.

So when God spoke matter and energy into existence and set all the bodies of the universe into movement, He *must have* had a reason for doing so. When He planted a garden and caused trees to shoot up from the ground, He did so with an intention. When God formed man from the dust of the ground, breathed life into his nostrils, and fashioned into him the divine image, God had a purpose. This notion that creation has a design and purpose from its Creator is called *teleology*.

It's somewhat easier to understand why God would create an unconscious universe than living, breathing, divine-image-bearing creatures. Why does a painter paint a beautiful landscape? Why does a musician string notes together into a lovely melody? Why does a poet painstakingly craft lines and lyrics? Why does an architect design elegant buildings?

The answer to each of these questions is the same as the answer often given for why God created: *for the pleasure of the creator*. It's a reasonable conclusion. The primary reason why anyone creates something beautiful is to enjoy it, to take pleasure in its existence. Looking at pictures of the universe captured by the Hubble Space Telescope or watching high-definition documentary footage of nature, it's easy to grasp that the One who created it all did so for His pleasure. No other answer seems necessary.

But for humans—conscious, intelligent creatures who bear the image of their Creator—more needs to be said. Yes, of course God created us for His pleasure the same as the rest of creation, but He had more in mind than that. His intentions ran deeper than simple satisfaction with the final product.

David wonders about this in Psalm 8:3-4: "When I look at your heavens, the work of your fingers, the moon and the stars, which you have set in place, what is man that you are mindful of him, and the son of man that you care for him?"

In contrast to deistic depictions of a god who sets creation into motion and then sits back, aloof, watching indifferently as history unfolds, David's question presupposes a God who cares intimately about these special creatures called humans.

Despite the size and wonder of creation—at least 93 billion lightyears in diameter—God takes an interest in these five- or- six-foot-tall, bipedal, mostly hairless mammals that roam the plains of the third planet in their solar system. And yet, small and seemingly insignificant as we humans are, "You have given him dominion over the works of your hands," says David in Psalm 8:6, "you have put all things under his feet."

Here we find the first aspect of man's intended purpose.

Dominion. Specifically, dominion over creation—"the works of [God's] hands."

It's an often misunderstood concept in the Bible. It doesn't mean unrestricted or unlimited power over creation. It isn't total freedom to do with creation as we wish, though some of the language used in Genesis seems to imply that. "Be fruitful and multiply and fill the earth and *subdue it and have dominion over the fish of the sea and over the birds of the heavens and over every living thing that moves on the earth*" (Gen. 1:28). It certainly *sounds* as if God gave the first humans free reign over creation to do whatever they wished with it and with its creatures. But pay attention to the very next thing God said: "Behold, I have given you every plant yielding seed that is on the face of all the earth, and every tree with seed in its fruit. You shall have them for food" (v. 29). Within the span of one breath God has placed limitations on man's dominion over creation and its creatures in the form of a dietary restriction. The humans can't eat the animals over which God has given them dominion.

Dominion does not equal ultimate ownership. God remains the owner of the animals. "Every beast of the forest is mine," God says in Psalm 50:10-11, "the cattle on a thousand hills. I know all the birds of the hills, and all that moves in the field is mine." God never gave away ownership of creation or its creatures, but He did endow humans with the privilege of exercising control over it. And, of course, with privilege comes responsibility.

Jump ahead to Genesis 2:15, where, "The Lord God took the man and put him in the garden of Eden to work it and keep it."

Here we find not just a boundary to man's dominion, but a duty that God has assigned him to fulfill. Humans are to be God's groundskeepers, the stewards of His land. It makes sense why God would command His people later in the Bible that "[t]he land shall not be sold in perpetuity, *for the land is mine. For you are strangers and sojourners with me*" (Lev. 25:23). Of course, it wasn't God's intention to denigrate His people in this verse, merely to communicate what He effectively communicated to Adam: Your dominion over this land is like a tutor's dominion over a pupil; it is not ultimately yours, but nevertheless you are responsible for it.

* * *

God With Us

So we know that one of God's original intentions for humanity (which was never taken away in the Fall, by the way) was to exercise *dominion* over His creation. And we know that "dominion" here refers to responsible care for God's land and animals. But is that the only intention God had for humans? Did God create them simply to maintain the grounds of His earthly estate while He admires their work from a distance?

No. We are given a hint of another intention God had for humans in Genesis 3:8, which comes just after Adam and Eve had eaten the fruit from which they had been commanded not to eat and then made fig-leaf clothing to hide their nakedness. "And they heard the sound of the Lord God walking in the garden in the cool of the day—" Let's pause right there. We know what happens next. God questions the humans, receives a few blame-shifting confessions, and then banishes them from the garden for their disobedience. But we can't overlook the significance of verse 8. The idea of God walking in the garden doesn't immediately stand out as noteworthy because it falls in the midst of a dramatic and tense story—the Fall of creation and the introduction of sin into the world. But think about the verse itself, the idea of God taking a stroll through the garden to visit His image-bearers. This divine being of awesome, unimaginable power is "walking in the garden in the cool of the day." It's a surprisingly humble act for a divine being to lower himself to the level of humans and walk amongst them, especially for the age when Genesis was written. In the ancient Near East, the gods were petty, frequently squabbling with each other for power, and often, creation or various parts of creation came about as a byproduct of the gods 'infighting. In the Babylonian *Enuma Elish* story, the god Marduk kills a goddess named Tiamat, then splits her carcass in half and uses part of it to create the heavens and the other part to create land.[3]

Not only was the idea of only *one* God unique to the religion of the Hebrews at the time Genesis was written, the idea of God taking casual walks on earth to visit His human creatures was unheard of. Yet that is what we find in the Bible. From what we can tell from the text, God has no ulterior motives for visiting His humans. He's just popping in to see them. Unlike the common theme in Sumerian and Mesopotamian creation myths of humans being formed to provide for the gods in some way, God doesn't *need* humans or use them as His laborers. "If I were hungry," God says in Psalm 50:12, "I would not tell you, for the world and its fullness are mine." God, of course, doesn't get hungry, but what He's saying here is that *even if He did get hungry*, He wouldn't need humans to work or provide for Him. As the Apostle Paul said to the men of Athens, "The God who made the world and everything in it, being Lord of heaven and earth, does not live in temples made by man, nor is he served by human hands, as though he needed anything, since he himself gives to all mankind life and breath and everything" (Acts 17:24-25).

God wasn't walking through the garden to make sure his human peons were hard at work to provide for Him. Nor, by the way, was He visiting out of loneliness. We know God

____

[3] See https://www.metmuseum.org/toah/hd/epic/hd_epic.htm.

wasn't lonely before humans or before anything in creation was made because *God wasn't alone.* No, I'm not referring to the angels who predate the creation of the heavens and the earth. I'm referring to the uniquely Christian mystery of the Trinity. God the Father, God the Son, and God the Spirit existed in an eternal relationship before humans came about. As Jesus prayed in John 17:5, "Father, glorify me in your own presence with the glory that I had with you *before the world existed*" (see also verse 24). We see a hint of this divine relationship in Genesis 1:26 when God says in the plural, "Let *us* make man in *our* image, after *our* likeness."

So we know that God purposely created humans in His own image, but He didn't do so because He needed workers, and neither did He need someone to soothe His loneliness. Why did He make us, then? Why did He come to walk in the garden (presumably a regular occurrence) and visit His human creatures?

The key idea here is that *God simply wants to be with us.* We humans have been made in the image of God so that we can live in a harmonious, intimate relationship with our Creator. He made us to be *like* Him so that we could *relate* to Him like none other of His creatures. That is why God would go for walks in the garden of Eden in the cool of the day. That is why, in the new heavens and the new earth, after Satan has been defeated and sin and death have been wiped out, an announcement will be made from the throne of God saying, "Behold, the dwelling place of God is with man. He will dwell with them, and they will be his people, and God himself will be with them as their God" (Rev. 21:3). God's ultimate goal for humanity, His ultimate desire for us, is simply to reside in His peaceful Kingdom as His citizens and relate to Him without any barriers or mediators. God longs for the day when His servants (those of us who have submitted our lives to Him) will worship Him, not from afar, but right before His throne. "They will see his face, and his name will be on their foreheads. And night will be no more. They will need no light of lamp or sun, for the Lord God will be their light, and they will reign forever and ever" (Rev. 22:4-5). Never before in history, except perhaps in the garden of Eden, have humans seen the face of God— whatever form that takes. But in the new heavens and the new earth we will. We will be marked as belonging to God, and we will reign (presumably over creation) with Him for all eternity, just as we were designed to from the beginning.

This concept of God simply wanting to be with us is uniquely Judeo-Christian. The attentive reader of Scripture will find it in both Old and New Testaments.

"I will make my dwelling among you," God says to His people, "and my soul shall not abhor you. And I will walk among you and will be your God, and you shall be my people" (Lev. 26:11-12). Just like in the garden of Eden, God longs simply to dwell with His image-bearers, to walk among them, and to be their God. (See also Ezek. 37:26-28.)

Even after His people sin and go astray, God's love for them remains. "But now thus says the Lord, he who created you, O Jacob, he who formed you, O Israel: Fear not, for I have redeemed you; I have called you by name, you are mine. When you pass through the waters, I will be with you. . . For I am the Lord your God, the Holy One of Israel, your Savior. I give Egypt as your ransom, Cush and Seba in exchange for you. Because you are precious in my eyes, and honored, and I love you. . . . Fear not, for I am with you" (Is. 43:1-5). The sentiments expressed here from God to His people, Israel, are moving. It almost feels like a private reassurance between lovers that we should not be overhearing, but no, God included this passage in Scripture for a reason: He wanted to communicate that He cherishes those who trust in Him and will always be with them. "The Lord your God goes with you," says Deuteronomy 31:6, "he will never leave you nor forsake you."

This concept is amplified in the New Testament with the coming of Jesus. Very early in the Gospel of Matthew, Jesus is called "Immanuel" by the angel of the Lord, a name which means "God with us." How beautifully appropriate!

In John 1, Scripture says of Jesus, the embodied Word of God, that "the Word became flesh and dwelt among us, and we have seen his glory, glory as of the only Son from the Father, full of grace and truth" (v. 14). This word for "dwelt" more literally means "tabernacled." In the Old Testament, after Israel fled from slavery in Egypt, they took with them a movable tent to set up wherever they made camp. This tent would hold the Ark of the Covenant, which itself held the most precious artifacts from their history—the very words of God passed down to them by Moses on stone tablets. The tent also acted as a makeshift temple until a permanent building could be built. Within its fabric walls resided the glory of God—hence John's emphasis on seeing the glory of the Father in the Son. But this sanctuary, this tabernacle, also served the purpose of allowing God to "dwell in their midst" (Ex. 25:8). "There I will meet with you," God says to His people in Exodus 25:22, "and from above the mercy seat. . . I will speak with you about all that I will give you in commandment for the people of Israel." Hence, also, John's mentioning that Jesus is "full of grace and truth." Jesus also sits above the mercy seat and imparts truth in the form of his teachings.

Now it is the church, the body of Christ, the new covenant congregation of God's people, that are "God's building" (1 Cor. 3:9). God is actively crafting us into a temple—the consummate form of tabernacle—in which He will dwell (Eph. 2:21-22). Indeed, Christ *already* dwells in our hearts (Eph. 3:17), along with the Holy Spirit (1 Cor. 3:16) as a promise of the fuller presence of God we will enjoy someday.

Interestingly, in Revelation 21, when the voice from the throne says, "Behold, the dwelling place of God is with man," the word for "dwelling place" there is "tabernacle." In the new heavens and the new earth, when God has set everything right in creation, He will *tabernacle* with His human creatures forever and ever.

* * *

King of Kings and Lord of Lords

While Scripture does not portray God as thirsting for power over His creatures, it *does* teach that God naturally holds a position of authority over creation and His creatures. It makes sense. How can anything created from nothing be equal to or greater than its creator? How can the finite stand up to the infinite? How do creatures of extremely limited knowledge and power fare against a Being of unlimited knowledge and power? They can't.

But wait, what about the verses in the Bible that describe God as our friend? Doesn't God simply want to dwell with us and be our friend?

The answer to that question is, in one sense, yes. Absolutely, God wants to dwell with us and to be our friend. In John 15:14-15, Jesus told his disciples that he no longer calls them servants but rather *friends*. Likewise, because of his faith, Abraham "was called a friend of God" (Jam. 2:23; see also 2 Chron. 20:7 and Is. 41:8). But, of course, in another sense, the answer to that question is a resounding *no*. Is the relationship God wants with us mere friendship? No. *Mere* friendship implies some extent of equality between peers. Our relationship with God, however, is marked by an undeniable hierarchy — God the Creator is high above us human creatures. "You are my friends *if you do what I command you*," Jesus tells his disciples in John 15:14. God's friendship with us necessarily involves submission to His will and authority.

Think of your pet — your dog, cat, hamster, turtle, goldfish, whatever it is. Granted, you did not speak that animal into existence like God did to us, but still, you are its owner, its master. If you have a good relationship with your pet (and why would you have one if you didn't?), you undoubtedly think of the animal as your little furry (or scaly) friend, a member of your family. But your pet is, of course, not *merely* your friend, as if it were in some sense your equal. It relies on you, depends on you, and as much as an animal can, looks up to you. It is easily controllable by you, and you determine the course of its life, whether it fights your decisions or not. You hold a natural position of authority in that animal's life.

Now, I am not suggesting that we are the equivalent of God's pets! After all, our pets are not made in our image, and we cannot relate to them in the same way that God can relate to us. The illustration is useful, though. We find a commonly used metaphor in Scripture of God as the Shepherd and we humans as His sheep. "The Lord is my shepherd," David, himself a shepherd, says in Psalm 23:1, "and I shall not want." Despite all the dangers of the world, David says, "I will fear no evil, for you are with me"—there's that theme again — "your rod and your staff, they comfort me" (v. 4). The rod and staff, to a sheep, are symbols of the shepherd's authority and power, and yet they do not cast fear or dread into the sheep who trust in their master. Rather, they are a comfort.

So, too, is God's authority to the Christian. We, Jesus's sheep, follow our "good shepherd" because we know his voice (John 10:4), and we know that Jesus lays his life down for us to keep us eternally secure (John 10:14). Indeed, "Greater love has no one than this, that someone lay down his life for his friends" (John 15:13). Because Jesus is the Son of God, the Word which was with God in the beginning, he is rightfully in authority over us. But since he loves his creatures and lays his life down for them, we can take comfort in his authority. This relationship is what God intended for humans from the beginning.

What's more, from even a cursory reading of the Bible, it's easy to see that God did not design or desire His authority over humans to be shared. God commands His people not to worship or serve other gods because "I the Lord your God am a jealous God" (Ex. 20:5). He even tells the Israelites that His very *name* is Jealous (Ex. 34:14)! God yearns for that authority over His creatures because, as the Old Testament shows time and time again, calamity and chaos ensue when people forsake their singular submission to God.

Thus, we find in the Old Testament again and again and

again that God is, not just the King, but *the King of kings and Lord of lords* (see, for instance, Deut. 10:17; Is. 43:15, 52:7; Zech. 14:9). All other kings and lords and governing authorities on earth are, in some sense, *subordinate* to God. As the psalmist says in Psalm 47:7-8, "For God is the King of all the earth; sing praises with a psalm! God reigns over the nations; God sits on his holy throne."

Someday, God will reclaim all authority after Christ destroys "every rule and every authority and every power" and then "delivers the kingdom to God the Father" (1 Cor. 15:24).

This truth ought to be very, very comforting. God doesn't want authority in order to stroke His own ego. He wants authority so that He may better care for His creatures — to lead His sheep into green pastures and by still waters (Ps. 23:2-3). Precisely *because* God is benevolent, He deserves our submission and faithfulness. We should "give thanks to the Lord of lords," then, "for his steadfast love endures forever" (Ps. 136:3). God's love and power intertwine beautifully.

* * *

From the Beginning

What does all this mean for our exploration of the church's role in the political realm?

So far, we have only a few of many puzzle pieces, but they are important pieces. Knowing *why* God created humanity and *what kind of relationship* He desires to have with us will help define how God wants to redeem humanity and what that future state will look like. It will also help us understand how humans should relate to each other in the meantime.

God is an intentional God. He is an infinitely intelligent and purposeful Creator. As we will explore further in the following chapter, God did not intend to share His authority with anyone or anything, gods or governments. God gave humans the authority to reign, yes, but only over His creation, not over our fellow humans. Only when the relationship between God and His people eroded did God — grudgingly — allow the formation of a government.

One final note about the Kingship of God. We Christians often spiritualize God's Kingship and speak of it only in lofty, abstract terms. This is perhaps partially due to the fact that we live in the 21st century when monarchies are, for the most part, a thing of the past. The few kings and queens still extant in today's world bear scarcely any resemblance to the kings and queens and lords of the ancient Near East. Those rulers were not abstract. They did not hold their titles as mere symbols of glory and power. Rather, kings and lords had direct authority over their subjects. They commanded their subjects 'ultimate loyalty and respect. They reigned over defined territories on *this* earth.

It is in this context that the Bible says God is our King and Lord — our direct, governing authority who commands our ultimate loyalty and respect and who will one day reign over all the earth. And not only that. God is said to be the King of all other kings and Lord of all other lords. His authority takes precedence over any other authority, and in fact, He desires a world where He is the *only* authority. Someday, thankfully, He will have it.

* * *

"Know that the Lord, he is God!
It is he who made us, and we are his;
we are his people, and the sheep of his pasture."
Psalm 100:3

CHAPTER TWO

"They Have Rejected Me": Man's Desire for Earthly Power and God's Accommodation

The first mention of any sort of government in the Bible comes in Genesis 10. At this point, the Great Flood has purged the earth, leaving Noah and his family as the only human survivors. God has "started over" with humanity after man's evil had become so thorough and pervasive as to warrant a comprehensive divine intervention. The result is a cessation in the reign of evil on the earth, but alas, only a very temporary one. Sin creeps back in and causes conflict among Noah's family. They disperse, and the earth gradually repopulates.

"These are the generations of the sons of Noah, Shem, Ham, and Japheth," reads Genesis 10:1. "Sons were born to them after the flood." The account proceeds to lay out the genealogies of each of Noah's three sons.

Ham fathered a son named Cush, and Cush fathered a son named Nimrod, who "was the first on earth to be a mighty man" (v. 8). Nimrod was a great hunter, a profession of enormous value a few generations after the almost total annihilation of humanity. People needed to eat, and in an age long before humans had gained agricultural skill, the products of a proficient hunter were in high demand. This skill apparently propelled Nimrod to a position of leadership among his cousins and second cousins. "The beginning of his kingdom was Babel, Erech, Accad, and Calneh, in the land of Shinar" (v. 10.).

Interestingly, nearly all of Israel's historic enemies descend from Ham. Among the sons of Ham are Egypt and Canaan (v. 6). "Babel" is the same word often used in the Old Testament for Babylon. Nimrod's family also populated Assyria and in that land built the city of Ninevah, which the Lord describes in Jonah 1:2 as a "great city" whose "evil has come up before me." The man named Egypt fathered a son named Casluhim "from whom," the author of Genesis says in an aside, "the Philistines came" (v. 14). Some of Ham's other descendants are the founders of various Canaanite tribes that Israel fought at one point or another.

Needless to say, Nimrod comes from the bad side of the family. And his kingdom, as we will see in Genesis 11, is the antithesis of what God desires for His creation.

* * *

The Tower of Babel

> Now the whole earth had one language and the same words. And as people migrated from the east, they found a plain in the land of Shinar and settled there. And they said to one another, "Come, let us make bricks, and burn them thoroughly." And they had brick for stone, and bitumen for mortar. Then they said, "Come, let us build ourselves a city and a tower with its top in the heavens, and let us make a name for ourselves, lest we be dispersed over the face of the whole earth. (Genesis 11:1-4)

Who knows whether it was Nimrod's idea to build a city and tower there on the plains of Shinar, but since it was in his kingdom, it's safe to assume Nimrod at least knew about it and approved of it. It would certainly fit his character as one called a "mighty man," and it would also fit his history given that Genesis 10:11 says he built the city of Ninevah. Josephus, a Jewish historian of the first century AD, writes in *The Antiquities of the Jews* that Nimrod wished to outsmart God in the case that

God decided to take revenge on humanity again. "[I]f he should have a mind to drown the world again," Josephus says, Nimrod "would build a tower too high for the waters to be able to reach." Josephus even says that Nimrod had a mind to "avenge himself on God for destroying their forefathers!"[4]

Now, we should pause here to reflect on the limits of human accomplishment. Biblical scholars theorize that the Tower of Babel was a ziggurat, a three- or four-layered pyramid-like structure, typically topped by a small shrine or altar for burnt offerings to the gods. A long stone stairway, or several stairways, would angle up to the highest level of the temple-tower. One of the greatest of these ancient Mesopotamian wonders was the Ziggurat of Nanna at Ur (the land from which Abraham would later hail). This structure sat about 200 feet wide and 80 feet tall.[5] But Genesis 7:20 says that the waters of the flood "prevailed above the mountains, covering them fifteen cubits [22.5 feet] deep." It says in chapter 8 that Noah's ark came to rest on the mountains of Ararat as the water receded enough for their tops to be seen (v. 4-5). Mount Ararat in modern day Turkey reaches an elevation of 16,854 feet at its peak. Maybe Nimrod's tower stood a good bit taller than the one in Ur. But did it stand over 16,800 feet tall? Doubtful.

Of course, Josephus was not inspired by the Holy Spirit in his writings, so we must take his additions to Scripture with a hefty grain of salt. We must rather interpret Scripture on its own terms. What does the Genesis account say was the motivation for those who built the Tower of Babel? The answer, in short, is *pride* and *fear*.

"Let us make a name for ourselves [pride], lest we be dispersed over the face of the whole earth [fear]."

Pride. The land of Shinar, recall, boasted not only the first tower after the flood but also one of the first cities. In cities, it is easier to feel reliant only on other humans rather than the

---

[4] Josephus, *The Antiquities of the Jews*. Book 1, Chapter 4.
[5] ESV Study Bible, 68.

garden of nature, which was God's means of material providence in Eden. Their tower may have been an attempt at spiritual independence, as is indicated by their goal of building it up into the heavens, but their desire to construct a city indicates an attempt at something else—material and political independence. It's Nimrod's kingdom, after all. Their king needs a city from which to reign. Perhaps they figured with Nimrod's skills as a great hunter and reputation as a mighty man, he could take care of them—if they serve him, of course. They wouldn't need to trust in the God who wielded control over the elements of nature.

The people of Shinar felt a sense of pride in themselves. Their leader, Nimrod, was strong, so they assumed they were strong by association. They trusted in their leader and in themselves and spurned God. Their city and their tower symbolized a rejection of God's providence and authority.

Fear. With this independence, they also felt afraid. As if sensing that God would oppose their plans, they wanted to make a name for themselves *so that* they could avoid being dispersed across the world. Again, we see the pride inherent in the idea that a group of people can build a city or tower or nation that is strong enough to resist God's will. But we also hear fear in their voices—fear of losing their power, independence, and status. Pride is often accompanied by this deep fear of losing the object of pride. The city and the tower created a sense of *security* to combat their fear of losing power and status.

Despite the people of Shinar's efforts (or, perhaps, *because* of them), their fears *did* become reality. They did end up losing their object of pride—their power and status.

"And the Lord came down to see the city and the tower, which the children of man had built" (v. 5). Notice here that, despite whatever delusions of grandeur the people of Shinar entertained, God had to *come down* from heaven to see this city and its tower that was being built with its top to reach the heavens. "And the Lord said, 'Behold, they are one people, and they have all one language, and this is only the beginning of what they will do. And nothing that they propose to do will now be impossible for them" (v. 6). Why did God disapprove? Because in God's sin-stained creation, humanity had coalesced into "one people" with "one language"—in other words, they had become concentrated and unified. Power had become centralized. So much so that "nothing they propose to do will now be impossible for them." Why would this be a bad development? Because the people are not placing their trust in God but instead selfishly seeking to affirm their pride and assuage their fear of losing status. Power of this kind magnifies the scope of sin and its effects.

What does this have to do with kingdoms or governments? For now, we'll simply note that the first kingdom mentioned in the Bible was not associated with the protection of justice or human wellbeing. Rather, its actions were motivated largely by pride and fear and its goals centered on the accrual of power, status, and earthly security.

* * *

The Introduction of Mediators

A handful of generations after the Babel incident, God called Abram out of his homeland and into another, promising to make him into a great nation. The word "nation," here, doesn't refer to government but rather to an expanded tribe or collection of related families. In fact, this is almost always what is meant by "nation" in the Bible—a group of people with a common familial heritage. That is what God wanted to create from Abram (eventually to become Abraham) and his descendants. Unlike Babel, the purpose of this nation would be to bless all families of the earth (Gen. 12:3).

It is interesting to notice that, even though Abraham led a number of people between his family and his servants, God did not establish a government for His people in Abraham's generation. Neither did He do so in Isaac's generation, nor in those of any of Abraham's descendants until far down the road when Israel demanded a king. We will get to that soon. For now, we note that even as the children of Abraham grew in numbers, even as they interacted with other kings and governments, even as they settled in the land of Israel, God maintained a direct leadership over them, guiding the people Himself rather than through any governing authorities. Even though God instituted the rule of fair retribution for bloodshed ("Whoever sheds the blood of man, by man shall his blood be shed") after the Great Flood, He *did not* institute any kind of governmental structure to enforce that rule.

Fast forward to the period of Israel's history *after* God had secured their freedom from Egypt but *before* they had entered the promise land. During this period, Israel still had no government, but an arrangement had developed around their leader, Moses, to resolve disputes. Moses, having been the man God specially used to speak on His behalf before Pharaoh, was known among the Israelites as a man of God. He could discern the will of God in a way no one else could. Moses would sit "to judge the people, and the people stood around Moses from morning till evening" (Ex. 18:13). While not a government and with no defined laws to interpret (the Ten Commandments hadn't even been given yet), Moses acted as a mediator between God and the people of Israel insofar as he resolved their disputes and used the opportunity to teach the people about God. He acted, in a way, like a judge in a courtroom.

(Interestingly, before Israel had a legislature or executive to form a three-winged government, they *did* have a judiciary.)

The father of Moses's wife, a man named Jethro, observed this gathering and asked what was going on. "Because the people come to me to inquire of God," Moses told him, "when they have a dispute, they come to me and I decide between one person and another, and I make them know the statutes of God and his laws" (Ex. 18:15 16). Jethro found this arrangement unsatisfactory. He told Moses, "What you are doing is not good. You and the people with you will certainly wear yourselves out, for the thing is too heavy for you. You are not able to do it alone" (v. 17-18). The alternative arrangement Jethro suggested was this:

> You shall represent the people before God and bring their cases to God, and you shall warn them about the statutes and the laws, and make them know the way in which they must walk and what they must do. Moreover, look for able men from all the people, men who fear God, who are trustworthy and hate a bribe, and place such men over the people as chiefs of thousands, of hundreds, of fifties, and of tens. And let them judge the people at all times. Every great matter they shall bring to you, but any small matter they shall decide themselves. (v. 19-22)

Rather than coming from some sort of political philosophy, Jethro's advice stems from a desire to lighten the load on Moses: "So it will be easier for you, and they will bear the burden with you" (v. 22). Nevertheless, the wisdom of Jethro's idea is readily apparent.

The Israelites numbered in the tens of thousands or more. How could one man properly make decisions about all the disputes that arose between that many people? It would be enough to wear anyone down. What's more, resolving disputes almost always requires knowledge of personal details, and thus these cases would be easier to handle by someone closer to the individuals involved. Hence Jethro advises Moses to appoint a hierarchy of leaders: some to reside over groups of a thousand, some over groups of a hundred, others over groups of fifty, and even some over groups of ten people. This way, those appointed men can get to know (if they aren't already familiar with) the people they are to judge. Having such a familiarity will help the judges arrive at fairer, more effective, more personalized decisions.

Moreover, in being chosen specifically by Moses, these men would carry a sense of legitimacy. Moses would carefully choose only men who were trustworthy and unswayable by bribery. Of course, we know from the book of Deuteronomy that the process of picking leaders didn't happen exactly as Jethro had advised. Rather than Moses picking men himself, he opted to go about the election process democratically[6]: "Choose for your tribes wise, understanding, and experienced men," he told the people of Israel, "and I will appoint them as your heads" (Deut. 1:13).

Regardless what the best way was (or would have been) to appoint these leader-judges, we can derive an applicable principle from Jethro's advice. We'll call it the **Jethro Principle**:

> *It is preferable to solve problems and resolve disputes at the most local level possible.*

The flip side of this principle is what Catholic thinkers call *subsidiarity*, which is the idea that central authorities ought to serve a subsidiary function and perform only those tasks that cannot be performed at a more local level. Jethro's arrangement is a fitting example of subsidiarity: lower-tier authorities would listen to the people's disputes and, if possible, resolve them on their own. But if they could not resolve them, they would appeal to a higher-tier authority, and if that authority could not resolve it, they would appeal to a yet-higher authority, and so on up to Moses, the highest human authority. But Moses would not get involved unless all other channels of resolution had been exhausted.

How applicable is the Jethro Principle (and its reverse, subsidiarity) in the grand scheme of history? We have already stated that Israel did not have anything like what we would think of as a government at the time. Perhaps this arrangement of Moses and the leader-judges existed merely as a temporary fix to conflicts and disputes and would later be replaced with some form of government once the Israelites had progressed enough to be ready for it. Perhaps they would establish a

---

[6] The word "democratically" is used loosely here, as women, children, and servants likely had little to no say in the election of leaders.

permanent arrangement once they had entered the promised land. After all, God did not give Moses this idea. Jethro did.

As we will see, the above way of thinking doesn't fit with Scripture. In fact, while God didn't directly initiate this hierarchy of judges, He did make it part of the Mosaic Law and seemed happy to work with it and through it. Throughout this period, God raised up individual leaders to serve certain purposes, but all the while, direct and ultimate authority over Israel remained with God.

* * *

The Gideon Principle

After the death of Moses, his handpicked successor, Joshua, led the people of Israel and acted as the mediator between them and God. For all the days of Joshua's life, he and his house served the Lord (Josh. 24:15), and under his leadership an entire generation of Israelites did the same. But when he grew old and died, "there arose another generation after them who did not know the Lord or the work that he had done for Israel" (Judg. 2:10). The Israelites turned away from the God of Joshua and Moses, having forgotten the stories told to them by their parents and grandparents of how God had worked mightily to save them. They served the gods of neighboring tribes, the Baals and Ashtareth, and God gave them over to be plundered by their rivals. Having completely lost the material blessing their parents and grandparents enjoyed during the time of Joshua, "they were in terrible distress" (Judg. 2:15).

It is during this time of distress that "the Lord raised up judges, who saved them out of the hand of those who plundered them" (v. 16). But the people's loyalty and faith had already fled from God. Any loyalty God earned by delivering them from their enemies through a judge would be quickly reversed once the people returned to relative comfort. "[W]hen the judge died, they turned back and were more corrupt than their fathers, going after other gods, serving them and bowing down to them. They did not drop any of their practices or their stubborn ways" (v. 19). God grew increasingly frustrated with His people, to the point where He withdrew and would not intervene in their wickedness or suffering unless they cried out to Him again.

This pattern continued for many, many generations. The Israelites' slide toward unfaithfulness would lead to God's lifting of providential protection, a foreign power would threaten Israel, the people would cry out to God, and then God would raise up a judge to perform (often) a singular, supernaturally empowered task in order to save His people. No continuously extant human defense or governmental structures were present.

The period of the judges spanned several centuries from the Late Bronze Age (1550 - 1200 BC) to the Early Iron Age after 1200 BC. At the beginning of this period, the tribes of Palestine were relatively small and disorganized. Gradually, over time, city-states and villages began to be subsumed into the larger empires of the Hittites (who dominated modern-day Turkey) and the Egyptians. The Israelites, Canaanites, and a handful of neighboring tribes, however, resided between these two empires and had little contact with them.[7] For the time, the great kingdoms remained far off, but kings and governments were not unheard of. Tribes of the Levant increasingly evolved into little kingdoms themselves, and this put pressure on Israel to follow suit.

Enter Gideon, a farm boy from the Israelite tribe of Manasseh. God called this young man who was heavily lacking in self-confidence to perform a great task: save the Israelites from the fearsome Midianites, who were led at the time by two princes named Oreb and Zeeb. Gideon doubted and questioned God at every turn, carrying out several tests before he decided that he was indeed hearing God correctly. Finally, Gideon

---

[7] See ESV Study Bible. Introduction to Judges, 434.

obeyed the voice of the Lord and began his new role as a judge by destroying the altars and idols to Israel's false gods (Judg. 6). Israel had to be purified in heart before God would physically save them from their enemies.

Next, Gideon gathered a respectable army of around 32,000 men. But God saw their numbers and was displeased. He said to Gideon, "The people with you are too many for me to give the Midianites into their hand, lest Israel boast over me, saying, 'My own hand has saved me'" (Judg. 7:2). *God* wanted to be the leader of Israel, its authority and protector. He wanted Israel to know that *He* had saved them and *He alone* was worthy of their faith and worship. So He instructed Gideon to narrow down his army until only 300 remained — roughly 1/100th of its original size. With this scant number, God promised to deliver victory.

How did he do it? He gave the Midianites dreams that Gideon would ambush their camp and conquer them. This left the Midianites crippled in fear (Judg. 7:12-14). And Gideon saw that God was coming through on His promise. "As soon as Gideon heard the telling of the dream and its interpretation, he worshiped. And he returned to the camp of Israel and said, 'Arise, for the Lord has given the host of Midian into your hand'" (v. 15). They then surrounded the Midianite camp at night and scared them away with torches and trumpets.

We see here that God's direct authority and provision inspired in Gideon exactly the response that was intended: worship. When God leads His people, their faith is affirmed and fortified. Their relationship with God is strengthened.

Thus, we may extrapolate another worthy principle to remember, which we'll call the **Gideon Principle**:

> *God wants direct authority over His people, individually and as a corporate body, so as to increase their faith in Him rather than in earthly power.*

We find multiple passages of the Old Testament that

condemn trusting in the power of a human king and the sense of safety they afford. "Some boast in chariots and some in horses, but we will boast in the name of the Lord our God," says Psalm 20:7. Chariots were equivalent to armored tanks in the ancient world. They weren't owned by average people. They were only ever produced by governmental authorities as instruments of war. So, also, was the accumulation of many horses emblematic of building up a large army. Thus, in Isaiah 31:1, we read, "Woe to those who go down to Egypt for help"— denoting reliance on a foreign power— "and rely on horses, and trust in chariots because they are many and in horsemen because they are very strong, but they do not look to the Holy One of Israel, nor seek the Lord!" (See also Isaiah 22:18 and 36:9.)

In short, the whole of Scripture urges God's people, "Put not your trust in princes, in a son of man, in whom there is no salvation" (Ps. 146:3). Rather, put your trust in God— spiritually, materially, and politically— and *He* will be your warrior (Ex. 15:3).

Often the people's hearts and minds reflect that of the highest authority in society. Presidents are chosen by the "will of the people" through elections, and kings operate roughly the same way. If they lose the support of their people, they will be ousted. Thus, the highest authority's heart melds to his people, and his people's hearts meld to his. The same is true with God's kingship. When we submit to His rulership, our hearts sync up with His. That is why Deuteronomy 10:17-18 proclaims that "the Lord your God is God of gods and Lord of lords, the great, the mighty, and the awesome God, who is not partial and takes no bribe. He executes justice for the fatherless and the widow, and loves the sojourner, giving him food and clothing." It uses the same language about impartiality, taking no bribes, and executing justice that the Old Testament uses about the responsibilities of judges and, later, kings.

It is because of the human inability to rule over others this way that Zechariah 14:9 promises that someday "the Lord will be king over all the earth. On that day the Lord will be one and his name one." The NASB translation inserts the word "only" to communicate the intention in this verse that God *alone* will claim rulership over the world: "in that day the Lord will be the *only* one, and His name the *only* one."

But after the Israelites obtained victory over the Midianites with the war cry, "A sword for the Lord and for Gideon" (Judg. 7:20), they apparently forgot about the Lord and only remembered Gideon. "Then the men of Israel said to Gideon, 'Rule over us, you and your son and your grandson also, for you have saved us from the hand of Midian'" (Judg. 8:22). *You have saved us*, they say with no mention of God's rather large role in delivering them from Midian. In fact, to say God had a "rather large" role to play is a massive understatement. Gideon's army had only a small role to play in *God's* victory over the Midianites. Surely the men of Israel knew that Gideon had routed the huge force of Midianites with an army of 300 men, even if they didn't know about the dreams. Surely they knew about the war cry those 300 men uttered: "A sword *for the Lord* and Gideon!" But their memory was selective. Perhaps seeing the kind of power the two princes of Midian wielded made them envious.

Gideon, to his credit, had none of it, telling them, "I will not rule over you, and my son will not rule over you; *the Lord will rule over you*" (Judg. 8:23). The word order in Hebrew is important here. It might be paraphrased as, "It is the Lord, and no other, who shall rule over you."[8] Gideon recognized the request as a step on the path toward Babel—a rejection of God's authority over them, a desire to take pride in their accomplishment, and a fear of losing this newfound sense of security. They believed a King Gideon could give them these on his own.

But having experienced God's supernatural leadership and provision firsthand, Gideon knew that to accept the role as king

---

[8] See note for verses 22-23 in ESV Study Bible, 453.

would be self-deception and opportunism. Having torn down Israel's idols to false gods, he had earned the moniker of Jerubbaal, which means "Let Baal contend against him." He didn't want to then become another idol for the people of Israel to worship and revere in place of God. Neither did he want to rob them of enjoying the blessings of the Gideon Principle—strengthened faith as a result of God's direct rulership over them.

Alas, no man or woman on Earth is above corruption. While Gideon wisely refrained from accepting kingship, he gave in to the temptation to act like a king. He took many wives and at least one concubine (Judg. 8:30-31), behavior typical of an ancient ruler. He also used a portion of the pillaged gold from the Midianites to make a ceremonial garment called an ephod, typically worn by the high priest of a certain god. This ephod became an object of worship for Israel and "a snare to Gideon and to his family" (v. 27). After Gideon's death, "the people of Israel did not remember the Lord their God, who had delivered them from the hand of all their enemies on every side" (v. 34).

* * *

Gideon vs. Abimelech

Abimelech was the son of Gideon and Gideon's concubine. He may have been a bastard son, but he had great ambitions. He wanted to rule over Israel as their king. His name in Hebrew literally means, "my father, the king." He evidently viewed himself as the son most worthy of carrying on the authoritative name of his father.

So he went to the leaders of his family and said, "Which is better for you, that all seventy of the sons of Jerubbaal [Gideon] rule over you, or that one rule over you?" (Judg. 9:2). Perhaps, if Jethro had been around, someone could have spoken for the wisdom of a balanced and orderly hierarchy of leaders rather than power concentrated in one individual. But alas, Jethro was not present, and in his absence, Abimelech persuaded the leaders of his family to back his seizure of rulership.

Of course, since Abimelech was starting from scratch, he needed some kind of force to help carry out his coup. So he hired a posse of "worthless and reckless fellows" and went with them to the house where Gideon had lived. There he killed all seventy of Gideon's legitimate sons (his half-brothers) "on one stone"—implying death by execution. Only one son of Gideon—Jotham, the youngest of his brothers—escaped this massacre. Afterward, the leaders of the Manasseh tribe of Israel gathered by an oak tree and made Abimelech their king. Judges 9:22 tells us that "Abimelech ruled over Israel three years," but the word for "ruled" here is not the usual Hebrew word for ruling as a king. Instead, the word here carries the nuance of ruling as a prince or commander. It undermines the legitimacy of Abimelech's authority.

Jotham cried out on a mountaintop with a parable simultaneously condemning Abimelech and calling for unity in support of him for the sake of peace and order (Judg. 9:7-15). The parable goes like this: The trees of the forest want to anoint a king over them, so they go to various noble trees trying to convince them to accept the role as king. They go to an olive tree, a fig tree, and a grapevine, but in each case they are denied because each of these trees already has a productive and honorable role to play in the forest. Their produce brings joy to those for whom they provide. Why would they want to give that up in order to rule?

The trees finally go to the bramble to ask it to reign over them. Bramble is a fast-growing shrub with thorny, tangled vines and little to no productive value. It often chokes the life out of other plants, and once established, it is difficult to get rid of. The bramble, in this parable, is Abimelech. Yet rather than merely condemning the bramble and calling for the trees to revoke their support of it, Jotham used the parable to send a different message. "If in good faith you are anointing me king over you," says the bramble, "then come and take refuge in my shade, but if not, let fire come out of the bramble and devour the cedars of Lebanon."

In other words, as Jotham explained, "if you then have acted in good faith and integrity with Jerubbaal and with his house this day, then rejoice in Abimelech, and let him also rejoice in you" (v. 19). If this arrangement is satisfactory to you and leads to a cessation of bloodshed and infighting, says Jotham, then may it be. The youngest son of Gideon gave up any desire for vengeance and justice that he had for the good of his people. Accepting a less-than-ideal situation was better than continued bloodshed. After three years of rule, however, both Abimelech and the clan leaders who made him king got what was coming to them. For Abimelech, it was having his skull crushed by a boulder dropped from a tower—by a woman, no less.

The story of Abimelech is important to note for three reasons. First, it serves as a foil to the virtue of Gideon's denial of authority. Abimelech's ambition contrasts with Gideon's (at least ostensible) lack of ambition. Abimelech's desire to gather more followers, even if they were "worthless and reckless," contrasts with Gideon's willingness to let God narrow his army down to only the most worthy and prudent. Abimelech's hubris and premature death contrast with Gideon's humility and long life.

Second, the story encapsulates Israel's thoroughgoing apostasy from God during the generations of the judges. God's people became religiously, morally, and socially corrupted, leading even to civil war between the tribe of Benjamin and the other tribes. Thus we find the author of Judges giving several repeated editorial comments toward the end of the book, saying that "[i]n those days there was no king in Israel. Everyone did what was right in his own eyes" (17:6, 21:25; also 18:1, 19:1). The Israelites did not live as if God was their king, which God had made clear was His preference, so the author looks forward to a time when a human king might root out and police this corruption. Surely the author, like Gideon, knew that God was the proper King of Israel, but given Israel's growing record of failures, it is understandable that the author would think there needed to be a change in order to set the nation back on the right track.

This leads to the third reason to cover Abimelech, which is to observe the paradoxical attitude Jotham takes about his rulership—condemnable yet necessary to support for the sake of unity and peace. We see a similar attitude taken by God Himself when Israel finally demands a king, which we will turn to next.

* * *

God's People Demand a King

The period of the judges had lasted many, many generations by the time a young, faithful man named Samuel appeared on the scene in Palestine. Samuel ministered to God and the Israelites under a priest named Eli, and (perhaps because of Eli's faithful and persistent service) God intervened less frequently in the affairs of Israel. "And the word of the Lord was rare in those days; there was no frequent vision" (1 Sam. 3:1).

After Eli died, Samuel became the judge of Israel, carrying the mantle of Joshua and Moses as the man with the most intimate relationship with God among the Israelites. Samuel would travel around the villages and towns of Israel to decide their disputes with justice and fairness (1 Sam. 7:15-16). "When Samuel became old, he made his sons judges over Israel" (1 Sam. 8:1). But alas, his sons didn't take after him. They "did not walk in his ways but turned aside after gain. They took bribes and perverted justice" (v. 3). This prompted the elders of Israel to gather before an aged Samuel to say to him, "Behold, you are old and your sons do not walk in your ways. Now appoint for us a king to judge us like all the nations" (v. 4-5).

Just as in the case of Gideon, the people had grown weary of the judge system and asked for a king. Maybe they understood the Gideon Principle but had weak faith in God to lead them. Or maybe they agreed with the logic of the Jethro Principle but thought that a strong, central governing authority would work better in practice. After all, their immediate reason in asking for a king was the corruption of judges. Maybe they figured having one leader with the combined power of all the judges would work better than a decentralized system of leadership.

Notice, though, that corruption of the local authorities was not the only reason the Israelite elders called for a king. They also said they want a king to judge them "like all the nations." Implied in this phrase is one of two things—or both of them. Perhaps the elders meant that they wanted a king for the status and consolidated power that neighboring nations enjoyed. Maybe they looked at the Philistines and Canaanites and Ammonites and others who all had monarchial governments and envied the way they had evolved from networks of tribal villages to little self-sufficient kingdoms. Maybe they had become enamored by those kings who would lead their people to victory in battle, forgetting the many times God had led them to victory in battle. Maybe they wanted to take the same pride in a Kingdom of Israel as their neighbors did in their own kingdoms.

The other potential meaning embedded in this phrase "like all the nations" could be fear. Perhaps they wanted a king because they were afraid of the surrounding nations that *were* ruled by kings. After all, kingship often came with it a standing army and accumulations of war instruments such as weapons and chariots.

This interpretation would certainly fit with the context. Later, the elders reiterate their desire for a king over them so that "our king may judge us and go out before us and fight our battles" (v. 20). Throughout the period of the judges, God had always been the one to fight Israel's battles. And God had raised up judges of his own choosing to judge the people. Later, in his final address to the people before his death, Samuel chastised the Israelites, saying, "And the Lord sent Jerubbaal and Barak and Jephthah and Samuel and delivered you out of the hand of your enemies on every side, *and you lived in safety*. And when you saw that Nahash the king of the Ammonites came against you, you said to me, 'No, but a king shall reign over us', *"when the Lord your God was your king"* (1 Sam. 12:11-12). Despite how many times their Divine King had delivered them victory against their enemies, the people of Israel were still afraid of the threat of a neighboring nation's king. They didn't want to trust in their invisible, often silent God. They wanted an earthly king to protect them. They wanted to place their faith in swords and spears and chariots—and kings.

It's important to understand how counter-cultural the idea of God's direct rulership over His people was in the ancient Near East. In that context, the king *was* divine, or else part of the gods' original design for the world and specifically chosen as an instrument of that design. Not so in Israel. As pointed out by Moshe Halbertal and Stephen Holmes in the introduction of their incisive book, *The Beginning of Politics: Power in the Biblical Book of Samuel,*

> Rather than declare that "the king is a God," the new theology postulated instead that "God is the king." The sole or exclusive kingship of God was fundamentally irreconcilable with a consolidated political monarchy. The kingship of God entailed, as we see in the biblical Book of Judges, a divine monopoly on sovereign authority that essentially precluded the creation of self-sustaining political institutions.[9]

This is why it "displeased Samuel when they said, 'Give us a king to judge us'" (1 Sam. 8:6). Samuel was perturbed for an obvious reason—because they wanted to replace their Divine

---

[9] Halbertal, Moshe and Holmes, Stephen. *The Beginning of Politics: Power in the Biblical Book of Samuel* (Princeton: Princeton University Press, 2017), 4.

King with a human one. But it likely also irked Samuel because he himself had judged Israel for his entire life. He obviously believed in the judge system. He believed in the Jethro Principle and the Gideon Principle. By asking for a king, the people were disrespecting his life's work and core beliefs. They were essentially putting him and all future judges like him out of work!

But Samuel's displeasure went beyond mere personal rejection. The phrase "the thing displeased Samuel" literally translates to, "the thing was evil in Samuel's eyes." Samuel felt frustration and anger that the people could betray God like this.

So he went to the Lord in prayer, asking what to do. God responded, "Obey the voice of the people in all that they say to you, for they have not rejected you, but *they have rejected me from being king over them*. According to all the deeds that they have done, from the day I brought them up out of Egypt even to this day, forsaking me and serving other gods, so they are also doing to you" (1 Sam. 8:7-8). Even though Samuel naturally feels slighted over this call for a king, God tells him not to despair. This isn't a rejection of Samuel's leadership; it's a rejection of God's leadership.

Though heavy-hearted, God acquiesces to His people's demand for a king. For all His stern warnings that He would remove His blessing if His people lost faith in Him, God is still an accommodating God. He meets His creatures where they are, sinful hearts and all. He works through the desires of their flesh to hopefully bring about some good. As we know from a much later passage of the Bible, "God works all things together for good for those who love him" (Rom. 8:28). Even at our best, human love and loyalty for God is imperfect.

God revealed to Samuel that Saul, a tall and handsome young man pursuing some of his father's lost donkeys, would be the one for Samuel to make "prince over my people Israel" (1 Sam. 9:16). The Hebrew word for "prince" (*negid*) connotes a lower form of ruler than a king—more of a chief or captain, implying that God had not given up His status as Israel's true king. Indeed, when God says that Saul will "rule" over His people (1 Sam. 9:17), the Hebrew word there (*asar*) typically means "to restrain," indicating that Saul's job would be more to restrain Israel's worst impulses rather than to lead and guide them.[10] Continuing God's tendency to use what is small, weak, and modest to demonstrate His power, God chose a leader from the smallest tribe of Israel as well as the smallest family clan within that tribe (v. 21).

As Halbertal & Holmes write, contrary to other ancient Near Eastern monarchial mythologies,

> The biblical king, enthroned before our eyes, is a thoroughly human being, not a God. He is not a pillar of the cosmic order. He plays a negligible and wholly dispensable role in religious ritual, does not convey divine commands to his people, does not maintain the order of nature, and is not the prime lawgiver.[11]

After privately anointing Saul as Israel's king (1 Sam. 10:1), Samuel called the people together to announce Saul's kingship publicly. But even then, he reminds them what choice they have made: "Thus says the Lord, the God of Israel, 'I brought up Israel out of Egypt, and I delivered you from the hand of the Egyptians and from the hand of all the kingdoms that were oppressing you'. But today you have rejected your God, who saves you from all your calamities and your distresses, and you have said to him, 'Set a king over us'" (1 Sam. 10:18-19).

Clearly, Samuel was still unhappy about this shift in the course of Israel's history. But he went along with it anyway, making the best of the situation. He "told the people the rights and duties of the kingship, and he wrote them in a book and laid it up before the Lord" (v. 25). This book presumably acted as a sort of constitution by which the king would rule, knowing his limits and responsibilities. Perhaps the contents of this book

---

[10] See Dr. Thomas Constable's commentary (https://netbible.org/bible/1+Samuel+9).
[11] Halbertal & Holmes, 7

were a copy of a relevant passage from the Mosaic Law concerning Israel's future kings. In this passage it is instructed that any future king of Israel do just that: "he shall write for himself in a book a copy of this law, approved by the Levitical priests. And it shall be with him, and he shall read it all the days of his life, that he may learn to fear the Lord his God by keeping all the words of this law and these statutes, and doing them" (Deut. 17:18-19).

* * *

Did God Plan for Israel to Have Kings?

But wait, you might be thinking, if God wants direct authority and kingship over His people, why did He include in the Mosaic Law instructions for when and how Israel might eventually set a king over themselves and how that king was supposed to conduct himself? Don't those two ideas conflict? If God is upset in 1 Samuel 8 that His people have rejected Him by demanding a human king, why did He make these provisions in the Torah several centuries earlier? Here are the (stunningly prescient) provisions to which we're referring:

> When you come to the land that the Lord your God is giving you, and you possess it and dwell in it and then say, 'I will set a king over me, like all the nations that are around me', you may indeed set a king over you whom the Lord your God will choose. (Deut. 17:14-15)

How do we reconcile these two seemingly contradictory passages of Scripture? Did God plan for Israel to later have kings?

One very common answer to this is to say *yes*, God did plan and desire for Israel to someday have a human king. His rulership over them before and during the period of the judges was a temporary arrangement meant to last until the people had become deeply obedient and trusting in God, and thus ready for God to usher in the new age of a human king. According to this view, it didn't really matter what form of governance Israel had—central or decentralized, judges or kings—as long as they remained wholeheartedly obedient and faithful to God. So when Samuel chastised the people of Israel for demanding a king, he disapproved of their *motivations* rather than the request itself. It wasn't wrong merely to ask for a king. What made it wrong was the fear and/or national pride behind asking for a king.

I take a different view. In one sense, God certainly planned for Israel to have a king. We read in Hannah's Prayer from before the people demanded a king, "The Lord will judge the ends of the earth; he will give strength to his king and exalt the power of his anointed" (1 Sam. 2:10). This poetic verse looks forward to a time when Israel does have a king, so, clearly, human government and God's authority over His people *are* at least somewhat compatible. Going back even further to the time when God established His covenant with Abraham, we see God promising Abraham that He "will make you exceedingly fruitful, and I will make you into nations, and *kings shall come from you*" (Gen. 17:6; see also Gen. 35:11). Pay attention to the grammar here. It says that God will directly make Abraham exceedingly fruitful and into a multitude of nations but not that *He* will make Abraham's descendants into kings. The verb becomes passive tense here—*predictive* but not *prophetic*. God reveals what the future holds for Abraham's descendants but refrains from saying that *He* will be the one to bring it about.

We see a similarly passive response from God in the Deuteronomy 17 passage quoted above. He is predicting that at a certain point in the future Israel will decide to appoint a king "like all the nations" around it. God takes a permissive stance toward this, saying "you may indeed set a king over you whom the Lord your God will choose." Notice that God does not *command* His people to appoint themselves a king at a certain point in time. He only says that when they decide to declare a king, He will allow it under certain conditions.

Contrast this passive, permissive stance toward kingship with the way the Mosaic Law deals with the judge system:

> You *shall* appoint judges and officers in all your towns that the Lord your God is giving you, according to your tribes, and they shall judge the people with righteous judgement. You *shall not* pervert justice. . . . Justice, and only justice, you *shall* follow, that you may live and inherit the land that the Lord your God is giving you. (Deut. 16:18-20; see also 17:8-13)

God instructs the Israelites to adopt this judge system in strong, imperative language, and it is not in response to a desire of the people. God doesn't merely *allow* this; He *commands* it.

If God is indifferent to whether His people have a human government or what that government looks like, then why does He have separate approaches to judgeship and kingship — one passive and permissive, the other active and imperative?

Furthermore, the conditions set by the Mosaic Law on how the king must be chosen and must behave cast an air of negativity over the system as a whole. First, to counter the people's decision to set a king over themselves, God insists that *He* will choose the king (Deut. 17:14-15). Second, it cannot be a foreigner (v. 15). Third, the king cannot acquire many horses for himself or go to a foreign land to acquire horses (v. 16), which implies building up a large standing army. Neither shall he acquire many wives or excessive silver and gold (v. 17), implying the king must not have conflicts of interest or amass great wealth. And most crucially, he should devote his life to following the law of God (v. 18-20). With all these restrictions, the future king sounds like not much more than a glorified judge!

On their own, these limitations don't seem to cast an air of negativity over a future king, but in combination with the warning Samuel gives in 1 Samuel 8 about how kings will behave, it's clear that these conditions are meant to be restraints on the evil that kings can carry out.

"Now then, obey their voice," God told Samuel after they demanded he appoint them a king (1 Sam 8:9), "only you shall solemnly warn them and show them the ways of the king who shall reign over them." Samuel then goes to the people and this is what he says to them:

> These will be the ways of the king who will reign over you: he will take your sons and appoint them to his chariots and to be his horsemen and to run before his chariots. And he will appoint for himself commanders of thousands and commanders of fifties, and some to plow his ground and to reap his harvest, and to make his implements of war and the equipment of his chariots. He will take your daughters to be perfumers and cooks and bakers. He will take the best of your fields and vineyards and olive orchards and give them to his servants. He will take the tenth of your grain and of your vineyards and give it to his officers and to his servants. He will take your male servants and female servants and the best of your young men and your donkeys and pet them to his work. He will take the tenth of your flocks, and you shall be his slaves. And in that day you will cry out because of your king, whom you have chosen for yourselves, but the Lord will not answer you in that day. (v. 10-17)

Harsh.

Among the vices of this potential king are conscription of the people's sons for war — to "run before his chariots," acting as human shields for the king, being the first to make contact with the enemy and presumably the first to die. Also we find the king enacting forced labor, using some to plow his ground and reap his harvest, others to make weapons and military equipment, still others to cook and clean and beautify for him. Worst yet, he will take "the best" of the people's produce — "a tenth" of it — to give to his servants and cronies, the politically well-connected. One-tenth of one's produce is only ever used in the Old Testament to refer to what the people owe to God.

By this, Samuel implies that the king will, at least to some degree, take the place of God in society and in the people's hearts.

As if to hammer his point home, Samuel concludes his tirade by saying that the people who called for a king will become his slaves and will cry out for mercy from God, only to have their cries fall on deaf ears.

Part of Samuel's message, relayed to the Israelites from God (v. 10), was that *greater power leads to greater abuse of power.* After all, "The heart is deceitful above all things, and desperately wicked" (Jer. 17:9). Why wouldn't this apply also to kings and other governing authorities? This makes sense of why Deuteronomy 17 put such emphasis on the king faithfully following God's law — it's the only bulwark against corruption and abuse of power.

We may call this **Samuel's First Principle**:

> *Because of sin, greater power in the hands of any one person or small group of people tends to lead to a greater abuse of power.*

As the English Lord Acton put it, "Power tends to corrupt, and absolute power corrupts absolutely. Great men are almost always bad men." Recall Jotham's parable of the trees trying to find one of their number to rule over them, only to be rejected by all the noble, productive trees of the forest and taken up by the ignoble, destructive bramble. With this parable in mind, Lord Acton's quotation makes sense on multiple levels. Yes, power — the ability, for example, to conscript soldiers and force laborers to provide for the state apparatus — tends to corrupt sin-prone humans. But also, powerful positions tend to attract those who already have a bent for corruption.

Notice that throughout Israel's history as a monarchy, exceedingly few kings are considered good. David, called a "man after God's own heart" in Acts 13:22, is one of them, though he was by no means perfect. Josiah, who "walked in all the way of David" (2 Kings 22:2), was another. Solomon, wise but corrupted by great wealth and many wives, might be considered a third. Besides these, however, the lion's share of Israelite kings were indeed bad men. Of the 40 Israelite kings mentioned in the biblical record (counting both Northern and Southern kingdoms), only eight are portrayed in an even somewhat positive light.

But Samuel's other point, implied in his message, was that the king would claim at least some of the loyalty and sacrifice that was supposed to be reserved for God alone. One's "best" and the "tenth" of one's produce, according to the Old Testament, were tithed in the presence of the Lord as a ritual of faithfulness and loyalty (Deut. 14:22-27). Samuel applied that language to the king taxing his citizens and taking a portion of their harvest. From this we may extrapolate **Samuel's Second Principle**:

> *Governing authorities have the tendency to demand*
> *the same loyalty and sacrifice from their citizens as*
> *God does from His people.*

It is in this context that the Israelites' call for a king is said to be "evil in Samuel's eyes" and deemed by God to be a rejection of His kingship over them. It does not stand to reason, then, to suggest that God willed Israel to establish a monarchy all along, or that He was indifferent to their form of governance. The rationales given for why Israel's demand for a king so displeased God and Samuel do not match up with these ideas. How can we say that God desired Israel to have a line of human kings all along if He felt that His people had rejected Him when they asked for just that?

Moreover, the Israelites didn't simply take matters into their own hands to enact this desire for a king. They went to Samuel, the most well-known judge and speaker for God in his day to make this request. They did not go through nefarious channels to acquire a king; they went through the most righteous channel available to them. And yet still Samuel told them in his final address that "you shall know and see that your wickedness is great, which you have done in the sight of the Lord, in asking for yourselves a king" (1 Sam. 12:17). The people even acknowledge the veracity of Samuel's indictment when they respond, "Pray for your servants to the Lord your God, that we may not die, for we have added to all our sins this evil, to ask for ourselves a king" (v. 19).

Later in Scripture, in a moment when God fulminates against His unfaithful people, He scoffs at the Israelites' request for human government when He says:

> You are destroyed, Israel, because you are against me, against your helper. Where is your king, that he may save you? Where are your rulers in all your towns of whom you said, "Give me a king and princes"? So in my anger I gave you a king, and in my wrath I took him away. (Hos 13:9-11)

It fits better with the Scriptural account of Israel's slide toward monarchy to say that the verses in Genesis promising Abraham that kings would come from him, along with the instructions for a future king in Deuteronomy, demonstrate God's *foreknowledge* of Israel's future but do not prove God's *desire* for such a future. God can know that something is coming and prepare His people for it without willing it or intentionally bringing it about. After all, it is difficult to avoid the plain message of Scripture that Israel's desire for a human king *in itself* was evil. It violated the Psalmist's wisdom that "[i]t is better to take refuge in the Lord than to trust in princes" (Ps. 118:8-9; see also Ps. 146:3).

But God and His servant Samuel remained ever faithful. After the Israelites asked for prayer for the sin of asking for a king, Samuel replied to them, "Do not be afraid; you have done all this evil. Yet do not turn aside from following the Lord, but serve the Lord with all your heart. . . . For the Lord will not forsake his people, for his great name's sake, because it has pleased the Lord to make you a people for himself. Moreover, as for me, far be it from me that I should sin against the Lord by ceasing to pray for you, and I will instruct you in the good and right way" (v. 20, 22-23).

Amen. What a merciful and loving God we serve! Even in the midst of our sinful, corrupted state, God lowers Himself to accommodate us in order to gradually steer us back in the direction that we ought to go. Even though we do not know or want what is best for ourselves, God does. He will continue to guide us on the path of righteousness, even if our own choices make that path more painful and circuitous than God would have preferred.

* * *

"If we are faithless, he remains faithful."
2 Timothy 2:13a

CHAPTER THREE

Kingdom Come: What God's Kingdom Looks Like

"The time is fulfilled, and the kingdom of God is at hand; repent and believe in the gospel" (Mark 1:15).

What did Jesus mean when he uttered these earth-shaking words? What exactly *is* the Kingdom of God?

The Kingdom of God is a concept that is talked about constantly in some Christian circles and rarely in others. But it isn't the clearest concept in Scripture, at least to a 21st century reader, and thus there remains much confusion about it among both those who like to talk about it and those who don't. Does it refer to God's omnipotence? Or His right to determine the course of His creation? Or the sphere of His influence over the world? Is it merely another term for the church? On top of all that, what exactly does it mean to say that Jesus is Lord or Jesus is King? He's obviously not anything like the medieval lords — or is he? He's obviously not anything like a human king — or is he?

Were these terms — lord, king, kingdom — chosen by the biblical authors merely as metaphors for spiritual truths, or do they have some tangible, real-world basis of truth? Does the Kingdom of God exist in some parallel world to our own, or does it have some bearing on our physical reality of here and now? What does it mean for believers to be citizens of heaven (Phil. 3:20), and does that citizenship conflict in any way with our earthly citizenships?

The concept of the Kingdom of God is a vast one in Scripture, and we don't have the space in this humble volume to plumb its depths. But like an expertly cut diamond, we can turn it slightly one way and then another to examine a few of its aspects. Understanding a few of these key aspects of the Kingdom of God as ushered in by Jesus will help determine if that reality has political implications, and if so, what they are.

* * *

Jesus as King

The Old Testament contains several prophesies of Jesus not only as the coming Messiah and Savior but also as King. And these prophecies do not speak of Christ's ruling as merely spiritual or abstract. "Of the increase of his government and of peace there will be no end," says Isaiah 9:7, "on the throne of David and over his kingdom, to establish it and to uphold it." A few things should be immediately apparent about this verse.

First, it says the "increase of his government and of peace" will be unending. This likely pertains to the way in which the Kingdom of God will come into power—not all at once, but rather gradually increasing forever and ever. How exactly God's government and the peace of His Kingdom can extend indefinitely is not clear. Maybe this simply indicates that nothing can or will stop its expansion.

Second, notice that Christ will reign from *David's throne*—a real human king from history, who sat on a physical throne. This not only indicates that Christ would be born into the royal lineage of David but also that he would rule His Kingdom in the same way that David ruled his. Is it any wonder that many Jews interpreted this to mean that the Messiah would return as a warrior-king and restore Israel to a monarchy like the one it had before?

In the next book of the Bible, Jeremiah 23:5 says that "the days are coming, declares the Lord, when I will raise up for David a righteous Branch, and he shall reign as king and deal wisely, and shall execute justice and righteousness in the land."

This prophesied King would reign the righteous way that God had commanded of Israel's kings and judges. And the phrase "in the land" ought to steer us clear of any over-spiritualized interpretations. Of course, even though we know from Peter's sermon at Pentecost that God has already fulfilled His promise to "set one of [David's] descendants on his throne" (Acts 2:30), we must grapple with the *already* and *not yet* aspects of God's Kingdom. The Kingdom has *already* been inaugurated by Christ and is *already* "in the midst of you" (Lk. 17:21). In other words, it is available to enter into *now*, and it is steadily growing like good crops among the weeds (Matt. 13:24-30). And yet, while the Kingdom of God already exists on earth, the earth is *not yet* entirely in its domain. Most of the world still exists outside the Kingdom of God and apart from submission to Christ.

However, since God, through Jesus, has successfully completed the work required to redeem creation and bring it under His authority, we can summarily state that Jesus Christ is the "Lord of lords and King of kings" (Rev. 17:14), the "ruler of kings on earth" (Rev. 1:5), as well as the king of God's historic people, the Jews (Matt. 2:2).

Even the phrase "good news" (gospel) has kingly connotations. Luke summarizes the ministry of Jesus as "proclaiming and bringing the good news of the kingdom of God" (Lk 8:1). The term often signified in an ancient Hebrew context that a new king had been crowned or that a battle had been won by the king (e.g. 1 Sam 31:8-9; 2 Sam 4:10; 2 Sam 18, esp. v. 7). Hence we find that when King David was old and his son Adonijah claimed to be his successor (despite the fact that he had promised heirship to Solomon), David sent messengers throughout the land to proclaim the good news of the new king's reign. The messenger arrived as Adonijah and his guests were feasting, and Adonijah said, "Come in, for you are a worthy man and bring *good news*." But the messenger answered, "No, for our lord King David has made Solomon king" (1 Kings 1:41-44).

This is why we find Jesus immediately tying the gospel

("good news") with the Kingdom of God in the New Testament accounts: "Jesus came into Galilee, proclaiming the gospel of God, and saying, 'The time is fulfilled, and the kingdom of God is at hand; repent and believe in the gospel'" (Mk 1:14-15).

Moreover, it's also why Jesus was praised by crowds of people as he entered into Jerusalem riding a donkey (Matt. 21:1-11), alluding to the prophecy from Zechariah 9:9 that Israel's king would come riding a donkey. Interestingly, the prophecy specified that their king would be "gentle," coinciding with the choice of a donkey, a creature of peace and production, rather than a horse, a creature of war and destruction. Jesus would not be like Israel's past kings, ruling through physical power and force. Yes, he would rule as a king, but he would rule in the tradition of the judges from Israel's early days, who also shared the characteristic trait of riding on donkeys (Judg. 10:4, 12:14).

* * *

The Purpose of the Kingdom

It is interesting to observe that we only begin to see prophecies of the coming Kingdom of God long after the height of Israel's kings, during the era of their exiles. It's as if during the reign of kings, the people had forgotten Samuel's Second Principle—that governing authorities have the tendency to demand the same loyalty and sacrifice from their citizens as God does from His people—and placed their faith and hope in their current king. We see from the annals of the kings of Israel that this was very often the case. But after foreign empires swept through the land, destroyed Israel's kingdom, and dispersed the Israelites from their homeland, what would they place their faith in? What hope would they find through their prophets?

Many of them undoubtedly longed for the glory days of Israel as an independent kingdom, prosperous and answerable to no foreign power. Certainly, some passages of Scripture such as Micah 5:1-6 make it seem as though God wanted to return just this to His people. God is an accommodating God, after all. He wants to give His people the desires of their heart when they delight in Him (Ps. 37:4). But in His infinite wisdom, God knows better what is good for us and what we are designed for than we do. When we long for a benevolent and just governing authority, God knows that there is only one way to provide that: *He* must be our governing authority. God must become King over His people again, just as He once was before Saul became king of Israel. Thus we find in Scripture that when God promises to raise up a new king in Israel who will rule with justice and benevolence, He intends to make His Son—the second member of the Trinity, co-Creator of the universe—this King.

In other words, the solution is to go back to the relationship God had with His people in the Garden of Eden. Direct divine authority must be reestablished. God must be the sole King of His people again!

Philippians 2 says that after Christ's work on earth was complete, God "highly exalted him and bestowed on him the name that is above every name, so that at the name of Jesus every knee should bow, in heaven and on earth and under the earth, and every tongue confess that Jesus Christ is Lord, to the glory of God the Father." This language serves a reminder of the Gideon Principle: God wants direct authority over His people, individually and as a corporate body, so as to increase their faith in Him rather than in earthly power. Just as God's miraculous leadership evoked a reaction of worship from Gideon, Christ's authority over creation evokes submission among those who know him.

Through his work on earth, Jesus assumed the role of mediator between God and His people that had been borne by Moses, Joshua, Gideon, Samuel, David, and many others throughout history. Christ became the "*one* mediator between God and men" (1 Tim. 2:5), and after his sacrificial death on the cross, the thick veil inside the temple (which separated humanity from the place where God was said to dwell) "was torn in two from top to bottom" (Matt. 27:51). For most of Israel's history, that special dwelling place of God — the holy of holies — could only be entered by the high priest, and only rarely. The high priest acted as a mediator, of sorts, trying to maintain peace between his people and God. But now Jesus has become our High Priest (Heb. 4:14).

This, then, is the purpose of the Kingdom of God — to reestablish God's authority over His creatures, to reclaim His right to their ultimate loyalty, and to make Him the One in whom they place their trust and hope.

* * *

The Substance of the Kingdom

In John 10:10, Jesus says that he came so that we may have abundant life — life to the fullest. I am reminded of the title of a book by the popular megachurch pastor, Joel Osteen: *Your Best Life Now*. Jesus told his audience that he "came that they may have life and have it abundantly." It certainly sounds as if God wants His people to have their best lives now! Isn't that why Jesus came?

Not really. At least not the way we usually think of it.

The problem with saying that Jesus came to make possible our best lives now is that our ideas of the "best life" are inevitably subjective and worldly. They are often tied to cultural values and traditions that may or may not be what Jesus intended. We Americans can't help but think of the American Dream when we consider what our "best lives" would look like. We think of working our way up the socioeconomic ladder, accruing wealth, and attaining those material possessions — whatever they may be and however expensive they are — that make us feel like we have "made it" to the "good life." From a biblical perspective, however, this "best life" sounds identical to the accrual of earthly recognition and rewards about which Jesus says "woe to you," for "you have received your consolation" (Lk. 6:24).

And yet it is undeniable that this abundant life Christ made possible *does* have a material component.

Consider the way the Gospel of Luke records the beginning of Christ's ministry, right after he returned from his temptations in the wilderness. Jesus goes to the synagogue in his hometown of Nazareth and reads a scroll from Isaiah that says:

> The Spirit of the Lord is upon me, because he has anointed me to proclaim good news to the poor. He has sent me to proclaim liberty to the captives and recovering of sight to the blind, to set at liberty those who are oppressed, to proclaim the year of the Lord's favor. (Lk. 4:18-19)

After he finished reading the passage of Scripture, Jesus said to his audience, "Today this Scripture has been fulfilled in your hearing" (v. 21). Jesus proclaimed that he was the fulfillment of these Old Testament prophecies looking forward to a future Golden Age of freedom, fairness, health, and prosperity. Notice the phrase "*good news* to the poor," which uses the word "gospel." While many Christians believe the gospel is *merely* spiritual—that Jesus came to save us from our sins—Jesus himself indicates that there is also a material aspect to his good news. "Liberty to the captives" probably harkens back to God's deliverance of Israel from slavery in Egypt—certainly a real change in their material status! "Recovering of sight to the blind" signifies physical health and wholeness of life, as well as freedom from ailments and defects. "Liberty to those who are oppressed" probably refers to religious, economic, and political oppression, all of which the Israelites experienced in abundance during the first century. Finally, "the year of the Lord's favor" alludes to the year of Jubilee (Lev. 25), which certainly aimed to spread material abundance among God's people but was probably not practiced much if at all in

Israel's history.

The passage Jesus read from Isaiah 61 looks both forward and backward. It looks forward to the time when God would decisively act to deliver His people from spiritual and material oppression, but it also looks back to the spiritual and material blessings God intended for His people to enjoy under the Mosaic Covenant (Lev. 26:3-13). *If* the people trusted God obediently, they would enjoy a supernatural peace and prosperity in the land that God had given them. They would remain free of the yokes of slavery (v. 13) and of the fear of invading armies (v. 8-9). Their bellies would remain full (v. 10), and they would live in harmony with nature (v. 4-5). God even says he would "remove harmful beasts from the land" (v. 6)! Most importantly, though, because of their wholehearted trust in Him, God would dwell among them, walking with them as their God (v. 11-12). That, as we have already seen, is God's ultimate goal with humanity, the end toward which all of history arcs.

Jesus, the Word who became flesh and dwelled among His people (John 1:14), inaugurated the fulfillment of these prophecies. When Jesus proclaimed the good news that "the kingdom of God is at hand" (Mk. 1:15), it was *this* state to which he referred. God was enacting His long-held plan to once again dwell among His people—those human creatures who trust in Him and walk with Him in obedience. No longer would God lead His people through human mediators. Rather, His people would reign with Him (1 Tim. 2:12) as a "royal priesthood" (1 Pet. 2:9) with the Divine Son himself as their only mediator (1 Tim. 2:5). And in this state, humanity would enjoy freedom not only from bondage to sin but also the material consequences of sin, such as ill health, demonic influence, and poverty.

This is why we witness Jesus healing people with various ailments almost everywhere he went. He wasn't simply proving his bonafides as the Messiah; he was ushering in the physical blessings of the kingdom of God. This is why Jesus miraculously fed large crowds of people and also told Peter to feed his sheep (John 21:17). It wasn't simply a way to prevent attrition among his followers; it was a glimpse of the Kingdom of God breaking into the world.

But God does not want all of the material blessings of His Kingdom to come directly from Him, hence Jesus's instruction to Peter to feed his sheep. Jesus wants his followers to care and provide for each other, and in a broader sense, God wants His image-bearers to care and provide for each other just as He provides for them. Yes, in an ultimate sense, "every good and perfect gift is from above" (Jam. 1:17), but we who are called members of the body of Christ (1 Cor. 12:27) are meant to be the foremost channels of those gifts.

God's people bore the same responsibility in the Old Testament. In Deuteronomy 15, God proclaims that within the community of His people "there will be no poor among you" (v. 4). Rather, if someone in the community "should become poor, in any of your towns within your land that the Lord your God is giving you, you shall not harden your heart or shut your hand against your poor brother, but you shall open your hand to him and lend him sufficient for his need, whatever it may be. . . . You shall give to him freely, and your heart shall not be grudging when you give to him, because for this the Lord your God will bless you in all your work and in all you undertake" (v. 7-8, 10). The reason for the lack of poverty among God's people is because they provide for each other's needs, just like the godly woman of Proverbs 31:20 and the church body in the new covenant (Rom. 12:13).

When God condemns His people for their unfaithfulness to the covenant in Ezekiel 16:49, He associates Israel with sinful and corrupt Sodom: "Behold, this was the guilt of your sister Sodom: she and her daughters had pride, excess of food, and prosperous ease, but did not aide the poor and needy." The Sodomites practiced many sins, as we find throughout Scripture, but one important sin was the neglect of those in need. This isn't a small matter in God's eyes.

As Jesus teaches in Matthew 6, we are not to be anxious

about money or possessions but rather to "seek first the kingdom of God and his righteousness" (v. 25-33). Why is one contrasted with the other here? It's because of Jesus' prior instructions not to "lay up treasures" for ourselves on earth but rather to store our treasure in heaven (v. 19-20). How does one store treasure in heaven? One way is to give to the poor, which Christ commands us to do "in secret" (v. 2-4). In this way, our material giving is an act of investing in the unseen, heavenly storehouses of God's eternal Kingdom. To give, then, is one way to seek God's Kingdom. It creates a culture of generosity among God's people that is indeed "good news to the poor" (Lk. 4:18).

Thus, in Matthew 25:34-40, we find Jesus saying to those "who are blessed by my Father" to come and "inherit the kingdom prepared for you from the foundation of the world." Why does Jesus say that these blessed people will inherit the Kingdom? Is it because of their personal relationship with him? No, not exactly. It is because "I was hungry and you gave me food, I was thirsty and you gave me drink, I was a stranger and you welcomed me, I was naked and you clothed me, I was sick and you visited me, I was in prison and you came to me." When the faithful believers ask in confusion when they did these things, Jesus replies, "Truly, I say to you, as you did it to one of the least of these my brothers, you did it to me."

Paradoxically, those who will inherit the Kingdom of God are the same ones who used their time on earth to build it up and serve in it.

Let us state this as a principle, which we'll call the **Kingdom Community Principle**:

> *We—the church, the body of Christ on earth—are meant to be the primary channel through which the material blessings of the Kingdom of God are distributed.*

When Jesus walked this planet, *he* fed people, befriended the lowly, and healed the sick in order to manifest the Kingdom of God. Now that job belongs to the church, which is called the "body of Christ" (1 Cor. 12:27).

Thus, we find in the gospels both the concepts that God will *give us* His kingdom (Lk. 12:32) as an inheritance (Matt. 5:3, 10) and also that *we ought to seek* His Kingdom (Lk. 12:31, also Matt. 5:20). In Luke 12:22-34, Jesus reassures his audience that "if God so clothes the grass, which is alive in the field today, and tomorrow is thrown into the oven, how much more will he clothe you, O you of little faith!" Here the wording implies God will directly provide for people, but a few verses later, the wording shifts. "Seek his kingdom, and *these things will be added to you* . . . for it is your Father's good pleasure to give you the kingdom." Who will do the adding of basic necessities? The next verses imply that God gives these *through* His people:

> Sell your possessions, and give to the needy. Provide yourselves with moneybags that do not grow old, with a treasure in the heavens that does not fail, where no thief and no moth destroys. For where your treasure is, there your heart will be also.

This concept of providing for the needy as a form of eternal investment is further fleshed out in Luke 18:18-30 in the story of Jesus's interaction with the rich ruler. In this story, the law-following ruler wants to know how to attain eternal life. Sensing the man's unwillingness to part with his wealth, Jesus instructs him to sell his possessions, give to the needy, and follow him. Of course, the ruler does not obey Jesus's instruction, but Jesus uses it as a teaching opportunity, saying, "Truly, I say to you, there is no one who has left house or wife or brothers or parents or children, *for the sake of the kingdom of God*, who will not receive many times more in this time, and in the age to come eternal life." In other words, what you have to give up in service to the Kingdom of God (which in this case involved giving to the needy) is an investment that will pay dividends in the age to come *as well as* this present life.

The sacrifices Jesus is referring to are material ("house")

and relational ("wife or brothers or parents or children"), and he says it is of *these* things that believers will receive more in the Kingdom. It isn't as if they are asked to trade material possessions and real-world relationships for spiritual rewards *only*. Jesus implies that they will receive the same kinds of things that they sacrificed. This, of course, does not mean that a little bit of sacrifice will score one a greater amount of personal possessions or better blood relatives in a prosperity gospel-style get-rich-quick scheme. It means sacrifice of worldly wealth will result in access to the shared, communal wealth of the Kingdom. Share your possessions with a believer in need today, and they (or perhaps another believer) will share their possessions with you when you are in need in the future. Likewise, sacrifice of worldly relationships (when beyond the power of the believer to keep along with one's faith) will result in entrance to the family of God. What relationships a believer has to cut off or let fizzle out will be offset by membership in the Kingdom community with the new friendships it offers.

The prosperity of God's Kingdom as a whole is far greater than what any individual could enjoy on their own. But this is true only if the body of Christ shares resources and possessions with each other and embraces each other as a family.

Everyone who enters the Kingdom of God has some kind of value to add, and we are to make the best of what we can offer. "As each has received a gift, use it to serve one another, as good stewards of God's varied grace," Peter instructs in 1 Peter 4:10. For pastors, their gift is a teaching ability. For musicians, it is their ability to make beautiful music. For administrators, it is their organizational skills. For the rich, it is (among other things) their wealth and/or income-generating abilities. Just as God uses those with a talent for teaching to shepherd congregations, God uses the relatively well-off to provide for the needy. Jesus warns that "only with difficulty will a rich person enter the kingdom of heaven" (Matt. 19:23) not because the rich are necessarily or inherently more sinful than other kinds of people, but because there are so many temptations to use one's wealth in alluring, worldly ways—ways that do nothing to build up the Kingdom.

Of course, God also desires and uses the generosity of the less well-off for His Kingdom (such as in the parable of the Widow's Offering in Mark 12:41-44), but "to whom much is given, much will be required" (Lk. 12:48). In other words, God wants all of His people to give generously and sacrificially, but those who have more ought to give a proportionately higher amount.

Compare the story of the rich ruler with the story of Zacchaeus (Lk. 19:2-10), a rich tax collector who eagerly found Jesus to tell him, "Behold, Lord, the half of my goods I give to the poor. And if I have defrauded anyone of anything, I restore it fourfold." To this declaration Jesus replied, "Today salvation has come to this house, since he also is a son of Abraham." Salvation did not come to Zacchaeus because of works. Rather, Jesus declared that it had come because Zacchaeus demonstrated faith in God and an understanding of the substance of God's Kingdom. Not only does Zacchaeus do justice to those of whom he unjustly took advantage, he also sees to it that the needy obtain some of the abundance of the Kingdom.

Though the New Testament often focuses on the attitude and motivation of the individual giver ("God loves a cheerful giver" [2 Cor. 9:7]), there is also a broader principle of fairness which the church should be seeking. In 2 Corinthians 8, Paul encourages the recipients of his letter to give generously to their fellow believers in other regions of the world. He wants them to give only what they can afford to without excessively burdening themselves (v. 12). "For I do not mean that others should be eased and you burdened, but that *as a matter of fairness* your abundance at the present time should supply their need, so that their abundance may supply your need, that there may be fairness" (v. 13-14).

Paul here asks those who have more than what is necessary to meet their basic needs to give to those who do not have enough to meet their basic needs. He contrasts the words "abundance" and "need," leaving open to interpretation what exactly qualifies as either. However, we know from earlier in the chapter that the churches of Macedonia, who were suffering a "severe test of affliction" and "extreme poverty" still wanted to take part in "the relief of the saints" and thus "overflowed in a wealth of generosity" (v. 1-5). Given that the Macedonians gave from a position of "extreme poverty" and Paul did *not* encourage the Corinthians to give to them as well (only to the needy believers in Jerusalem), it is safe to assume that the recipients of the Corinthians' alms were in at least as bad a state.

Here we can identify another principle to keep in mind — **Paul's Principle of Fairness**:

> *Those who have the ability to provide for the material needs of others have the responsibility to do so.*

While somewhat vague on its own, this principle will be fleshed out when added with other principles which we will get to.

To connect this principle with the bigger picture, remember that *the substance of the Kingdom of God is spiritual and material wholeness of life*. It is the abundant life that God intended us to have from the beginning. Some aspects of this whole, abundant life can only be provided by God's supernatural intervention, such as freeing people from bondage to sin. But for other aspects of the abundant life, God expects His people to participate with Him in their provision. Sometimes that means prayers for healing illnesses (as in James 5:14-15), other times evangelizing those who have not heard the gospel (as in Romans 10:13-14), and still others giving clothes to (as in Luke 3:11) and sharing money with (as in 2 Corinthians 9:10-15) those in need. The Kingdom functions best when each of its members recognizes their unique abilities and gifts and capitalizes on them to serve others. That includes the materially well off, who are instructed to "be generous and ready to share, thus storing up treasure for themselves as a good foundation for the future so that they may take hold of that which is truly life" (1 Tim. 6:17-19).

The benefit of giving is always a two-way street. It is a benefit to the one who has genuine needs, but it also benefits the heart and faith of the one who gives. The point of giving, as Paul points out in the 2 Corinthians passage, is not to make ourselves poor. Nor does fairness imply literal, material equality. Rather, the goal is to ensure that the whole family of God takes part in the prosperity of the Kingdom. (See Prov. 3:9-10.) In this way, the substance of the Kingdom, for both giver and receiver, is "that which is truly life."

* * *

The Method of the Kingdom

Again and again in Scripture, especially the New Testament, we find that God wants His people to serve His Kingdom *wholeheartedly* and *voluntarily*. Following Jesus's example, we believers are to live out the Kingdom through love of others and sacrificial giving. Whether this giving is of time, money, resources, or some sort of labor, it should not be done begrudgingly or by coercion. "Show hospitality to one another without grumbling," says Peter in 1 Peter 4:9.

"Each one must give as he has decided in his heart," says Paul in 2 Corinthians 9:7, "not reluctantly or under compulsion, for God loves a cheerful giver." Earlier in 2 Corinthians, Paul even conditions his instruction to give on the individual's readiness to give: "For if the readiness is there, it is acceptable according to what a person has, not according to what he does not have" (8:12). Notice the word "acceptable" here. If the gift is acceptable only when the giver is ready to give, then it would be better for a believer to give nothing at all than to give reluctantly or out of compulsion. Two more times in 2

Corinthians 8, Paul suggests that the Corinthians themselves must make the decision to give. First, he says that the Macedonians gave "of their own accord" (v. 3), then a few verses later, Paul says to the Corinthians, "I say this *not as a command,* but to prove by the earnestness of others that your love also is genuine" (v. 8). Genuine love can only exist if freely chosen and heartfelt. Compulsion destroys genuine love and compassion.

Clearly, voluntarism is important.

This emphasis on voluntary and heartfelt giving is not unique to the New Testament. We can find almost identical instructions given in the Old Testament, such as in the Deuteronomy 15 passage (mentioned above) about giving generously to members of the community that have become poor: "You shall give to him freely, and *your heart shall not be grudging* when you give to him." God has always desired His people to provide for each other willingly and generously, with open hearts as well as open hands.

Leadership among God's people ought to model this commitment to voluntarism, using one's own example as the method of influence rather than coercion. Just as Jesus led by example (see John 13:12-17) rather than compulsion or manipulation, so, too, should his followers. Paul wrote in Philippians 3:17, "Brothers, join in imitating me, and keep your eyes on those who walk according to the example you have in us." (See also 1 Thess. 1:6-7 and 2 Thess. 3:6-9.) Moreover, Paul encourages both Timothy and Titus to lead by example as well — "set the believers an example" he says to Timothy (1 Tim. 4:12), and to Titus, "Show yourself to be a model of good works" (Tit. 2:7).

Indeed, every member of the church who exercises some measure of leadership must lead this way. As Peter exhorts elders in 1 Peter 5:2-3, "shepherd the flock of God that is among you, exercising oversight, not under compulsion, but willingly, as God would have you. . . not domineering over those in your charge, but being examples to the flock." We find this modeled by Paul in his letter to Philemon, appealing to him to free his slave, Onesimus, who had begun to serve Paul while he was imprisoned. Paul even sent Onesimus back to his master, Philemon, so that it would truly be Philemon's choice whether or not to free his slave. Paul told him, "I preferred to do nothing without your consent in order that your goodness might not be by compulsion but of your own accord" (v. 14).

Scripture makes clear that God wants our service to His Kingdom to be authentic and heartfelt, and that requires choice. We must *choose* to serve and to give of our own accord. Moreover, we must do so not to meet some quota of service hours or percentage of income but rather out of heartfelt obedience to God and a desire to help others. It must be natural, sustainable, and led by the Spirit. This is the proper method of living out the Kingdom of God.

We may call this the **Kingdom Principle of Voluntarism**:

> *Service and charity in the Kingdom of God must always be heartfelt and voluntary.*

* * *

The Example of the Christians After Pentecost

We find a powerful example of the Kingdom of God in practice as carried out by the believers just after the coming of the Holy Spirit at Pentecost. Acts 2:41 tells us that three thousand people in Jerusalem became believers that day.

> And all who believed were together and had all things in common. And they were selling their possessions and belongings and distributing the proceeds to all, as any had need. And day by day, attending the temple together and breaking bread in their homes, they received their food with glad and generous hearts. . . (Acts 2:44-46)

> Now the full number of those who believed were of one heart and soul, and no one said that any of the

> things that belonged to him was his own, but they had
> everything in common. . . . There was not a needy
> person among them, for as many as were owners of
> lands or houses sold them and brought the proceeds of
> what was sold and laid it at the apostles' feet, and it
> was distributed to each as any had need. (Acts 4:32,
> 34-35)

Some read these passages and combine them with the story of Ananias and Sapphira, two believers who were stricken dead for dishonestly withholding some of the proceeds of the sale of their property from the church (Acts 5:1-11), and conclude that living out the Kingdom of God is incompatible with owning *any* property or possessions at all. Those who reach this conclusion do so based on several points of observation:

In both Acts 2 and Acts 4, Luke (the author of the book) says that the believers "had everything in common." What's more, in Acts 4:32, he says "no one said that any of the things that belonged to him was his own." The wording for both phrases certainly suggests that the believers considered everything they owned (or formerly owned) as freely available to the group rather than merely themselves. Having all things in common implies no claims of ownership whatsoever.

Luke tells us that the believers sold their possessions and belongings as well as any land or houses that they owned. Thus, it's clear that this attitude of holding all things in common was met with action—actually disposing of material possessions.

The deaths of Ananias and Sapphira indicate that failure to comply with this state of common ownership was a punishable offense, and thus compliance was not voluntary.

What are we to say to this? Are we to conclude that believers should not own anything and that God desires the church to enforce complete material egalitarianism? I don't think so. Though Scripture does prescribe sacrificial generosity for Christians, as we've already covered, it is not likely condemning any and all ownership of possessions. Rather,

Luke is describing the radical generosity that came over the church shortly after Pentecost as well as their *attitude* of withholding nothing from each other. The way in which his language suggests a *total* abandonment of property is an example of First Century Jewish hyperbole intended to emphasize his point but probably not meant to be taken as wholly literal.

Let us go through the reasons to embrace this view one by one:

1. Luke indicates that the believers' selling of property was done *as needed*, not for its own sake. Acts 2:45 says they sold their possessions and distributed the proceeds to all "*as any had need.*" Likewise, Acts 4:34-35 puts it, "There was not a needy person among them" because owners of property sold it and brought the proceeds to the apostles, who then "distributed to each *as any had need.*" The text stops short of suggesting that believers sold everything they owned regardless of need. It communicates only that they sold what was necessary to provide for fellow believers in need. Radical generosity, certainly, but not technically communal ownership.

2. Believers clearly still owned personal possessions, because Acts 4:32 informs us that the Christians had belongings even though they didn't claim them as solely their own. For instance, after Pentecost Luke says they met "in their homes" (Acts 2:46), and the New Testament mentions many other Christians who owned homes (Acts 12:12, 17:5, 18:7, 20:20, 21:8, 16; Rom. 16:5; 1 Cor. 16:19; Col. 4:15; Philem. 2; 2 John 10). As if owning homes wasn't enough, Philemon apparently owned at least one slave, and yet Paul did not chastise him for owning possessions (and people!) but rather urged him to voluntarily free his slave, Onesimus.

3. Peter's condemnation of Ananias and Sapphira indicates that their sin was not withholding some of the proceeds of the sale of their land. Rather, their sin was lying to the Holy Spirit. Peter asks Ananias in Acts 5:4, "While it remained unsold, did it not *remain your own*? And after it was sold, was it not *at your* *disposal*?" Ananias probably felt the peer pressure to give the entire sum like many other believers were doing. But Peter stresses here that both before and after the land was sold, it remained in the ownership of Ananias, implying that he did not have to give anything.

Though it's difficult to comprehend how the punishment fits Ananias and Sapphira's crime, their story serves as a potent reminder of the Kingdom Principle of Voluntarism: Service and charity in the Kingdom of God must always be heartfelt and voluntary.

It's important to focus not just on what Luke is *not* saying in these passages but also on what he *is* saying. What does Luke want us to take away from these approvingly recorded events? More importantly, what does *God* want us to take away from them?

The lesson here is that God has always wanted His people to provide for each other's needs, even if that comes at great personal sacrifice (Deut. 15:4, 7-11). We aren't merely to be generous with our excess—the money or possessions we didn't really need in order to sustain our normal lifestyle with all of its luxuries. Giving what is left over after enjoying today's many luxuries is not enough. Not in a world where many, including and *especially* our brothers and sisters in Christ, do not have their basic needs met. "If we have food and clothing," says Paul in 1 Timothy 6:8, "with these we will be content." Our attitude with money and possessions ought to acknowledge that "we brought nothing into the world, and we can take nothing out of the world" (v. 7).

Rather, everything in creation belongs to God, and we are mere temporary stewards of some of God's resources. We ought to be *willing* to give it all to provide for each other's needs, even if God does not necessarily call each of us to do so. Just as Jesus calls *all* of his followers to "bear his own cross and come after me" (Lk. 14:27) and yet not all his followers *will* be called specifically to die, so also does Jesus call *all* of his followers to "renounce all that he has" (Lk. 14:33), even if not all of his followers will be called specifically to do so. It is the willingness, the posture of the heart, the openness to God's will, that matters.

Luxuries should *never* be prioritized over helping to meet the basic needs of others. As C.S. Lewis put it in *Mere Christianity*:

> I do not believe one can settle how much we ought to give. I am afraid the only safe rule is to give more than we can spare. In other words, if our expenditure on comforts, luxuries, amusements, etc, is up to the standard common among those with the same income as our own, we are probably giving away too little. If our charities do not at all pinch or hamper us, I should say they are too small. There ought to be things we should like to do and cannot do because our charitable expenditure excludes them.

Of course, the point is not to give for the sake of giving. Charity and generosity may be matters of the heart, but they are not *merely* matters of the heart. We are also to give for the sake of helping and serving, and indeed we have a duty to give where there is need. But for those of us who live in material comfort, Lewis's message is a convicting one, for we have greater knowledge of those in need than ever before, as well as a greater ability to use our resources to help and serve them. This is the way God rules in His Kingdom. Jesus humbled himself and gave out of his abundance in order to be glorified and lifted up to kingship. He came to earth "not to be served but to serve" (Matt. 20:28). We, his followers, are to do the same (Matt. 20:26-27).

We are not God's involuntary slaves, laboring all our lives to provide for Him. Neither will God directly provide everything for us. Rather, God delegates His people the "front line" role in bringing about the material and communal wholeness of life that Jesus came to deliver.

" Your Kingdom come, your will be done, on earth as it is in heaven." - Matthew 6:10

CHAPTER FOUR

Servants of Wrath: The Role of the State in the Church Age

If you are a Christian who has spent some time in Scripture, you are probably confused at this point. If all of the previously stated principles are true, and if God really does want to reclaim direct authority over His people—indeed, over all humanity and creation—then why would God inspire Paul to write a passage like this?:

> Let every person be subject to the governing authorities. For there is no authority except from God, and those that exist have been instituted by God. Therefore whoever resists the authorities resists what God has appointed, and those who resist will incur judgement. For rulers are not a terror to good conduct, but to bad. Would you have no fear of the one who is in authority? Then do what is good, and you will receive his approval, for he is God's servant for your good. But if you do wrong, be afraid, for he does not bear the sword in vain. For he is the servant of God, an avenger who carries out God's wrath on the wrongdoer. Therefore, one must be in subjection, not only to avoid God's wrath but also for the sake of conscience. For because of this you also pay taxes, for the authorities are ministers of God, attending to this very thing. Pay to all what is owed to them: taxes to whom taxes are owed, revenue to whom revenue is owed, respect to whom respect is owed, honor to whom honor is owed. (Rom. 13:1-7)

If God wants direct authority over His creatures, why would He "institute" earthly governing authorities—the very thing in which He instructs us *not* to put our trust in Psalm 146:3—and tell us to live our lives in subjection to them? Not only that. Why would God call those governing authorities a "servant for good" that His people must obey "for the sake of conscience"? How does this square with the Gideon Principle ("God wants direct authority over His people, individually and as a corporate body, so as to increase their faith in Him rather than in earthly power")? What about Samuel's First Principle ("Because of sin, greater power in the hands of any one person or group of people tends to lead to a greater abuse of power")? What about Samuel's Second Principle ("Governing authorities have the tendency to demand the same loyalty and sacrifice from their citizens as God does from His people")?

To put it simply, it seems contradictory to affirm all of what we have already affirmed *as well as* Romans 13. How do we explain the coexistence of these two?

The simple answer, in my view, is that God has delegated earthly governments a certain role in the present age that is compatible yet wholly distinct from His own Kingdom. Like weeds growing alongside the wheat, earthly governments do not hinder the growth of the Kingdom—not, at least, as long as they are fulfilling the role implicitly designated to them by the New Testament. Rather, they exist alongside it.

The role of governments, as we will flesh out further in this chapter, is to act as a bulwark against human evil until humanity has been redeemed. After all, humans are sinful and prone to great acts of wickedness, as both history and Scripture attest. "All have sinned and fallen short of the glory of God," says Romans 3:23. And as Jeremiah 17:9 puts it, "The heart is deceitful above all things, and desperately sick; who can understand it?" Governments restrain and punish evil so as to prevent unredeemed humans from behaving as atrociously as we otherwise would if we didn't have any fear of reprisal. They serve as a temporary stopgap to prevent society from degrading into chaos. Such conditions existed before the Flood, when God "saw that the wickedness of man was great in the earth, and that every intention of the thoughts of his heart was only evil continually" (Gen. 6:5). In those days, "the earth was corrupt in God's sight, and the earth was filled with violence" (v. 11). Though governments are not God's ideal for humanity, they do prevent and punish this wickedness, evil, and corruption by carrying out "God's wrath on wrongdoers."

In the late 50s or early 60s AD, when the book of Romans was written, Christians were almost entirely excluded from government positions, both in the regional Jewish governmental structure and the Roman Empire (with the exception of converted Roman soldiers). Thus, when the New Testament addresses governments, it is referring to secular institutions of sinful, unredeemed people governing other sinful, unredeemed people.

Why, then, would Paul use such positive language to describe governing authorities? One reason, in my estimation, lies in the nature of an epistle. Epistles are letters of encouragement and teaching. The book of Romans is a prime example of this as it includes a hefty share of teaching but also plenty of encouragement for the believers of Rome. Romans 13 falls in the "encouragement" section of the epistle which begins in Romans 12:1 and continues through 15:13. Of course, Paul provides some teaching in the encouragement section of the book and some encouragement in the teaching section, but the main thrust of chapters 12 through 15 are encouragement and moral instruction. His instruction to "be subject" to the governing authorities is one of many exhortations given one after the other starting in chapter 12.

Why would the Christians of Rome need to be encouraged to be subject to the governing authorities and reminded of their merits? Consider the historical context. The emperor of Rome at the time was Nero, undoubtedly one of the harshest persecutors of Christians among Rome's emperors. He blamed the Great Fire of Rome in 64 AD on Christians and used that as justification for all kinds of "fearful tortures," according to the Roman historian Tacitus.[12] In his writings, Tacitus speaks of Christianity as a "pernicious superstition" whose adherents were convicted after the fire "not so much on the charge of burning the city, as of 'hating the human race.'"[13] It's inconceivable to believe that disdain of the Christians by Nero or the Roman people as a whole began at the time of the Fire. Nero likely blamed it on the Christians because they were already a loathed class of people.

Scripture itself gives hints that this was indeed the relationship of the Christians to the broader Roman culture. When Paul is received by the Jews in Rome, for instance, they tell Paul, "we desire to hear what you think; for concerning this sect [Christianity], we know that it is spoken against everywhere" (Acts 28:22). The book of Acts was almost certainly written after the book of Romans, but this verse still demonstrates that when Paul was in Rome during the 60s AD, the Christians were "spoken against everywhere."

If these were the circumstances under which the Christians of Rome received Paul's letter, it is understandable why they would need encouragement to live in subjection to the government. The Roman authorities and culture were unfriendly, if not outright hostile, to the Christians. Paul's aim here is to assure them that the Kingdom of God would not be served by resisting earthly authorities or starting an uprising. After all, God's Kingdom, though it is attainable *in* this world, is not *of* this world. "If my kingdom were of this world," Jesus says to Pilate in John 18:33, "my servants would have been fighting. . ." Living in subjection to the government, rather than bucking against it, was a practical way in which the Roman believers might "live peaceably with all" (Rom. 12:18). Likewise, reminding them that God uses the governing

---

[12] Tacitus, *Annals*, Vol. 15.
[13] "Nero Persecutes The Christians, 64 A.D.," EyeWitness to History, www.eyewitnesstohistory.com (2000).

authorities to play a useful role in society—namely, maintaining order and preventing crime—would diminish the temptation to think that the government was purely evil and deserved no respect at all.

In order to further assess how Romans 13 fits into the broader story of Scripture, let's examine a few specific aspects of the passage.

* * *

Subjection vs. Submission

When Paul calls believers to *"be subject* to the governing authorities," he is using a form of the Greek word "hupotasso." Literally, the word refers to soldiers moving to the orders of their commander, but in non-military use, the word refers to "a voluntary attitude of giving in, cooperating, assuming responsibility, and carrying a burden."[14] The concept is about voluntarily yielding one's preferences to others. It's the same word used elsewhere in the New Testament for "submit."

"Submit yourselves to God," says James 4:7. In Ephesians 5:21, Paul encourages believers to always be *"submitting* to one another out of reverence for Christ." He follows up that exhortation by telling wives to *"submit* to your own husbands, as to the Lord" (v. 22). Likewise, the author of Hebrews instructs believers about elders and pastors in the church: "Obey your leaders and *submit* to them, for they are keeping watch over your souls, as those who will have to give an account." Clearly, the concept of "hupotasso" as it is used in the New Testament is about voluntarily putting oneself under another and acknowledging their authority or dignity. It is done to serve the other, to promote the other's welfare or wants above one's own.

Notice, however, that when the New Testament addresses

---

[14] Thayer and Smith. "Greek Lexicon entry for Hupotasso". "<u>The NAS New Testament Greek Lexicon</u>". 1999.

believers' relationship to the government, the wording shifts. "Let every person *be subject* to the governing authorities" (Rom. 13:1). "Remind them to *be submissive* to rulers and authorities" (Tit. 3:1). "*Be subject* for the Lord's sake to every human institution, whether it be to the emperor as supreme, or to governors as sent by him to punish those who do evil and to praise those who do good" (1 Pet. 2:13-14). "Therefore, one must *be in subjection,* not only to avoid God's wrath but for the sake of conscience" (Rom. 13:5).

In the context of believers and the government, the verb "hupotasso" becomes passive ("be subject") rather than active ("submit to"). What does this mean?

Fortunately, Paul gives us the antithesis of "being subject" in the same passage of Romans 13 when he tells us that "whoever *resists* the authorities resists what God has appointed." The opposite of being in subjection, then, is resistance. Resistance is active, but subjection or submissiveness is passive. It need not be *doing* anything at all. It is rather a lack of doing something. Thus, being in subjection does not carry the same connotation of intentional service as does submission. Paul is not calling on us to be servants of the government or to promote its welfare and wants above our own. Rather, he is saying: Don't resist the government. Don't avoid your taxes. Comply with the government as much as possible while remaining Christlike.

It is useful to compare the various wording that is used in reference to slaves with their unbelieving masters and wives with their unbelieving husbands. In instances in which the authority figure is not morally pure or not a follower of Christ, we find that the verb "hupotasso" indicates passivity and compliance rather than intentional submission.

"Servants, *be subject* to your masters with all respect, not only to the good and gentle but also to the unjust" (1 Pet. 2:18). "Bondservants are to *be submissive* to their own masters in everything. . . so that in everything they may adorn the doctrine of God our Savior" (Tit. 2:9-10). Adorning the doctrine of God here refers to making it attractive to outsiders. It aligns with the principle found in 1 Peter 2:12 that all of our behavior around unbelievers should be honorable so that "they may see your good deeds and glorify God."

We find the same subtle distinction of "submit to" versus "be subject" with regards to wives with unbelieving or unrighteous husbands. Whereas Paul instructs wives to "submit to your own husbands. . . as the church submits to Christ" (Eph. 5:22, 24), clearly referencing a mutually Christian marriage, in 1 Peter 3:1-2 Peter writes, "Likewise, wives, *be subject* to your own husbands, so that even if some do not obey the word, they may be won without a word by the conduct of their wives, when they see your respectful and pure conduct." Peter references Sarah who was subject to her husband Abraham, obeying him and "calling him lord" (v. 5-6). He is likely drawing an allusion to the instance when Abraham tried to pass Sarah off as his sister instead of his wife for fear of being killed by powerful men. Clearly, it took some serious faith to obey and "be subject" to her husband in that situation! In any case, Peter says that "you are her [Sarah's] children, if you do good and do not fear anything that is frightening" (v. 6). This indicates that Sarah's obedience and subjection (v. 5) was done out of respect rather than heartfelt, active, self-giving service.

The common denominator of each usage of "be subject" is passivity and compliance. The New Testament instructs wives not to resist their unbelieving husbands nor slaves their unjust masters but rather to have a "gentle and quiet spirit" (1 Pet. 3:4) as well as "respect and fear and sincerity of heart" (Eph. 6:5). In 1 Peter 5:5, being in subjection is also linked to humility. And the purpose of being subject always seems to be "that the word of God may not be reviled" (Tit. 2:5).

Most importantly, being subject does *not* mean rendering service or actively promoting the other's welfare or preferences. Case in point: after Jesus sent out the seventy-two, they returned to him and joyfully proclaimed that "even the demons are *subject to* us in your name" (Lk. 10:17). Obviously, the demons' subjection to Christ did not refer to active service but rather a passive nonresistance or compliance.

So when Paul tells us in Romans 13:1 to "be subject to the governing authorities," he is telling us to be humble, respectful, fearful, gentle, quiet, and sincere before them. Render them obedience when they require it (so long as doing so doesn't violate our Christian ethics, as we will discuss later). Do not resist them.

* * *

Delegated Authority

"For there is no authority except from God, and those that exist have been instituted by God. Therefore whoever resists the authorities resists what God has appointed. . ." (Rom. 13:1b-2). How does this square with the idea that God wants direct authority over His people? If "God is the King of all the earth" (Ps. 47:7), why would He appoint earthly authorities who will claim large swathes of His territory and the loyalties of His creatures?

We should try to understand what it means for God to "institute" or "appoint" governing authorities, because if we understand that, it will be easier to answer these questions.

Theologian John Howard Yoder outlines three broad views of what it means for governments to be instituted by God. One view, which Yoder calls the *positivistic view* holds that "whatever government exists, it is by virtue of an act of institution, that is, a specific providential action of God, that it came into being." In other words, whatever governments we find throughout the world, both now and historically, are and were in power by the specific will of God. "Whatever is, is the will of God," as Yoder puts it. Some of the language of Romans 13 seems to support this view, for instance, when it says "there is no authority except from God, and those that exist have been instituted by God." However, as Yoder points out, though

Romans 13 does use broad language to address *all* governing authorities, it also "makes no affirmative moral judgement on the existence of a particular government and says nothing particular about who happens to be Caesar or what his policies may be."[15] Paul refers to governing authorities in a broad, abstract sense rather than as any one government or person or group of people. This leaves open the possibility that God does not necessarily sanction each and every government that has ever existed.

Yoder calls the common alternative view the *normative view* because it interprets Romans 13 as highlighting what government *should be* rather than what it *is*. In this view:

> What is ordained is not a particular government but the concept of a proper government, the principle of government as such. As long as a given government lives up to a certain minimum set of requirements, then that government may properly claim the sanction of divine institution. If, however, a government fails adequately to fulfill the functions divinely assigned to it, it loses its authority.[16]

The problem with this view is that the passage makes no distinction between "proper" government and "improper" government. As Yoder puts it, "Who is to judge how bad a government can be and still be good?" Indeed, there's not even a hint of an exclusion to Christians being subject to government found in the passage. Again, Yoder: "In the social context of the Jewish Christians in Rome, the whole point of the passage was to take out of their minds any concept of rebellion against or even emotional rejection of this corrupt pagan government."[17]

Yoder's solution, which is the commonly held view among Anabaptist denominations, is that God's "institution" of

---

[15] Yoder, John Howard. *The Politics of Jesus* (Grand Rapids: Eerdmans, 1994), 199.
[16] Ibid.
[17] Ibid. 200

government is much broader and more in line with God's constant, ever-present providence in the world. Yoder thinks it is inaccurate to say that God specifically creates, institutes, or ordains the governing authorities. Rather, he thinks God *orders* them, organizing them in a way that suits His purposes.[18] This organizational providence looks less like micromanagement than it does like the expansive superintendence of history described by Paul to the men of Athens in Acts 17:26-27:

> And he made from one man every nation of mankind to live on all the face of the earth, having determined allotted periods and the boundaries of their dwelling place, that they should seek God, in the hope that they might feel their way toward him and find him.

Paul speaks here of God's overarching direction of history, how He bends the broad trends, epochs, and balances of political power toward His ultimate ends. The language does not entail management of every detail, every shift in power, or every influential figure. Rather, it paints a picture of a God who, though He may not be controlling every dash of the waves or shift in the winds, is still steering the ship of history. God's "institution" of governments as described in Romans 13 is part of this overarching superintendence of history.

In my judgement, Yoder's view comes closest to Paul's intention in Romans 13 but doesn't quite capture it. Paul does address government in abstract, all-inclusive terms rather than as a specific organization or person. He likely has Nero and the Roman government in mind, and that is certainly what the audience would think of. But he intentionally leaves out any references to the Roman government (unlike Peter in 1 Peter 2, who mentions the emperor). This lends credence to the notion that Paul's meaning here is of government *as a concept* rather than *every individual government in aggregate*. Paul is saying that God has established government *as a concept* to fulfill a certain role, and He has appointed governing authorities *as a concept* to

---

[18] Ibid. 201

carry it out. Thus, it would not necessarily be accurate to say that God appointed Nero, or that He appointed Hitler, or that He appointed Barack Obama or Donald Trump. Who sits in positions of governmental power and what those individuals do with that power is not necessarily sanctioned by God. The fact that government and the positions of authority within it exist, however, *is* sanctioned by God.

The weakness of Yoder's view of Romans 13 pertains to his assertion that God merely "orders" or "organizes" governments. While the language used about governing authorities is broad and conceptual rather than specific and concrete, there clearly *is* a sense in which God has established governments for His purposes, even if those purposes are limited and temporary. To say that God merely "orders" or "organizes" governments stretches the words "institute" and "appoint" beyond their natural meaning. Yoder, a pacifist, seems intent on finding a way to absolve God of any close association with governments that, by their nature, use force ("the sword") to function. But in doing so, he embraces an unnatural reading of these verbs.

It makes more sense to read Paul as saying that God has instituted government *conceptually*, and that He has appointed governing authorities *conceptually*. This avoids the distinction (not found in Romans 13) of proper vs. improper government, and it also avoids the problem of the myriad evil, unredeemable governmental authorities that have held power throughout history. Since governing authorities are sinful people, we should not expect all of their policies or governing decisions to be good. But God has delegated them a role to play, and that role is to prevent and punish evil, thereby acting as a vehicle for God's wrath on evildoers (Rom. 13:4).

Of course, God has the prerogative to intervene in history whenever He chooses to alter the balance of earthly power, and sometimes He does. We find evidence for this particularly in the book of Daniel, as Daniel had many interactions with King Nebuchadnezzar and his government. On multiple occasions,

Daniel informed Nebuchadnezzar that God "rules the kingdom of men and gives it to whom he will and sets over it the lowliest of men" (Dan. 4:17). Indeed, "It is He who changes the times and the epochs; He removes kings and establishes kings; He gives wisdom to wise men and knowledge to men of understanding" (Dan. 2:21). Both of these passages use exalting, poetic language in reference to God's authority, so it is unclear just how involved God is in the everyday politics of humanity. However, Daniel 5:18-21 suggests that sometimes God will decide to remove a ruler based on the ruler's actions or attitude. The passage makes clear that while God delegates earthly authority (in this case, to Nebuchadnezzar), He does not want the truth to be lost that "the Most High God rules the kingdom of mankind and sets it over whom he will" (v. 21).

In this way, the Bible affirms both that "kingship belongs to the Lord" *and* that "he rules over the nations" (Ps. 22:28; see also Ps. 47:8). Indeed, God retains the highest authority in the universe and all authority comes from Him, and thus those who have earthly authority did not obtain it outside the will or power of God. Rather, it is *by the will of God*, broadly speaking, that they hold the authority they do. Hence Jesus's statement to Pontius Pilate in John 19:11: "You would have no authority over me at all unless it had been given you from above."

How, then, does this fit with God's overarching plan to restore His own direct authority over His creation and His human creatures? How does it conform to Christ's goal to give people wholeness of life?

We must remember that, even though the Kingdom of God is available to enter into now, we are also living in an age of *already* and *not yet*. We believers are *already* part of the Kingdom and can *already* experience the wholeness of life that Christ brought, but the Kingdom has *not yet* become the sole organizing structure of the world. It is *not yet* here in its entirety. For now, it is like crops growing amongst the weeds. Practically, this means that even though God's ultimate goal is to retake direct authority over humanity, a change is required that has not yet occurred—it requires every knee to bow to Jesus and every tongue to confess that he is Lord (see Phil. 2). It requires all human hearts to be sanctified through submission to Christ and the indwelling of the Spirit. It also, unfortunately, requires all those who are unwilling to accept Christ to experience the "second death" (Rev. 20:11-15). Until then, the power structures of our world are mixed. The Kingdom of God, which eschews worldly hierarchies of power and embraces leadership through service (see Matt. 20:20-28), is developing alongside those worldly hierarchies.

In short, in a world in which not everyone has been redeemed and regenerated through faith in God, governments are still necessary. Where there are sinful, unredeemed people, there needs to be an earthly force to prevent and punish evil, if only to hinder people from harming each other as much as they otherwise would.

Thus, we read that "rulers are not a terror to good conduct, but to bad. Would you have no fear of the one who is in authority? Then do what is good, and you will receive his approval" (Rom. 13:3). Paul knows that governments do not always approve of good behavior and disapprove of bad. Nero's government certainly didn't do this. But, broadly speaking, Paul wants his audience to know that God has delegated governments a useful role to play in society, and that is the authority to suppress human evil. When governments fulfill this function, which they by and large *must* do in order to remain in power, they are indeed a "terror" to bad conduct.

* * *

The Sword

How exactly does government carry out its role in society? What means does it use that set it apart from other types of social organizations? In short, what defines government?

The answer lies in a sentence in verse 4: "But if you do

wrong, be afraid, for he [the government] does not bear the sword in vain". The "sword" here (Greek: *machaira*) alludes to the weapon worn on the belt of the Roman soldier during the first century. At this time, in Judea-Samaria, there were no organized armies that stood in opposition to the Romans. The Jewish zealots certainly opposed the Roman occupation, using mostly guerrilla tactics, but they did not have the capability to go toe-to-toe with the Romans in open battle. The same situation, more or less, pervaded all the Mediterranean regions of the Roman Empire. The city of Rome, especially, housed no military threats to the empire. Paul's use of the word "sword," then, would not draw to his audience's mind the military application of the weapon. He wasn't making any comment, approving or disapproving, of Rome's military expansionism or imperialism.

Instead, the image that would come to mind for Paul's audience in Rome is the short sword worn by the domestic soldier who acts as a policeman. As John Howard Yoder points out, the reference being made is to "judicial authority." It doesn't refer to "the instrument of capital punishment, since the Romans crucified their criminals. It was not the instrument of war since it was but a long dagger." Rather, "it was more a symbol of authority than a weapon."[19] In other words, Paul is using the symbol of the sword as a way of showing the *means* by which government fulfills its function. "The power of the sword," writes Pastor Greg Boyd, "is the ability to coerce behavior by threats and to make good on those threats when necessary: if a law is broken, you will be punished."[20] The symbol of the sword, then, "is the way a given government exercises dominion over its subjects by appeal to violence."[21]

Violence or the threat of violence is *how* governments operate. It is how they punish bad conduct and exercise God's

---

[19] Yoder, *Politics of Jesus*, 203.
[20] Boyd, Gregory. *The Myth of a Christian Nation* (Zondervan: Grand Rapids, 2005) 18.
[21] Yoder, 204.

wrath on evildoers. This may seem like an obvious point, but it helps us form a biblical definition of government.

Boyd puts it well when he writes, "Wherever a person or group exercises power over others—or tries to—*there* is a version of the kingdom of the world."[22] To Boyd, governments are all "kingdoms of this world," and the power of the sword mentioned in Romans 13:4 is tantamount to "power over" others—the ability to use force or the threat of force to carry out one's will. "The sword is part of our common curse," Boyd states, "yet God uses it to keep law and order in the world." He goes on to conclude, "The government 'does not bear the sword in vain, 'therefore, for it is a divine means of keeping fallen people from wreaking havoc on each other." Boyd agrees with our conclusion that, though God's ultimate goal is to reclaim full and direct authority over His creation, He uses government to mitigate human evil in the present age.

We might formulate our own definition of government (or the state) as this: Government is the institution of society that God has appointed to punish and prevent evil through the threat or use of force.

Of course, the Bible is not a political science textbook and Paul is not explicitly laying out a definition of the government in Romans 13. However, it is possible to piece together each word and phrase of this definition from Scripture without sacrificing our faithfulness to the intent of the biblical authors. When any of the New Testament authors talk about government or governing officials, it makes sense to assume that the above definition is what they have in mind.

* * *

God's Servant

Some read Romans 13 and conclude that Paul must have a

---

[22] Boyd, 18.

far more favorable view of government than the one we have presented. Government is called "God's servant for your good" and "ministers of God." Surely if the Bible awards any person or institution such designations, it does so approvingly.

We must remember that Paul is addressing governments and governing authorities *conceptually* in this entire passage. Romans 13 discusses the general purpose God has for governments. Hence being called "God's servant for your good" is tied to rulers being a terror not to good conduct but to bad (v. 3-4). Likewise, the authorities being called "ministers of God" is tied to their "attending to this very thing" (punishing evil and approving of good). Thus, while the passage doesn't draw a distinction between good government and bad government, it *does* inform us about the purpose of government and how believers ought to relate to it when it is fulfilling its purpose. We might think of it as an idealistic portrayal of government — a picture of how earthly authorities *should* look in this age. The text is silent, however, about what to do when government has radically departed from its God-given role.

In two separate occasions in the Old Testament — the cases of King Nebuchadnezzar of Babylon and Cyrus the Great of Persia — Scripture uses similar and even some identical language to describe governing authorities as Romans 13 does. In both of these cases, the king responded to God's prodding and conformed to His will. In the case of Nebuchadnezzar, the king responded to Daniel's interpretations of his dreams by acknowledging God's authority (Dan. 2:46-47; 4:34-37) as well as "practicing righteousness" and "showing mercy to the oppressed" (Dan. 4:27). Hence, in the book of Jeremiah, God refers to Nebuchadnezzar as "my servant" to whom He has given land and authority (Jer. 25:9, 27:6, 43:10).

Likewise, Cyrus of Persia responded to God's moving in his heart to release the Jews from captivity and allow them to return to their homeland (Ezra 1:1; see also 2 Chron. 36:22). "Thus says Cyrus king of Persia, 'The Lord, the God of heaven, has given me all the kingdoms of the earth and He has appointed me to build Him a house in Jerusalem, which is in Judah'" (Ezra 1:2; see also 2 Chron. 36:23). Cyrus even restored the treasures of the temple in Jerusalem from the royal treasury (Ezra 6:4-5). This is the reason that God took favor on Cyrus and called the king "His anointed" (Isa. 45:1) and said of him, "He is my shepherd, and he shall fulfill all my purpose" (Isa. 44:28).

Despite these two glowing exemplars, they are exceptions to the rule and not the rule itself. God does not always or even typically have this kind of positive influence on governments. More often in Scripture, we find that governments are made up of "wicked rulers" who "frame injustice by statute" (Ps. 94:20), "decree iniquitous decrees" and write oppression into law (Isa. 10:1-3), request and accept bribes (Mic. 7:3), deny justice and evade responsibility (Eccl. 5:8), delight in evil and treachery (Hos. 7:3), hurt others with their power (Eccl. 8:9), and lord their authority over others while pretending to be benefactors (Lk. 22:25). This is to say nothing of the vast amount of anecdotal evidence from both the Old and New Testaments of governing authorities doing these and even worse things.

Cases like that of Nebuchadnezzar and Cyrus, then, are quite rare in the landscape of Scripture. Thus, Paul's invoking of language that harkens back to them, such as calling authorities God's servants and ministers, presents an idealized version of government. Paul speaks of government as it *should be*, as it is *meant to be*, not necessarily as it *is*. That is, government should be just and fair and should refrain from oppressing the vulnerable. It should punish evil and approve of good. In this way, God uses governments, even if not everything governments do conforms to God's role for them. Just as many of Nebuchadnezzar and Cyrus's actions did not conform to God's will (as is obvious from a cursory reading of Daniel 1-4) and some of their actions conformed to God's will without their even knowing it (compare Isa. 44:28 to Isa. 45:4), God can use governments in surprising ways.

There are other examples in Scripture of God using even

evil or corrupt governments to fulfill His purposes. For instance, in Isaiah 10:5, God pronounces "woe" on Assyria even as He proclaims Assyria "the rod of my anger" and says that "the staff in their hands is my fury!" God used Assyria to punish the "godless nation" of Israel (Isa. 10:6), but in the very next verse, God says, "But he [Assyria] does not so intend, and his heart does not so think; but it is in his heart to destroy, and to cut off nations not a few" (v. 7). In other words, God used the actions of the Assyrians to fulfill His purposes (executing His wrath) even though He did not morally approve of the Assyrians' intentions. What the Assyrians meant for evil, God meant for good (see Gen. 50:20). Thus, the passage goes on, "When the Lord has finished all his work on Mount Zion and on Jerusalem, he will punish the speech of the arrogant heart of the king of Assyria and the boastful look in his eyes" (Isa. 10:12). The very same actor who played into God's purposes of executing wrath and vengeance was held accountable for his own sin!

Circling back to Romans 13, Paul gives us no reason in this passage not to assume that God holds the same stance toward all governments in the present age. They might be fair and morally upright like Cyrus and Nebuchadnezzar, or they might be corrupt and unjust like the Assyrians, but God uses them all the same. In either case, they exist to fulfill God's purposes.

* * *

"For the Sake of Conscience"

If governments can be either good or evil and yet still serve the function God intends for them, why does Paul say we must "be in subjection, not only to avoid God's wrath but also *for the sake of conscience*" (Rom. 13:5)? If our government is evil, how can we be subject to it and keep a clean conscience?

First, remember that "being subject" comes closer in meaning to "not resisting" than to "actively serving." Also, remember that the original recipients of this letter lived under a cruel, corrupt, wicked government themselves. We do not conscientiously subject ourselves to government because of *everything* it does but rather only because of a specific role assigned to it by God. Recall that the state's servanthood and status as "minister of God" is tied to its "attending to this very thing"—i.e. carrying out God's wrath on the wrongdoer and approving of good conduct. Governing authorities remain God's servants appointed to do these things even if they do many things that violate God's moral will. Thus, even though governments are imperfect (some much more so than others), they have a God-given role to play in society and accordingly deserve our subjection and honor.

In short, we conscientiously live in subjection to government, not because of our faith in the governing authorities, but because our faith in our True King—the King of kings—is so strong that we trust in His power over His secular human agents. If we truly trust that state actors are God's servants, we will see God's provision in their peacekeeping duties in society. We will see that *God* is bringing justice upon evildoers *through* them.

But what if the authorities in power *don't* fulfill their God-given role in society? As we pointed out earlier, the text is silent about how believers ought to relate to government when it has radically departed from its task of punishing evil and approving of good. Readers of Paul's epistles find themselves in the same predicament when Paul addresses wives submitting to husbands, children obeying their parents "in everything," and slaves obeying their masters "in everything" (Col. 3:18-4:1). Here, though Paul gives instruction to both wives and husbands, children and parents, slaves and masters, he does not address difficult circumstances in which submission or obedience would require abandoning one's Christian principles. What if a husband instructs his wife never to read her Bible or go to church? What if a father wants to molest his daughter? What if a master commands his servant to steal?

It is imperative in these cases to seek the *whole counsel of Scripture* in order to garner the wisdom to handle such hard situations. Even though Paul often speaks in absolutes, we should not necessarily interpret him as saying that there are no exceptions to his teachings. For instance, was it right that Sapphira submitted to her husband's plan to lie to Peter and the Holy Spirit about the proceeds of their land sale? Was it wrong for the Jewish slaves to flee their wicked masters in Egypt?

Similar cases can be found in Scripture about disobedience and even outright revolt against government, and these cases are mentioned approvingly! Think of the Hebrew midwives who refused to kill Jewish babies despite being ordered to do so by the Egyptian authorities (Ex. 1). Think of Rahab lying to the King of Jericho about the Hebrew spies (Josh. 2). Think of Ehud infiltrating the king's palace and assassinating him (Judg. 3). Think of Daniel and his friends refusing to obey the king's decrees and dietary norms (Dan. 3, 6). Think, finally, of the wise men disobeying Herod's orders to report back to him any news of a Jewish king (Matt. 2). Clearly, it is sometimes justified to defy the governing authorities and their laws.

How does a believer distinguish when one ought to be subject to the authorities and when it is justifiable to defy them? We find only one principle in Scripture that can explain this: the **Acts 5:29 Principle**. In this passage from Acts 5, shortly after Pentecost, the Jewish authorities had some of the apostles arrested and taken before a council, who ordered them "not to teach in this name" (the name of Jesus) (v. 28). "But Peter and the apostles answered, '*We must obey God rather than men*'" (v. 29). Here we find one more instance of godly people *disobeying* governing authorities, but in this case we are also given a principle that justified their disobedience. Put simply, the principle is this:

> *If there is any disagreement between God's law and
> the laws or orders of the government, God's law
> always takes precedence.*

Thus, whether it be obedience to parents or masters or submission to husbands or the state, *submission/obedience is a general principle, not an unbending rule.* Though Paul may command obedience to parents and masters "in everything," we must read his teachings in light of the New Testament and Scripture as a whole. When we encounter instances in which the will of man and the will of God clearly conflict, we must follow the will of God. As this is true for wives, children, and slaves, it is also true for believers in relation to government.

Even though governing authorities are God's servants appointed to fulfill a certain task, their natures are no less sinful than any other unsaved human being. State leaders are no less prone than anyone else to moral failures. The same is true of those individuals whom God appointed various tasks in the Old Testament. Think of Abraham, Isaac, Moses, Gideon, or David. Were any of them flawless? No. They all violated God's moral will at times—sometimes often. But God used them for specific purposes all the same.

That God has established government a role to play in society is not to say that He morally approves of its actions or intentions. We believers honor it and conscientiously subject ourselves to it not for its own sake, but because of the necessary role God has assigned it to play.

* * *

The Sovereignty of God vs. the Influence of Satan

How does this picture of government as God's servant of wrath fit with Satan's proclaimed possession of earthly governments? Recall that during the wilderness temptations, Satan said that the authority over "all the kingdoms of the world . . . has been delivered to me, and I give it to whom I will"

(Lk. 4:5-6). How can it be the case that Satan has authority over earthly governments *and* that "there is no authority except from God" (Rom. 13:1)?

Was Satan lying when he indicated that all of the earth's kingdoms are in his possession and under his authority? The theologian Wayne Grudem believes so. In his book, *Politics According to the Bible*, Grudem cites Jesus' explanation in John 8:44 that Satan "has nothing to do with the truth" because "there is no truth in him. When he lies, he speaks out of his own character, for he is a liar and the father of lies." Grudem goes on to ask: "Do we believe *Satan's words* that he has the authority of all earthly kingdoms, or do we believe *Jesus' words* that Satan is a liar and the father of lies?"

Asking the question this way uses a clever rhetorical method of persuading readers to adopt his viewpoint without presenting any evidence for it. The question assumes that we either side with Grudem's view that Satan was lying about his authority over earthly governments or that we must reject one of Jesus' teachings. But the truth is more nuanced than Grudem's narrow dichotomy would imply.

Grudem does not develop an argument from the passages in which Satan tempts Jesus with all the kingdoms of the earth but rather cites a verse from a different context and then applies it to this passage. In John 8, Jesus rebukes the Jews who rest on their laurels because they are physical descendants of Abraham. No, says Jesus, Abraham may be their father genetically, but their spiritual father is Satan, who has deceived them. The Jews do not accept the truth Christ came to bring because their spiritual father "has nothing to do with the truth, because there is no truth in him" (v. 44). This passage does not fit with what Grudem is trying to use it for. Grudem takes the statement that Satan "has nothing to do with the truth" and implies that the Devil is *incapable* of telling the truth. Jesus' teaching in John 8, on the other hand, suggests that Satan's overarching goal is deception but not that Satan cannot or does not use individual statements of truth in order to accomplish that.

Take the case of Job. When Satan appears with the other angels before God and God asks where Satan has come from, Satan answers, "From going to and fro on the earth, and from walking up and down on it" (Job 1:7). Was Satan lying about where he had been? Probably not. We have no indication of that from the passage. But it is clear from the next thing Satan says that his overarching goal is deception, as he suggests that Job will curse God if his possessions are taken away (v. 11). Job, we know from the story, did not end up cursing God.

We find the same thing happening in the three temptations in the wilderness. In the second temptation in Matthew's account, Satan takes Jesus to the top of the temple, tells him to throw himself down, and accurately cites Psalm 91:11-12: "He will command his angels concerning you. . . On their hands they will bear you up, lest you strike your foot against a stone." But while the Scripture is truthful, Satan misuses it in an attempt to derail Christ's messianic mission. Certainly, the angels could have saved Jesus, and such a feat would earn Jesus great popularity, but it would not adhere to the humble and sacrificial plan laid out for Jesus.

Contrary to Grudem's claim that Satan was lying about his authority over human governments, there is ample Scriptural evidence to support the Devil's claim. First, notice that Jesus does not dispute Satan's claim of authority. He merely disputes the Devil's attempt to get Jesus to worship him. Second, keep in mind that on three separate occasions Jesus calls Satan the "ruler of this world" (Jn 12:31, 14:30, 16:11). As Greg Boyd points out in *Myth of a Christian Nation*, "The term 'ruler' (*arche*) was a political term used to denote the highest ruling authority in a given region—and Jesus applied it to Satan over the whole world!"[23]

Third, two other biblical authors, John and Paul, agree with Jesus' teaching about Satan's authority. As John puts it in 1 John

---

[23] Boyd, Greg. *Myth of a Christian Nation*, 21-22.

5:19, "the whole world lies in the power of the evil one." By the "world," here, John likely means the unbelieving world, which includes most of the human population of the world. Paul refers to Satan as "the god of this age" (2 Cor. 4:4) and as "the ruler of the power of the air" (Eph. 2:2), describing the Devil's thoroughgoing influence over every aspect of the world including human culture, religion, and government.

Put all of this together and it's difficult to avoid the conclusion that Satan does indeed wield the kind of authority that he claims to in the third temptation.

So how, then, do we make sense of both Satan and God's authority over human governments? A few things are important to remember here.

First, the broader narrative of Scripture indicates that creation is engaged in a fierce spiritual battle between God and Satan. As God is working out His plan in the world, Satan seeks to undermine it at every turn. The goals of Satan are both macro and micro; he wishes to derail God's ultimate objectives, and he also wishes to erode and destroy every individual piece of creation that is meant to comply with God's beautiful plan. The entire creation "has been groaning" in anticipation of the new creation that Christ came to inaugurate (Rom. 8:22), but we also see God's purpose even down to individual stones (Lk. 19:14). Likewise, we find in Scripture that Satan's attention is focused *both* on the world as a whole, which is said in 1 John 5:19 to be "in the power of the evil one," *and also* on individuals, such as in instances of demon possession (e.g. Lk. 8:26-33). To whatever extent Satan can prevent people from experiencing the spiritual and material blessings of the Kingdom of God, he will do so.

This battle, however, is certainly a two-way one. As the Creator of everything, including Satan, God knows exactly what He is up against and how to combat it. This is an important reason why He sent His Son into the world: "The reason the Son of God appeared was to destroy the works of the devil" (1 Jn. 3:8). As Jesus himself explained: "Now is the judgement of this world; now the ruler of this world will be cast out. And I, when I am lifted up from the earth, will draw all people to myself" (Jn. 12:31-32). Even though Christ's work on earth has sealed the eventual demise of Satan, and Christ is actively drawing people away from Satan's influence, the spiritual battle that rages between the demonic forces and God's forces continues in this age.

Second, we have already seen how God can have an intention for a person or group of people's actions that does not align with the intentions of the person(s) themselves. We see this in the case of Joseph and his brothers who sold him into slavery. Joseph says to his brothers that "you meant evil against me, but God meant it for good, to bring it about that many people should be kept alive, as they are today" (Gen. 50:20). We also see this in the case of the prideful Assyrians, whom God used to punish His faithless people even though the Assyrians themselves did not share God's intentions (Isa. 10).

So, too, do we see this with earthly governments. Though God established a useful role for them to play in this present age, Satan bears a more immediate influence over them. The general role that God intends for good, Satan can twist for evil. Indeed, although all of the governing authorities' power comes from God and can be revoked by God, the freedom to use their delegated power is real. This freedom leaves humans susceptible to influence from multiple forces and actors. Satan, who, as we have seen, Paul calls the "god of this world" in 2 Corinthians 4:4, uses every means at his disposal to manipulate, deceive, and control humanity and human power structures. Non-believers naturally slip into his influence as they are caught "in the snare of the devil" (2 Tim. 2:26) and lie in the "power of the evil one" (1 Jn. 5:19). "And no wonder," Paul writes in 2 Corinthians 11:14, explaining why humans are so easily deceived, "for Satan himself masquerades as an angel of light."

This is how it can be simultaneously true that "God is the King of all the earth" (Ps. 47:7) *and* that Satan is the "ruler [or prince] of this world" (Jn. 12:31). God maintains ultimate authority and sovereignty, but Satan has been allowed immediate influence over the non-believing world and its power structures. Satan has no power over the Kingdom of God, but all other earthly governments, which by their nature lie outside the Kingdom of God, are within Satan's grasp.

With this paradoxical truth in mind, it is now even clearer why Paul instructs the Roman believers to "be subject" to (not resist) their governing authorities. Even if the Roman government and broader culture hated and persecuted the Christians, the *people* were not the church's enemies. The true enemy was the energizing spiritual force behind the persecutors. "For our struggle is not against flesh and blood," Paul writes in Ephesians 6:12, "but against the rulers, against the authorities, against the powers of this dark world and against the spiritual forces of evil in the heavenly realms." Paul lived this out when he stood before Herod Agrippa, spoke to the king with respect, and attempted to persuade him of the truth of the gospel (Acts 27). He addressed the emperor not merely as a pawn of Satan, but as a human being that Christ died for, a person with whom God yearned for reconciliation.

Of course, Paul also knew that the emperor would make a terrible foe to the church. Perhaps the apostle had recently meditated on Proverbs 19:12: "The king's fury is like a lion's roar; to rouse his anger is to risk your life. Avoiding a fight is a mark of honor; only fools insist on quarreling." But Paul also recognized that, rather than the emperor himself, Paul's real enemy was the spiritual actor who wielded influence over him.

* * *

Conclusion

Government is the institution of society that God has appointed to punish and prevent evil through the threat or use of force. Even though God's direct authority over humanity has already broken into the world through His Kingdom, earthly authorities continue to serve a useful function because sin still exists and continues to pervade our world. God's Kingdom has not yet become the sole governing structure of creation, but someday it will.

Though human governments in the present age are under the influence and authority of Satan, God has designated them a necessary role to play. We Christians are like ambassadors living in a foreign land under our respective human governments. We abide by its laws and participate in its government to whatever degree we are invited (so long as that participation does not conflict with our Christian ethical standards), but our citizenship is ultimately in Heaven. Besides being subject to governing authorities, there is more to be said about the church's relationship to the government, which will be the subject of the following chapter.

* * *

"And you were dead in the trespasses and sins in which you once walked, following the course of this world, following the prince of the power of the air, the spirit that is now at work in the sons of disobedience."
Ephesians 2:1-2

CHAPTER FIVE

Pray for Kings: The Church's Relationship to the State

In the previous chapter, we explored the negative relationship of the church to the state — in other words, how the church should *not* relate to the governing authorities (resisting them). In this chapter, we discuss the positive relationship of the church to the state — that is, the duties that believers have to the government and governing authorities. Beyond simply refraining from resisting the state, the New Testament authors assign Christ-followers a few strategic yet sincere tasks that are meant to complement the role of the state as well as enable the church to thrive.

There are three main passages which address this topic: 1 Timothy 2, 1 Peter 2, and Romans 12-13.

* * *

Pray For

Paul describes the first duty of the church to the state in 1 Timothy 2:1-2:

> First of all, then, I urge that supplications, prayers, intercessions, and thanksgivings be made for all people, for kings and all who are in high positions, that we may lead a peaceful and quiet life, godly and dignified in every way.

Supplicate, pray for, intercede, and give thanks for the

governing authorities. Paul here lists various terms associated with prayer on behalf of someone else in order to drive home his point that we are not to pray for those in "high positions" as if they are merely enemies but rather as whole persons, capable of good and evil. Yes, Paul says at first that we are to pray "for all people," but the primary point he is making here is about prayer for those in positions of authority. Sometimes our prayers about them take the form of supplications—earnestly asking God for a certain outcome. Sometimes they take the form of intercessions, or asking God to bring about or prevent a certain outcome. And sometimes they take the form of thanksgiving, praising God that a certain outcome did (or did not) come to pass. And, of course, all of our prayers should acknowledge the leaders as human beings for whom Christ died, regardless of their political affiliation, policies, or decisions.

Notice in verse 2 that Paul suggests the sort of outcome we are to pray for when praying for our leaders and authorities: "that we may lead a peaceful and quiet life, godly and dignified in every way." What we ought to pray for when we pray for our authorities is not necessarily a certain policy agenda or increased influence in the government, but rather that Christians be given the ability to "lead a peaceful and quiet life"—suggesting a separation from the strife and hostility of politics—that is "godly and dignified in every way." In other words, we pray for the governing authorities to leave the church alone so that it can carry out its primary purpose on earth.

What exactly is that purpose? Verses 3 and 4 lay it out: "This [leading a peaceful, quiet, godly, and dignified life] is good, and it is pleasing in the sight of God our Savior, who desires all people to be saved and to come to the knowledge of the truth." That is why we pray specifically for those in positions of authority. They wield the greatest ability to prevent or distract the church from carrying out its Great Commission work. This was especially true at the time that the epistle to

Timothy was written, but it is still true today. Then and now, we pray for a separation of church and state so that state affairs do not become intermingled with our Kingdom duties—and so that we Christians do not become too intermingled in state affairs.

As Paul put it later in 2 Timothy 2:4, "No soldier gets entangled in civilian pursuits, since his aim is to please the one who enlisted him." Indeed, we believers ought to pray for both our political leaders and ourselves that we do not become so entangled in the affairs of government that our Kingdom-building and disciple-making efforts suffer.

* * *

Respect

Peter writes this in his first epistle:

> Be subject for the Lord's sake to every human institution, whether it be to the emperor as supreme, or to governors as sent by him to punish those who do evil and to praise those who do good. For this is the will of God, that by doing good you should put to silence the ignorance of foolish people. Live as people who are free, not using your freedom as a cover-up for evil, but living as servants of God. Honor everyone. Love the brotherhood. Fear God. Honor the emperor.

The first two verses of this passage sound very much like Romans 13. Perhaps Peter had heard Paul's teaching about governing authorities before writing this letter, or perhaps Paul had heard Peter's teaching on this subject before writing the book of Romans. Or, perhaps, the Spirit simply guided both men to write similar language in their treatments of the state. In any case, 1 Peter 2 and Romans 13 echo each other's teachings, each adding richness to the other.

Just as Paul instructs believers in 1 Timothy 2 to pray for everyone but highlights those in positions of authority as subjects of prayer, Peter likewise instructs believers to "honor everyone" but highlights honor for the emperor, and by extension all governing authorities under him, in particular. "Honor" is a term rarely used in today's world, but Peter's meaning here comes very close to "showing respect." Show respect to everyone, and yes, that includes the emperor and other state authorities.

Once again, we find a motivating factor behind this Christian duty to the government. Peter says that "by doing good you should put to silence the ignorance of foolish people." We show respect to the governing authorities not only because they are human beings for whom Christ died and thus are not our true enemy, but also because we want to quell the legitimacy of any accusations against us.

Here we must remember that Peter is addressing various churches in Asia Minor, part of the Roman Empire, who were facing religious persecution. Recall that the Jews in Rome told Paul that, though they knew little about Christianity, "with regard to this sect we know that everywhere it is spoken against" (Acts 18:22). As a passionate and fast-growing religious minority that abstained from emperor worship and pagan festivals, it is not difficult to see why the broader culture would find them loathsome and intolerable. Thus we find Peter, earlier in the letter, instructing believers to "[c]onduct yourselves with such honor among the Gentiles that, though they slander you as evildoers, they may see your good deeds and glorify God on the day He visits us" (2:12). Likewise, in the next chapter, Peter tells believers to respond to their detractors "with gentleness and respect, having a good conscience, so that, when you are slandered, those who revile your good behavior in Christ may be put to shame" (3:15b-16).

The motivation behind Peter's instruction to honor—show respect—to the governing authorities agrees with Paul's motivation from 1 Timothy 2. The goal is neither to gain political influence nor to give undue praise, but rather to keep good relations so that the government will leave the church alone to focus on the more important matters of spreading and defending the faith. As members of the early church suffered constant slanderous charges against them, related to any number of issues surrounding their counter-cultural lifestyle, it was imperative to show respect to the Roman authorities so as to squelch any claims of political subversion. The church wanted to keep the peace with the state *because* of its lack of total coalescence and adherence to it. Showing respect and even praying for it was their way of doing so.

* * *

Complement

To complement is to combine two separate and unique things together in order to improve or enhance the qualities of each. This is the relationship we find between the church and the state in Romans 12-13. In the second half of chapter 12, Paul identifies some of the marks of the true Christian, followed immediately by Romans 13:1's instruction that "every person be subject to the governing authorities." Considering that Paul's original letter contained no chapter or verse breaks, we must remember to read chapter 12 and 13 as one continuous line of thought. Sometimes Paul gives transitional words such as "therefore" or "then" to mark a shift from one line of thought to another, but we find no such transitional word between these chapters.

Here's the relevant passage in full (Rom. 12:14-13:8):

> Bless those who persecute you, bless and do not curse them. Rejoice with those who rejoice, weep with those who weep. Live in harmony with one another. Do not be haughty, but associate with the lowly. Never be wise in your own sight. Repay no one evil for evil, but give thought to do what is honorable in the sight of all. If possible, so far as it depends on you, live peaceably with all. Beloved, never avenge yourselves, but leave

it to the wrath of God, for it is written, "Vengeance is mine, I will repay, says the Lord." To the contrary, if your enemy is hungry, feed him; if he is thirsty, give him something to drink; for by so doing you will heap burning coals on his head. Do not be overcome by evil, but overcome evil with good. Let every person be subject to the governing authorities. For there is no authority except from God, and those that exist have been instituted by God. Therefore, whoever resists the authorities resists what God has appointed, and those who resist will incur judgement. For rulers are not a terror to good conduct, but to bad. Would you have no fear of the one who is in authority? Then do what is good, and you will receive his approval, for he is God's servant for your good. But if you do wrong, be afraid, for he does not bear the sword in vain. For he is the servant of God, and avenger who carries out God's wrath on the wrongdoer. Therefore one must be in subjection, not only to avoid God's wrath but also for the sake of conscience. For because of this you also pay taxes, for the authorities are ministers of God, attending to this very thing. Pay to all what is owed to them: taxes to whom taxes are owed, revenue to whom revenue is owed, respect to whom respect is owed, honor to whom honor is owed. Owe no one anything, except to love each other, for the one who loves another has fulfilled the law.

Where you choose to begin or end this passage is more or less arbitrary. One could find the marks of the true Christian beginning in 12:9 or even the beginning of chapter 12, and Paul's line of thought continues well beyond 13:8.

Several contrasts between the church and the state could be drawn from this passage, but the most important deals with vengeance and how to relate to one's enemies. While Paul instructs believers to "live peaceably with all" and do good to their enemies, the state is a terror to "bad conduct" and does not "bear the sword in vain." While believers are never to avenge themselves but rather to leave it to God, we are told just a few verses later that the state acts as God's avenger who carries out His "wrath on the wrongdoer." Believers are to "overcome evil with good" by blessing our enemies and persecutors, whereas the state subdues evil by fostering the fear of resistance to it. Believers are to "live in harmony with one another," while the state bears the sword precisely because it does not expect to live harmoniously with all of its subjects. In short, the church exists to draw all people into the Kingdom of God, while the state exists to keep the evil people in society in check.

Paul makes clear in this passage of Romans that both institutions have distinct roles to fulfill in society and the world. Whether or not an individual believer can remain true to his or her faith while "bearing the sword" in a governmental role, it must never be forgotten that the church and the state have radically different goals as well as methods of carrying out those goals. While the state uses force to achieve its ends, the church body operates under the Kingdom Principle of Voluntarism: "Service and charity in the Kingdom of God must always be heartfelt and voluntary." Thus, any impact the church seeks to make on the world, foremost being the conversion of unbelievers into believers, must be made outside the domain of government. Moreover, the moral behavior which follows faith in Christ cannot be spurred by any mechanism of government.

Paul gives no indication as to whether these two roles can be simultaneously fulfilled by the same person, which raises some tough questions for the contemporary Christian. What about Christians in the police force or the military or other offices which command forceful power over others? They "bear the sword" for the purpose of keeping evil people in check. Can one live peaceably with all and bless one's enemies while also acting as God's agent of wrath? Can one forsake vengeance while also using "the sword" to avenge those who do evil?

Some believers, who represent a view known as "Just War," say yes, that a Christian in the police or military can enter the role of agent of the state in carrying out God's wrath on evildoers while personally denying vengeance. Acting under the mantle of government, Just War advocates would say, gives a believer certain privileges and responsibilities (including the use or threat of force) that one would not have outside of government. Other Christians (who would be considered pacifists) would say no, that living peaceably with all, blessing one's enemies, forswearing vengeance, and overcoming evil with good are fundamentally incompatible with any kind of sword-bearing, even in government. The contrast between believers' restriction from vengeance in Romans 12 and the state's duty of carrying out vengeance in Romans 13 certainly lends support to this view. After all, the text gives no indication that Romans 12 refers to a different form of vengeance than that spoken of in Romans 13. And neither does Paul suggest an exception to the prohibition on vengeance for Christians in governmental offices.

As we will see shortly, the early church fathers writing in the first few hundred years after the life of Christ predominantly held the latter view.

While this is an important debate worth considering, both sides of the divide are susceptible to overlooking the complementary relationship between the church and the state. Yes, the church and the state have different goals as well as different methods of achieving those goals, but these two also provide things for each other that each would otherwise lack. The church, in its mission to make disciples and teach them to live the same peaceable and morally upstanding life as Jesus, provides the state with a more harmonious and civil populace than it would otherwise have. The state, on the other hand, ideally provides space in society for the church to operate, free from the threat of cruel and unjust persecutors.

"Ideally" is an important word here, as we know that many times in history (and continuing today, in some countries) the state did not provide the church with such space but rather sanctioned, encouraged, or carried out the cruel and unjust persecution themselves. However, Paul does not mention the potential for state persecution of the church here, even though he was intimately familiar with it. Rather, in his body of writings taken as a whole, we find that Paul instructs believers to pray for, honor, and be subject to the governing authorities *so that* the authorities will be more inclined to provide the church with this space and freedom. It is not as if it was a necessary evil for the church to relate to the state in such an arm's-length way until the state could be Christianized. The goal, in Paul's age as well as our own age, is to live at peace with the government so that they will grant the church freedom and fair treatment but otherwise ignore it, allowing the church to go about its business.

We may articulate this as the **Principle of Separation of Church and State**:

> *The church seeks to maintain a good relationship*
> *with the state so that the state will give the church*
> *the freedom, fair treatment, and independence to*
> *carry out its mission.*

Whether or not a believer can follow the New Testament's teachings while also wearing a police or military uniform or hold an office that commands the use of force, we must never forget that God's preference, demonstrated time and time again throughout Scripture, is to work through the weak, the lowly, the poor in spirit, *not* the ones who wield the most power. "God chose what is foolish in the world to shame the wise; God chose what is weak in the world to shame the strong; God chose what is low and despised in the world, even things that are not, to bring to nothing things that are, so that no human being might boast in the presence of God" (1 Cor. 1:27-29). The most profound example of this, of course, is Jesus, who emptied himself of all power and took on the form of a servant in order to carry out his mission (Phil. 2:5-8).

* * *

Early Church Views of the State

The last of the New Testament books and epistles were written as late as the 90s AD (although it is my opinion that they were all completed much earlier than this). A dearth of writings exists from that period until around the middle of the second century, perhaps because local churches were still circulating copies of the apostles' epistles and the gospels and, as such, there was little need to produce new writing. Perhaps, likewise, all efforts at preservation of texts went into preserving what was perceived as the more important documents — what we now know as the New Testament canon. Moreover, in the generation after the apostles' death, the disciples of the apostles could still pass on their teachings more or less intact, without the need to produce new writings to clarify or bolster the original teachings.

However, in the mid to late second century, we find many Christian writers such as Polycarp, Justin Martyr, and Theophilus essentially echoing, sometimes simply quoting, the New Testament's teachings about the state and believers' duties to it. As early as 175 AD, Athenian philosopher and Christian convert, Athenagoras, writes in his *Embassy for the Christians*:

> Who are more deserving to obtain the things they ask for than those who, like us, pray for your government? ... We pray that your empire may receive increase and addition—and that all men may become subject to your sway. And this is also for our advantage, that we may lead a peaceable and quiet life and may readily perform all that is commanded us.

Notice that Athenagoras reiterates the Principle of Separation of Church and State in that he explains Christian prayer for the government is both for the good of the authorities *and* for another motive: "that we may lead a peaceable and quiet life." That is, so that the government would leave us alone to pursue the cause of our Heavenly Kingdom.

Around the time that a Carthaginian thinker named Tertullian began writing in the late second century, the character of Christian writing changed. Tertullian, along with his slightly earlier contemporary Irenaeus, synthesized and elucidated Christian teachings in new yet (mostly) orthodox ways. He was, for instance, the first Latin writer to use the term "trinity." Christian writing no longer merely echoed or quoted New Testament language on the state. Tertullian strove to further illuminate the reasoning behind the separation of church and state. For instance, we find it stated many times that Christians pray for their governing authorities not for imperial conquests but rather for peace.

> We offer prayer for the safety of our rulers to the eternal, true and living God. . . . We pray for protection of the imperial house, for brave armies, a faithful senate, a virtuous people, *and a world at peace.*[24]

Though each of these taken together could be interpreted as a general blessing on the Roman Empire, it is important to note the culmination of the list, the greatest prayer request of all, is world peace. Likewise, Tertullian writes,

> You, then, who think that we do not care for the welfare of Caesar, look into God's revelations, examine our sacred books. . . . Most clearly, Scripture says, "Pray for kings, rulers, and powers, that all may be peace with you."[25]

Here it is important to note that Tertullian's summary interpretation of 1 Timothy 2:2-4 reiterates the purpose of prayer for government as the maintenance of peace. There is no hint of a desire for political influence, other than to preserve the church's ability to live out the gospel. Despite the frequent disparagement of the church in Roman society, it was in the church's best interest, according to Tertullian, that the Roman

---

[24] Bercot, *A Dictionary of Early Christian Beliefs*, 320-321.
[25] Ibid. 152

Empire thrive:

> There is also another and a greater necessity for our offering prayer on behalf of the emperors—in fact, for the complete stability of the empire and for Roman interests in general. For we know that a mighty shock impending over the whole earth—in fact, the very end of all things threatening dreadful woes—is only retarded by the continued existence of the Roman empire. We have no desire, then, to be overtaken by these dire events. In praying that their coming may be delayed, we are lending our aid to Rome's duration.[26]

In other words, the Romans may not have been perfectly amenable to the Christians, but they were better, in Tertullian's estimation, than barbarian or regional rule. The Roman legal system afforded them certain rights, which we see Paul taking advantage of in Acts 22, that were not guaranteed outside of the empire. Not to mention the fact that the church could take advantage of the Pax Romana throughout the empire. As church father Origen reasoned half a century later, "The existence of many kingdoms would have been a hindrance to the spread of the doctrine of Jesus throughout the entire world . . . because of the necessity of men everywhere engaging in war, and fighting on behalf of their native country, which was the case before the times of Augustus."[27]

Despite the desire for peaceful relations, Tertullian draws a sharp disparity between church and state, later commenting that "Peter, no doubt, had said that the king indeed must be honored. But he means that the king is honored *only when he keeps to his own sphere*."[28] This is the sphere of governing, keeping the peace, and promoting justice in society. The church's sphere, on the other hand, is fundamentally different. Writes Tertullian:

---

[26] Ibid. 152
[27] Ibid. 321
[28] Ibid. 153

> In us, all ardor in the pursuit of glory and honor is dead.
> So we have no pressing inducement to take part in your
> public meetings. *Nor is there anything more entirely
> foreign to is than affairs of state.*[29]

Why does Tertullian view "affairs of state" as foreign to believers? He explains this in a later document, dated to 200 AD:

> Therefore, very recently, there arose a dispute as to whether a servant of God should take upon himself the administration of any dignity or power—if he can keep himself (through adroitness or some special grace) from every type of idolatry. . . . Let us suppose that it is possible for anyone to succeed in operating under the mere *name* of the office, in whatever office. Let us also suppose the following: He neither sacrifices nor lends his authority to sacrifices. He does not farm out sacrificial victims. He does not assign to others the care of the temples. . . . He does not even take oaths. Furthermore, he does not sit in judgement on anyone's life or character (for you might allow his judging about money). He neither condemns nor indicts. He chains no one. He neither imprisons nor tortures anyone. Now, is it believable that all this is possible?[30]

Tertullian seeks to prove that the life of a Christian and the office of a governing authority are incompatible by listing many of the duties of state officials. Some of these are applicable only to the Roman government of his day, such as state sponsorship of the pagan sacrificial system and funding of the temples. But others, such as taking oaths, judging another's character, determining the life-or-death fate of others, and potentially imprisoning or using force upon others, are all duties of state officials which are equally applicable to today. And none of them are compatible with the lifestyle we are

---

[29] Ibid. 321
[30] Ibid. 545

called to in Christ.

To put the point a different way, how can a Christian live out the Kingdom Principle of Voluntarism ("Service and charity in the Kingdom of God must be heartfelt and voluntary") while also carrying out the coercive duties of the state? Likewise, how can a Christian who eschews vengeance take up the role of avenger? As Tertullian puts it in an early third century text, "Shall he apply the chain, the prison, the torture, and the punishment—he who is not the avenger even of his own wrongs?"[31]

This point is made in unambiguous terms by Clement of Alexandria writing in the late second or early third century:

> Christians are not allowed to correct with violence the delinquencies of sins. For it is not those that abstain from wickedness from compulsion, but those that abstain from choice, that God crowns. It is impossible for a man to be steadily good except by his own choice. For he that is made good by compulsion of another is not good; for he is not what he is by his own choice. For it is the freedom of each one that makes true goodness and reveals real wickedness.[32]

A similar statement was given by church father John Chrysostom much later, in the late fourth century, when he wrote:

> For Christians above all men are not permitted forcibly to correct the failings of those who sin. Secular judges indeed, when they have captured malefactors under the law, show their authority to be great, and prevent them even against their will from following their own devices: but in our case the wrongdoer must be made better, not by force, but by persuasion. For neither has authority of this kind for the restraint of sinners been given us by the law, nor, if it had been given, should

---

[31] Ibid. 545

[32] "Fragments of Clemens Alexandrinus." https://st-takla.org/books/en/ecf/002/0020441.html

we have any field for the exercise of our power, inasmuch as God rewards those who abstain from evil by their own choice, not of necessity. . . . For it is not possible for any one to cure a man by compulsion against his will.[33]

This is perhaps the clearest, most powerful statement from an ancient church father encapsulating both the Principle of Voluntarism and the Separation of Church and State. Since believers are not permitted to correct the failings of sinners by force, what use is it to us to participate in the offices of government? How can the peaceable, disciple-making cause of God's Kingdom be furthered through the forceful authority of the state? And, likewise, how can the necessary job of forcefully restraining and punishing criminal behavior be adequately carried out through the church's voluntarist way of life?

Perhaps this is why Tertullian draws such a sharp contrast between Caesar and Christianity when he writes: "The Caesars too would have believed on Christ, if either the Caesars had not been necessary for the world, or if Christians could have been Caesars."[34] Notice that the language used here indicates not just a *difficulty* or *implausibility* of authorities being faithful Christians, or of faithful Christians taking on offices of authority, but an *impossibility*. Tertullian views the mission and *modus operandi* of believers as being fundamentally incompatible with the mission and *modus operandi* of governing authorities.

It is because of this sharp contrast in Christian theology that Tertullian can give the Romans this assurance:

No conspiracy has ever broken out from our body. No Caesar's blood has ever fixed a stain upon us in the senate or even in the palace. No assumption of the

---

[33] John Chrysostom, *On the Priesthood*, Book II, Chapter 3.
[34] Bercot, *A Dictionary of Early Christian Beliefs*, 320.

purple has ever in any of the provinces been affected by us.[35]

In other words, since we Christians uphold in our thinking a fundamental separation of church and state, the state has no need to fear that we might jockey for power. We have not pursued or taken on seats of power, symbolized by the royal color of purple, in any area where Christians live. And the reason for this is not because we are too few or too weak to ascend to positions of power but because it goes against our calling.

As Origen put it around the middle of the third century, responding to a pagan critic of Christianity named Celsus who called for Christians to "take office in the government of the country":

> So it is not for the purpose of escaping public duties that Christians decline public offices. Rather, it is so they may reserve themselves for a more divine and necessary service in the church of God—for the salvation of men.[36]

For Origen, those Christians who were intellectually gifted and skilled in leadership could perform a much greater service to the church than to the state, which led him to "exhort those who are mighty in word and of blameless life to rule over churches."[37] And yet, Origen, like other church fathers before him, recognized the need to remain on good terms with the government, despite the church's total lack of political ambitions:

> We are to scorn trying to ingratiate ourselves with kings or any other men—not only if their favor is to be won by murders, licentiousness, or deeds of cruelty— but even if it involves impiety towards God, or any servile expressions of flattery and fawning. For those

---

[35] Ibid. 153.
[36] Ibid. 154.
[37] Ibid.

> things are unworthy of brave and high-principled men.
> . . . However, although we do nothing that is contrary
> to the law and Word of God, we are not so insane as to
> stir up against us the wrath of kings and rulers, for they
> will bring upon us sufferings, tortures, or even death.[38]

Put differently, though Christians have no desire for political influence or power, we must do everything we can short of violating our Christian principles to keep up an amicable, if arm's-length, relationship with the state.

Even as late as 305 AD, we find a canon (56) in the Council of Elvira stating: "A magistrate [local official or judge] is ordered to keep away from the church during the one year of his term." Why go to such lengths to remain separate from the governing authorities? Perhaps because Christians viewed themselves as belonging to a separate Kingdom and owing allegiance to a different Lord and King. As church father Lactantius explained around this same time, "There is no occasion for violence and injury, for religion cannot be imposed by force; the matter must be carried on by words rather than by blows, that the will may be affected."[39] As the primary goal of the church is to live out the Kingdom of God, and since participation in God's Kingdom must be heartfelt and voluntary ("that the will may be affected"), it made little sense to the early church to participate also in an earthly kingdom whose goal and means of attaining that goal is different than the Heavenly Kingdom.

Though more examples from early church writings could be given illustrating this theology of the separation of church and state, held universally among church writers for at least the first few hundred years of its existence, what we have already covered will suffice.

Certainly, these quotations from early church fathers signify *principles* rather than unbendable rules. Some of their

---

[38] Ibid.
[39] Lactantius, *Divine Institutes*, 5.20

statements demonstrate an attitude that is not *totally* separationist in character, such as the sentiment of Clement of Alexandria that "[b]y the counsel of holy men [i.e. the influence of the church], states are managed well."[40] Likewise, Origen asked rhetorically through his writing whether it would be "an act of impiety to do away with those laws that prevail in the Tauric Chersonese, regarding the offering up of strangers in sacrifice to Diana? Or what about the sacrifice of children to Saturn by certain of the Libyan tribes?"[41] Christians did weigh in on matters of law and policy, whether or not their voices had any sway, pertaining to issues of basic human rights and cruelty. To give another example, Athenagoras wrote a letter in 177 AD to Emperor Marcus Aurelius explaining the Christians' disapproval of both the bloody gladiatorial games and abortion.[42] But on these matters, Christians had no specific biblical teachings that they wanted the state to impose; rather, they were simply some of the only ones with a strong enough moral compass to recognize and criticize these aspects of the broader culture. They were not seeking to live out the Kingdom of God through the channels of government but rather to universalize the freedom and fair treatment that they themselves requested from the state. Overall, they held the view articulated by Augustine that, originally and ideally, "God did not intend that man should have power over his fellow man,"[43] and they sought to embody this truth as best they could.

This Principle of the Separation of Church and State prevailed for centuries, but something changed during the fourth century. The inciting incident was the conversion of the most powerful figure in the Roman Empire—the emperor himself—to Christianity. This surprising event altered the course of Christianity in history and gradually reshaped

---

[40] Ibid. 320.
[41] Ibid. 321.
[42] Ibid. 2, 85.
[43] Saint Augustine, *The City of God*, Book 19, Chapter 15

Christian thinking about the use of state power. It is to this momentous shift we turn in the next chapter.

* * *

"Honor everyone. Love the brotherhood. Fear God. Honor the emperor."
1 Peter 2:17

CHAPTER SIX

The Constantinian Shift: God's People Embrace a Human King Again

Constantine the Great was the son of a Roman warrior-emperor who ascended to the throne and united much of the divided empire in the fourth century.

Some have depicted Constantine in a harshly negative light, as a bellicose and cynical despot, or even, as in the case of James Carroll's *Constantine's Sword*, as the intellectual predecessor of European anti-semitism and the Holocaust. Others portray Constantine as a genuine convert who acted basically as we should expect and *want* a Christian ruler to act, as Peter Leithart argues in *Defending Constantine*. Clearly, these disparate characterizations cannot both be wholly accurate, even if they each contain bits and pieces of truth.

If history is going to serve any useful purpose in our present task of rethinking the role of the church in the political realm, we cannot paint a figure as fascinating and complex as Constantine, or the many interesting figures of his century, with a broad brush. There are countless nuances to history that must be acknowledged, whether we have the space to cover them here or not. Moreover, we must recognize that Constantine and his contemporaries in the church were human beings who, though flawed, often did what they thought was right in the complicated circumstances in which they found themselves. There are no absolute villains or untainted paragons in history—only people, motivated by the same things that people have always been motivated by.

I say all of this because, at this point, it would be easy to paint any shift in church thinking away from a commitment to separation of church and state, no matter how subtle or well-intentioned it may have been, as apostasy — the abandonment of principles which defined Christians as Christians. Indeed, as we will see, Constantine did initiate a chain of events which ultimately led to a change in church thinking as well as the justification of behaviors which would have horrified Christians of prior generations. But not every outcome of this shift was bad. Some of the results proved a blessed relief for the marginalized and persecuted church. And there's little reason based in the historical record to impugn Constantine's sincerity or sympathy toward Christianity. While he was flawed, he could not have known all the effects his actions would have on the empire after his death.

Likewise, the Christians who broke from church-state separationism (as laid out in the previous chapter) to participate in this newfound church-state synergism did not leap immediately from one absolute to another. Historian Ramsay MacMullen points out that, even prior to Constantine, "it was not unusual for Christians to serve in real, active civic magistracies."[44] Although, given the prevailing separationist view among Christian leaders and intellectuals, MacMullen adds that "[c]hurch councils had to reflect on the problems raised by such service."[45] In any case, we must read the Constantinian Shift as a gradual evolution over several generations, one that the church had not anticipated or prepared for. And we must acknowledge the difficulty of identifying exactly the point at which the church had moved from separationism to something more synergetic between itself and the state.

In short, we must not judge our Christian ancestors too

---

[44] MacMullen, Ramsay. *Christianizing the Roman Empire: AD 100-400*. (New Haven: Yale University Press, 1984), 40
[45] Ibid.

harshly until we put ourselves in their sandals and ask: What temptations have I given into because the rewards seemed too great to pass up? In what ways do I — or would I — compromise my principles because I believe it will ultimately benefit the church?

But before we answer these questions, we must travel further back in time to gain a greater grasp of context.

* * *

Centuries of Persecution

It is the mid-60s AD. Several texts of the New Testament are still being written. The church is tiny but spreading rapidly through the provinces and into the heart of the Roman Empire.

Nero is emperor. Roman historians of his age or shortly after depict him in their writings as tyrannical, compulsive, and corrupt, which is odd, considering that Roman historians nearly always depicted emperors in glowing, complimentary language. The emperor's life bears out why almost anyone who knew him hated him. For one, at age 22, Nero killed his own mother for the audacity of urging him not to divorce his wife to marry his mistress. After divorcing his wife, he banished her, and when he received criticism for this, he accused her of infidelity and had her executed. He also executed several political rivals. He also threw lavish parties in his gardens, and during one of these events, he participated in a marriage ceremony between himself and a male former slave in which he took the role of the bride. He drained the treasury and raised taxes to complete extravagant public works projects and entertainment which earned him admiration from the lower classes but ire from the middle and upper classes. When he ran low on funds, he devalued the currency for the first time in the history of the empire by reducing the amount of silver in each coin.[46]

In short, Nero comes close to disproving my earlier caveat that there are no absolute villains in history.

In 64 AD, a great fire broke out in the middle of Rome, completely consuming three of the city's fourteen districts and causing damage in several others.[47] It burned for over a week. Three contemporary Roman historians—Suetonius, Cassius Dio, and Pliny the Elder—all agreed in their writings that Nero himself was responsible for starting the fire. A fourth historian, Tacitus, claimed uncertainty about how the fire started but didn't rule out Nero's involvement. Suetonius asserts that Nero started the fire to clear up room in the crowded urban center of Rome for the lavish and costly palace he built there afterward. This glittering new palace would be called *Domus Aurea*, the "Golden House," and would feature beautifully designed landscaping and a ninety-eight-foot-tall bronze statue of—who else?—Emperor Nero.[48]

After this great fire, which consumed countless Roman lives along with their homes, as well as the subsequent construction of his opulent new palatial estate on the grounds those homes once occupied, Nero came under the suspicion of arson. Stories circulated that the emperor had hired street dwellers to feign drunkenness and start the fire. In the wake of these rumors, Nero sensed the people turning on him, and he realized that he needed a scapegoat—someone to take the blame off of him, someone the majority of Romans could easily turn against.

What group would work better as Nero's scapegoat than the members of this strange, counter-cultural religious sect

---

[46] See Will Durant, *Caesar and Christ* (New York: MFJ Books, 1944), 276-282. Also https://web.archive.org/web/20010210220413/http://www.tulane.edu/~august/han douts/601cprin.htm

[47] Tacitus, *Annals*, XV.40.

[48] Edward Champlin, *Nero*. (Cambridge: Harvard University Press, 2003) pp. 36–52. Will Durant, in *Caesar and Christ*, p. 280, attests that the statue was 120 feet in height.

called Christianity? They may have been a harmless bunch, but they did not participate in (drunken and debauched) religious feasts or worship of the emperor, and thus they seemed rebellious enough to have been capable of mass arson. Will Durant writes that "Christians were charged with demonic magic, secret immorality, drinking human blood at the Paschal feast, and worshipping an ass."[49]

Just as Nero made false accusations and ultimately executed his wife in order to protect his reputation, he likewise made false accusations against the Roman Christians and sentenced many to "fearful tortures" in order to advance his lie. Some were thrown to the beasts in the arena. Others were crucified. Still others were burned alive.[50] Tacitus provides a horrifying description of the Christians' treatment at this time:

> Mockery of every sort was added to their deaths. Covered with the skins of beasts, they were torn by dogs and perished, or were nailed to crosses, or were doomed to the flames and burnt, to serve as a nightly illumination, when daylight had expired.[51]

From the sources available to us, it appears that this terrible persecution lasted four years, the final four years of Nero's mentally deranged life before the emperor, friendless and beset by enemies, killed himself. With Nero gone, the Roman people eased off their persecution of Christians. "At length," writes Tacitus, "the brutality of these measures filled every beast with pity. Humanity relented in favor of the Christians."[52]

Persecution of the church for the next few hundred years was varied, sporadic, and mostly localized to certain cities or regions. Social and cultural marginalization served as the primary source of Roman pushback against Christianity during this period. However, it was also in this era that many Christian

---

49 Durant, *Caesar and Christ*, 647
50 Champlin, *Nero*, 121-122
51 Tacitus, *Annals*, XV
52 Durant, *Caesar and Christ*, 281

luminaries such as Justin Martyr, Clement of Alexandria, Tertullian, Irenaeus, Origen, and other early church fathers appeared on the scene, writing passionately to defend the Christian faith or re-articulate its message. They serve as proof that Christianity did not merely prey on the weak-minded and uneducated, as the late second- and early third-century critic of the faith, Celsus, argued in his writings. The vitriol is sharp in the pagan aristocrat's words when he writes:

> Their [the Christians'] injunctions are like this: "Let no one educated, no one wise, no one sensible draw near. For these abilities are thought by us to be evils. But as for anyone ignorant, anyone stupid, anyone uneducated, anyone who is a child, let him come boldly." By the fact that they themselves admit that these people are worthy of their God, they show that they want and are able to convince only the foolish, dishonorable and stupid, and only slaves, women, and little children.[53]

Ouch.

It is true, as MacMullen notes, that "the church's teachings were offered most often to the unsophisticated or uneducated, and by people of low standing in the community."[54] But this may have been due to paganism's strong hold on the middle and upper classes of Roman society. Slaves, laborers, and socially powerless women would naturally find solace in a message of hope for all humanity. Besides, it fits with the theme of God using the lowly and weak to shame the worldly-wise and strong. And yet, paradoxically, as MacMullen also notes, "Christianity after New Testament times is presented to us almost exclusively in pages addressed to upper-class readers."[55] This is not only because most of the population was illiterate but also because many Christian writers such as Justin

---

[53] MacMullen, *Christianizing the Roman Empire*, 37.
[54] Ibid.
[55] Ibid. 38

Martyr and Origen were well-versed in Greco-Roman philosophy and directed their apologies of the faith toward fellow thinkers. Just as Paul was a Jew to the Jews and a Gentile to the Gentiles (1 Cor 9:20-21), the early Christians tailored their message to their audience. This undoubtedly helped Christianity grow at such a rapid pace in spite of unrelenting marginalization and persecution.

State discrimination against Christians spiked in 257-258 AD when Emperor Valerian ordered the senate to impose several sanctions and ultimatums, at first only on Christian clergy but later on Christians more broadly. Church leaders were forced to make sacrifices to Roman gods on pain of banishment or even execution. Wealthier Christians faced the choice of performing acts of worship to the gods or else losing their title and property. Not even servants were exempted—if they didn't recant their Christian exclusivity and worship the Roman gods, they would be sold into slavery or sent to the mines.[56]

For the next 45 years after Valerian's persecution in the late 250s, the Roman central government mostly left the church to its own devices. Religious and cultural tension remained, but in this period, persecution more likely came from local pagan mobs, with soldiers looking the other way, than from the Roman state itself. Despite this environment, by 300 AD, the church body swelled impressively to as much as 10% of the Roman population[57]—some five million people by one historian's estimate.[58] Tertullian spoke truthfully, then, when he wrote that "the blood of the martyrs is the seed of the church."[59] Basil of Caesarea concurred, writing in the mid-300s: "The blood of martyrs watered the churches and reared up

---

[56] W.H.C. Frend, *The Rise of Christianity.* (Philadelphia: Fortress Press, 1984) 326.

[57] Kreider, Alan. "'Converted 'but Not Baptized," *Constantine Revisited.* (Eugene: Pickwick Pub, 2013), 47

[58] MacMullen, 86

[59] Tertullian, *Apologeticus*, ch. 50.

many times as many champions of piety."[60]

As secular historian Will Durant put it,

> There is no greater drama in human record than the sight of a few Christians, scorned or oppressed by a succession of emperors, bearing all trials with a fierce tenacity, multiplying quietly, building order while their enemies generated chaos, fighting the sword with the word, brutality with hope, and at last defeating the strongest state that history has known. Caesar and Christ had met in the arena, and Christ had won.[61]

Emperor Diocletian had much more distaste for Christianity than most of his predecessors, who seemed content merely to marginalize the church. Diocletian, more so than the average emperor, favored the traditional set of gods, especially the ultra-masculine Olympians. He associated himself closely with the head of the pantheon, the hurler of lightning bolts himself—Jupiter (the Roman equivalent of Zeus). He even referred to himself in writing and speeches as "Iovius," the Latin name for Jupiter.[62] Seeing the unabated rise of Christianity, Diocletian undoubtedly wanted to stamp it out and restore the empire to its former piously pagan glory.

The emperor started with the military, first purging any Christian in the imperial court who refused to make sacrifices, then moving to officers more broadly, then to the entire military.[63] Later, after consulting an oracle, Diocletian instituted general persecutions of the Christians, inaugurated by the destruction of the church in Nicomedia (located in Northern Asia Minor), but continuing with other thrashings: burning Christian scriptures, prohibiting assembly for worship, pillaging items of value belonging to the church, confiscating property from individual believers, rescinding the

---

[60] MacMullen, 29

[61] Durant, *Caesar and Christ*, 652

[62] Bowman, Alan. "Diocletian and the first tetrarchy, a.d. 284-305", 70-71.

[63] Lactantius, *De Mortibus Persecutorum*, 10.1-5.

right to have one's voice heard in court, and eventually sentencing Christians to death or imprisonment.[64] Roman prisons subsequently became so filled with Christians that they could no longer hold the vast numbers of people forced into them. Instead of limiting the number of Christians imprisoned, the Romans began releasing ordinary criminals to make room for more Christians![65]

Diocletian's final edict against the Christians — given for all citizens to obey but directed primarily against the Christians — commanded everyone regardless of gender or social class to congregate in public spaces in order to offer collective sacrifices. Naturally, many Christians refused to join these ceremonies and paid the price for it in blood.[66] In the Eastern portion of the empire, where a particularly strong hater of Christianity named Galerius ruled, the preferred method of execution was burning.

Just how many Christians were martyred during Diocletian's reign is unknown, but it is widely agreed to have been the harshest and most coordinated period of persecution during the Roman Empire's existence. It may have been the worst in the history of the church.

With this dark and bloody backdrop in view, it is not hard to understand a yearning among Christians to be free of this oppression, once and for all, and to welcome any step in that direction.

* * *

"By This Sign, You Will Conquer"

At this time, the vast Roman Empire covered the majority of Europe, a large swathe of North Africa, and a carving of the Middle East. It proved, at times, too unwieldy for one emperor

---

[64] Eusebius, *Historia Ecclesiastica*, 9.10.8
[65] Eusebius, *Historia Ecclesiastica*, 8.6.8–9
[66] Eusebius, *De Martyribus Palestinae*, 3.1

to control, so multiple emperors would reign over different regions, maintaining a tacit, symbiotic alliance with each other. After Diocletian abdicated the throne, rule of the empire bifurcated between Galerius in the East, where persecution continued, and Constantius Chlorus in the West, where it largely subsided. After the death of Constantius, the empire splintered even further.

In 311, in his old age, Galerius grew weary of his war on the Christians and issued the Edict of Serdica, granting toleration toward the Christians over his portion of the empire (the last portion to sustain persecution in full force). The 61-year-old emperor died shortly thereafter.

Rewinding back to 306, the son of Constantius Chlorus, a warrior named Constantine, was chosen by the military to take his father's place as their leader. But in order to cement his status as Emperor of the West, Constantine would have to defeat his major rival to the throne, Maxentius (the son-in-law of Galerius). In 312, both armies positioned themselves on opposite sides of the Tiber River in the province of Britain, poised for battle. But before the battle, Constantine received a vivid vision in the sky—a symbol combining the Greek letters "Chi" and "Rho," the first two letters of Christ. A voice that Constantine interpreted as that of Jesus spoke to him, saying, "By this sign, you will conquer."

Constantine, though not a Christian himself, must have been familiar with the religious sect. He must also have known that most of the Christians in the military had been purged during the Great Persecution of Diocletian.[67] But the vision had such a strong effect on him that he complied with its demand despite not worshipping the Christians' God. He commanded his army to paint or otherwise affix this newly invented symbol combining the "Chi" and "Rho" letters—called the Christogram—to their shields. When Constantine decisively won the Battle of Milvian Bridge, in which his rival Maxentius

---

[67] MacMullen, 44

was killed, the young warrior-emperor was convinced. He converted to Christianity, at least to a degree (he was not baptized until a few weeks before his death[68]), having seen the power of its God.

By 313 AD, the power of the emperorship had consolidated to two emperors: Constantine in the West and Licinius (successor to Galerius) in the East. Still motivated by what he saw as a God-given victory, Constantine met with Licinius in Milan in order to draft and issue a joint, empire-wide edict declaring the return of Christian property that had been confiscated during the Diocletianic Persecution[69] as well as to grant freedom of religion:

> . . . we have given to those Christians free and unrestricted opportunity of religious worship. When you see that this has been granted to them by us, your Worship will know that we have also conceded to other religions the right of open and free observance of their worship for the sake of the peace of our times, that each one may have the free opportunity to worship as he pleases; this regulation is made that we may not seem to detract from any dignity of any religion.[70]

It is fascinating to note that two Roman emperors both signed a document expressing their will that *freedom of religion,* a right never before embraced by the Roman Empire, would become the law of the land, which affected roughly one-fourth of the world's population. Surely the prevailing Christian principle of separation of church and state had much to do with this.

Nevertheless, it is also important to keep in mind that this statement—the Edict of Milan—was jointly composed by two emperors of opposing faiths: Constantine, a Christian, and

---

[68] Kreider, Alan. "Converted 'but Not Baptized," *Constantine Revisited.* (Eugene: Pickwick Pub, 2013), 28

[69] Eusebius, *Ecclesiastical History,* 5.15–17

[70] Lactantius, *De Mortibus Persecutorum,* ch. 48

Licinius, a pagan. It is written in such a way as to be agreeable to both parties, but the language of the edict did not necessarily determine how either emperor would behave. In the East, Licinius still favored pagans and looked the other way as his favored religious groups marginalized Christians. In the West, it took no time at all for Constantine to begin funding new church buildings and showing favoritism to Christians in political appointments.

Constantine reigned for a quarter of a century, quite long compared to most other Roman emperors. "In so long a reign," writes MacMullen, "though its Christian years had begun without the least intent to propagate the Faith, his [Constantine's] violent energies were gradually and to some degree drawn into a more truly Christian posture of active aggression: error, he saw, must be confronted and given its right name. . . ."[71] Christians needed to recognize and exert their rightful authority lest, in the words of Constantine, "the Highest Divinity should be aroused not only against the human race but even against me, myself."[72]

Unfortunately, along with the emperor's aggression came error. Though initially persuaded by Trinitarian Christianity, Constantine eventually gave an audience to Arius (a denier of Christ's divinity) and, upon hearing him out, became an Arian, banishing the prominent Trinitarian, Athanasius, from the empire. Moreover, we also know that he had his eldest son Crispus killed by poison and his second wife, Fausta, killed by over-heating in a bath, the reasons for both being unknown.[73]

Constantine's three sons continued narrowing the gap between church and state after their father died in 337 AD, though the three did not exactly behave like Christ-followers. The oldest, Constantine II, attempted to assert full control of the Roman Empire from his brothers in 340 AD but was defeated

---

[71] MacMullen, 50
[72] Ibid.
[73] Guthrie, Patrick. The Execution of Crispus, *Phoenix*, vol. 20, no. 4, 325-331

and killed by his brother, Constans. Constans, the only Trinitarian Christian of Constantine's successors, was a homosexual, despite issuing an edict threatening punishment for "unnatural" marriage. According to Roman historians, Constans "indulged in great vices" and took advantage of "handsome barbarian hostages."[74] Further, well into his reign, Constans apparently succumbed to corruption, auctioning government positions to the highest bidder and favoring his own bodyguards for military appointments.[75] Constantius II boasted the longest reign but late in life declared war on his cousin Julian over a dispute about who held higher authority.

In short, the Roman emperors more or less continued to behave how they always had. The church, however, began conforming to its newfound political influence.

The Constantinian shift, which began with freedom of religion in 313 AD, culminated in 380 AD when the three co-emperors of the empire at the time convened to promulgate the Edict of Thessalonica, making Christianity the official religion of the Roman Empire. The edict affirmed the unified deity of the Father, Son, and Holy Spirit, "in equal majesty and in a holy Trinity,"[76] thus specifying *Trinitarian* Christianity over and against its major rival of Arianism (which denied the deity of Christ). The edict also promised "the punishment of our authority in accordance with the will of Heaven which we will decide to inflict" upon the "foolish madmen" who denied Trinitarian faith.[77]

Compare this government mandate with the sentiment of Tertullian, which, 168 years prior, so succinctly expressed the predominate attitude of the early church: "It is a fundamental human right, a privilege of nature, that every man should worship according to his own convictions. One man's religion neither harms nor helps another man. It is assuredly no part of

---

[74] DiMaio, Michael. *Constans I (337–350 A.D.)*
[75] DiMaio, https://www.roman-emperors.org/consi.htm
[76] *Codex Theodosianus*, xvi. 1.2
[77] Ibid.

religion to compel religion, to which free will and not force should lead us."[78] When presented with the opportunity, the church by and large abandoned Tertullian's wisdom, the same wisdom handed down to us in the form of Samuel's First and Second Principles.

The church, through small changes one after the other, had completely penetrated and taken over the organization that they once considered foreign to them. The year following the Edict of Thessalonica, Emperor Theodosius ramped up persecution of paganism, banning sacrifices and rituals on pain of death. From 389 to 391 AD, he went further, issuing decrees which effectively made traditional Roman paganism a *religio illicita* (illegal religion), outlawing and disbanding every practice and belief related to paganism.[79] Pagan temples across the empire were systematically torn down and destroyed or converted into churches. Despite this, the empire remained half or more pagan even into the fifth century.[80] Pagans pleaded with the emperor again and again to return to a state of religious toleration, but Theodosius refused.[81]

Rather than condemning the government's compulsion and persecution of heretics and unbelievers, prominent church leaders such as Ambrose of Milan encouraged Theodosius's actions and sometimes pushed him to go further.[82]

In less than a hundred years, Christians had evolved from a powerless, persecuted minority to the empowered persecutors themselves.

* * *

---

[78] Tertullian, *Ad Scapulam*, circa 212.
[79] Theodosian Code 16.10.11
[80] MacMullen, 83
[81] Symmachus, *Relatio* 3.
[82] *Theodosian Code* 16.10.10

Merging Church and State

To be fair, some of the historical developments following the merging of church and state into one symbiotic duo were admirable. As Constantine grew to understand himself as a Christian, the role of emperor gradually became stripped of its aura of divinity. Emperor worship gradually faded (though veneration of the emperors continued in the military[83]). Constantine made an effort in his legal reforms to provide justice and fair treatment of women and poor litigants.[84] Gladiatorial combat was officially outlawed during his reign, though it continued on unofficially for a time afterward. Likewise, the return of confiscated property to Christians is surely an example of justice served. And we Trinitarians ought to be grateful that Nicene Christianity, always the majority but not always represented in positions of authority, prevailed over Arianism.

However, if the test is faithfulness to the biblical principles we have described thus far, especially the Principle of the Separation of Church and State, the Constantinian shift had much more downside than upside. The negative impacts on the church's ability to carry out its mission are incalculable, but it is important to identify and describe them as best we can.

(1) State preference for Christians over non-Christians. Constantine "exempted church lands from taxation; he ordered provincial officials to make available materials and labor for construction; set up a system of gifts of food to churches, grain allowances to nuns, widows, and others in church service; excused clerics from shouldering onerous, sometimes ruinous, civic obligations."[85] Those taxes and onerous civic obligations then had to be provided more heavily by non-Christians. What's more, consistently after Constantine's conversion, the Roman government exhibited "a clear if not very aggressive

---

[83] MacMullen, 76
[84] Kreider, 45
[85] MacMullen, 49

preference for Christians in office."[86] Besides putting more Christians in sword-bearing roles, this also led, in part, to the next negative impact on the church.

(2) *An epidemic of inauthentic or questionable conversions.* Historian Ramsay MacMullen notes that, in those days, "office was sought for material reward" which made it "manifestly profitable in worldly terms to declare yourself a Christian." He cites an ancient Roman historian who describes the mindset of some Christian converts who, "envious at the honor in which Christians were held by the emperor, deemed it necessary to follow in the emperor's path."[87] In fairness, this imperial favoritism was carried out with the best of intentions. The Christian emperors wanted to make the Christian faith more attractive to outsiders, even if that meant incentivizing church membership with social and material rewards. "Constantine's sons continued and extended their father's gifts to the church — gifts of exemptions from taxes and inheritance rights. . . . through which he [Constantius II] supposed he might bring his subjects over to the faith."[88] Similarly, later on, "Theodosius assumed that people, at any rate some people, could be turned into coreligionists with his party and himself simply because it would cost them too much money to refuse."

Perhaps these emperors overlooked Paul's teaching that it is "*with the heart* one believes and is justified" (Rom. 10:10), and that those "who were once slaves of sin have become *obedient from the heart* to the standard of teaching to which you were committed" (Rom. 6:17). The wisdom of the Principle of the Separation of Church and State is all the more evident when it becomes politically expedient to claim Christianity or feign Christian faith. Authentic faith becomes much harder to discern when there are earthly rewards on the line.

Material benefit was only one side of the non-religious

---

86 Ibid. 56
87 Ibid.
88 Ibid. 53

motivation to convert after the Roman Empire became Christianized. The other factor, in the words of Eusebius, was "fear of the emperor's menaces."[89] These "menaces" sometimes took the form of pillaging or destroying pagan temples, oppressive taxes on non-Christians, state threats, or Christian riots in predominantly pagan cities.[90] And these state actions were widely accepted and encouraged by church leaders and Christian statesmen alike. One of them, writing to Constantine's sons after Constantine's death, made this aggressive plea: "There remains only a very little for your laws to accomplish, whereby the devil may lie prostrate and overthrown before them. . . Need commands you, most sacred emperors, to exact vengeance and punishment upon this evil! This is prescribed to you by the law of the supreme deity, that Your Severity should follow up on all fronts the crime of idolatry."[91]

Whereas the church had formerly gained converts mainly through the preaching of the word, wonder-working by certain gifted individuals, and extraordinary care for the lowly, when the church became empowered with the sword of the state, they began "countenancing the use of force at the local level." MacMullen references an instance when a pagan of Minorca (a small island in the Mediterranean) recalled being pressured to convert by a riot of Christians: "I therefore am thinking of the danger to my life, and so I go off now to the church, to evade the death that otherwise awaits me."[92] Likewise, the church insisted that masters "should enforce their religious conformity [upon their slaves] by means of a good beating, or, if one weren't enough, 'by progressively heavier beatings.'"[93] In the fifth century, "the emperors announced that they would confiscate the lands of any man who so much as allowed, even

---

[89] Ibid. 56
[90] See MacMullen, 49-50, 90-91
[91] Ibid. 91
[92] Ibid. 82
[93] Ibid. 65

in ignorance, a meeting for prohibited worship on his acres."[94]

MacMullen tells a story that illustrates this symbiotic relationship between church and state in the late fourth century: "Intrigues and the pulling of the right strings in the capital" produced for a bishop in Gaza "a high churchman's help, then a high official's, and then help still closer to the throne, until at last a letter is obtained from the emperor himself to be read aloud to the populace of Gaza by a commander at the head of his troops." The help that the bishop sought from the governing authorities was the use of their armed forces. "All Gaza's temples are torn down and burned and the city is cleansed of every belief but the Christian. The most stubborn opponents. . . are tied up, marched away to the provincial capital, severely tortured, and all killed. . . ." Those pagans who complied with the Christian authorities helped to build a "grand new church" in the city.[95]

What excuse is given for those "who had not left their mistaken ways of their free will but in fear and terror of the emperors"? The bishop answers this objection by citing Paul's words from Philippians 1:18: "Whether falsely or truly, Christ is preached, and I rejoice in that."[96] Saint Augustine and other church fathers living after the Christianization of the empire used this reasoning to defend their abandonment of the Kingdom Principle of Voluntarism—"that they are false is not for us but for God to judge," said Augustine.[97] Of course, Paul never dismissed the importance of accepting Christ wholeheartedly and voluntarily. The situation described in Philippians 1, in which some preached the gospel—accurately, from what we can tell—out of some sort of selfish motivation, is not commended or given as an example of something allowable. And even if it was, Paul's situation in which the gospel was being preached truthfully, albeit from vain

---

[94] Ibid. 66
[95] Ibid. 88-89
[96] Ibid. 89
[97] Ibid. 57

motivations, is entirely different from a situation in which unbelievers flock to the church out of fear, self-interest, or under compulsion.

While such disregard for the authenticity of conversions was, up to the time of Constantine, foreign to Christians and to Christian thinking, it fit comfortably with traditional pagan culture. "The idea that any sort of day-to-day service or perpetual allegiance was owing to divinity had little currency" in Roman paganism. "Neither was there the least uneasiness about the self-interested nature of worship. You only made offerings, or promises of offerings, in order to gain favor from powerful beings."[98] Perhaps the emperors, church leaders, and other Christian authorities who operated with a more coercive posture toward non-Christians imported this cultural understanding of religion from paganism. If personal devotion didn't matter as much as outward conformity, a verbal confession, and the ritual of baptism, Christians could watch with pride as their ranks swelled.

Once again, contrast this newfound acceptance of the sword with the words of church father Lactantius, writing during the Diocletianic Persecution: "There is no occasion for violence and injury, for religion cannot be imposed by force; the matter must be carried on by words rather than by blows, that the will may be affected."[99] Prior to the Constantinian shift, writes Alan Kreider,

> The church grew, not because imperial campaigns promoted it, but despite the fact that imperial authorities opposed it. The church grew, not because Christianity was a way to prosperity or respectability, but because the Gospel made a practical difference to people's lives so that people espoused the message freely. As liberated and transformed people, the Christians were attractive. . . . With Constantine the

---

[98] Ibid. 13
[99] Lactantius, *Divine Institutes*, 5.20

church's missional approach began to change—from bottom-up to top-down, from attraction to advantage.[100]

(3) Erosion of religious freedom in favor of Christianity. Though Constantine began his reign as a Christian emperor with the goal of "concord" with non-believers and instructed some of his provincials not to "use what he has received by inner conviction as a means to harm his neighbor" or to "enforce it with sanctions,"[101] the emperor and his successors steadily moved away from this policy of religious freedom. It began during Constantine's reign with a ban on pagan rituals performed in order to learn the future, such as haruspicy.[102] Later, in 341 AD, Constantine's son, Constantius II, banned pagan sacrifices. And in 356 AD, worshipping images was outlawed. Erosion of religious freedom continued with the widespread, state-sponsored destruction of pagan temples or conversion of the buildings into churches.[103]

(4) Little noticeable moral effect on the broader culture. In contrast to Christ and Paul, who told their audiences that "you will know them by their fruit" (Matt 7:20) and instructed them to bear the fruit of the Spirit (Gal 5:22-25), Roman society demonstrated little change in cultural mores even after many decades of Christianization. Despite Christian emperors and increasing Christian presence in high offices, gladiatorial combat remained popular, although it was "offensive to more refined non-Christian sensibilities as well as Christian." Homosexuality continued openly, "though with somewhat uneasy toleration." Slaveholding also remained, as did "sexual indecency in theatrical performances."[104] Not to mention the myriad abuses of pagans, heretics, and Jews.

(5) Pagan traditions and practices creeping into the church.

---

[100] Kreider, 57-58
[101] Ibid. 60-61
[102] MacMullen, 50
[103] Ibid. 96-101
[104] Ibid. 79

Historian Johannes Geffcken notes that, as the Roman Empire became Christianized, a "vast mass of cultural forms passed from paganism into Christianity . . . a huge stream of tradition."[105] George Barna and Frank Viola detail some of these cultural forms that passed into Christianity in their book, *Pagan Christianity?* Many pagan festivals and celebrations, for instance, were incorporated into Christian holiday observance. According to Kreider, "many pagans were put off Christianity by the church's disapproval of their pagan feasting and drinking. So bishops decided to *inculturate* — to insert Christian values into Roman culture by allowing Christian feasting and drinking 'in honor of the holy martyrs'" that was "equally lavish" as pagan celebrations.

Also, it was during this period when the term "church" took on a second meaning besides its original denotation for the corporate body of believers; "church" came to signify the special building in which believers gathered to worship. Due to extravagant basilicas Constantine commissioned for the church's use, Christians began to mimic pagan temples in their building designs. As opposed to the humble, domestic settings in which believers formerly met, "[t]hese were large buildings, whose basilica form and splendid ornamentation communicated Christianity's triumph in the Roman world."[106]

Constantine also changed the Christian day of worship from the traditional Jewish Sabbath on Saturday to Sunday, the day of the Sun god, Sol Invictus ("Unconquered Sun"). For roughly half of his reign (a decade or so after converting to Christianity), Constantine harbored an affinity for the Sun god, even minting coins with his face alongside that of Sol Invictus. He initially gave Sundays off to Christians in the military, as Sol Invictus was the patron god of soldiers, but that practice eventually spread into the church as a whole.[107]

---

[105] Cited in MacMullen, 157-158
[106] Kreider, 48
[107] MacMullen, 44-45

"While Christianity converted the world," Will Durant writes, "the world converted Christianity, and displayed the natural paganism of mankind."[108]

(6) *Association of Christians with the Roman Empire by Rome's enemies.* When Constantine converted to Christianity and began his generous patronage of the church (and corollary stifling of paganism), the major rival of the empire to the east, the Persian Sassanid Empire, took notice. Prior to this point, they practiced a policy of toleration toward Christians living within their territory. But when Constantine threw his support behind the church, the Sassanids began viewing Christians with suspicion. The Persian Christians were accused of being pro-Roman partisans, even though they by and large had nothing to do with the Romans.[109] Even before 380 AD, non-Romans began to associate Christianity with the government that had adopted it as its preferred religion. And that government was their longstanding enemy — Rome.

When military conflict sparked between the Sassanids and Romans in 341 AD, the Sassanid king, Shapur II, ordained a harsh persecution against those he deemed to be Roman sympathizers, including double taxation on any self-identified Christians.[110] With the blessing of their governing authorities, Zoroastrian priests rounded up church leaders and monks to be executed.[111] This period of persecution in Persia continued for over half a century. A Palestinian Christian and historian of the fifth century named Sozomen estimated that at least sixteen thousand believers were martyred in the Persian Empire

---

[108] Durant, *Caesar and Christ*, 657

[109] Bowman, Alan; Peter Garnsey; Averil Cameron, eds. *The Cambridge Ancient History: Volume 12, The Crisis of Empire, AD 193-337* (Cambridge: Cambridge University Press, 2005), 474.

[110] D. T. Potts, *The Archaeology of Elam: Formation and Transformation of an Ancient Iranian State*, (Cambridge: Cambridge University Press, 1999), 422.

[111] Joel Thomas Walker, *The Legend of Mar Qardagh: Narrative and Christian Heroism in Late Antique Iraq.* (Los Angeles: University of California Press, 2006), 111.

during this period.[112]

---

[112] Sozomen, *Ecclesiastical History,* Book II, Ch. 9

(7) *Evolution of thinking about Christian participation in the military and the government.* Prior to Constantine, church fathers and writings uniformly condemned any and all killing of other people. Origen, for example, asserted that Christ "did not consider it compatible with his inspired legislation to allow the taking of human life in any form at all."[113] Lactantius agreed: "It is always unlawful to put to death a man, whom God willed to be a sacred animal."[114] Cyprian went so far as to argue that, for Christians, "it is not lawful for the innocent even to kill the guilty."[115] Similar sayings could be found in the writings of Tertullian, Athenagoras, Justin Martyr, and others.

If the early church interpreted and applied New Testament teachings accurately, then Christian participation in the military and government would be limited to non-violent roles. This is precisely what we see in numerous church orders and ethics manuals. Even early in and midway through the fourth century, after Constantine began his support of the church, Christian documents forbade Christian soldiers from killing. "A soldier who has authority, let him not kill a man," reads one church order from the mid-300s. "If he is ordered, let him not go to the task nor let him swear. . . . One who has the authority of the sword, or is a ruler of a city who wears the purple, either let him cease or be cast out."[116] Christians could remain in their posts if they could refrain from the use of the sword, but those who could not carry out their jobs without the use or command of force had to resign. Here we see the Acts 5:29 Principle come into play—where there was disagreement between God's law and the role of the governing authorities, God's law had to take precedence.

"Concerning the Magistrate and the Soldier they are not to kill anyone, even if they receive the order," reads a church order from Egypt, dating to around 336 AD. "Whoever has received

---

[113] Origen, *Contra Celsum*, 3.7
[114] Lactantius, *Divine Institutes*, 6.50.15-17
[115] Cyprian, Letter 56
[116] *Apostolic Tradition 16*, cited in Kreider, 33

the authority to kill, or else a soldier, they are not to kill in any case, even if they receive the order to kill."[117] Another order from the late-middle fourth century says, "If anyone be a soldier or in authority, let him be taught not to oppress or to kill or to rob, or to be angry or to rage and afflict anyone. . . . But if they wish to be baptized in the Lord, let them cease from military service or from the [post of] authority."[118]

As more and more Christians took on positions of authority or filled the ranks of the military, however, church instructions for them softened. The *Apostolic Constitutions*, compiled in 385 AD (five years after Christianity was declared the official religion of the Roman Empire), provides a clear example of this: "If a soldier come, let him be taught to do no injustice, to accuse no one falsely, and to be content with his allotted wages; if he submit to those rules, let him be received; but if he refuse them, let him be rejected."[119] Notice that, while there are still biblically inspired standards given for soldiers to follow, the prohibition on killing is gone. As is the call to resignation for those who are required by their positions to use or command force.

Rather than remaining steadfast in their distinction between those whom God has called *never* to avenge and those whom God has called to act as His agents of vengeance, the church lowered their standards and gave in to the temptation of political power. Rather than affirming that participation in the Kingdom of God, in which believers are citizens and ambassadors, must always be heartfelt and voluntary, the church simply invented a distinction between Christian morality in personal versus political matters. Turning the other cheek and abstaining from vengeance and the use of the sword became ethics merely for the personal sphere, while those Christians who acted as agents of the state were allotted a different set of ethics, exempted from the stricter personal

---

[117] *Canons of Hippolytus* 13-14, cited in Kreider, 35

[118] *Testament of our Lord*, 2.2, cited in Kreider, 35

[119] *Apostolic Constitutions*, 8.32.10, cited in Kreider, 36

standards. Rather than honoring and praying for the state so that Christians might lead a peaceful and quiet life, the church did so because the Christianized state had effectively become an extension of itself.

* * *

A New Age

Though Constantine lived only to 337 AD, his actions and decisions after his conversion had deep and indelible effects on the church. By the end of his century, Christianity had completely infiltrated and seized the power structures of the Roman Empire. Church membership exploded, but not for the same reasons as its growth prior to Constantine. Of course, not every convert to Christianity joined the faith for suspect or self-serving reasons after this, but the Christianization of the state created a newfound—and powerful—motivation to convert that had nothing to do with the Spirit's moving in a person's heart or voluntary submission to Christ. The sword that Jesus had commanded Peter—the rock on which the church was built—to sheath, the church of the fourth century eagerly unsheathed.

Though Christians interpreted this turn of history as God's vindication of them after centuries of persecution, it didn't take long for Christians to abuse this perceived vindication by becoming the persecutors themselves. And though they often took on the power of the state with the best of intentions, the temptation to use that power to benefit the church at the expense of outsiders was too great to pass up. That which was meant to strengthen the church diluted and corrupted it.

A new age of church history had begun. God's people had accepted a human king for themselves again. They had been offered (what must have seemed to them like) all the kingdoms of the world in exchange for a compromise of their principles, and they said yes.

* * *

"Do not be conformed to this world, but be transformed by the
renewal of your mind, that by testing you may discern what is the
will of God, what is good and acceptable and perfect."
Romans 12:2

CHAPTER SEVEN

Political Principles: Compatible But Not Overlapping Kingdoms

At this point, before moving on to specific applications, it will be helpful to summarize and clarify the principles we have garnered from our tour through Scripture thus far. Hopefully, by assembling the pieces, a general framework for how the church ought to encourage the state to act will emerge into a coherent whole. The goal is to discover the political philosophy—or rather, the political *theology*—of the Bible, if there is one to be found.

In other words, if the political-theological principles covered so far are true, how should the church act in the political realm?

To answer this question, we must build out the foundations of Christians 'identity and purpose in this world as well as our role in both the salvation of souls and moral instruction. *Please note*: Some sections of this chapter get a bit technical or philosophical. Feel free to skim through or skip past them, if you need to.

* * *

In But Not Of

The book of John records Jesus 'final prayer in the Garden of Gethsemane before being arrested, in which he prays this for his followers:

> I have given them your word, and the world has hated them because they are not of the world, just as I am not of the world. I do not ask that you take them out of the world, but that you keep them from the evil one. They are not of the world, just as I am not of the world. (John 17:14-16)

Twice in the span of two verses Jesus says that his followers are "not of the world," by which he means that through faith they have gained enough purity of heart to stand out in a corrupt and sinful world. They are counter-cultural just as Jesus was counter-cultural. They are also counter-political in the sense that they consider themselves citizens of a Heavenly rather than earthly kingdom (Phil. 3:20) and proclaim Jesus, rather than Caesar or any other earthly authority, as Lord (Rom. 10:9, Phil. 2:11).

It is a kingdom of paradoxes, a kingdom that is *in* but not *of* this world. As Jesus put it, the Kingdom is "in your midst" (Lk 17:21) and yet is also "not of this realm" (Jn 18:36). His is a kingdom bent on conquering the entire world "so that at the name of Jesus every knee should bow" (Phil. 2:10). Yet the citizens of this kingdom are taught to put away their swords (Matt 26:52) and love their enemies (Lk. 6:27) because their fight is not "against flesh and blood" (Eph. 6:12) but rather against the "ruler of this world" (Jn 12:31) who is Satan (Lk. 4:6). The King of this kingdom "desires all people to be saved" (1 Tim. 2:4) and to obey all of His teachings (Matt. 28:20) so that they may enjoy the blessing of abundance and wholeness of life in His Kingdom (Jn. 10:10).

This Heavenly Kingdom, though it has already broken into the world, has not arrived to its fullest extent. Rather, it coexists with earthly kingdoms like weeds growing among the wheat (Matt. 13:24-43). We believers are thus "ambassadors for Christ" (2 Cor. 5:20) in the sense that we reside in foreign territory. An ambassador is a representative of one government who is living in the territory of another government. They speak for their government and remain ultimately loyal to it even while they honor and live in subjection to the governing authorities of the foreign land. They reside *in* the foreign government's territory but they are not *of* its authority structure or morals. Of course, this does not mean that *every* aspect of earthly government or morality is evil and must be rejected, only that they are secondary in importance behind our Home Country's government and morality. When there is any disagreement between them, our loyalty and obedience must remain with the (Heavenly) Homeland.

We as ambassadors of our Lord Jesus are to honor, pray for, and live in subjection to the governing authorities of the land in which we live no matter what form of government, political party, or individual leaders are in power. Even if the worst authorities imaginable hold power, as they did during the time when Paul and Peter wrote their epistles (i.e. Nero), we still have these obligations to them. How much more, then, are believers of today obliged to honor, pray for, and live in subjection to the authorities when the political party we disfavor holds power! Of course, we abide by these obligations not because our loyalties are divided between earthly and Heavenly governments, but because we desire these governments to be at peace with one another. Peace between our earthly and Heavenly governments will allow more freedom to advance the cause of our (Heavenly) Lord.

* * *

Dual Citizenship

In a sense, we ambassadors of our Lord Jesus have dual citizenship in both Heaven and the earthly country in which we reside. Though our ultimate loyalty lies in our Heavenly citizenship, we can take advantage of our earthly citizenship when it suits the mission of our Heavenly Government, as Paul did when he used his Roman citizenship to prolong his life and ministry (Acts 22:22-29, 25:10-11).

What if the foreign (earthly) government gives us as citizens of Heaven a voice in their political process? What if they give us the opportunity to take jobs in their government or run for their political offices? When this is the case, as it is for the majority of Christians in the world (since most of us live in at least semi-democratic countries), our first priority ought to be to prevent conflicts between the extensive mission of our Heavenly Government (to spread the gospel and live out the Kingdom) and the limited role of our earthly government (to keep order in society by preventing and punishing evil). The mission of our Heavenly Government is nothing less than to bring all mankind into its citizenry, or at least as many as are willing, and to provide them a spiritual, material, and communal abundance in life. And the primary channel for delivering the material and communal abundance is the citizenry of Heaven themselves!

Put another way, the church's primary purpose on earth is to make disciples of all earthly nations and to manifest the Kingdom blessings as best we can. If we can make our political voices heard through voting for candidates or policies that expand our ability to spread the gospel or make the Kingdom of God more attractive and important in society, we should.

Granted, we would be participating to a degree in the government's use of the sword because our votes, if in the majority, would override the will of voters in the minority through state force. After all, this is how voting works. "Consent of the governed" in democratic countries means "consent of the majority." Those in the minority are forced to go along with the will of those in the majority. But if Christians express their will through the electoral process that the government follow the role assigned to them in Scripture, they would (paradoxically) *not* be seeking the power of the sword. Just the opposite! If Christians voted according to the biblical principles outlined in this book, they would be voting for the separation of church and state. They would be voting for religious freedom as well as the space to let the Kingdom community operate in society. In this way, we believers would be taking advantage of our rights as earthly citizens in a similar way as Paul — not *using* government to make disciples or realize Kingdom blessings, but *swaying* government to make room for the church to do these things.

What about political office? Should Christians run for political office in order to advance the collection of biblical principles we've covered so far? If a Christian should vote for a candidate or policy that they perceive to be in harmony with the Principle of the Separation of Church and State, would it follow that some Christians should go further and run for office on this platform?

First, we must distinguish between administrative or otherwise non-policymaking roles in government and the judiciary, legislative, or executive decision makers who determine the policies by which the nation operates. There's also a useful distinction between those in government who serve purely cooperative roles versus those whose jobs sometimes necessitate the use of force, such as police officers or soldiers. Little in Scripture would suggest that there is anything wrong with serving in a non-policymaking role that doesn't require the use of force or violence. This may refer to advising, administrative tasks, or other supportive roles. Think of the faithful Jew Mordecai from the book of Esther, who served the king (Esther 2:21). Think also of Nehemiah, cupbearer to King Artaxerxes of Persia (Neh. 1:11).

About roles of government in which the use of force or violence is sometimes necessary, on the other hand, Scripture is less clear. In fact, there is evidence to support an argument *against* Christians entering these roles, including the disparate attitudes that the church and the state are to take about vengeance which Paul wrote about in Romans 12-13. Likewise, when Peter drew his sword and struck a Roman who was about to arrest Jesus, the Messiah told him to put away his sword, also giving a principle for *why* Peter was to do so — because "all who take the sword will perish by the sword" (Matt 26:52). Lastly, we must remember that Jesus 'teachings about turning the other cheek, not resisting the evildoer, and refraining from retaliation were never qualified by caveats for those bearing the authority of government or any other authority (Matt 5:38-39).

If this seems radical, *it is!* Everything about Jesus was radical. Remember, Jesus told his followers that if "anyone would come after me, let him deny himself and take up his cross and follow me. For whoever would save his life will lose it, but whoever loses his life for my sake will find it" (Matt. 16:24-25). Jesus warned his followers that life would be difficult as a Jesus-follower. The cross, being the very same device of execution on which Jesus would later die, acts as a symbol of the sacrifice that believers would have to make if they follow in Christ's footsteps. Rather than prepare his followers to defend themselves or the oppressed with the use of force, Jesus told them that they are blessed when they are *persecuted* for the sake of righteousness (Matt. 5:10). How, after all, can a Christian forgo vengeance, choose not to resist evildoers, and love and bless one's enemies while also wearing a uniform and carrying a gun with the willingness to kill, if necessary?

At the very least, we must recognize that there is a strong tension between some of the teachings of the New Testament and the role of policemen and soldiers in society that Christians must acknowledge and wrestle with. Following Christ, ultimately, is *meant* to be radical. If being a Christian results in only a slight modification of the life one would otherwise lead as non-Christian, that person is likely not living faithfully to their calling as a believer.

None of this is to suggest that Christians need to be absolute and legalistic pacifists. Violence itself is never denounced outright in Scripture. What *is* denounced for believers is vengeance (or retribution) (Rom 12:19). We are told to leave that to God, and we are also told how God will primarily exercise His vengeance — through governments (Rom

13:4). Putting two and two together, it would seem that the roles of those directly involved in exacting vengeance — soldier, policeman, prison guard, and perhaps judge — are incompatible with our Christian calling. We are to be a people known for loving and reconciling with our enemies and thereby drawing them into the Kingdom community. That goal is simply not compatible with the jobs of those who use force or violence to subdue others.

That is not to say, however, that these jobs are ignoble or shameful. On the contrary, they often require virtues such as bravery and selflessness, and that makes many people who serve in these positions praiseworthy. But there are other roles in society Christians can play which require the same or similar virtues. Think of firemen, emergency medical technicians, international aid workers, or missionaries to hostile countries.

What about politicians or those with the power to make or shape policy in the judiciary, legislative, or executive spheres of government? To answer this, we should take a page out of Tertullian's playbook. Assuming there's nothing inherently incompatible with the Christian calling to hold the office itself, we should ask if it's possible to fulfill the duties of that position without: attempting to advance Christianity or distinctly Christian morals through force or compulsion, taking any explicit or implicit bribes (Ex. 23:8, Deut. 16:19, Prov. 15:27), doing something wrong even if done to bring about something good (Rom. 3:8), deceiving or giving false witness (Ex. 20:16, Prov. 16:28), slandering one's enemies or political opponents (Ps. 101:5, Jam. 4:11, 1 Pet. 2:1), boasting in oneself or one's accomplishments (Prov. 27:2, Jam. 4:16), showing partiality to the poor, to the rich, or to those who might benefit oneself (Lev. 19:15, Prov. 28:21, Jam. 2:1-4), acting hypocritically (Matt. 7:1-5, Lk 6:41), condemning others to death (Jn 8:1-7), or any other sinful behavior prohibited in Scripture.

Is it possible to take on the role of a judge, legislator, or government executive while avoiding each of these pitfalls? Perhaps. Is it possible to imitate Christ (1 Cor. 11:1, 1 Jn. 2:6) while successfully performing the duties of political office? Again, through great difficulty, perhaps it is. We have no New Testament examples of faithful Christians seeking political power, but neither do we find any instructions against it.

What about the Old Testament examples of Joseph and Daniel, both of whom held high positions in government in which they exerted great power over others? We must remember that *neither man ever sought the offices that they held*. It was their kings who appointed them. Joseph and Daniel merely sought to live faithfully to God and make the best of their less-than-ideal situations. And in any case, no mention is made in either account that God wanted the circumstances in which Joseph or Daniel found themselves to be permanent.

However, given the New Testament's silence on this specific issue, it should be left up to the conscience of each believer whether the most faithful path could involve personally taking political office. Some may conclude that political office should be avoided altogether, while others may view it as a way to influence government—from the inside—toward greater compatibility with the Christian political theology. Those who do seek political office ought to be prayed for and, if they abide by the principles we've discussed, supported. But believers that engage in politics should always be wary of giving in to the Third Temptation and allowing the political realm to grow more important than the Kingdom of God.

* * *

Morality vs. Legality

At this point it would be beneficial to highlight a point that has already been made implicitly but should be made explicitly, and that is the fundamental difference between morality and legality. That distinction might sound trite, but it is of utmost importance in understanding both the overarching story of Scripture and why Christians ought to establish and maintain a healthy separation of church and state.

"Attempting to advance Christianity or a distinctly Christian morality through force or compulsion" was just listed as one of the things that Christians ought to avoid, but many Christians (most vocally evangelicals) would likely disagree with that idea. Many Christians think that the church ought to have a significant influence on government policy with the goal of crafting biblically inspired laws, even while not trying to completely take over or merge with the government.

Evangelical theologian and political conservative Wayne Grudem, for instance, cites Jeremiah 29:7 in support of his view that "Christians *should* seek to influence civil government according to God's moral standards."[120] The verse reads, "Seek the welfare of the city where I have sent you into exile, and pray to the Lord on its behalf, for in its welfare you will find your welfare." Grudem interprets this to mean that believers should seek to "bring good" to their earthly government because the "true 'welfare' of such a city will be advanced through governmental laws and policies that are consistent with God's teaching in the Bible, not by those that are contrary to the Bible's teachings."[121] While acknowledging that "[m]erely passing good laws and having good government will never be enough to change a society," Grudem asserts that "many or perhaps most of the people in a society, if the government passes laws that say something is legal . . . will also think that it is morally right. If the government says that something is illegal, then many people will think that it is morally wrong."[122]

On the other side of the political spectrum, theologian and political liberal Jim Wallis also believes Christians should have significant influence on government, albeit with very different goals than Grudem. Wallis believes that "[p]ersonal and social

---

[120] Grudem, *Politics According to the Bible*, 55
[121] Ibid. 59
[122] Ibid. 96, 98

responsibility are *both* at the heart of religion."[123] By this he means that the government ought to promote both "personal moral values *and* a commitment to social justice and peace" through its laws, policies, and budgets. To Wallis, "[government] budgets are moral documents, revealing our true priorities, and must be judged morally, not just economically."[124] This leads him to seek out political candidates and policies that "show compassion for poor families" rather than "reward the rich," as well as those which "protect creation" rather than "serve corporate interests that damage it."[125]

Both of these viewpoints fail to realize that, in biblical terms, there is a fundamental difference between morality and legality. And that difference is crucial to understand when it comes to what exactly believers should be urging the state to do.

Some time into Christ's ministry, a group of scribes and Pharisees, "holding to the tradition of the elders" which had been enshrined in their law, noticed Jesus's disciples eating with ceremonially unclean hands. "Why do your disciples not walk according to the tradition of the elders, but eat with defiled hands?" they asked him. But in Jesus's reply, he distinguishes between the traditional laws and morality: "There is nothing outside a person that by going into him can defile him, but the things that come out of him are what defile him" (Mark 7:15).

In other words, morality starts in a person's heart and mind and then leads to actions. Actions alone do not make a person moral or immoral. Jesus makes this distinction again numerous times in the Sermon on the Mount. For instance, it is *immoral* both to murder and to be angrily vindictive at someone, yet it is not *unlawful* merely to be angry (Matt 5:21-26). Likewise, it is immoral both to commit adultery and to lust,

---

[123] Wallis, Jim. *God's Politics*. (San Francisco: Harper, 2005) xxiii
[124] Ibid. xxv
[125] Ibid. xxvii

yet it isn't unlawful to lust, despite being the equivalent of committing adultery in one's mind (Matt 5:27-28).

In another story recorded in the book of Matthew, Jesus and his disciples were hungry on the Sabbath and "began to pluck heads of grain and to eat" (12:1). When the religious leaders saw this, they said, "Look, your disciples are doing what is not lawful to do on the Sabbath" (v. 2). Jesus responded by citing a few instances in which breaking the law of rest on the Sabbath is *not* wrong: David entering the temple and eating bread that was supposed to be reserved for the priests, and the Levitical priests who *had to work* on the Sabbath (v. 3-5). Since the Pharisees did not distinguish between morality and legality, they failed to see that Jesus and his disciples were "guiltless" for plucking grain and eating it (v. 7). While technically against the Mosaic Law, the disciples were not doing anything immoral.

Paul makes a similar distinction. Without being under the Mosaic Law, "all things are lawful," he writes in 1 Corinthians 10:23, "but not all things are profitable. All things are lawful, but not all things edify."

Paul here distinguishes between that which is "legal" for the Christian and that which is profitable or edifying (moral). They are not the same. Not everything that is "legal" is morally good or praiseworthy, and not everything that is immoral is unlawful.

The Mosaic Law (along with any other mandated laws) could enforce or encourage certain behaviors but could not enforce morality. It could make people line up at the altar to offer sacrifices for their sin, but it couldn't make them penitent for their sin. Hence God says that those deeds which are righteous by the standards of law are like "filthy rags" to him coming from those who have gone astray (Is. 64:6). God prefers genuine, heartfelt morality over strict adherence to any law: "I desire steadfast love and not sacrifice, the knowledge of God and not burnt offerings" (Hos. 6:6).

We must remember that those who have not submitted

their lives to Jesus and been redeemed as a new creation are still "dead" in sin, "following the prince of the power of the air" (Satan), and are thus "by nature children of wrath" (Eph. 2:1-3). In fact, technically, "no one is good except God alone" (Mk. 10:18) and those whom God has redeemed and purified (Tit. 2:14). "The natural person," by which Paul means the person who does not follow Jesus, "does not accept the things of the Spirit of God, for they are folly to him, and he is not able to understand them because they are spiritually discerned" (1 Cor. 2:14). Instead, in our natural, unredeemed state, "the desires of the flesh are against the Spirit, and the desires of the Spirit are against the flesh" (Gal. 5:17). We who have been redeemed give thanks to God, because we "who were once slaves of sin have become obedient from the heart" to God's moral standards (Rom. 6:17).

Morality comes from the heart, not from actions alone. But the heart, without faith in God, "is deceitful above all things, and desperately sick" (Jer. 17:9). Indeed, "a healthy tree cannot bear bad fruit, nor can a diseased tree bear good fruit," says Jesus in Matthew 7:18. Submission and allegiance to Jesus, along with the indwelling of the Holy Spirit, *have to happen* before moral change or growth can come. Thus, it is futile to try to change human behavior before the heart has been changed. Redemption of the heart comes first, and only then can there be reformation of morals.

Our goal as Christians should not be to transform our government (or our culture through government) into a Christian nation. We should not be trying to "take America back for God" through the channels of government, nor should we try to legislate morality. That completely misunderstands how lives are changed and commits the same error as that of Constantine and his successors in the fourth century. They misinterpreted *outward behavior*, motivated by fear or self-interest, as a sign of the church's success. This was also the error committed by the Pharisees in Jesus' day. They thought that stricter adherence to the law equated to greater morality, but

Jesus rebuked them because their actions were not heartfelt. They were not motivated by faith.

As a corollary to the inability to legislate morality, it is also impossible to *prevent* immorality by making it illegal. While it is tempting to think that we might be able to discourage, and thus lessen the occurrence, of immoral behaviors through government force, this also misunderstands unredeemed human nature. Besides the difficulty of preventing (victimless) immoral behavior through force (e.g. the Prohibition), we must also remember that morality comes from the heart and mind. An immoral heart will produce immoral actions ("fruit"), even if those actions are done in secret rather than in the open. If the heart has not been renewed by faith in Christ, it is futile to try to prevent immoral behavior through force, because the behavior is the *manifestation* or *extension* of the immorality, not the source of the immorality. Laws cannot change the moral status of a person's heart. Only God can do that.

Rather than influence the morality of our culture and society through laws or government policies, we must seek that reform the same way Christ did. "For I have given you an example," Jesus says to his disciples, "that you also should do just as I have done to you" (Jn. 13:15). We as Jesus 'followers must transform society by persuasion, teaching, helping, serving, loving, giving, sacrificing, and, finally, *by example*. As John put it, "Whoever claims to live in him must live as Jesus did" (1 Jn. 2:6). We imitate Christ, and in so doing we make ourselves an attractive example for others to imitate.

This leads us back to the Kingdom Principle of Voluntarism: Service and charity in the Kingdom of God must always be heartfelt and voluntary. We seek to maintain a separation of church and state because the state operates through force and compulsion, whereas the church operates through persuasion, example, and voluntary service. The church, not the state, is the primary method of moral reformation in society. Even William Wilberforce, the British politician who worked tirelessly to abolish the slave trade, acknowledged this:

> Let true Christians consider it their duty to perform a still more extensive service to society; not by busy interference in politics—in which it cannot but be confessed that there is much uncertainty—but rather by that sure and radical benefit of restoring the influence of the faith and raising the standards of morality.[126]

Laws cannot bring about morality. They can promote fairness and justice in society, or diminish unfairness and injustice as in the case of the abolition of slavery. But laws are made by humans, and humans are prone to sin and faulty thinking. Laws *can* do good in society, but they can't *make* society good. And even the good they can do in society is precarious and uncertain.

Thus, with Paul we must ask, "What business is it of mine to judge those outside the church? Are you not to judge those inside?" (1 Cor. 5:12).

* * *

What *Should* the Government Legislate?

If the preceding line of reasoning is correct and laws *cannot* legislate morality (because morality comes from the heart), then what *should* the government legislate? If not the morality of society, what is the aim of the law?

While Scripture does not directly address this question, we find some helpful principles which can guide our thinking.

First, we find in Romans 13 that the government's role is to use the sword to "avenge." The word for "avenge" here (Greek: "*ekdikeo*") suggests exacting punishment or retribution for a wrong committed against someone. John uses the word in the book of Revelation to denote God's just retribution upon those

---

[126] Wilberforce, William. *A Practical View of Christianity.*

who shed His people's blood (Rev. 6:10, 19:2; see also Deut. 32:43). In the book of Acts, the same root word is used to describe retribution against an oppressor in defense of the oppressed (Acts 7:24). And Paul says in 1 Thessalonians 4:6 that "the Lord is an avenger" against those who exploit or take advantage of their brothers and sisters in Christ.

The wrongs that call for vengeance, then, are those that cause (or threaten to cause) *intentional, tangible,* and *undeserved* harm to someone else. The harm must be intentional, because it seems intuitively wrong to call for vengeance against someone who caused harm unintentionally. It must be tangible, involving some detrimental effect on the victim's body or property. Emotional harm—saying something mean, for instance—wouldn't count as tangible. Lastly, the harm must be undeserved, committed against someone who had done nothing to warrant it, as is demonstrated by the biblical examples above.

Criminal behavior, by this definition, would be roughly defined as that which harms another person, whether that harm is physical, financial, or perhaps even against one's reputation. Much debate could be had parsing the specifics of what constitutes a harmful offense worthy of retribution, of course, but we can broadly say that the purpose of the law is to forbid behavior against which retribution would be warranted. It must be referring to crimes *against* another person or persons because harm to oneself doesn't call for retribution. How would it be just, for instance, to punish someone for attempting to commit suicide? Likewise, "victimless crimes" would not count as criminal behavior because there would be no one for the government to avenge. We will return to the idea of the retributive purpose of law in later chapters as it relates to various political issues.

"Praising good behavior," the other duty of government mentioned in Romans 13 and 1 Peter 2, may simply refer to the tacit approval afforded to those who do not commit retribution-worthy offenses, or it may imply honoring and calling public attention to those who are especially meritorious of praise. But there's nothing in the text to suggest that the government's "approval" refers to material rewards or incentives for good behavior.

So the foremost aim of secular law is to punish and prevent harmful wrongs committed against others.

The second useful guideline can be found in the verse cited by Wayne Grudem earlier: "But seek the welfare of the city where I have sent you into exile, and pray to the Lord on its behalf, for in its welfare you will find your welfare" (Jer. 29:7). First, it's necessary to make the observation that there's no mention of seeking the secular city's welfare specifically through political means. Presumably, the primary meaning of "seeking the city's welfare" here is to work for the overall wellbeing of fellow citizens, not showing partiality merely to one's own religious group, ethnicity, or socioeconomic class. And it would mainly refer to nonpolitical activities such as teaching, helping, serving, giving, and exemplifying a godly lifestyle. Only secondarily (because the exiled Jews likely had little political clout anyway) would it apply to how God's people ought to influence government policy when their opinion is welcomed.

The principle we can garner from this, then, is that the church should not act like a special interest group but should rather seek the wellbeing of the nation and citizenry as a whole. We should not seek special treatment but rather the same treatment under the law as everyone else.

In this regard, we would also do well to remember the wisdom garnered from our brief tour of the Old Testament:

Jethro Principle: It is preferable to solve problems and resolve disputes at the most local level possible.

Gideon Principle: God wants direct authority over His people, individually and as a corporate body, so as to increase their faith in Him rather than in earthly power.

Samuel's First Principle: Because of sin, greater power in the hands of any one person or small group of people tends to lead to a greater abuse of power.

Samuel's Second Principle: Governing authorities have the tendency to demand the same loyalty and sacrifice from their citizens as God does from His people.

* * *

The Early American Example

It is interesting to review the varying attitudes about separation of church and state among America's founding fathers. On one hand, many American colonists inherited the English view of church and state as synergetic and overlapping societal institutions. To them, God was sovereign over both the church and the state, and as such, it was the role of statesmen to act as "nursing fathers" to the church (citing Isa. 49:23). These thinkers approved of "freedom of conscience" in matters of religion, but they also saw no issue with state sponsorship of the Christian faith, whether that meant state-level establishment of a certain denomination or public funding of ministers. Up to the ratification of the Constitution, for instance, some states still had requirements that those who held political office must be Christian (Maryland and Massachusetts), or Protestant (the Carolinas and New Jersey), or Trinitarian (Delaware), but the Constitution specifically forbade any religious tests for political office.[127] According to Constitutional scholar Leonard Levy, "after the American Revolution seven of the fourteen states that comprised the Union in 1791 authorized establishments of religion by law"—by which he means "meaningful support to religion."[128]

On the other hand, another strain of thought in early

---

[127] Church, Forrest. *The Separation of Church and State: Writings on a Fundamental Freedom by America's Founders* (Boston: Beacon Press, 2004), 78-79

[128] Cited in Hutson, James. *Church and State In America: The First Two Centuries* (New York: Cambridge University Press, 2008), 104-105.

America was very similar (if not identical) to the separationist stance we have presented above. Early American thinkers, especially those from the Baptist, Unitarian, and Quaker traditions, largely recognized and embraced the wisdom of keeping matters of faith and morality separate from affairs of the state. Freedom of religion was preached and practiced up and down the colonies, even though the various colonies (and later, states) worked out different ways of interpreting that principle. Over time, this separationist viewpoint gradually edged out the more Constantinian norm. According to historian James Hutson, separationism and voluntarism did not prevail across the United States until 1833.[129]

Some, such as signer of the Declaration of Independence and co-drafter of the Constitution, Oliver Ellsworth, held an essentially conservative position concerning the state's role in enforcing certain moral standards. For instance, he wrote,

> ... while I assert the rights of religious liberty, I would not deny that the civil power has a right, in some cases, to interfere in matters of religion. It has a right to prohibit and punish gross immoralities and impieties; because the open practice of these is of evil example and detriment. For this reason, I heartily approve of our laws against drunkenness, profane swearing, blasphemy, and professed atheism.[130]

Ellsworth's political instincts differ from the traditional Christian conservatism of today only in the actions worthy of state punishment. Some immoral behaviors, according to this view, must still be punishable by the government.

Ellsworth's view, however, was an outlier; it was strongly contested in the early years of the republic. Contrary to a belief that is popular among American conservatives, America was not founded as a Christian nation. As George Washington put it in the Treaty of Tripoli (a Muslim nation):

---

[129] Church, 188
[130] Ibid. 86

> As the government of the United States of America is
> not in any sense founded on the Christian Religion,—
> as it has in itself no character of enmity against the
> laws, religion or tranquility of Musselmen [Muslims].
> . . it is declared by the parties that no pretext arising
> from religious opinions shall ever produce an
> interruption of the harmony existing between the two
> countries.[131]

Early American thinkers largely followed in Thomas Jefferson's minimalist attitude toward government, which held that the "legitimate powers of government extend to such acts only as are injurious to others." Conflicting religious beliefs or moral standards that did no harm to others were to be tolerated on an equal basis. "[I]t does me no injury," said Jefferson, "for my neighbor to say there are twenty gods, or no god. It neither picks my pocket nor breaks my leg."[132]

Separation of church, faith, and morality from affairs of state was supported for several reasons beyond Jefferson's minimalist principles. First, they saw that *faith (and, by extension, morality) cannot be enforced.* George Mason, delegate of the Constitutional Convention and neighbor of George Washington, wrote in the "Virginia Declaration of Rights" that "religion, or the duty which we owe to our Creator, and the manner of discharging it, can be directed only by reason and conviction, not by force or violence." Thus, he concluded, "it is the mutual duty of all to practice Christian forbearance, love, and charity towards each other."[133] Likewise, writing in protest against a proposed bill that would establish a tax-funded provision for religious teachers and preachers, James Madison agreed with Mason's sentiment: "It is the duty of every man to render to the Creator such homage, and only such, as he believes to be acceptable to him."[134]

---

[131] Ibid. 123
[132] Ibid. 55
[133] Ibid. 30
[134] Ibid. 61

Thomas Jefferson described the American commitment to make no law establishing or favoring any given religion as the "wall of separation between church and state."[135] The Virginia Statute for Religious Freedom, penned by Jefferson, began with these stipulations:

> Whereas Almighty God has created the mind free, that all attempts to influence it by temporal punishments or burdens, or by civil incapacitations, tend only to beget habits of hypocrisy and meanness, and are a departure from the plan of the Holy Author of our religion, who, being Lord both of body and mind, yet chose not to propagate it by coercions on either, as was in His almighty power to do. . .[136]

Indeed, in matters of faith, Jefferson firmly held that "[r]eason and persuasion are the only practicable instruments. To make way for these, free enquiry must be indulged; and how can we wish others to indulge it while we refuse it ourselves?"[137]

On the other hand, would it even be possible to impose faith or morality through sheer force? Jefferson thought not: "Is uniformity attainable? Millions of innocent men, women, and children, since the introduction of Christianity, have been burnt, tortured, fined, imprisoned; yet we have not advanced one inch towards uniformity. What has been the effect of coercion? To make one half the world fools, and the other half hypocrites."[138]

A second reason why the early Americans rejected any merging of church and state, however minimal, was that *the state enforcement of religion (or morality) is uncertain and always subject to change under different leadership.* As Jefferson gloomily put it, "the spirit of the times may alter, will alter. Our rulers

---

135 Ibid. 130
136 Ibid. 74
137 Ibid. 54
138 Ibid. 53

will become corrupt, our people careless."[139] James Madison put his trepidation about the changing hands of power like this:

> Who does not see that the same authority which can establish Christianity, in exclusion of all other religions, may establish with the same ease any particular sect of Christians, in exclusion of all other sects? That the same authority which can force a citizen to contribute threepence only of his property for the support of any one establishment may force him to conform to any other establishment in all cases whatsoever?[140]

In other words, government is fickle because the governing authorities can change. Ones who would grant the church special favors or privileges could easily be followed by others who would strip away those benefits and instead straddle the church with burdensome policies. And note that it would be just as easy to make this criticism of state-enforced *morality* as it is for state-enforced *religion*. While Christians may sway the governing authorities one moment to punish drunkenness, profane swearing, and atheism (to use Ellsworth's examples), it could easily swing the other way with leaders who grant special favors to alcohol producers, openly swear themselves, or promote hostility in schools and government halls to any influence from Christians.

The belief that the state can enforce religion (or morality), in the words of Madison, "implies either that the civil magistrate is a competent judge of religious truths, or that he may employ religion as an engine of civil policy. The first is an arrogant pretension falsified by the contradictory opinions of rulers in all ages and throughout the world; the second an unhallowed perversion of the means of salvation."[141] In other words, it is unwise to attempt to legislate either religious truths

---

[139] Ibid. 55
[140] Ibid. 63
[141] Ibid. 64

or morality because governing officials are no less human (and thus no less faulty) than anyone else, and also because such an endeavor misunderstands how a person arrives at religious truths and morality in the first place (through salvation).

Third, the founding fathers of America recognized the biblical and historical truth that *the church does not need the help of government to thrive*. In the words of Madison:

> . . . the establishment proposed by the bill [state funding of ministers and religious teachers] is not requisite for the support of the Christian religion. To say that it is, is a contradiction to the Christian religion itself; for every page of it disavows a dependence on the powers of this world. It is a contradiction to fact, for it is known that this religion both existed and flourished not only without the support of human laws but in spite of every opposition from them.[142]

Here Madison refers to the period in church history prior to Constantine, a time when "this religion" (Christianity) "both existed and flourished" while utterly lacking in any government support. The only tools the church had in this time were teaching, helping, serving, praying, giving, sacrificing, and exemplifying Christ. The founding fathers of America saw these tools as the only ones necessary for the success of the faith. Jefferson asserted "that truth is great and will prevail if left to herself, that she is the proper and sufficient antagonist to error, and has nothing to fear from the conflict, unless by human interposition disarmed of her natural weapons, free argument and debate, errors ceasing to be dangerous when it is permitted freely to contradict them."[143] Indeed, as Jefferson wrote elsewhere, "It is error alone which needs the support of government. Truth can stand by itself."[144]

Fourth, the early Americans realized that *Christianity has*

---

[142] Ibid. 65
[143] Ibid. 76
[144] Ibid. 53

been corrupted by intermingling with the state. Once again, Madison makes the keen observation:

> . . .experience witnesses that ecclesiastical establishments, instead of maintaining the purity and efficacy of religion, have done a contrary operation. During almost fifteen centuries has the legal establishment of Christianity been on trial. What have been its fruits? More or less in all places, pride and indolence in the clergy; ignorance and servility in the laity; in both, superstition, bigotry, and persecution. Inquire of the teachers of Christianity for the ages in which it appeared in its greatest luster; those of every sect point to the ages prior to its incorporation with civil policy.[145]

Once again, the only time in which it could accurately be said that Christianity had not incorporated with civil policy was prior to Constantine. And the early church fathers predominantly held the same view about church and state relations as the early Americans. Both groups had one thing in common: neither had been corrupted by the seductive allure of power yet. Writing in the Boston *Independent Chronicle* in 1780, a columnist writing under the pseudonym "Philanthropos" argued that, as a result of Constantine's misguided favor of the church,

> . . . the Christian religion, which for 300 years after the ascension of Jesus, had been spreading over a large part of Asia, Europe and Africa, and without the assistance of secular power and . . . was almost everywhere in a flourishing condition, in the space of another 300 years, or a little more, was greatly corrupted in a large part of that extent, its glory debased, and its light almost extinguished.[146]

Philanthropos echoed a sentiment articulated by Roger

---

[145] Ibid. 65-66
[146] Hutson, 121

Williams in the 1640s that the "unknowing zeal of Constantine and other emperors did more to hurt Christ Jesus' crown and kingdom than the raging fury of the most bloody Neros."[147]

But the intermingling of church and state does not merely corrupt the church. Both organizations become corrupt together. Madison asked, "What influence in fact have ecclesiastical establishments had on society? In some instances they have been seen to erect a spiritual tyranny on the ruins of civil authority; in many instances they have been seen upholding the thrones of political tyranny; in no instances have they been seen the guardians of the liberties of the people."[148] There can scarcely be a more damning judgement than this! These few sentences are rich with wisdom. History is replete with examples of authorities, imbued with the mantle of divine privilege, committing all kinds of heinous offenses and justifying every form of aggression imaginable.

Ergo we read from Jefferson that intermixing church and state "tends only to corrupt the principles of that religion it is meant to encourage, by bribing with a monopoly of worldly honors and emoluments those who will externally profess and conform to it."[149] Again we find a lesson from the Constantinian Shift echoed in the wisdom of the American founders. Recall that some church fathers of the fourth century lamented a rise in false or inauthentic conversions due to the material benefits of outwardly professing faith and acting like a Christian—as well as the threat of punishment for those who resisted this agenda. Jefferson discerned that such an environment could produce only "fools" or "hypocrites." Either the false Christian is a fool for being unaware of the selfish motivations behind his own actions, or he is a hypocrite for knowing his selfish motivations and feigning sincerity anyway.

Fifth and finally, James Madison rejected church-state

---

[147] Ibid.
[148] Church, 66
[149] Ibid. 75-76

integration because, *rather than aiding or incentivizing the faith, it instead embitters outsiders to it.* Madison writes that such integration is "is adverse to the diffusion of the light of Christianity." If Christians managed to sway the government to favor it somehow or to impose moral standards expected of Christians upon all of society, what effect would that have on nonbelievers? Would it drive nonbelievers to repentance and a genuine faith in Christ? "No," says Madison, "it at once discourages those who are strangers to the light of revelation from coming into the region of it; and countenances by example the nations who continue in darkness, in shutting out those who might convey it to them."[150]

In other words, those who are forced to support a religion they don't follow or comply with moral standards to which they don't adhere are *alienated* and *discouraged* from that ideology rather than attracted to it. As humans, we treasure our freedom. Our free will dignifies us. When that freedom is curtailed by a certain group or ideology, we naturally become embittered toward them. Our view of them is immediately soured. And this is just as true for the nations that don't follow the ideology imposed in one's own nation. They become even more closed off to the members of that faith which are associated with their rival government (as we saw with the Sassanids after the conversion of Constantine).

The founders, by and large, *did* view morality as a prerequisite for a peaceful society and an effective government. As George Washington put it, "virtue or morality is a necessary spring of popular government." He went on to assert that "reason and experience both forbid us to expect that national morality can prevail in exclusion of religious principles."[151] And yet, morality does *not* and *cannot* come from the government. As John Adams put it, "The laws of man may bind him in chains or may put him to death, but they can never make

---

[150] Ibid. 68-69
[151] From George Washington's *Farewell Address*

him wise, virtuous, or happy."[152]

In short, the American founding fathers advised the church to remain satisfied with its role of spreading the gospel and thereby reforming moral behavior, while the state remains content with its task of preventing and punishing harmful wrongs.

* * *

But Aren't *All* Laws Based on Some Morality?

Norman Geisler and Frank Turek, in their book *Legislating Morality*, point out that laws are by nature *prescriptive*; they inform society what ought and ought not to be done. Indeed, "all laws declare directly, or by implication, that one behavior is right and its opposite is wrong."[153] Since right and wrong is the language of morality, laws by necessity dictate that which is morally permissible or impermissible. Thus, "legislating morality is inescapable. The only question is, whose morality will be legislated?"

How should we respond to this? Isn't it intuitively true that the law assumes some behaviors to be wrong and others to be right? Doesn't a law against drunk driving, for instance, exist because it presumes driving while intoxicated is morally wrong?

First, we must acknowledge that Geisler and Turek are correct in that there is *some* moral element to law: actions that are illegal must also be immoral. Or, at least, they should be. Why else would something be illegal? Murder, theft, fraud, and vandalism are all *wrong* in addition to being harmful offenses against which the government should legislate and police. A law against something morally good would not be a law that

---

[152] *Letter from John Quincy Adams to George Washington Adams*, 15 September 1811
[153] Geisler, Norman and Turek, Frank. *Legislating Morality: Is It Wise? Is It Legal? Is It Possible?* (Minneapolis: Bethany House Publishers, 1998), 25

Christians should support.

But as the authors tacitly grant in the book, not *everything* that is immoral must be made illegal. The law should be limited to that which causes harm, but the authors define harm more broadly than what "vengeance" would imply. They say that "[a] person's liberty . . . ends where the exercise of his liberty threatens his life or the life of others."[154] But they go even further than that. Besides harm to oneself, Geisler and Turek expand the proper scope of law as forbidding "what is objectively wrong."[155] However, without clear definitions, the authors use the Prohibition as an example of why we should not "over-legislate." They generally view harm to oneself or others as the principle guiding law, but "harm" in their view would include more indirect, tenuously connected cases of harm than merely what would call for retribution.

For instance, they argue that homosexuals (specifically men) harm themselves and each other through sodomy, even if their sexual relations are consensual. Even if there is no *direct* harm in gay sexual relations, they make the case that sexually active gay people indirectly harm themselves and their partners due to increased risk of disease and shortened lifespan.[156] We will return to the topic of homosexuality in a later chapter, but suffice it to say for now that their argument crumbles if there is a drastic reduction in diseases and shortened lifespans among homosexuals, which there has been since the publication of their book in 1998. However, even if these negative side effects of gay sexual relations persisted to today, the harm would still be indirect, unintended, and consensual not something that would call for vengeance or retribution. Any harm is either to oneself or to someone who is complicit in the harmful behavior.

But, once again, isn't it true that the law assumes some

---

154 Ibid. 32
155 Ibid. 30
156 Ibid. 150-152

behaviors to be wrong and others right, thus legislating against immoral behavior? If gay sexual relations are legal, does that imply that the government or its citizenry have given it their imprimatur? Does it imply that all legal behavior is morally permissible?

In short, this is simply not the implication we find in Romans 13, in which Paul writes that the government bears the sword to act as God's *avenger* against the evildoer. Laws promulgated and enforced by secular states (like the one Paul undoubtedly had in mind when he wrote the book of Romans) exist for the purpose of punishing and preventing harmful behavior that warrants retributive action. The sort of harmful behavior that the Bible indicates as worthy of retributive action, as we have seen, is direct and tangible. Murder, assault, theft, fraud, vandalism, slander, and libel would be intuitive examples of this. Laws against such actions *do* imply the government and its citizenry's moral condemnation of these actions. However, it does *not* imply that everything allowed by the law is morally permissible. Many behaviors which could be deemed directly harmful to oneself or indirectly harmful to others were prevalent at the time Paul wrote the book of Romans, but he said nothing of the state's legal permission of these actions. The state's role in society, it seems, according to Paul, is to protect the peaceful and innocent against violent attackers, aggressors, swindlers, or vandals.

Surely purposeful deception, dishonoring one's parents, taking the Lord's name in vain, coarse joking, using profane language, committing adultery, drunkenness, and any number of other sins are morally wrong and yet also *not* the proper realm of government involvement.

What about drunk driving? It certainly endangers the lives of others, which is morally wrong, but the harm they do is a threatened harm—indirect, not direct. Drunk driving *correlates* with harm to oneself and others, but does not *necessarily* bring it about. One *can* drive while intoxicated and not hurt anyone. But it is true that the fear of punishment establishes a strong disincentive to drink and drive. Moreover, it does seem intuitively true that any intentional action which endangers the wellbeing of others is worthy of punishment.

The key here is the threat of harm to innocent people—those who are not complicit in the harmful behavior. Cases in which there is no threat of harm to the innocent would not intuitively call for punishment. For instance, if a person was drunk alone at home and stumbled, hurting themselves somehow, would this warrant retribution? No. The pain caused to themselves would be punishment enough. Only harm or the threat of harm to *others* is worthy of punishment for those whose freely chosen actions or negligence brought about that harm. Driving while intoxicated would be an example of this.

So, in sum, that which is illegal is (or, at least, *should be*) also morally wrong. But Geisler and Turek go too far when they argue that the proper role of the law is to prohibit everything that is "objectively wrong"—a concept that is increasingly difficult to agree upon in a multicultural, pluralistic, secularized country. Rather, the purpose of the law is to create and retain a peaceful and orderly society. It does that by preventing and punishing behavior that is harmful to innocent people or that threatens the innocent with harm. To say something should be legal is *not* to say that it is morally permissible but rather that it does no harm to those who did nothing to deserve it. The wisdom of Proverbs 3:30 is relevant here: "Do not contend with a man for no reason, when he has done you no harm."

* * *

Brief Outline of the Bible's Political Theology

Jesus turned down earthly political power because it was fundamentally incompatible with his mission on Earth and because it would require a steep compromise: forsaking God's will and vision for the world so that an intended good might come. Even a *good* goal with *good* intentions carried out through *bad* means is wrong. All it takes is the tiniest touch of arsenic to ruin an otherwise marvelous dessert. Likewise, all it takes is a small compromise in principles to ruin a good, well-intended cause.

As Christians, we want to draw outsiders into our faith. We want others to participate in the Kingdom of God. We want others to live moral and Christlike lives according to the standards God has given us to live by. But we must recognize that none of these goals can possibly be accomplished through the channels of the state. That is because the state bears the God-given role of using the sword (the use or threat of force) to punish and prevent harmful wrongs in society. The church, on the other hand, operates only through non-coercive means because faith and morality cannot come about through coercion. If it is forced faith, it is not true faith. And if it is forced morality, it is not true morality.

The two must remain separate and distinct. The church cannot carry out its mission by means of the sword, and the state cannot carry out its mission by means of the cross. To assume that Christians can flex their political influence in order to make their earthly government or society into a "Christian nation" would be to commit the same error as Constantine. The only "Christian nation" that has ever existed or will ever exist is the Kingdom of God. We believers, its citizens, are called by God the "holy nation" (1 Pet. 2:9). As such, we have only one political slogan, and that is the same one proclaimed two millennia ago: "Jesus is Lord!"

Indeed, because God's ultimate goal is to reassert His rightful role as King of His people, ruling without deputies or proxies, He has inaugurated Christ (the second member of the Trinity) as Lord, making certain Christ's eventual authority over all of humanity (Phil. 2:9-10). But He wants to exert direct authority over His people even now, in this life, because it increases their faith in His supernatural power and providence. While it is difficult to put our trust in God rather than fellow humans or governing authorities (Ps. 118:8-9), we are promised that when we do so, God works all things together for good (Rom. 8:28).

Therefore, the best kind of earthly government that we could work and pray for would be the one most compatible with our Kingdom mission, allowing the church maximal freedom to carry out its tasks of material, communal, and spiritual life-giving—and crucially, not attempting to get involved in those tasks. If the government legally forbids behaviors which also violate Christian standards, we need not necessarily fight to have those laws removed. But we do make it clear that the laws are not in place to enforce Christian morality or to forbid that which our Scriptures reveal to be immoral. Rather, as Christians, we make it known that morality is distinct from legality (though they overlap), and that the standards of *morality* go far beyond the limited scope of *legality*. As Paul put it, "All things are lawful for me, but not all things are helpful" (1 Cor. 6:12). Not everything that is immoral should be or needs to be illegal.

In fact, there is very little that Christians ought to encourage government to do. The essential function of the state is to keep order in society by avenging harmful wrongs committed against others. Beyond that, we have little else to assign to the authorities. We as the church do not want to outsource our own jobs to the state. Moreover, we ought to be wary of the state crowding the church out of tasks such as caring for the needy, feeding the hungry, and clothing the naked. (We'll return to the "crowd-out effect" in a later chapter.) We must remember that God's method of realizing the material and communal abundance of the Kingdom is through the church, not the state. When the government provides anything that could have been provided by the church, the importance and relevance of the church in society is diminished, and one of the most powerful tools for attracting outsiders into the community of faith is blunted.

We as the church should never forget that our mission is an

expansive one. Not only are we called to evangelize and make disciples, but we are also called to provide for the needy, advocate for the oppressed, heal and care for the sick, help the weak, lend freely while expecting nothing in return, show radical hospitality, and strive to be peacemakers. Though much of the New Testament's passages on these subjects focus on believers giving or sacrificing to help others in the church (because fellow believers have entered into the Kingdom and have access to its abundant life and Sabbath rest), Jesus himself provides an example of using material provision as a way to draw in outsiders in order to hear his teachings. Think of those who sought Jesus for his ability to heal, as well as the feeding of the five thousand in Matthew 14 and the four thousand in Matthew 15. Jesus said to those people, "you are seeking me, not because you saw signs, but because you ate your fill of the loaves" (Jn. 6:26). Our generosity and sharing are directed primarily at fellow believers, which itself makes the Kingdom community attractive to outsiders. But, secondarily, generosity can also be directed at nonbelievers as a form of outreach. Paul says that "as we have opportunity, let us do good to *everyone*, and especially to those who are of the household of faith" (Gal. 6:10).

As far as the church is concerned, then, to quote Henry David Thoreau, "that government is best which governs least"—or at least one which protects religious freedom and doesn't poach the earthly mission to which the church is called. A smaller government that provides fewer services against which the church would have to compete gives more urgency to the church's calling to provide material abundance.

A smaller government also coincides with the Jethro Principle practiced by the Israelites' judge system: "It is preferable to solve problems and resolve disputes at the most local level possible." A larger government providing more services requires more administration and bureaucracy, which typically requires more centralization of authority and decision-making. But the wisdom of the judge system was that collective decisions should be made, and disputes settled, at the most local level possible. When more power resides higher up the chain of command, Samuel's Second Principle (which can be summarized as "power corrupts and attracts the already corrupt") is in danger of being ignored.

Finally, we ought to remember Samuel's Second Principle: "Governing authorities have the tendency to demand the same loyalty and sacrifice from their citizens as God does from His people." Often debates about patriotism revolve around loyalty—whether an action or political stance shows loyalty or disloyalty to one's country. Many people, especially in America, become inflamed at any perceived sign of disloyalty to the nation, believing that their fellow citizens should be willing to sacrifice for the good of their country. But while it is not wrong to honor or even love one's country, the fervent loyalty that is shown to one's country, political party, or favored politicians often *replaces* loyalty to God in that it drives us to commit and rationalize actions which violate biblical morality. Likewise, the sacrifices that such loyalty drives us to make for the sake of our country, political party, or favored politicians often come at the expense of sacrificing for the Kingdom of God. After all, the more we sacrifice for our country—or for any earthly cause—the less we have left to offer to God's Kingdom. Ultimately, we cannot serve two masters.

We Christians ought to be aware that patriotism and partisanship verge on the same God-replacing zeal that Samuel warned about in 1 Samuel 8. He said that Israel's king would take a tenth of their produce, the same amount God reserved for Himself in the tithe. In fact, their very *desire* for a government is condemned as a form of idolatry—replacing God with some created (and thus lesser) object of their hope and allegiance. When our hope is found in earthly authorities, our hearts have gone astray. In the words of Aleksandr Solzhenitsyn, a man who experienced firsthand this God-replacing political zeal in Soviet Russia, "We have placed too much hope in political and social reforms, only to find out that we were being deprived of our most precious possession: our spiritual life."

Encouraging a smaller government that generally provides less moral instruction and fewer services, at least as far as the church is concerned, acknowledges that *God* is our Sovereign, our Provider, our Hope, and our Peace. It also acknowledges that we, as the hands and feet of Christ, are meant to provide and care for each other. We are meant to teach and administer the moral principles of the Bible. And we are meant to manifest the first fruits of God's new creation. When we are doing these things faithfully, whether the church consists of two people or two hundred million people in our home country, there is less need for government intervention in areas of moral instruction or material provision for the needy, the elderly, or children. To the extent that the government *needs* to step in and provide these things, at least as far as concerns the church body and those whom the church has the ability to bless, Christians have failed to live out the Kingdom of God as fully as we are called to.

Now that some political-theological vision of the Bible, however broad, has been sketched out, let us apply this framework to various contemporary political issues and try to discern specific policy implications.

* * *

"Who is it that overcomes the world except the one who believes that Jesus is the Son of God?"
1 John 5:5

CHAPTER EIGHT

Marriage and Family

When it comes to politics and the Bible, contemporary Christians often approach the subject from one of two frames of mind. Either they assume the Bible has nothing to say about modern politics, or they assume that the Bible fully supports the views that they already hold. Both are, in all likelihood, inaccurate.

To assert that the Bible has nothing at all to say — no relevant principles — about a given political issue is to diminish the value of the Bible, at least to some degree. But then, to say that the Bible fully backs any contemporary political party or partisan set of political beliefs would be an anachronism. Jesus was neither a Republican nor a Democrat, for these political parties didn't even exist until after the formation of the United States in the 18th century. Besides, political parties are fluid; the stances they hold in one generation or election cycle may evolve — and, indeed, *do* evolve — in the next. Even the dichotomous systems of thought known as *liberalism* and *conservatism* shift over time and hold different meanings in different parts of the world. A "liberal" in 18th century Europe would stand for a far different set of political values than would a "liberal" of 21st century America or Great Britain. In fact, a contemporary" liberal democrat" in Great Britain would not always agree with a "liberal democrat" in the United States!

Neither was Jesus (or any other biblical author or figure) a capitalist or socialist. Capitalism as an economic philosophy didn't come about until sometime in the 18th century, and socialism followed after it. It makes no sense to superimpose a philosophy onto figures or writings that existed at least 18 centuries prior to the founding of that philosophy! The same could be said of the theory of property rights put forward by John Locke during the Enlightenment of the 17th century or of the "veil of ignorance" theory of justice espoused by John Rawls in the 20th century. Indeed, it could also be said of liberation theology, feminist theology, black theology, or any other philosophy of the modern era that is superimposed upon the thinking of Jesus or the biblical authors. Of course Jesus came to "liberate" the captives, but we must understand that as he meant it in the first century. Of course Jesus supported the equal dignity of women, as evidenced by the fact that the first two people to witness his resurrection were *women*, but that doesn't mean Jesus was a "feminist" with all the connotations the label involves today. And *of course* Jesus would readily affirm that black lives matter, but that doesn't mean that he would affirm everything that the contemporary and varied political movement would assert.

We Christians must vigilantly guard against allowing ourselves to recruit — or rather, *conscript* — Jesus or Scripture in support of our preconceived politics. "Many have substituted Liberalism or Conservatism or some other ism for Christ and coopted Christ for their cause," writes philosopher Peter Kreeft, "Christ cannot be coopted for any cause; all causes must be coopted for Him."[157]

That said, we must also recognize the Bible as the rich source of practicable wisdom that it is. So much of this wisdom centers around the proper functions of *marriage*, *family*, and *community*.

Let us begin our exploration of how to apply our political-theological principles to the church's role in the political realm, then, by sketching out a Scriptural framework of these three social organizations. Then we'll compare the state of modern

---

[157] Kreeft, Peter. *The Philosophy of Jesus* (St. Augustine's Press: 2007), 147

American culture to the Bible's ideal for marriage and family and see how they match up. In the following chapter we'll look at the erosion of American community compared to God's ideal for it. The results will be depressing but ever so important for understanding our societal problems.

* * *

The Function of Marriage

The original function of marriage was to cure man's lonesomeness. About Adam God says in Genesis 2:18: "It is not good that the man should be alone. I will make a helper fit for him." The word for "helper" here (Hebrew: *'ezer*) does not denote a subordinate or someone lesser in value. That is why none of the multitude of animals brought to Adam to be named are suitable for him as his "helper." They are in many ways subordinate to Adam, which disqualifies them from being able to be his helper. Scripture has a high view of this word, as it refers to someone who supplies strength in an area that is lacking. It is one whose own qualities complement and complete the qualities of the other. That is why Jesus refers to the Holy Spirit as our "Helper" in John 14:16.

The woman, later to be called Eve, was crafted by God from one of Adam's ribs. Not from his head so as to be above him, and neither from his leg so as to be below him, but from his rib, so as to be as close as possible to his heart and vital organs. Thus, in marriage, the man and woman become bonded to each other physically, mentally, and emotionally. They are "one flesh"—interdependent in every way. This interdependence involves obligations to one another, as Paul mentions in 1 Corinthians 7:3-4. They are to "submit to one another out of reverence for Christ" (Eph. 5:21). Here in Ephesians 5, we find a second purpose of marriage: Paul says that the mystery of man becoming one flesh with his wife in fact "refers to Christ and the church" (v. 32). Marriage between man and woman is a symbol of the relationship between Christ and his people—two complementary entities coming together to form one body, one covenantal union.

In the marriage between man and woman, just as in the marriage between Christ and the church, each participant has obligations to the other. Just as the church respects and submits to Christ as its leader, so too does the wife respect and submit to her husband (v. 22-24). And just as Christ "submits" to the church in the sense of loving, serving, and giving self-sacrificially for her, so too does the husband love, serve, and give self-sacrificially for his wife (v. 25-30). They *both* have obligations to each other, even though those obligations are not identical.

Up until recently in human history, the wife's obligation to submit to her husband did not rub people the wrong way. It wasn't interpreted as misogyny or male chauvinism because women were biologically and culturally the "weaker vessel" (1 Pet 3:7) in society. The female body is simply less physically strong, generally speaking, than the male body, and in a world where physical strength determines power and ability to generate income, women are at a disadvantage. Such a state dominated most of human history. Likewise, pregnancy, childbirth, and breastfeeding puts women at a disadvantage. It diminishes time that a woman can work and get an education. Only recently in history has "work" shifted from largely physical to largely mental labor, which has put women on a more level playing field with men. And only recently in history has education become so beneficial to income generation.

Even so, only a woman's body can become pregnant, gestate, give birth, and nurse a child. This still makes a wife dependent on her husband to some degree, even if she works and is well-educated. This makes the husband the "head" of the marriage, loving his wife self-sacrificially in order to provide for her as she provides for their child. She owes him her respect, just as he owes her his self-sacrificial provision.

Notice, then, that there is a third function of marriage: not only is it the most basic, God-honoring, Christ-symbolizing social unit, it is also the primary relationship of shared resources. The wife provides something that her husband cannot—care for their unborn and infant child. The husband provides something that his wife cannot—protection of and provision for her when she is vulnerable during pregnancy and nursing. What charity or state benefits are needed when this relationship exists and functions properly? None. Granted, there are situations in which struggling couples need financial help to get by, but one of the functions of marriage is to establish a relationship of shared resources in order to avoid these situations. Marriage is God's foremost method of fairly, lovingly, and voluntarily redistributing wealth.

* * *

The Function of Family

If marriage is the primary *relationship* of shared resources, the family, as an extension and product of marriage, is the primary *community* of shared resources. In terms of material possessions, families are little (sometimes not so little) communes. They are organizations in which their members share belongings and responsibilities. Its members feel an innate obligation to each other, to provide not just love, care, and attention, but also physical things—food, clothing, shelter, and so on.

This obligation, according to Paul, is to what we'd call in modern lingo "extended family"—grandparents, grandchildren, aunts, uncles, nephews, nieces, cousins, and in-laws. But if the obligation exists for extended family, it exists even stronger for one's "nuclear family." As Paul writes in 1 Timothy 5:8, "But if anyone does not provide for his relatives, and *especially for members of his household,* he has denied the faith and is worse than an unbeliever." The word "relatives" here would include extended family, while "members of his household" would be the nuclear family of parents and children.

So strong is this obligation to provide for one's family that if anyone fails to accomplish it, they have "denied the faith" and are "worse than an unbeliever." Why such a harsh denouncement of those who don't materially provide for their families? How has one denied the faith by failing to properly feed, clothe, or provide shelter for their relatives? First, we must remember that *family* is an extension of *marriage*. Children are products of that relationship, and if either spouse is neglecting their duties to provide for their family, God is not being honored and the relationship between Christ and the church is not being put on display. But marriage is broader than simply two individuals becoming one flesh; it also includes the enjoining of two families. When the branches of humanity's vast family tree grow back together through a marriage, the opportunity to display Christian love and self-sacrifice becomes *communal* rather than merely *individual*.

Second, remember God's special compassion for those who are in need. Jesus says of those whom the King will welcome into the eternal Kingdom: "For I was hungry and you gave me food, I was thirsty and you gave me drink, I was a stranger and you welcomed me, I was naked and you clothed me, I was sick and you visited me, I was in prison and you came to me" (Matt 25:35-36). The righteous ask in confusion when it was that they did these things, and the King replies: "Truly, I say to you, as you did to one of the least of these my brothers, you did to me" (v. 40). There is a connection, Jesus asserts, between loving God and loving one's neighbor. After all, "Religion that is pure and undefiled before God," writes James, includes "to visit orphans and widows in their affliction" (Jam 1:27). How much truer is this for God's people when it is their own relatives?

All human beings are made in the image of God. The phrase—"image of God"—carries multiple connotations in Scripture, but one of the most important is the notion of being a *representation* of God. In the ancient world, only kings and great rulers were said to bear the image of God (if they didn't claim divinity themselves). These rulers had infinitely more value than those they ruled over. The subjects who served the king had little to no worth compared to the great, god-in-the-flesh ruler. But in the Judeo-Christian faith, one reason why God's people were originally to have no human king ruling over them (and were not even to make any "carved images" of God to worship [Ex. 20:4]) was because *all* human beings bear the image of God. *Every* person, however rich or poor, displays the divine image and possesses unsurpassable worth. Therefore, *every* person deserves love, care, attention, and material provision. Every person deserves to be served just as subjects serve their ruler. The family is designed to provide this mutual service within one community.

The family is God's primary social safety net. To let someone within one's own household slip through that safety net is truly to deny an essential part of our faith, for "loving God" is only one-half of Christ's greatest commandment. The other half is to "love your neighbor as yourself" (Mark 12:30-31).

* * *

Function of the Church

As we have already covered, God has designated the church, the hands and feet of Christ, to be the primary channel through which the material blessings of the Kingdom of God are distributed. The most basic social unit and primary relationship of shared resources is the marriage, and the primary *community* of shared resources is the family. The church body is simply one further extension of that family. Just as one's family may expand by getting married and embracing one's in-laws as relatives, so much more can one's number of relatives expand by embracing the family of faith!

As Christ said of his disciples, "Here are my mother and

my brothers! For whoever does the will of my Father in heaven is my mother and sister and brother" (Matt 12:49-50). We followers of Christ, then, are part of a larger family—God's family. We "are no longer strangers and aliens, but . . . members of the household of God" (Eph 2:19). Elsewhere, Paul calls it the "household of faith" (Gal. 6:10), signifying a family that lives under one roof together.

A believer's highest obligation is to provide for one's spouse, and then one's nuclear family, and then one's extended family, *and then* one's family of faith. The order is important. One cannot properly provide for others in one's faith community if their family's needs are not met. When Paul described the traits required of those who would take up the office of "overseer" in the church, he says, "He must manage his own household well, with all dignity keeping his children submissive, for if someone does not know how to manage his own household, how will he care for God's church?" (1 Tim. 3:4-5). The same qualification is given for deacons: they must manage "their children and their own households well" (1 Tim. 3:12). Part of that family management is making sure each member is provided for. Only then can we be like the centurion, Cornelius: "a devout man who feared God with all his household [and] gave alms generously to the people" (Acts 10:2). The alms were the overflow of a household that was already provided for and that feared God.

We have already explored how, in the wake of the Spirit indwelling believers at Pentecost, the church practiced radical generosity in giving to those in need, selling property if necessary, and holding all material things in common (Acts 2, 4). It was as if the scales had been lifted from their eyes to see each other now as family members, and *as* family members, how could they *not* provide for each other's needs, even at great cost?

The example of the post-Pentecost church serves a reminder that our fellow believers' needs should not be overlooked. It should show the benefit of living in solidarity with those possessing both greater and lesser resources than us. If we associate only with believers in our own socioeconomic class, we will be incapable of blessing the family of faith as well. When wealthy and poor believers intermingle, both have greater opportunities to bless each other with the gifts God has given them. As Paul says,

> we, though many, are one body in Christ, and individually members one of another. Having gifts that differ according to the grace given to us, let us use them: if prophecy, in proportion to our faith; if service, in our serving; the one who teaches, in his teaching; the one who exhorts, in his exhortation; the one who contributes, in generosity; the one who leads, with zeal; the one who does acts of mercy, with cheerfulness. (Rom. 12:5-8)

When believers serve each other with their unique gifts, all the needs of the faith community are met. Those who provide for their family are given the instruction, "Contribute to the needs of the saints and seek to show hospitality" (Rom. 12:13). Just as one with a gift for teaching ought to seek out opportunities to teach, so also should one who has resources seek opportunities to contribute and show hospitality. This is not an instruction *only* for the wealthy, but it *is* more weighty for the wealthy. "To whom much is given, much is required" (Lk. 12:48).

* * *

Conditions for Church Financial Support

Though we are to exhibit the generosity of family members, providing for each other out of love and kinship, we are instructed *not* to do it indiscriminately. Just as if one's son or daughter abuses financial support from his or her parents, believers should be careful to give only to the *deserving* and only when support is *necessary* and *helpful* to the recipient. In the same breath, Paul encourages the Thessalonians both to "help the weak" *and* to "admonish the idle" (1 Thess. 5:14).

In the ancient world, widows were among the most vulnerable and weak in society. Yet, even for them, Paul instructs Timothy to be discriminating with church support.

> Honor widows who are truly widows. But if a widow has children or grandchildren, let them first learn to show godliness to their own household and to make some return to their parents, for this is pleasing in the sight of God. She who is truly a widow, left all alone, has set her hope on God and continues in supplications and prayers night and day, but she who is self-indulgent is dead even while she lives. (1 Tim. 5:3-6)

First, notice that *it pleases God* for immediate and extended family members to take care of each other. Recall the Jethro Principle: It is preferable to solve problems and resolve disputes at the most local level possible. This is true also of caring for those in need. If the church provided for needy members who have family capable of doing that, they are effectively usurping an opportunity to bless one's own family. God designed families to be the most basic social safety net, and when they actually operate that way, He is pleased. But notice, also, that Paul recognizes some truly are "left all alone" and need help. He does not take the view that everyone who is poor must necessarily be poor because of laziness or some other vice. Some — the "self-indulgent" — *do* remain poor because of character flaws, but not all of the impoverished are that way. The widow who is truly needy but who "has set her hope on God" *does* deserve help from her church family. Paul goes on:

> Let a widow be enrolled if she is not less than sixty years of age, having been the wife of one husband, and having a reputation for good works: if she has brought up children, has shown hospitality, has washed the feet of the saints, has cared for the afflicted, and has devoted herself to every good work (1 Tim. 5:9-10)

Paul's qualifications for those truly deserving of help are rather strict. First, the widow must be over 60 years old, which was quite old in the first century. The average lifespan rose above 70 in the United States only in the last century. However, this qualification likely wasn't meant to be exercised legalistically. Rather, it's meant to make the point that those who are more or less able to work and provide for themselves ought to do so (and be given the opportunity to do so). There were some things a younger widow could do in those days. Look at Ruth, for example. Older widows who could no longer work or remarry, on the other hand, were truly, desperately needy.

> But refuse to enroll younger widows, for when their passions draw them away from Christ, they desire to marry and so incur condemnation for having abandoned their former faith. (1 Tim. 5:11-12)

Remarriage was an option for younger widows in those days, one that Paul doesn't condemn *per se*. But what Paul has in view here is a widow who remarries a non-Christian and is thus drawn away from her faith, since it was common in those days for wives to take on the religions of their husbands. (Christians were a tiny minority in the first century, and thus a Christian widow may have few or no eligible men to marry.) Paul doesn't want the church's scarce resources used on a person like this when those resources could have gone to someone more deserving.

> Besides that, they learn to be idlers, going about from house to house, and not only idlers, but also gossips and busybodies, saying what they should not. (1 Tim. 5:13)

An unintended outcome of indiscriminate financial support is turning recipients into "idlers"—those who are lazy or listless. Having one's basic necessities provided in such a way strips a person from the natural sense of purpose in life derived from having a job to do or family members to care for.

Without that sense of purpose, recipients exhibit behaviors that are harmful to the community, like gossip and meddling, in order to ease the boredom and purposelessness in life. Boredom spawns all kinds of bad conduct. Paul expresses the profound and hard truth here that, sometimes, even heartfelt and compassionate giving can be harmful rather than helpful to the recipient. We are instructed to admonish the idle, but in a larger community setting like the church, it is easier for idlers to slip through the cracks than it would be within a family. Thus, Paul concludes, "If any believing woman has relatives who are widows, let her care for them. Let the church not be burdened, so that it may care for those who are truly widows" (1 Tim. 5:16).

Notice that the reason for the qualification on financial support is not stinginess. It does not arise from an indifference to the plight of the poor, nor from a desire to let wealthier believers keep more of their money. Rather, God wants all people to enter into the Sabbath rest of His Kingdom and to enjoy the abundant life that Christ came to bring. Indiscriminate giving, even if well-intentioned, actually *hinders* that goal. The church is called to generosity, but not a *careless* generosity. As Paul wrote to the Thessalonians,

> If anyone is not willing to work, let him not eat. For we hear that some among you walk in idleness, not busy at work, but busybodies. Now such persons we command and encourage in the Lord Jesus Christ to do their work quietly and to earn their own living. (2 Thess. 3:10-12)

Work, which we may interpret broadly here as referring to any activities of value to others (employers, customers, family members, the needy, etc.), gives us purpose and meaning in life. Without work, which can include parenting or serving the church but mainly refers to earning a living, people naturally gravitate toward troublesome behaviors like being a busybody (meddling in others 'affairs). We naturally yearn for the sense of meaning that only labor or service can bring, and if we don't labor or serve then we tend to intrude upon others 'affairs. At least that relieves the boredom. But no, says Paul, the ideal is to "work with your own hands . . . so that you may walk properly before outsiders and be dependent on no one" (1 Thess. 4:11-12).

Ideally, no able-bodied person would be dependent on others. That is why work is so important. The connection between work and a sense of meaning in life is innate in us because we were *created* to work, even in the idyllic Garden of Eden: "The Lord God took the man and put him in the garden of Eden *to work it and keep it*" (Gen. 2:15).

The ideal, then, is for everyone in the family and church community to have some kind of meaningful work to do—some activity of value to others. Generosity and hospitality of family members or fellow believers is limited only by the degree to which help is truly necessary as well as helpful rather than harmful. Because those closest to individuals requesting help have the greatest ability to discern between deserving and undeserving needs, larger communities play a subsidiary role to smaller communities in the provision of help. The church body steps in only when family cannot. Extended family steps in only when immediate family cannot. Immediate family steps in only when one's spouse cannot.

This is the way God's people ought to live in order to create a social safety net that provides *holistic* support for each other. We are more than mouths to feed or bodies to clothe and shelter. We are human beings, crafted from the dust of the earth and imbued with the yearning for meaningful work that is, having a significant role to play that will improve the lives of others.

And since God desires *all people* to experience this abundant life, we should expect these principles to be just as true outside the church as they are in it. Granted, if individuals do not follow Christ, then this ladder of communal safety nets will work less well. But we should still expect it to work better than any alternative because it is a matter of human nature—how God created us to live and relate to one another.

* * *

Erosion of the Family

Alas, the Western family has looked increasingly less like the New Testament vision in the last half century or so.

For most of human history, holding families together has been challenging, to be certain, but also quite natural. It was practical as well as virtuous. Divorce, for instance, carried an aura of shame not just for moralistic reasons but also because it meant impairing society's most basic social safety net. Single motherhood was a tragedy not merely because it implied premarital sex but because it so strongly correlated with poverty and dependence on others (not to mention the negative effects of a child growing up in a single-parent home). Church attendance signified not only that one desired to please God or hear a good sermon but also that one was willing to engage in community and share their resources. What was once accepted as the sequence of success in life—getting at least a basic education, getting a job, getting married, taking part in a broader community, *then* having kids—is now viewed as passé. Social tolerance now trains Western societies to believe that success can come by rearranging the order however one would like.

But the consequences of this societal shift highlight the intended function of the family as the most basic safety net. In his book, *Home Economics: The Consequences of Changing Family Structure*, Nick Schulz cites a study by researchers at the Brookings Institution (a left-of-center think tank) which found that "if young people finish high school, get a job, and get married before they have children, they have about a 2 percent chance of falling into poverty and nearly 75 percent chance of joining the middle class by earning $50,000 or more per year."[158] Surely no small part of the reasoning for this is because one has better job prospects with a high school degree and by spending some time in the job market prior to having children, but it also pertains to the stability of the household. Less stable households (families) do less well economically, and couples that have children prior to getting married are statistically less stable. "Researchers at the University of Michigan find that over 65 percent of cohabiting couples with kids are separated by the time the child turns ten years old."[159]

The correlation between single parenthood (most often single motherhood) and poverty is very strong. Robert Rector uses data from the Census Bureau to conclude that "marriage drops the probability of child poverty by 82 percent." The poverty rate for single parents with children in 2008 was 36.5%, whereas the same rate for married couples with children was only 6.4%. By 2011, the rate for single parents had climbed to 40.7%, whereas for married families it was 8.8%.[160] Less than one-third of all poor households/families are married, whereas three-quarters of non-poor households/families are married.[161] Columbia University's National Center for Children in Poverty corroborates these statistics. Using a slightly different metric for poverty, it "found that only 5 percent of married-family households were poor at some point within a given year, compared with almost 30 percent of single-parent households."[162]

But the problem goes deeper than material or financial deficiencies. Schulz quotes Sara McLanahan and Gary Sandefur's book *Growing Up with a Single Parent*:

---

[158] Schulz, Nick. *Home Economics: The Consequences of Changing Family Structure* (Washington D.C.: AEI Press, 2013), 39.

[159] Ibid. 26-27

[160] http://www.familyfacts.org/charts/327/two-in-five-single-mother-families-are-poor

[161] https://www.heritage.org/poverty-and-inequality/report/marriage-americas-greatest-weapon-against-child-poverty-0

[162] Schulz, 52

> [A]dolescents who have lived apart from one of their parents during some period of childhood are twice as likely to drop out of high school, twice as likely to have a child before age twenty, and one and a half times as likely to be "idle"—out of school and out of work—in their late teens and early twenties.[163]

It gets even worse for children of single parents, though. They are also more than twice as likely to be arrested for a juvenile crime, twice as likely to be treated for emotional or behavioral problems, and about twice as likely to be suspended or expelled from high school. Moreover, they are three times as likely to commit a crime and end up in jail by age 30 and are 50% more likely to live in poverty as adults than children from similar backgrounds with married parents. And sadly, "girls from single-parent homes are more than twice as likely to have a child without being married [than girls raised in similar married families], thereby repeating the negative cycle for another generation."[164]

It is telling that 26 of the 27 deadliest mass shooters in American history were fatherless men.[165]

Why exactly do single parents (especially single mothers) have it so much worse economically than married parents? For Christians, this is explained by the lack of mutual service to and provision for one another. But social scientists David Ellwood and Christopher Jencks approach it from another angle:

> Single mothers seldom command high wages. They also find it unusually difficult to work long hours, since they must also care for their children. Many get very little in child support from the absent father, and even generous child support payments provide less support than a resident father with the same income would

---

[163] Ibid. 40

[164] Rector, from the previously cited heritage.org article

[165] Meckler, Mark. "Of the 27 Deadliest Mass Shooters, 26 of Them Had One Thing in Common." (https://www.patheos.com/blogs/markmeckler/2018/02/27-deadliest-mass-shooters-26-one-thing-common/)

> normally provide. . . . The spread of single-mother families has therefore played a major role in the persistence of poverty.[166]

Evidently, this has been a reinforcing cycle among those in the bottom third of the income spectrum, as the statistics are much different for those in the middle and upper classes. Social scientist Charles Murray's book, *Coming Apart*, demonstrates that marriage is still quite strong among America's affluent and well-educated, but the further down the income and education spectrum one goes, the more erosion there has been in marriage and the family.[167] For instance, "[w]hile just 6 percent of children born to college-educated American mothers are born out of wedlock, the percentage for mothers with no more than a high school education is 44 percent."[168] Indeed, Brad Wilcox of the University of Virginia's National Marriage Project finds that "highly educated Americans, who make up 30 percent of the adult population, now enjoy marriages that are as stable and happy as those four decades ago" and that "the retreat from marriage has been regarded largely as a problem afflicting the poor."[169]

This was not always the case in the United States. According to Pew Research, whereas in recent years "64 percent of Americans with a college degree were married, [and] of those with a high school diploma or less, only 48 percent were married . . . [i]n the middle of the twentieth century, both the well educated and the less educated were just as likely to be married." Charles Murray corroborates this assertion using census statistics: "As of 1950, decennial census figures show that 88 percent of white families consisted of husband-wife households, compared with 78 percent of black families. Both figures had remained essentially unchanged since before the

---

[100] Schulz, 40-41

[167] Murray, Charles, *Coming Apart: The State of White America, 1960-2010* (New York: Crown Forum, 2012)

[168] Schulz, 17

[169] Ibid.

Second World War (the figures for the 1940 census were 86 percent and 77 percent, respectively)."[170]

Today, largely because the birth rate is higher among the poor than it is among the affluent, out of wedlock births have become something of a new normal, while a few generations ago they were exceedingly rare. "While only 5 percent of children were born out of wedlock in 1960, the percentage of births to unmarried women in 2010 was over 40 percent." In fact, in early 2012, the New York Times reported that "over half of births to women in the United States under the age of 30 are now out of wedlock."[171]

* * *

Causes of Family Erosion

What is the cause of this striking divergence in family structure between rich and poor in America over the last 50 years or so? Some (mainly those on the political Left) argue that stagnating wages in the working class and rising income inequality between rich and poor has put stress on lower-income families, and thus, a lack of money is the cause of the fracturing. Furthermore, this lack of money is the root of problems for children of single mothers or low-income families more generally. The problem can be solved, then, by transferring more cash or in-kind benefits to those at the bottom of the income spectrum. This would alleviate the relational tension of constantly worrying about money which, the theory stipulates, is tearing apart low-income families. It would also remedy the negative behaviors often seen in children of low-income families.

This approach, however, simply does not comport with the research about family structure and poverty. For one, it ignores

---

[170] Murray, Charles, *Losing Ground: American Social Policy, 1950-1980*. (New York: Basic Books, 2015), 129.
[171] Schulz, 21

the relative recency of weakening marriage among the poor. If poverty causes relational stress such that couples are incapable of holding their marriage together, why have we seen this phenomenon increasing in recent decades but essentially nonexistent before the 1960s? One might respond that, prior to the 1960s, women had less ability to enter the workforce and provide for themselves and were therefore more dependent on marriage. They *couldn't* leave the marriage, despite the stress of dealing with poverty, because it would leave them destitute. But this response ignores the strong correlation even today between out-of-wedlock births, single motherhood, and poverty. If the problem was simply that women had less access to jobs and that, if given such access, the correlation of single motherhood with poverty would decline, how does one explain the ever-rising levels of poverty for single mothers even as job opportunities for women simultaneously increase? The data shows that today, just like 50 years ago, low-income couples (especially parents) are better off together than separated, so the economic rationale for staying together has not changed.

Besides, we more often see low-income couples never marrying in the first place rather than marrying, struggling to make it work despite poverty, and ultimately separating.

Secondly, this theory treats all family structures as roughly equal in quality as far as the children are concerned; single-parent families are no worse than two-parent families, as long as they receive adequate income. But this ignores the non-economic roles that families play in the raising of children. Families are not *merely* economic support communities. They are also the "chief agency of socialization," writes social critic Christopher Lasch. As such,

> the family reproduces cultural patterns in the individual. It not only imparts ethical norms, providing the child with his first instruction in the prevailing social rules, it profoundly shapes his character, in ways of which he is not even aware. The family instills modes of thought and action that become habitual.

> Because of its enormous emotional influence, it colors
> all of a child's subsequent experience. . . . If the
> reproduction of culture were simply a matter of formal
> instruction and discipline, it could be left to the
> schools. But it also requires that culture be embedded
> in personality. Socialization makes the individual want
> to do what he has to do; the family is the agency to
> which society entrusts this complex and delicate
> task.[172]

In other words, the family is the primary force that shapes a child's character. It is the primary influencer of a child's social skills, work ethic, creativity, and ambitions. "Families are major producers of skills," writes economist James Heckman. "Skill begets skill; motivation begets motivation. Motivation cross-fosters skill, and skill cross-fosters motivation. If a child is not motivated to learn and engage early on in life, the more likely it is that when the child becomes an adult, he or she will fail in social and economic life."

> Thus, families do more than pass along their genes.
> Inequality in skills and schools is strongly linked to
> inequality in family environments. While the exact
> mechanisms through which families produce skills are
> actively being investigated, a lot is already known.
> Parenting matters. *The true measure of child poverty
> and advantage is the quality of parenting a child
> receives, not just the money available to the household.*
> [emphasis added][173]

Changes in family structure, then, "must have an enormous impact on the development of personality."[174] This is not to say that single mothers or fathers are necessarily bad parents, only that they are incapable of parenting as well as would be possible with a spouse.

Researchers at the Economic Mobility Project found from

---

[172] Ibid. 46
[173] Ibid. 48-49
[174] Ibid. 46

data stretching back to the late 1960s that "it is not true that parents 'income alone enables children to succeed." Rather, "the structure of the family in which a child grows up could have as large an impact as income, or larger, on subsequent economic outcomes."[175]

The issue of the eroding family—and all of the corresponding problems that go along with it—cannot be solved simply by transfers of money or benefits. If it could, we would expect to see a strengthening of the family during the decades from 1950 to 1980, when welfare programs and expenditures significantly increased. Instead, we find this: "In 1980, 48 percent of live births among blacks were to single women, compared with 17 percent in 1950. During the same period, white illegitimate births were increasing as well, from less than 2 percent in 1950 to 11 percent in 1980."[176] From 1968 to 1980, the number of intact marriages among black families dropped from 72 percent to 59 percent, while during the same period the figure for white families dropped only three percent.[177]

The difference in race is significant only because white families enjoyed significantly lower poverty rates than black families during this period. Looking specifically at poor black families in 1959, "Barely one in ten of the low-income blacks in families was living in a single-female family. By 1980, the 10 percent figure had become 44 percent."[178] Looking even further back to the turn of the century, "when blacks were just one generation out of slavery, the rate of marriage in the black population of the United States was slightly *higher* than that of the white population," writes economist and social theorist Thomas Sowell, using Census Bureau data. Sowell goes on to say:

---

[175] Ibid. 50
[176] Murray, *Losing Ground*, 126-127
[177] Ibid. 130
[178] Ibid. 132

> The catastrophic decline of the black nuclear family
> began, like so many other social catastrophes in the
> United States, during the decade of the 1960s. Prior to
> the 1960s, the difference in marriage rates between
> black and white males was never as great as 5
> percentage points.[179]

The same could be said for poor, white single-mother families, which went from 18 percent in 1959 to 31 percent in 1980. Meanwhile, in that time period, the percentage of all middle- and upper-income persons living in single-mother families inched up from 5 percent to 9 percent—a *drastically* slower rise than that of the poor.

Thus, it would be inaccurate to say that poverty *alone* (or even poverty in addition to expanded work opportunities for women) has caused the erosion of the family among those at the bottom of the income spectrum. What, then, *is* the cause (or causes) of such a drastic decline?

One possibility is the Sexual Revolution, which began sometime in the 1950s. This movement, likely spurred by the rise in new and effective birth control methods, increased the cultural acceptance and practice of non-traditional sexual relationships in certain demographics. Premarital and extramarital sex likely led to a rise in out-of-wedlock births and single motherhood, the theory says. Surely there is some truth to this. The trend lines of declining marriage began in the 1950s, which lends some credence to the theory. But it doesn't adequately explain the trends into the 70s and 80s. "If the trend line from 1950 to 1963 had remained unchanged," writes Murray, "the black illegitimacy rate would have increased another 6.8 percentage points by 1980. Instead, the slope of the trend line suddenly steepened. The increase was not 6.8 percentage points, but nearly four times that."[180] Besides, the

---

[179] Sowell, Thomas. *The Quest for Cosmic Justice* (Touchstone: New York, 1999), 16
[180] Murray, 126

most active participants in the Sexual Revolution were the educated, mostly in the middle and upper classes, not the lowest income individuals where we see the sharpest decline in marriage. And furthermore, the Sexual Revolution movement did not last further than the 70s, but the trends of declining marriage did.

Another theory put forth is that, during this period, the number of manufacturing and agricultural jobs declined, leading to less good employment for low-skilled males, which translated into fewer marriageable men. Of course, mothers would generally be better off with a man earning a low income than with no man at all, but women may be less enticed to marrying men with poor income prospects. There is likely some truth to this idea, but it falls far short of explaining the decline on its own. Around 40% of all births are now to unmarried mothers.[181] It would be quite a stretch to argue that 40% of American adult men are not marriageable! Besides, we know that most unmarried men are employed at the time that their child is born. Robert Rector puts the figure at 8 out of 10.[182]

The same could be said of the argument that men in today's world simply don't want to get married. It is a well-known trend that younger generations are delaying marriage, but that does not mean they do not want to get married at all. In a study on the personal value of marriage, 75% of the least educated reported marriage as either "very important" or as "one of the most important things" to them. Among the moderately educated, the number was 76%. Among the highest educated, 79%.[183]

What about changing cultural mores surrounding premarital sex? This element undoubtedly plays a role in the erosion of marriage, but arguably not a very large one. The main reason that this cultural shift is probably not a major

---

[181] https://www.cdc.gov/nchs/fastats/unmarried-childbearing.htm
[182] Rector, previously cited article on heritage.org
[183] Schulz, 25

factor is because it corresponds with the rise of effective birth control methods. The rise in premarital sex is likely offset by the growth in availability and use of contraception.

What about the decline in religiosity? Again, this factor likely plays a role in the decline of marriage and rise of single motherhood, but its explanatory power is limited. There are eight times as many babies born to unmarried mothers today than there were in 1960, but church attendance has not dropped nearly that much. According to sociologist Robert Putnam, writing in 2000, "the most reasonable summary is that attendance has slumped — modestly, but unmistakably — by roughly 10-12 percent over the last quarter century."[184] Church attendance has likely slid even more since 2000, but again, not nearly as much as the family has eroded in the lower echelons of society.

So, if none of these things — even working in concert — have the explanatory heft to demonstrate causation in the erosion of the family structure, then what caused it? Surely, there must be *some* primary motivating factor.

* * *

The Effect of Welfare on Low-Income Families

Probably the biggest reason for the decline of marriage and family in America over the last half-century is the rise of the welfare state. One of the most important changes in American society — at least for those in the lower class — was the initiation of the "War on Poverty" in the mid-60s. "In only three years, from 1964 to the end of 1967 . . . social policy went from the dream of ending the dole to the institution of permanent income transfers that embraced not only the recipients of the dole but large new segments of the American population."[185]

---

[184] Putnam, Robert. *Bowling Alone: The Collapse and Revival of American Community* (Simon & Schuster: New York, 2000), 70-71
[185] Murray, *Losing Ground*, 24-25

As a result, America saw a massive rise in government transfers to the needy: "Health and medical costs in 1980 were six times their 1950 cost. Public assistance costs in 1980 were thirteen times their 1950 cost. Education costs in 1980 were twenty-four times their 1950 cost. Social insurance costs in 1980 were twenty-seven times their 1950 cost. Housing costs in 1980 were 129 times their 1950 cost."[186] Disability expenditures through the Supplemental Security Income program shot up from 1960 to 1975. "During the same period that the number of [SSI] beneficiaries increased by 533 percent, the number of workers covered by the program increased by 30 percent."[187] The Food Stamp program began in 1965 with 424,000 enrollees. "By 1980, the number of participants had grown to 21.1 million."[188] That number reached as high as 47.6 million people in 2013 but has dipped somewhat in recent years.[189]

What did these new programs have to show for their burgeoning generosity? Very little, unfortunately. "In 1968, as Lyndon Johnson left office, 13 percent of Americans were poor, using the official definition. Over the next twelve years, our expenditures on social welfare quadrupled. And, in 1980, the percentage of poor Americans was—13 percent."[190] During this same period of time, the proportion of husband-wife families fell precipitously, especially in low-income families. Granted, low-income single-mother households increased from 1959 to 1964—the five years prior to the beginning of the War on Poverty—from 6% to 10%, but in the next five years, the pace more than doubled, putting the number at 19% in 1969. By 1980, a quarter of low-income households were headed by a single mother.[191]

How exactly did the dramatic welfare expansion affect

---

186 Ibid. 14
187 Ibid. 47
188 Ibid. 48
189 https://fns-prod.azureedge.net/sites/default/files/pd/SNAPsummary.pdf
190 Murray, *Losing Ground* 8
191 Ibid. 130

family structure? First of all, for middle- and upper-income families, it had no effect because they were not beneficiaries. This coincides with the data that shows the family structure eroding at a crawling pace among the mid-to-upper echelon families during the second half of the 20th century. If the reason for this decline were *merely* the combination of causes listed above — the Sexual Revolution, lack of marriageable men, birth control, changing cultural mores, changing attitudes about marriage, declining religiosity — then we would expect the pace of decline in the low-income family to mirror that of middle- and upper-income families. However, as we've already covered, it did not. The family eroded at a much faster pace among the poor.

The reason for this has to do with incentives. If the total welfare benefits package offered by the government is, let's say, $18,000, then very poor individuals and families are faced with a choice. Either they can continue to work the (probably unpleasant) minimum wage job, or seek one out if they don't have one already, *or* they can accept the government welfare benefits instead and not have to work the minimum wage job at all — or at least work fewer hours. For anyone with at least decent intermediate- to long-term job prospects, the choice is obvious: one must still take the minimum wage job in order to begin the climb up the career ladder. But for the very poor and minimally educated, the choice is not so obvious, especially for those with family members who are or have been enrolled in welfare programs, and *especially* those who are desperate for help because a new baby has entered the scene. It's crucial to remember that welfare benefits are given to the *household*, not the individual. So if a woman marries the father of her incoming baby, and if the father works, she is then eligible for far less in welfare benefits.

"The first effect of the new [welfare] rules was to make it profitable for the poor to behave in the short term in ways that were destructive in the long term," writes Charles Murray.[192] In other words, for millions of people, each in their own unique situations, the opportunity to collect government benefits became a more attractive option than trying to climb the ladder of careerism which would eventually lead to financial independence. It became more attractive than the less immediately tangible benefits of marriage, and it *certainly* became more attractive than the potentially shameful act of asking family or friends for financial support.

Welfare may not have compared favorably to where one might be in their working life or marriage in five or ten years, but it surely compared favorably to where many were in their lives at the time they enrolled. The same is true for many today. But for those who enroll in welfare programs, especially those who come from extreme poverty or unpleasant and low-paying jobs, it becomes increasingly difficult to go off of welfare because there is no immediate benefit to do so. And over time, one's marketable skills atrophy and one's resumé decays, making it more difficult to find a decent job, thus exacerbating the temptation to remain in the "poverty trap" of welfare dependency.

This is not an indictment against all people who accept government assistance. It is an observation about human nature: people tend to choose the most attractive option for them at the time. For those with little education, a poor work ethic, lack of good health, an unexpected baby on the way, or other bad circumstances, the allure of welfare benefits outshines whatever longterm benefits might (possibly) come from climbing up the career ladder, trusting in one person (a spouse) to provide, or relying on the temporary help of family or friends.

Many studies corroborate this line of reasoning. For instance, a study by two Oklahoma professors called "The Effect of Welfare on Work and Marriage: A View from the

---

192 Ibid. 9

States" concluded that "state-determined [welfare] programs discourage the involvement of the adult male in the family unit because they make the option of unmarried, unreported cohabitation (and possible unmarried, living apart) financially attractive relative to either marriage or unmarried, reported cohabitation. The size of the differentials can be quite large, with the former category achieving total family resources twice that of marriage."[193] In other words, there is a substantial financial incentive for the father of a baby whose mother collects government assistance to live with the mother *without* getting married. Remaining unmarried, if the father works full time and the mother works part time (just little enough to keep her full benefits), the couple can enjoy a much higher standard of living than they would if they were to marry.

This set of incentives has existed since the introduction of these welfare programs during the "Great Society" era of the 1960s. Hence why, for decades, among those couples who earn little enough to qualify for government assistance, marriage has been an unappealing option. This does not mean that the *values* of those who accept welfare benefits have changed. Recall the study cited earlier that even three-fourths of those with little education still consider marriage very important. But the costs of marriage, for couples in certain circumstances, is just too great. Another study, *Effects of Welfare Participation on Marriage*, finds that "welfare participation reduces the likelihood of transitioning to marriage. . . *but only while the mother is receiving benefits*. Once the mother leaves welfare, past receipt has little effect on marriage." The authors of the study infer, then, "that the negative association between welfare participation and subsequent marriage reflects temporary economic disincentives rather than an erosion of values."[194]

In short, in the words of Reverend Robert Sirico: "In many

193

http://citeseerx.ist.psu.edu/viewdoc/download?doi=10.1.1.515.7251&rep=rep1&type=pdf

[194] https://www.ncbi.nlm.nih.gov/pmc/articles/PMC3068203/

cases state assistance not only replaces the father's role as protector and provider but, going still further, creates perverse incentives for single mothers to *avoid* marriage—never mind that marriage provides substantial benefits to women and children, including some that the state is incapable of providing."[195]

Remember, also, that choosing cohabitation produces poorer results than marriage over time. For instance, the National Institute of Child Health and Human Development reports that "cohabiting relationships are less stable than marriages and that instability is increasing." It's no surprise, then, that in the US and the UK, cohabiting couples are at a greater risk for breakup than non-cohabiting couples. Likewise, couples who lived together before marriage are more likely to divorce early in their marriage. (Past seven years of marriage they are just as likely to divorce as non-cohabiting couples.) They are also five times more likely to separate than married couples, and if they do separate, their reconciliation rate is a third that of married couples who separate. They also experience more infidelity, depression, and substance abuse.[196] Sadly, this relational instability likely leads to a greater dependence on welfare over time.

* * *

Policy Implications

How do we help low-income people out of this cycle of welfare dependence and marriage avoidance? How do we change course and begin to rebuild the most basic social safety net—the family? How do we reinstate the family as society's "original and best Department of Health, Education, and

---

[195] Sirico, Robert. *Defending the Free Market: The Moral Case for a Free Economy* (Regnery. Washington DC, 2012), 119
[196] https://www.thespruce.com/cohabitation-facts-and-statistics-2302236

Welfare?"[197] If it is true that healthy marriages and families will produce a better outcome, then it is *vital* to deal with this issue.

The first and most obvious step must be to stop disincentivizing marriage among low income-earners—those who might view welfare as an option. The American welfare system discourages marriage by making it much more rewarding to refrain from marrying than to marry. Rather than marrying, couples will either cohabit or remain together in separate residences without marrying. Either way, the longterm stability of the relationship is substantially lower, making it more likely that the child will grow up without a father taking an active role in raising the child. *Or* that the child will have to switch back and forth between two households— the father's and the mother's—in a psychologically confusing situation of shared custody. This system of perverse incentives needs to end so that couples who desire to get married can do so without incurring a financial penalty from loss of welfare.

One potential step toward accomplishing this goal is suggested by the authors of *The Effects of Welfare on Work and Marriage*, and that is to allow mothers to keep receiving benefits for a time after they marry, then phase them out.[198] This may have some positive effect, but if mothers receiving benefits know that they will lose these benefits some period after getting married, there will be an extra weight added to the decision to marry which may act as a deterrent. And, of course, the mother will know that welfare is still an option if she gets divorced.

Another suggestion from Robert Rector of the Heritage Institute would be to "establish a broad campaign of public education in low-income areas" demonstrating "a clear factual understanding of the benefits of marriage and the costs and consequences of non-marital childbearing."[199] The point of such

---

[197] Quoting former Secretary of Education William Bennett, from Schulz, 73

[198]

http://citeseerx.ist.psu.edu/viewdoc/download?doi=10.1.1.515.7251&rep=rep1&type=pdf

[199] Previously cited heritage.org article

a campaign would not be to moralize low-income couples, but rather to inform them of some of the arguments, facts, and statistics covered above. Women of any level of income ought to be aware of the profoundly positive effects of a child having their father in the home longterm, as well as the increased likelihood that the father will *stay* longterm if the couple is married. However, as witnessed in the "stay-in-school" and anti-smoking public campaigns, progress is slow and hampered without other corresponding changes that disrupt the incentive structure.

Rector proposes a second suggestion: "increase the value of the earned income tax credit (EITC) for married couples with children."[200] An EITC is a cash benefit that a recipient can receive which corresponds to income earned from a job. It slowly phases in, then slowly phases out as the recipient makes a higher and higher income from their job. Rector argues that increasing this would offset the other welfare benefits lost if a mother chooses marriage over the panoply of various welfare programs (food stamps, housing assistance, day care, Medicaid, etc.) available through the route that does not include marriage. The problem with this idea is that, as long as that package of welfare benefits is available (if the mother doesn't marry), it will be more attractive than getting a job or working more hours. Considering the high costs of healthcare, the Medicaid benefit alone far outweighs any extra amount a couple could reasonably expect to add from additional EITC income.

Setting up mandatory job training or work requirements for the able-bodied might reduce the appeal of welfare as an alternative to marriage, but this idea has problems as well. For one, a mother would have to work full-time to even come close to making as much as she receives in welfare benefits, which few mothers will want to do when they have a baby. And for another thing, these requirements put a government

---

[200] Ibid.

bureaucracy in charge of evaluating the lives of strangers and determining who is capable of work and who is not—an incredibly difficult task. What about those with a criminal record? What about those with undiagnosed health issues or mental disorders? What about those who lack transportation or adequate education to qualify for available jobs? It's usually possible to find a job if someone is willing to work, but not always.

What about allowing welfare candidates to qualify for all means-tested benefits on a per-individual basis rather than a per-family or per-household basis? While this might improve the prospects for marriage among low-income couples, it would also likely increase longterm welfare dependency as it would effectively double the benefits a couple could receive without having to either endure the low-paying (and potentially unpleasant) first-rung-of-the-ladder job or taking on more hours or greater responsibility at work. Why work more or go up to that next rung of the career ladder if it actually means *losing* benefits that did not require work?

Another potential solution would be to deal with the *effects* of family erosion rather than the problem itself by instituting universal day care. This would be free and encouraged for low-income mothers, giving the mother a chance to work while attempting to reverse many of the long-lasting negative effects of fatherlessness in young children. Studies of this kind of early childhood intervention have shown *some* positive effects, such as slightly more schooling and lower teen pregnancy rates. The problem is that these children experience "fadeout"—that is, the benefits of day care gradually fade over time. "Once any intensive intervention is lifted," writes Nick Schulz, "kids will spend an enormous amount of time influenced by peers, relatives, and neighbors, the effect of which may be to undo or overwhelm the benefits of the early intervention."[201] The ideal is not for a stranger to care for a child for half of the day from

---

[201] Schulz, 78

ages 1 to 5 but rather for the child to receive such care from one or both parents. The best way to do that would be through an intact, father-and-mother family.

It should be clear by now that any potential tweaks to our current system of (predominantly federal) government assistance to the poor will probably not have the desired effects of regaining the ground that the low-income family has lost. If the primary reason for the erosion of the family among the poor is the set of incentives created by the package of available welfare benefits, then those welfare benefits ought to be eliminated. There should be no replacement for them at the federal level. If there was a better federal welfare alternative that accomplished the goal of poverty relief without the deleterious effects on workforce participation and marriage, it would have been tried or proposed already. Rather than attempting to alleviate poverty at the most distant possible level from the average family, the federal government ought to allow states, municipalities, and cities to handle the alleviation of poverty.

Cities and municipalities in particular ought to take the lead rather than the state. Recall the Jethro Principle, which may be thought of as the Principle of *Localism*. At the local level, taxpayers pay more attention to the effectiveness of poverty relief programs. Ineffective programs can much more easily be changed in one's city than simultaneously across the nation. But more importantly, local authorities are much more likely to be persuaded to delegate churches and private charities a significant role in attending to the needy. This would undoubtedly be a boon to the church, as it would be an opportunity to distribute the material and communal blessings of the Kingdom to fellow believers who are less fortunate. It would also give unbelievers a taste of the abundant life that Kingdom citizens enjoy, and perhaps intrigue them to the gospel.

And it would eliminate, at least in some places, the perverse incentives of the present welfare system to avoid marriage.

Some cities or states may end up with more or less the same welfare system that we have now, but many others would not. Researchers would study the varying systems and come up with conclusions about what works and what doesn't, where low-income couples are more likely to marry and where they're less likely to marry, where children from low-income families are better off and where they're not. Believers would have greater ability, at least in some localities, to practice distinctly Christian forms of compassion and charity.

In short, *specialized* and *holistic* methods of alleviating poverty and assisting others to lead more comfortable, happy, and healthy lives are always preferable to *formal* and *one-size-fits-all* methods. As stated before, human beings are more than mouths to feed and bodies to clothe and shelter. The less specialized and holistic the approach, generally speaking, the less beneficial is the assistance. As Timothy Terrell puts it,

> Formulas and bureaucratic procedures become more necessary the further the source of the assistance is from the recipient. The more localized the administration of the charitable assistance, the less need there is for these cumbersome complications. On-the-spot care, such as that provided through the family and the local church, has the benefit of being able to discern the nuances of particular situations and make much more informed judgment calls. Some of the most important information needed in administering charity cannot be compressed onto a form sent to a central office.[202]

If there are problems that local authorities along with the church and charities cannot adequately address, Christians should encourage state governments to act as a backstop—but *only* as a backstop, a safety net under the primary safety net. Churches or denominations may still play some part in state-

---

[202] Terrell, Timothy. "The Church and Charity Pt. 2"
https://chalcedon.edu/resources/articles/the-church-and-charity-part-2

provided poverty relief, but the urgency of their participation is greater at the local level.

The church ought to be positioned as close as possible to the front lines of poverty alleviation, because that is part of our calling. When we have the opportunity to disperse the material blessings of the Kingdom, the spiritual blessings will follow. Just as one of the healed lepers returned to Jesus in order to worship him, so also would some of those who are materially helped by the contemporary body of Christ (the church) then repent and turn to God.

But, crucially, taxpayer funds should *not* go directly to churches or denominations because that would violate the Kingdom Principle of Voluntarism: Service and charity in the Kingdom of God must always be heartfelt and voluntary. Christians are called to be generous and compassionate, but neither of those are possible if forced. They must come from a willing heart.

* * *

Conclusion

The family has eroded at the lowest end of the income spectrum not primarily because low-income people are less moral than the rest of the population. Nor is it because they have drastically different values about marriage or family. Rather, it is because the incentives surrounding marriage and family formation are different for them than they are for the rest of the American population. Welfare changes the game. Therefore, it is the way we do welfare in America that needs to fundamentally change.

Local communities should take charge of the problems of poverty in their neighborhoods and cities rather than outsourcing responsibility to the federal government. Those *in* the community have the most knowledge about the specific issues involved with or causing the impoverishment. And when the responsibility to do something about it falls on the local community or fellow citizens of the city, Christians have an expanded capacity to provide Kingdom-oriented solutions. Some individuals will not be able to transition out of neediness through a job or marriage, even with the best of counseling and coaching, but others will. In both cases, a holistic and community-based response to poverty will have a significantly more positive outcome than what detached and disinterested government programs could provide.

And, importantly, these kinds of solutions are much more likely to avoid the disincentives to marriage that are so pervasive in the current system. With these disincentives gone, the damage done to the low-income family can — God willing — begin to heal.

* * *

"In the first centuries of Christianity, the hungry were fed at a personal sacrifice, the naked were clothed at a personal sacrifice, the homeless were sheltered at a personal sacrifice. And because the poor were fed, clothed and sheltered at a personal sacrifice, the pagans used to say about the Christians, 'See how they love each other.' In our own day, the poor are no longer fed, clothed and sheltered at a personal sacrifice but at the expense of the taxpayers. And because the poor are no longer fed, clothed and sheltered at a personal sacrifice, the pagans say about the Christians, 'See how they pass the buck.'"

Peter Maurin[203]

---

[203] Holben, Lawrence. *All the Way to Heaven* (Wipf & Stock: Eugene, 1997), 58

CHAPTER NINE

Community and Poverty

Everyone agrees that community involves friendship and fellowship. But the message of the New Testament that is so striking to individualistic, 21st century Americans is that community *also* involves provision for each other's material needs. The strongest social bonds are those that are formed in communities that share resources with each other wherever there is need.

In fact, though the word "fellowship" in modern Christian parlance is basically synonymous with socializing with fellow believers, it bore a more tangible and material connotation in the New Testament era. As D.A. Carson explains, "fellowship" was a term often used to denote commercial or business relationships, such as going in together to purchase a fishing boat or a piece of land. It referred to sharing resources in pursuit of a common goal. "The heart of true fellowship," Carson says, "is self-sacrificing conformity to a shared vision."[204] For Christians, that shared vision is the Kingdom of God.

Look at the post-Pentecost church in Jerusalem The believers practiced such open-handed, open-hearted generosity that they even sold property and possessions to provide for the needs of the poor (which were many). What was the result? Their community grew larger and stronger: "And day by day, attending the temple together and breaking bread

---

[204] Carson, D.A. *Basics for Believers*, 16-17

in their homes, they received their food with glad and generous hearts, praising God and having favor with all the people. And the Lord added to their number day by day those who were being saved" (Acts 2:46-47). Their gatherings in the Temple likely involved evangelism, but notice that the implied catalyst for the church's increasing numbers was not evangelism but the familial intimacy and generosity they regularly displayed!

Family may be the primary and most natural and practical social safety net, but hovering just beyond that is the family of faith. In either case, *community* is one of the blessings of the Kingdom of God. And God has designed His Kingdom such that when we participate in and belong to the community of faith, our material needs are met as well. In God's people, there are no rugged individualists. There are only brothers and sisters. Mutual dependence is a matter of both social well-being *and* financial prudence.

And just as help ought to come from immediate family before extended family, so also in the church should material provision come from the local community—one's own congregation, preferably, but also other nearby congregations or believers—before it comes from believers outside the local area. Paul's encouragement of the Corinthians to give generously to the desperately poor believers in Jerusalem is a good example of this (2 Cor. 8:1-5). Corinth is located some 1,800 miles away from Jerusalem if traveling by land. The Corinthian believers would likely never meet the Hebrew believers who would benefit from their charitable funds, and yet the same Paul who instructed families to care for the needy before the church exhorted the Corinthians to help their distant brothers. He reasoned that "as a matter of fairness your abundance at the present time should supply their need, so that their abundance may supply your need, that there may be fairness" (2 Cor. 8:13-14).

What Paul describes here is strikingly similar to the concept of "mutual aid"—a voluntary and reciprocal exchange of resources or other forms of support within a communal setting.

I do something for you today, trusting that you will someday return the favor. Or, alternatively, I contribute to an organization that renders assistance to you, with the understanding that the community will render me assistance when the day comes that I need it.

Delegation of specific duties or specialization of labor is not wrong so long as the community remains intact. In the early church, for instance, the twelve disciples appointed seven members of the community to oversee the "daily distribution" to the needy in order to free up more time to practice their own specialty of preaching the gospel (Acts 6:1-6). Efficiency is a good thing as long as the integrity and equity of the community is upheld.

Thus, we might add a clause to Paul's Principle of Fairness: Those who have the ability to provide for the material needs of others have the responsibility to do so, *trusting that their own present or future needs will likewise be met.* Though giving is not meant to be self-interested in the sense of expecting something in return, it is also not completely one-way. Since the church community provides for *whoever* has need, "the needy" as well as the nature of the need will surely change day by day. The church family cares for them regardless. This is a recipe for strong, healthy communities that display Christlike self-sacrifice and manifest the first fruits of the Kingdom. When the church practices mutual aid, its members experience much more of the abundance and wholeness of life that Jesus desires for us.

But mutual aid is not a practice that works exclusively within God's people. Non believers can and *have* experienced it as well. Although they lack the enormous benefit of the Holy Spirit's indwelling guidance and conviction, they are still divine image-bearers and have the moral law "written on their hearts" and embedded in their consciences (Rom. 2:14-15). In the agrarian society of the Old Testament, God's people were commanded to treat "sojourners" — those ethnically and religiously outside of God's covenantal people — with fairness and generosity (Deut. 24:14-15, 19-21). Likewise, God's people in the New Testament are to "always seek to do good to one another *and to everyone*" (1 Thess. 5:15). But the reverse is sometimes true; sometimes, as in the case of the Good Samaritan, it is the person *outside* the family of God that shows more propensity to compassion and mutualism than the one inside.

Indeed, then, mutual aid is a *human* concept, a *human* way of life. Submission to Christ is certainly helpful in practicing compassion, generosity, and mutualism, but the instinct toward it is innate in us. Sin is a corrupting force but not a totally destructive one. Besides, the instinct toward mutual aid may not arise out of a feeling of compassion at all; it could be motivated by self-interest. But in any case, the result is good: strong communities are formed, people work harder in order to provide for each other, and everyone's needs are addressed.

* * *

Mutual Aid

History teems with examples of mutual aid, both organized and informal.

Peter Kropotkin, a Russian aristocrat and philosopher of the late nineteenth and early twentieth centuries, detailed numerous examples of this. He argues that, far from the coldhearted, survival-of-the-fittest ideology of the social darwinists, humanity progressed and learned to thrive in groups not through a spirit of *competition* but of *cooperation*. Human civilization evolved *in spite of* the regular bouts of strife and war strewn throughout history, not *because of* them. Mutual aid, says Kropotkin, is the secret ingredient of the strongest communities and societies.

The elements of mutual aid — voluntary membership and participation, reciprocity, a sense of kinship, and a commitment to community virtues — can be observed in the most primitive human societies—the Inuits, Eskimos, and native populations on every continent. Truly, among these populations, it "takes a village" to raise a child, but also to care for the sick, provide for the weak or disabled, and inculcate a virtuous character and strong work ethic in the young. Far from the idea that, among native populations, only the strongest and fittest survive, most natives find it natural to care for fellow members of their tribe. Ethnologist Kenneth Little found in studying those in West Africa who had left the tribal village setting for more urban areas that a natural kinship formed between those from a similar background, and mutual aid ensued. "Such associations, comprising individuals brought up in a homogenous culture with a common interest in their place of origin, hold out considerable opportunities of friendship, sympathy, and solace, and help the migrant in various practical ways."[205]

Kropotkin argues that, in periods of history in which centralized governments are strongest, mutual aid is weakest. As the Roman Empire became larger and more centralized, more and more of its population became reliant on Rome rather than their village neighbors for assistance. Likewise, in the feudal era, as villages and towns were subdued under the banner of lords and kings, mutual aid faded. But in the latter stage of the Middle Ages, as parts of Europe gradually decentralized and governance became less formal (think of Northern Italy during the Medici era), mutual aid returned in the form of Medieval guilds. These weren't guilds merely of knights but also of common people with a common bond. Kropotkin writes that "we know of guilds among all possible professions: guilds of serfs, guilds of freemen, and guilds of both serfs and freemen; guilds called into life for the special purpose of hunting, fishing, or a trading expedition, and

---

[205] "Some Traditionally Based Forms of Mutual Aid in West African Urbanization." https://www.jstor.org/stable/3772873?seq=1" " *page_scan_tab_contents

dissolved when the special purpose had been achieved; and guilds lasting for centuries in a given craft or trade."[206]

Though they often organized around the trade or social class of their members, the services guild members provided each other were holistic, not merely social or professional. "If a brother's house is burned, or he has lost his ship, or has suffered on a pilgrim's voyage, all the brethren must come to his aid. If a brother falls dangerously ill, two brethren must keep watch by his bed till he is out of danger, and if he dies, the brethren must bury him. . . . After his death they must provide for his children, if necessary; very often the widow becomes the sister to the guild."[207] In short, these Medieval guilds looked and acted much like church congregations ought to look and act. They were not socialistic in the sense of literal common ownership of all property and possessions, but they cared and provided for each other as if members of one family. Sacrifice comes naturally when one regards fellow members of one's community as "brothers" and "sisters."

Kropotkin feels there is some innate sense of kinship shared among all humanity. As he put it, "Unless men are maddened in the battlefield, they cannot stand it to hear appeals for help, and not to respond to them. . . . The sophisms of the brain cannot resist the mutual-aid feeling, because this feeling has been nurtured by thousands of years of human social life and hundreds of thousands of years of pre-human life in societies."[208] Perhaps Kropotkin overstates the inherent goodness of the human heart, but to some degree he is right that the Good Samaritan instinct is present in all of us. Though we are prone to evil, we also have a conscience which convicts us toward the good. That conscience, however, can be trained or educated toward numbness and indifference to the plight of others, as in the case of the religious officials who perhaps felt

---

[206] Kropotkin, Peter. *Mutual Aid: A Factor in Evolution* (Ed. by Will Jonson, unknown edition), 111
[207] Ibid. 110
[208] Ibid. 175-176

compassion for the man on the road but passed by him anyway wishing to avoid uncleanness.

The Reformation in Europe ushered in bitter divisions between people, which led to associating almost exclusively with one's specific religious sect and subsequently (because most religious sects allied with European monarchs) with one's nation-state. For hundreds of years, one's religious and national loyalty defined and divided European Christians. But in the eighteenth and nineteenth centuries, as industrialism began a long process of intermixing various groups, a revival of mutual aid organizations swept across Europe and America. Associations committed to the principles of mutual aid, whether they used the term "mutual aid" or not, began to appear everywhere, in all corners of society. In Europe, they were called "Friendly Societies." In America, "Fraternal Societies" or simply "associations."

French diplomat and politician Alexis de Tocqueville marveled at these "associations" when he visited America in 1831.

> Americans of all ages, all conditions, and all dispositions, constantly form associations. They have not only commercial and manufacturing companies, in which all take part, but associations of a thousand other kinds,—religious, moral, serious, futile, general or restricted, enormous or diminutive. The Americans make associations to give entertainments, to found seminaries, to build inns, to construct churches, to diffuse books, to send missionaries to the antipodes; they found in this manner hospitals, prisons, or schools.[209]

Tocqueville observed that while European nations were already on a path toward centralization, the United States remained thoroughly decentralized. "Wherever, at the head of

---

[209] de Tocqueville, Alexis. *Democracy in America* (Penguin: New York, 1956), 198

some new undertaking, you see the government in France, or a man of rank in England, in the United States you will be sure to find an association."[210] Tocqueville considered this American way of social organization in the form of voluntary associations morally superior to the more centralized European approaches because of practicality. If you can't rely on the government to accomplish your goal, and if you lack the resources to accomplish it on your own, then you have to organize with your fellow citizens voluntarily. "Feelings and opinions are recruited, the heart is enlarged, and the human mind is developed," says Tocqueville, "only by the reciprocal influences of men upon each other. . . and this can only be accomplished by associations."[211]

Charles Murray cites one such example of voluntary associations coming together to solve an acute problem: "when Iowa mounted a food conservation program in World War I, it engaged the participation of 9,630 chapters of thirty-one different secular fraternal associations. It is a number worth pausing over: 9,630, in one lightly populated state."[212]

But Tocqueville wasn't the only European to admire the American tendency toward associational life. The German Max Weber, visiting in the early twentieth century, was also struck by it: "It has been a characteristic precisely of the specifically American democracy that it did *not* constitute a formless sand heap of individuals, but rather a buzzing complex of strictly exclusive, yet voluntary associations."[213]

These associations would include many that are well-known and some that are still around today, such as the Freemasons and the Benevolent and Protective Order of Elks, but also many countless others. Like guilds of the Middle Ages, mutual aid societies formed mostly among those in the lower

---

[210] Ibid.

[211] Ibid. 200

[212] Murray, Charles. *American Exceptionalism: An Experiment in History* (AEI Press: Washington DC, 2013), 29-30

[213] Ibid. 29

half of the income spectrum, both as social and financial networks as well as for various forms of insurance—life, disability, unemployment, medical, care for widows and orphans, and others. But, importantly, mutual aid was *not* charity, because all of the money within the organization came from its members. "The fraternal concept of reciprocity entailed mutual obligations between members and the organization to which they belonged," writes historian David Beito. "It was wholly antagonistic to the idea that the donor should dole out one-way entitlements."[214]

The manual of one such organization, an exclusively black association called the Knights of Pythias, declared that the "sick among our brethren are not left to the cold hand of public charity; they are visited, and their wants provided for out of the funds they themselves have contributed to raise, and which, in time of need, they honorably claim, without the humiliation of suing parochial or individual relief—from which the freeborn mind recoils with disdain."[215]

These mutual aid associations sought to preserve and magnify their members' dignity as human beings, and as such, they eschewed paternal or hierarchical ways of thinking about giving or receiving aid. On the one hand, they used rituals and ranks to instill good character and a strong work ethic in their members, and they "rigorously enforced rules against false claims."[216] This helped to keep their benefit expenditures down. But on the other hand, it allowed members in good standing to "honorably claim" their benefits when legitimate needs arose. Bina West, a leader in the Woman's Benefit Association, said in a speech to the National Fraternal Congress in 1901 that fraternity is "absolutely distinct from charity or philanthropy. It is liberalizing, self-sustaining, elevating, gives mutual rights and preserves independence of character," while charity

---

[214] Beito, David. *From Mutual Aid to the Welfare State: Fraternal Societies and Social Services, 1890-1967* (University of North Carolina: Chapel Hill, 2000), 57
[216] Ibid. 57-58
[216] Ibid. 56

"signifies condescension, a position of superiority on the part of the organization, and of dependency on the part of the recipient."[217]

Though they acknowledged that charity is sometimes necessary, members of fraternal organizations found their own way of fighting poverty superior — and for good reason. Rather than the relatively modest and temporary benefits that charities could provide, mutual aid societies focused on community, personal development, and holistic approaches to uplifting their fellow members. Compassion, reciprocity, and demonstrating a worthiness of others' help through commitment to the group were among mutual aid societies' highest virtues. A booklet of Masonic poems assembled by J.M. Hickman, dating to 1934, records a poem called "A Brother's Part":

> Help me to conquer self, dear Lord,
> And be to my fellow-man —
> More fully that which will accord,
> A golden rule of plan.
> To feel within my very soul,
> The anguish of his heart,
> When worldly troubles o'er him roll,
> And do a brother's part.[218]

Another poem expresses in a mere six lines the heart of the fraternal value of reciprocity:

> We feel, indeed,
> Should there be need,
> You would not fail the other,
> But onward go
> Through rain and snow,
> To aid a worthy brother.

This mutual care for one another and bearing of each

---

[217] Ibid. 58

[218] From a booklet owned by my great-grandfather, who was a Freemason. No publication information given except the year: 1934.

other's burdens did not extend only to fellow "brothers" but also to their families.

> There's a brother's widow striving,
> And she's somewhat behind;
> She has not asked for charity,
> But a Mason's never blind;
> Her crop is very grassy,
> And he has a day to spare;
> He's over in that widow's field,
> Relieving her despair.

Nowadays, the Freemasons are characterized primarily by their rituals and secretism, but in those days, they were known, like a great many other associations, for the mutual aid practiced among their members. Many rituals existed back then as well, but those were just its "exterior form," as Hickman put it in an introductory chapter to his book of poems. The many handshakes, signs, and phrases they used, along with their many communal rituals and special articles of clothing, acted as "a system of morals veiled in allegory." As Beito put it,

> By joining a lodge [local chapter of a mutual aid society], an initiate adopted, at least implicitly, a set of values. Societies dedicated themselves to the advancement of mutualism, self-reliance, business training, thrift, leadership skills, self-government, self-control, and good moral character. These values reflected a fraternal consensus that cut across such seemingly intractable divisions as race, gender, and income.[219]

As the associations' memberships and capabilities expanded, so did their services. Some opened free or low-cost schools for children of their members. Some, such as the Security Benefit Association, operated orphanages for children of deceased or incapacitated members. Some had homes for the

---

[219] Beito, 27

elderly. Some opened hospitals for their members (which also served non-members for a fee), while others kept doctors on retainer. Many had full-time doctors who worked exclusively for one organization, while other groups, mainly in less populated areas, would go in together to retain doctors. Not to mention the many instances of informal or one-time aid rendered for fellow members or non-members. And none of this even touches on the primary benefits of joining a fraternal association—sickness, old age, disability, childbirth, health, and life insurances.

All of this relied on the continuation of society virtues. Without its members embracing a strong work ethic, societies would not have the revenue to maintain their benefits to those who truly had need. Recall Paul's insistence that those who are able to work *ought* to work (1 Thess. 4:11, 2 Thess 3:10). And without heartfelt compassion for the most vulnerable, such as widows and orphans, societies would fracture into special interest groups, each lobbying to gain a larger share of the pie. The church operates the same way (Jam. 1:27). This melding of virtues and benefits is evident in the mission statement of the Security Benefit Association:

> Its prime object is to promote the brotherhood of man, teach fidelity to home and loved ones, loyalty to country and respect of law, to establish a system for the care of the widows and orphans, the aged and disabled, and enable every worthy member to protect himself from the ills of life and make substantial provision through co-operation with our members, for those who are nearest and dearest."[220]

Is this not a description of how the church itself ought to function?

One might think that the commitment to certain virtues would deter new initiates, but membership in these organizations was not rare. "A conservative estimate would be

---

[220] Ibid. 28

that one of three adult males was a member in 1920, including a large segment of the working class."[221] Beito cites a study which calculated that, in 1924, 48% of working class males belonged to at least one mutual aid association.[222] And in 1930, the President's Research Committee on Social Trends estimated fraternal membership as high as 35 million Americans.[223] This at a time when the entire population of the United States was only 123 million. Similar numbers could be found in Europe. "Membership in Great Britain surged from at least 600,000 in 1793 to as many as 4 million by 1874,"[224] and the number continued to grow to the end of the century. As Kropotkin put it around the turn of the century,

> All these associations, societies, brotherhoods, alliances, institutes, and so on, *which must now be counted by the ten thousand in Europe alone*, and each of which represents an immense amount of voluntary, unambitious, and unpaid or underpaid work—what are they but so many manifestations, under an infinite variety of aspects, of the same ever-living tendency of man towards mutual aid and support?[225]

As mentioned previously, these mutual aid societies were mostly populated by those in the lower half of the income spectrum, as those people were the ones most in need of mutual aid. "For every one who has any idea of the life of the labouring classes," wrote Kropotkin, "it is evident that without mutual aid being practiced among them on a large scale they never could pull through all their difficulties."[226] Two examples are the Knights of Pythias, "popular among middle-class working

---

[221] Ibid. 2
[222] Ibid. 222
[223] Ibid. 204
[224] Ibid. 6
[225] Kropotkin, 178
[226] Ibid. 181

men,"[227] and the Ancient Order of United Workmen, mostly made up of day laborers, mechanics, and firemen.[228] Society membership was especially high among African Americans, giving rise to groups such as the Free African Society in Philadelphia, the Free African Union Society in Rhode Island, and the Garrison Literary and Benevolent Association in New York. All of these provided material benefits to their members such as various forms of social insurance, medical care, education for children, and apprenticeship for young adults.

The Golden Age of these mutual aid groups, in America, began after the Civil War and lasted through the 1920s. Membership remained high even into the 1930s, despite the challenges of the Great Depression. In response to increased need, mutual aid societies ramped up their social service spending. "In 1935 societies allocated more in per capita dollars in combined spending for sickness, accident, disability, and old-age benefits than they had in 1930, although total spending declined" because members became increasingly unable to pay their dues.[229] One example: "In 1929 the Loyal Order of Moose spent $4.44 per member on sick and funeral benefits; by 1935 the expenditure had nearly doubled to a record-breaking $8.34 per member."[230] By 1940, however, social service spending was trending downward, especially old age benefits. Whereas over half of societies offered some old age benefits in 1935, only 35% offered them by 1940.[231] It became clear in the 1940s that mutual aid societies were on the decline, in terms of both benefits offered and total membership.

What caused this sudden reversal of a long, upward trend in membership, participation, and benefit payments in mutual aid associations that had begun in the 1860s? Beito views "the

---

[227] McBride, Harriett. "The Golden Age of Fraternalism: 1870-1910." (http://phoenixmasonry.org/Golden%20Age%20of%20Fraternalism.pdf)
[228] Schmidt, Alvin. *Fraternal Orders* (Westport: Greenwood Press, 1930), 82
[229] Beito, 224
[230] Ibid. 232
[231] Ibid. 226, Table 12.4

emerging welfare state" that surged to life in the New Deal as the primary culprit:

> There is reason to believe that a relationship existed between the emerging welfare state and the decline of fraternal services. Most notably, the first signs of benefit retrenchment appeared after 1935, the year the Social Security Act became law. Officials of the homes for the elderly and orphans of the SBA [Security Benefit Association] cited Social Security and other welfare programs as justifications not only for rejecting applicants but for closing down entirely. In 1939 Malcolm R. Giles, the supreme secretary and comptroller of the Loyal Order of Moose, urged the Supreme Council to consider restricting sick benefits to members under age sixty-five [the age at which one could begin collecting SS benefits].[232]

While some mutual aid leaders embraced Social Security and other welfare programs as "excuses to shed costly services," many others saw them as an affront to their mission and purpose. De Emmet Bradshaw, president of the Woodmen of the World, saw that, with ever-increasing state provision of welfare, what he called "Rugged individualism" would be "crowded out," and the people would "lose their ambition and become listless as they drop toward the valley of delusions called socialism." More succinctly and perhaps more poignantly, Bina West of the Woman's Benefit Society summed up her opposition to the New Deal by asking, "Is there any beautiful ritualism or human tenderness in a governmental bureau?"[233]

Indeed, as Beito puts it, "By assuming fraternal welfare burdens, governments had undermined much of the reason for the existence of societies and thus for people to join."[234] Nevertheless, societies changed and adapted to the new

---

[232] Ibid. 229
[233] Ibid. 229-230
[234] Ibid. 231

political climate, focusing instead on certain niches not yet touched by government programs, such as medical services and children's care. As a result, "by the middle of the 1940s, [membership] actually surpassed the levels of the 1920s."[235]

But over the course of the 20th century, governmental welfare continued to expand, and membership began falling steeply in the 1960s, never to recover. Aid to Families with Dependent Children, a government welfare program mainly for single mothers, along with the rise of the foster home system, rendered fraternal care for orphans largely obsolete. Likewise, federal laws in the 1940s making employer-provided health insurance fully tax exempt made fraternal-provided healthcare less attractive. Another amendment to the tax code exempted employer contributions to employee pension plans, which, again, made fraternal plans less necessary. And laws which restricted fraternal endowments and certain kinds of insurance forced some societies to convert to commercial companies, jettisoning their fraternal character.[236] "The fraternal has been legislated out of the plan," said one leader of a life insurance society.[237]

"Mutual aid was a creature of necessity," concludes Beito. "Once this necessity ended, so, too, did the primary reason for the existence of fraternalism."[238]

The fate of mutual aid societies is lamentable precisely because of the point made in the previous chapter that marriage and the family has eroded among the lowest-income segments of society due largely to the rise of welfare. In contrast to the anti-family effects of welfare dependence, societies "acted to reinforce, rather than supplant, the family as a social institution" and "also supplemented the extended kinship networks that supported the nuclear family."[239] Despite

---

[235] Ibid. 232
[236] Ibid. 206-214
[237] Ibid. 215
[238] Ibid. 234
[239] Ibid. 8

attempting to accomplish the same goal of providing a social safety net, mutual aid societies bolstered the strength of the family while welfare programs have effectively weakened it. The same could be said for community more broadly. In short, "Societies accomplished important goals that still elude politicians, specialists in public policy, social reformers, and philanthropists. They successfully created vast social and mutual aid networks among the poor that are now almost entirely absent in many atomistic inner cities."[240]

The "mutual" aspect of mutual aid gave every member a sense of equality, whether one was currently a net payer or net recipient of benefits. When those same benefits are almost exclusively provided by dispassionate state employees and funded by faceless taxpayers, the sense of equality and mutualism evaporates. "The old relationships of voluntary reciprocity and autonomy have slowly given way to paternalistic dependency. Instead of mutual aid, the dominant social welfare arrangements of Americans have increasingly become characterized by impersonal bureaucracies controlled by outsiders."[241] And with that loss of mutual aid, millions of people in the lower and middle classes lost the numerous social benefits of involvement in a strong community.

* * *

Downfall of Community

One of the most remarkable aspects of mutual aid societies was their knack for encouraging behaviors that would result in *trustworthiness*, which in turn fostered communities that were high in *social trust*. The term "social trust," while not used often in American vernacular, is an important concept.

"When each of us can relax her guard a little," writes Robert Putnam, "what economists term 'transaction costs' — the costs

---

[240] Ibid. 3
[241] Ibid. 234

of the everyday business of life, as well as the costs of commercial transactions — are reduced." Think about it. If your child can go over to a neighbor's house for a few hours after school, that saves money on an after school program. Or if the child can go over to grandma and grandpa's house before or after school, even better. If you are friends with your neighbor who knows how to change oil in cars and charges you only for the cost of the oil, that saves you money. If you befriend a coworker who lives nearby so that you can carpool to work, that saves money on gas. If you live with roommates, rent is much more manageable. If your small group at church volunteer their weekend to help you move, that saves you from hiring movers. The ways in which friendship and community can potentially make life easier and less expensive are myriad, but each of them requires some measure of *trust* — trust in your neighbors, trust in your family, trust in your friends, trust in your roommates. "This is no doubt why, as economists have recently discovered, trusting communities, other things being equal, have a measurable economic advantage."[242]

This is true even in countries where the population is very poor by modern standards. When a World Bank survey was conducted in Panama in 1998, for instance, three-fifths of all communities lacked sewer systems, more than half lacked any form of garbage collection, one-fourth did not have street lighting, and over a tenth did not have access to a nearby source of drinkable water.[243] But what they lacked in material comfort, they made up for in "social capital" — a term which denotes the resources and benefits available to someone through social connectedness and relationships. The World Bank found that

> the poor tend to participate more in community committees and associations than the non-poor,

---

[242] Putnam, 135

[243] World Bank, "Community Organization, Values, and Social Capital in Panama." http://documents.worldbank.org/curated/en/517911468083930982/pdf/multi-page.pdf, 7

whereas wealthier households tend to participate in cooperatives. The poor are 1.5 times more likely to join local committees and four times more likely to participate in local associations than the non-poor. In contrast, wealthier households were close to three times more likely to join cooperatives than the poor. These patterns seem to suggest that the poor see more benefits of participating in public good type community organizations, whereas the rich tend to enter into more production-oriented private good type unions such as cooperatives.[244]

Notice that the Panamanian poor are *four times* more likely to join a local association than the non-poor, demonstrating that poverty does not itself erode community, social capital, or social trust. Rather, where there is social trust, communities will form in order to ensure that its members' needs are provided for. In the World Happiness Report, Panama ranks disproportionately high in social support (roughly equivalent to social capital), even as it ranks poorly in terms of corruption and only modestly in GDP per capita.[245]

America once had many thriving pockets of social capital, especially among the working class. But, again, that has changed drastically over the last century. As Putnam reports, writing in the late 1990s,

> our evidence also suggests that across a very wide range of activities, the last several decades have witnessed a striking diminution of regular contacts with our friends and neighbors. We spend less time in conversation over meals, we exchange visits less often, we engage less often in leisure activities that encourage casual social interaction, we spend more time watching (admittedly, some of it in the presence of others) and

---

[244] Ibid. 22
[245] http://worldhappiness.report/ed/2018/

less time doing. We know our neighbors less well, and
we see old friends less often.[246]

In other words, social capital—the "networks and the
norms of reciprocity and trustworthiness that arise from
them"[247]— has waned in America. It has waned as much in
formal membership of communities or organization as it has in
informal networks. "During the last third of the twentieth
century formal membership in organizations in general has
edged downward by perhaps 10-20 percent. More important,
active involvement in clubs and other voluntary associations
has collapsed at an astonishing rate, more than halving most
indexes of participation within barely a few decades."[248] Note
that this period of change occurred in the "last third of the
twentieth century," implying that the initiation of change
happened sometime in the mid 1960s.

While it is unclear which comes first, social *capital* or social
trust, it is clear that they are linked. What happened to social
trust during this period that social capital was declining? "The
best evidence suggests that social trust rose from the mid-1940s
to the mid-1960s, peaking in 1964 just as many other measures
of social capital did. Middle-aged Americans in the 1960s were
probably living in a *more* trusting society than the one in which
they had grown up."[249] What happened thereafter? "In the mid-
1960s . . . this beneficent trend was reversed, initiating a longterm decline in social trust."[250]

Along with the decline in social capital and social trust
came a sharp rise in crime. Putnam's research shows that
"crime rates in America began to rise sharply in the middle
1960s, just about the time that other measures of social capital,
trust, and trustworthiness began to turn down."[251] And as

---

[246] Putnam, 115
[247] Ibid. 19
[248] Ibid. 63
[249] Ibid. 139-140
[250] Ibid. 140
[251] Ibid. 144

crime rates rose, so also did employment in industries which revolve around crime. In the late 1960s and early 70s, the number of police, guards, watchmen, lawyers, and judges exploded, rising steadily to the turn of the century.[252]

* * *

What Caused the Social Collapse?

Again, we must ask what caused this change of trends. What made America less community-oriented? What eroded our social capital? Putnam offers a few plausible culprits.

First, perhaps the most obvious—television and technology. As people have become enamored over the last seventy years with the myriad new entertainment options provided by TV, video games, the internet, and cell phones, communal and social engagement has become gradually less attractive. Surely there's much truth to this explanation. Technological entertainment tends not to be community-building. The more time spent enjoying technology, then, the less time there is for developing strong communities.

Another potential culprit is suburbanization, which results in longer commutes than previous eras. When one has to spend hours each day on the subway, in a bus, or stuck in traffic going to and from work, less time or energy is available to engage in community activities. For some, this is certainly true.

But these two culprits contain only a limited explanatory power when it comes to the dramatic drop in social capital. The reason for this, as mentioned in the previous chapter, concerns the difference between social/communal involvement in rich and poor. Putnam and Murray agree that the upper and middle classes of America have seen a far less pronounced drop in various measurements of social capital such as marriage rates, two-parent households, and male employment than the lower

---

[252] Ibid. 145

class.[253] Surely middle and upper class Americans have just as long of commutes (or longer) than the lower class. And surely they spend roughly equal time, on average, being entertained by various technological media as the less-well-off. It doesn't make sense, then, to posit these factors as the primary drivers of social collapse.

A third explanation offered by Putnam is that pressures of time and money have left less time for community engagement. As he puts it, "the emergence of two-career families over the last quarter of the twentieth century played a visible but quite modest role in the erosion of social capital and civic engagement." Since women in the household used to be the primary facilitators of community involvement, more women in the workforce and two-career households diminishes social capital. While there is some intuitive veracity to this claim, "the evidence also suggests that neither time pressures nor financial distress nor the movement of women into the paid labor force is *the* primary cause of civic disengagement over the last two decades."[254]

None of these explanations are fully satisfying, even taken together. What, then, can explain the breakdown of social capital, mainly among the less well-off?

Another explanation commonly given is that extreme levels of income or wealth inequality breed social distrust, which in turn erodes social capital. Proponents of this view point to Scandinavian countries, which have high rates of social capital as well as low income inequality, as evidence in support of the theory. But this idea has some problems. An example from American history demonstrates that the Scandinavian example is not transferrable to every nation and people group. Both Putnam and Beito show that, in spite of high income inequality, the period from 1890 to 1930 was the "Golden Age"

---

[253] Leo Dorin, "Erosion of Social Capital a Major Problem, Say Experts." https://www.insidesources.com/erosion-social-capital/
[254] Putnam, 202-203

of social capital and mutual aid in the United States. Tensions were certainly high between rich and poor, laborers and capitalists, but this did not result in a decline in the strength of communities. If anything, it *strengthened* social bonds because communities tend to form among members of the same socioeconomic class.

Rather than TV, longer commutes, women in the workforce, or income inequality, the factor that has most likely had the greatest negative effect on social capital is the rise of the welfare state. It may not have solely initiated the trend, but it almost definitely exacerbated it. Considering that the majority of the decline has occurred among the lower class—those who might view welfare as an option—the correlation is strong between the various measurements of falling social capital and rising welfare spending.

For instance, recall that the steepest portion of the decline in formal membership of organizations occurred in the last third of the twentieth century—a period beginning in 1966, right at the initiation of the War on Poverty. Likewise, the trend of *rising* social trust in the first half of the century *peaked in 1964*—the year that President Lyndon B. Johnson signed the Poverty Bill. After that came a long, steady decline in social trust, along with a rise in crime. Charles Murray explains that "in about 1964—the take-off year varies by type of crime—the crime rate started to climb steeply for both property and violent crime."[255] Thomas Sowell cites trends in other social pathologies such as infection with venereal diseases and teenage pregnancy which, after falling for most of the century, also reversed course in the 1960s.[256]

Homing in on the black population of this era, which was disproportionately poor, is insightful. The trend in violent crime among African Americans was not rising but *falling* prior

---

[255] Murray, *Losing Ground*, 114
[256] Sowell, Thomas. *Discrimination and Disparities* (Basic Books: New York, 2018)

to the mid-1960s. Murray considers "the experience of 1950-60, when homicide victimization dropped—22 percent for black males."

> It was a large reduction for a single decade. It was all the more remarkable when one considers that it coincided with a period of rapid black migration into urban centers—a 24 percent increase from just 1950 to 1960 in the proportion of blacks living in central cities, a much faster increase than in subsequent years.[257]

In the case of violent crime among the poorest Americans, then, the rise of the welfare state did not merely amplify an existing trend but appears to have initiated a reversal in the trend. Of course, proving *causation*, rather than mere *correlation*, is tremendously difficult. But considering the fact that African Americans were moving into urban areas where crime should have been higher and yet was the opposite, some new factor must have been at play to explain the sudden change. The new, aggressive federal push to address poverty through welfare programs in these years fits the data nicely as the explanatory factor.

As welfare benefits became an attractive option, the economic benefits of belonging to a community became less so. As the economic benefits of community waned, so did the strength of the social bonds. Recall the insight we garnered from the New Testament—which was once common wisdom but has become subdued in individualist America—that in strong communities, sharing resources should come naturally. When social bonds (and thus social trust) are solid, the needs of the community, whether they are as small as after-school childcare or as large as building a new barn or paying a large medical bill, are provided for. Welfare took away one of the strongest social adhesives keeping low-income families and communities together.

There are, of course, many more elements of community

---

[257] Murray, *Losing Ground*, 116-117

than just mutual aid or provision for each other's material needs. Enjoying a social safety net is not the only or even the primary motivation to be involved in a community. But the safety net *is* an important aspect of community that tightens social bonds and fortifies relationships. Sometimes, sharing life together *just means* sharing resources or doing favors that save each other money, and relationships become stronger as a result. If the government provides for such needs rather than one's community, the community erodes.

Thus, Marvin Olasky asks, after a book-length exploration of this topic, "When we hand out food and clothing indiscriminately, aren't we subsidizing disaffiliation?"[258] Indeed, when we don't follow Paul's instruction to give generously *but also* discriminately, we are apt to turn recipients not only into idlers and busybodies but also communal isolates. And as recipients gradually lose the inclination toward community (and thus mutual aid and self-help), they become more reliant on welfare. "It is easy to foresee that the time is drawing near," wrote Tocqueville in the 1830s, "when man will be less and less able to produce, of himself alone, the commonest necessaries of life. The task of the governing power will therefore perpetually increase, and its very efforts will extend it every day. *The more it stands in the place of associations, the more will individuals, losing the notion of combining together, require its assistance*: these are the causes and effects which unceasingly create each other."[259]

* * *

Crowding-Out Effect

Underlying our discussion in the previous few chapters has been the idea that government intervention in poverty relief

---

[258] Olasky, Marvin. *The Tragedy of American Compassion* (Regnery: Washington D.C., 1995), 225
[259] Tocqueville, 200

results in a reduction of private efforts and methods of poverty relief. This is called the *crowding-out effect*. The phrase envisions a limited space in which some new entity enters, joining other entities, and the entrance of the new entity makes the space too crowded for the original entities to remain. In the case of poverty relief, the thinking goes, the expansion of government welfare services and benefits "crowd out" non-governmental methods of alleviating poverty.

Crowd-out theory proponents argue that state-provided welfare is more attractive to recipients than non-state poverty relief alternatives for a variety of reasons. First, it is treated as an *entitlement* rather than *charity*. By way of being a citizen of the nation, one has the right to a certain standard of living, and if one does not or cannot achieve that standard on their own, the government provides it through welfare. Charity carries more stigma than an entitlement. In this way of thinking, charity is hierarchical while welfare is egalitarian. No one person or organization's generosity has provided the benefits; rather, they come from *society itself*. There is less shame in receiving benefits from society itself (especially if one considers it their right) than from an individual person or organization, who gave the help voluntarily.

Second, people generally prefer welfare to non-state methods of relief because there are fewer strings attached. Charitable and mutual aid organizations generally obligate their recipients or members to certain standards of behavior, like ceasing drug use or participating in job training, as a condition of receiving benefits. State-provided welfare is far less likely to make or enforce such demands of its recipients.

Third, state welfare is typically more discreet and formal, requiring fewer face-to-face interactions and discussions and more forms that can be filled out online or mailed in to a government office. Fewer awkward conversations about *why* the person needs help make the government's method of poverty relief more attractive.

Fourth, it is easier to game the system in order to receive

benefits even if one is not deserving of them. Consider disability benefits, for instance. Because the government does not want to exclude anyone in a unique situation that is genuinely disabled, the definition of a "disability" has steadily expanded over the decades (besides a brief period in the late 1970s and early 1980s). But this expanded definition has allowed an ever-growing number of the able-bodied to qualify and begin taking benefits, thus cheating the intent of disability insurance. As evidence of this welfare cheating, Avik Roy presents the strong correlation between the unemployment rate and applications for disability benefits — when unemployment rises, requests for disability benefits rise in tandem. Only 13 percent of this rise in applicants, according to researchers at the National Bureau of Economic Research, can be attributed to the rising age of the workforce.[260] Generosity of the benefits is most likely the main driver of the growth. As the OECD reports, "there is evidence that more generous disability policy is associated with higher numbers of beneficiaries while more comprehensive employment and rehabilitation programmes are associated with lower recipiency rates."[261]

In 1961, shortly after the program began, most disability conditions were the sort that could be objectively proven, such as cardiovascular conditions or neurological disorders. By 2011, however, musculoskeletal disorders (such as back pain) and mental conditions (such as anxiety), which are much more difficult to prove, made up over half (53%) of new awards.[262] This suggests that a substantial portion of disability applicants *are* capable of work when work is available. Rather than accepting a lower paying job or relying on family or one's

---

[260] Roy, Avik. "How Americans Game the $200-Billion-a-Year 'Disability Industrial Complex.'" https://www.forbes.com/sites/theapothecary/2013/04/08/how-americans-game-the-200-billion-a-year-disability-industrial-complex/* * *6634e6d74b6d

[261] http://www.oecd.org/employment/emp/43687710.pdf

[262] Winship, Scott. "How to Fix Disability Insurance." https://www.manhattan-institute.org/html/how-fix-disability-insurance-5402.html

community for support, welfare in the form of disability benefits is the more attractive option.

So there is some logic behind the idea that welfare is more attractive than private charity or mutual aid to prospective recipients and thus that the presence of welfare diminishes the demand for the other two. But is there data to back up this thesis? The answer is a qualified yes. (The real world is rarely as cut and clean as we'd like it to be.)

Charitable giving in total dollars has risen for centuries, but economist Russell Roberts provides evidence that the *nature* of charitable giving underwent a dramatic change in the 1930s, after the initiation of federal New Deal programs. Prior to the New Deal, the word "charity" almost exclusively connoted giving to help the poor. After the New Deal policies took effect, "charity" gradually came to bear the same meaning as the more generic "philanthropy," which suggests any benevolent use of funds such as patronizing the arts, the opera, libraries, university buildings, scholarships, etc. And, indeed, prior to the New Deal, the majority of charitable giving (excluding religious tithes) was directed at the poor. By 1955, about a third went to help the poor. By 1981, only a small fraction was earmarked for poverty relief.[263]

During the Great Depression specifically, private funds assigned to poor relief rose sevenfold from 1929 to 1932, the year Franklin Roosevelt was elected and the first year of the New Deal. In that year, public expenditures on poor relief more than doubled, then more than doubled again in 1933. Public funds for poverty alleviation rose nearly tenfold from 1931 to 1935. What happened to private funds directed to poor relief after 1932? In 1933, they halved. In 1934, they halved again. By 1935, private funding for poverty alleviation was only slightly higher than it had been in 1929.[264] The New York Association

---

[263] Roberts, Russell. "A Positive Model of Private Charity and Public Transfers." http://econweb.ucsd.edu/~jandreon/PhilanthropyAndFundraising/Volume%201/6%20Roberts%201984.pdf

[264] Ibid. 143

for Improving the Condition of the Poor (AICP), one of the largest private charitable organizations in New York City at that time, shows the same pattern in their data. Both donations generally and funds specifically earmarked for "material relief" more than doubled from 1928 to 1932, but the trend reversed thereafter. By 1936 (still during the Depression), donations totaled less than pre-Depression levels. Likewise, by 1937, spending earmarked for "material relief" had fallen back to pre-Depression levels.[265]

In the AICP's annual report for 1935, we find their explanation for this fall in spending on poverty relief: "The AICP has made major revisions of budgets downward. Many families formerly cared for by the AICP have been turned over completely to public relief departments. Nearly one-third of the present number of families under care are cooperative cases with public authorities, in which the cooperation consists in the AICP supplying social services not yet available in public departments."[266]

Others who have researched this era come to similar conclusions as Roberts. Jonathan Gruber and Daniel Hungerman found that total faith-based charitable spending fell by 30% in response to New Deal spending.[267] Richard Cloward and Irwin Epstein agree and offer an explanation for the drop: "Once publicly supported income maintenance programs came into existence, following the depression, private agencies began to refer economically deprived clients [to public agencies], thus conserving their resources for other services."[268] Those other services, such as health care and counseling, rarely involved direct material relief. Private

---

[265] Ibid. 144

[266] Ibid. 144-145

[267] Gruber, Jonathan and Hungerman, Daniel. "Faith-based charity and crowd-out during the great depression." https://economics.mit.edu/files/6424

[268] Cloward, Richard and Epstein, Irwin. "Private Social Welfare's Disengagement from the Poor—The Case of Family Adjustment Agencies." https://files.eric.ed.gov/fulltext/ED011895.pdf

charitable attention toward provision for the unemployed, the elderly, and widows and orphans largely disappeared and never returned.

The War on Poverty of the 1960s had a similar effect on charitable giving. Putnam documents trends in rising national generosity in the first half of the twentieth century. "As a share of income, personal philanthropy nearly doubled in the three decades between 1929 and 1960." Beginning in the 1960s, however, "philanthropy's share of Americans' income has fallen steadily for nearly four decades, entirely erasing the postwar gains."

> Total giving by living individuals as a fraction of national income fell from 2.26 percent in 1964 to 1.61 percent in 1998, a relative fall of 29 percent. In 1960 we gave away about $1 for every $2 we spent on recreation; in 1997 we gave away less than $.50 for every $2 we spent on recreation.[269]

Burton Abrams and Mark Schitz compare "the dramatic growth of government social-welfare transfers following World War II" with the stagnation of private transfers to conclude that "the puzzling failure of private charitable contributions per taxpayer to rise during recent decades is due, in part, to the growth in governmental social-welfare transfers."[270] Daniel Hungerman uses data from the 1996 welfare reform to show that government spending crowds out 20-38% of church charitable spending. Note that the number is not 20-38% of church charitable spending specifically on the poor. That's 20-38% of *total* charitable spending. "The results," writes Hungerman, "show that church activities substitute for

---

[269] Putnam, 123

[270] Abrams, Burton and Schits, Mark. "The 'Crowding-Out 'Effect of Governmental Transfers on Private Charitable Contributions."
https://www.jstor.org/stable/30023017?seq=1* * *page_scan_tab_contents

government activities."[271]

Anette Reil-Held of the University of Mannheim in Germany found that private financial support for the relatively small number of German seniors who receive it "negatively correlated with the public transfers they receive." She concludes that "the 'crowding-out' hypothesis cannot be rejected and it is possible that public transfers to older people by the German welfare state may displace private financial support which they would otherwise have received."[272]

What about healthcare spending on behalf of the poor? Prior to government involvement in healthcare, free and charitable clinics and hospitals (such as the Charity Hospital in New Orleans) were relatively common. Many of the largest medical networks even today were founded as religious non-profits. Think of the Catholic Health Initiative or the Baptist Health System. Samuel Hammond argues that, in the 1980s, "Medicaid and Medicare expansions interacted with the increasingly profit-oriented hospital sector, and many religious hospitals closed down or converted to secular ownership."[273] Nursing professor Barbra Mann-Wall explains that this period

---

[271] Hungerman, Daniel. "Are church and state substitutes? Evidence from the 1996 welfare reform."
https://www.researchgate.net/publication/222422024_Are_church_and_state_subs titutes_Evidence_from_the_1996_welfare_reform

[272] Reil-Held, Anette. "Crowding out or crowding in? Public and private transfers in Germany."
https://www.jstor.org/stable/20164343?Search=yes&resultItemClick=true&&searc hUri=%252Ftopic%252Fcrowding-out%252F%253FcurrentPath%253D%25252Ftopic%25252Fcrowding-out%25252F%2526amp%253DsearchType%253DfacetSearch%2526amp%253Bp age%253D2%2526amp%253Btopic%253Dcrowding-out%2526amp%253Bsd%253D%2526amp%253Brefreqid%253Dexcelsior%2525 3A1f3daa45d0d7925f1f4d30f686385d80%2526amp%253Bed%253D&seq=1* * *page_scan_tab_contents

[273] Hammond, Samuel. "Has Medicaid Made America Less Religious?"
http://abstractminutiae.com/post/834218925 30/has-medicaid-made-america-less-religious

witnessed the growth of for-profit hospital networks, resulting in increased vulnerability of smaller not-for-profit institutions. More than 600 community hospitals closed. It was at this time that both for-profit and not-for-profit institutions began forming larger hospital systems, which were significant changes in the voluntary hospital arena. . . . The balance of power in these institutions shifted from caregivers to the organized purchasers of care, with Medicare and Medicaid becoming a huge governmental influence in all types of hospitals.[274]

In other words, as a greater percentage of healthcare dollars came from the government (as well as large insurance companies), shrewd administrators saw an opportunity to benefit from this less discriminate spending. Healthcare providers became increasingly corporatized, seeking to claim as much of the government spending as possible. Religious and charitable providers who did not rely on government funds diminished as a result.

Of course, not all researchers agree with the crowding-out thesis. Nina Boberg-Fazlic and Paul Sharp, for instance, use data from the Poor Law system from historical England to argue for a crowding-*in* effect. Parishes controlled the amount of spending on poverty relief, and the researchers found a *positive* correlation between the amount spent by parishes and charitable spending. In other words, "areas with more public provision also enjoyed higher levels of charitable income."[275] While this is certainly not evidence for the crowding-out effect, it also isn't necessarily evidence *against* it. Since the Poor Laws were administered at the local level, it's difficult to say whether

---

[274] Mann-Wall, Barbra. "History of Hospitals." https://www.nursing.upenn.edu/nhhc/nurses-institutions-caring/history-of-hospitals/

[275] Boberg-Fazlic, Nina and Sharp, Paul. "Does Welfare Spending Crowd Out Charitable Activity? Evidence from Historical England Under the Poor Laws." https://onlinelibrary.wiley.com/doi/pdf/10.1111/ecoj.12251

parishes that spent more caused more charitable giving, or if there was simply greater need for poverty relief in those localities that even the above-average parish spending could not alleviate by itself.

Staffan Kumlin and Bo Rothstein observe the anomaly of Scandinavian countries, which have generous welfare states as well as high measures of social capital, to argue for a positive relationship between at least certain types of welfare and social capital. "Contacts with universal welfare-state institutions tend to increase social trust," they say, "whereas experience with needs-testing social programs undermine it."[276]

The logic here is that needs- (or means-)tested benefits seem more like simple transfers of wealth from one group of people to another, thus increasing social distrust between groups and classes. The haves distrust the have-nots, who are viewed as lazy and undeserving, and the have-nots distrust the haves, who are viewed as greedy and stingy. What's more, since one has to prove themselves needful of benefits, there is an opportunity and incentive to cheat the system (as in the "disability industry"), thus establishing an environment of distrust between those who dispense and those who receive benefits. All of this is avoided with universal programs, say Kumlin and Rothstein. To them, the Scandinavian countries prove that an increase in *universal* welfare benefits would actually increase social trust and social capital.

But there are reasons to doubt this argument as well. For one thing, the social cohesion that so strongly characterizes Scandinavian countries did not arise at the same time as their welfare institutions, which date to the mid-twentieth century. It has been around far longer than that. "High levels of trust, a strong work ethic, civic participation, social cohesion, individual responsibility, and family values are long-standing

---

[276] Kumlin, Staffan and Rothstein, Bo. "Making and Breaking Social Capital: The Impact of Welfare-State Institutions." https://www.medicine.gu.se/digitalAssets/1453/1453389_kumlin_rothstein.pdf

features of Nordic society that predate the welfare state," writes Nima Sanandaji of the European Centre for Entrepreneurship and Policy Reform.[277] Sanandaji's assertion is backed by research showing that Nordic immigrants to America and their children exhibit the same level of social trust as their fellow Nordics who stayed in Scandinavia.[278] Correspondingly, two economists from Sweden and Denmark approached the correlation between inequality and social trust head on and concluded that neither relative income equality nor larger welfare states have a positive effect on social trust.[279] So it's probably not true to say that Scandinavian countries have high social capital *because of* their mostly universal welfare programs but rather *in spite of* them.

Research by Larysa Tamilina of the University of Bremen might lend credence to Kumlin and Rothstein's argument. She found no evidence of crowding-out when it came to pensioners and the unemployed, but she *did* detect crowding out when it came to public spending on means-tested benefits.[280] Of course, this could be explained by the increase of social distrust surrounding means-tested benefits. Outside of government, there is less ability and incentive to cheat the system and take advantage of others' material aid, thus the presence of government programs tends to draw prospective recipients away from, and decrease demand for, private charity. Unemployment income and pension benefits, on the other hand, came more often from mutual aid than from charity prior

---

[277] Sanandaji, Nima. *Debunking Utopia: Exposing the Myth of Nordic Socialism.* (WND Books: Washington D.C., 2016), 27

[278] Uslaner, Eric. "Where You Stand Depends Where Your Grandparents Sat: The Inheritability of Generalized Trust." https://academic.oup.com/poq/article-abstract/72/4/725/1872415

[279] Bergh, Andreas and Bjornskov, Christian. "Trust, Welfare States and Income Equality: What Causes What?" https://pdfs.semanticscholar.org/7b1b/ee824a559223c4c60f364ec0b0c2aa78c013.pdf

[280] Tamilina, Larysa. "Welfare States and Social Trust: 'Crowding-Out 'Dilemma" https://link.springer.com/chapter/10.1007/978-3-540-92803-4_7

to welfare states. After all, unemployment insurance is something every employed person would benefit from, and an old age pension is something almost everyone will need. There is no need for a person to *prove* their need for either. This point would be easy to miss if one designed a study to compare contemporary government and private charitable spending, as Tamilina's study does.

Besides, not all of Sweden's social welfare programs are universal. Some, such as their disability insurance, housing assistance, and general anti-poverty assistance, are means-tested. And these are not small programs, either. OECD data reports that over 10% of Sweden's working age population are officially disabled and receiving benefits, which are quite generous.[281] The Swedes spend 4.3% of their GDP on disability benefits, whereas the OECD average is 2.1%. Similar rates of disability spending can be found in the other Scandinavian countries: Denmark (4.7%), Finland (3.8%), and Norway (3.7%).[282] Considering the necessary lack of universality of these programs, Kumlin and Rothstein's argument that universal welfare enhances social capital while means-tested programs have a detrimental effect becomes even more suspect.

Another reason stands out as to why Sweden in particular ranks so highly in social capital: its welfare system is largely decentralized. Many key social programs, including the financing and delivery of healthcare, are under the authority of the country's twenty-one County Councils. Welfare, disability, and elderly support are administered by municipalities. The top leaders of these local and municipal welfare agencies are elected every four years, and they make decisions that sometimes affect only a few towns. Aid to the needy comes from close to home, and the authorities in charge are far more

---

[281] http://www.oecd.org/employment/emp/43687710.pdf
[282] https://data.oecd.org/socialexp/public-spending-on-incapacity.htm* * *indicator-chart

reachable than America's distant bureaucrats. With this in mind, it would be reasonable to surmise that Swedish social capital has been sustained not because of the universality of its welfare programs nor because of any reason relating to government, but rather because they practice the wisdom of the Jethro Principle — the Principle of Localism. Decisions are made and problems solved at the most local level possible.

Sometimes the oldest wisdom is the best.

* * *

The Stakes Are High

What is at stake here for Christians? Why does it matter so much where the money comes from or who administers the aid, so long as the poor are being fed, clothed, and sheltered? An example from early church history illustrates the importance of the *church* providing relief to the needy rather than the government. It comes from the 360s AD, when the last non-Christian emperor of Rome — Julian — ruled the empire.

When Rome was predominantly pagan, the temples and pagan priests bore the primary burden of providing for the poor. But after Christianity swept across the empire, that societal role was "placed under new management" — that of the church. Emperor Julian did not like this development, seeing that it had led to much of the church's success. "It is generosity toward non-members, care for the graves of the dead, and pretended holiness of life that have specially fostered the growth of atheism" (i.e. Christianity; in that era, anyone who rejected the pagan panoply of gods was called an "atheist").[283] "For when it came about that the poor were neglected and overlooked by the [pagan] priests," wrote Emperor Julian, "then I think impious Galileans [another term for Christians]

---

[283] MacMullen, 54

observed this fact and devoted themselves to philanthropy."[284]

What solution did the emperor think of to change this situation? In short, he wanted to crowd the church out through state-provided poor relief efforts:

> In every city establish frequent hostels in order that strangers may profit by our benevolence; I do not mean for our own people only, but for others also who are in need of money. . . . for I have given directions that 30,000 modii of corn shall be assigned every year for the whole of Galatia, and 60,000 sextarii of wine. I order that one-fifth of this be used for the poor who serve the priests, and the remainder be distributed by us to strangers and beggars. *For it is disgraceful that, when no Jew ever has to beg, and the impious Galileans support not only their own poor but ours as well, all men see that our people lack aid from us.*[285]

Emperor Julian wanted to stop the Christians from helping the poor in their own personal, voluntary way both because it disgraced the pagans *and* because it was leading to more and more pagan attrition to these "impious Galileans." The emperor's plan was not to make Christian philanthropy illegal, but rather to render it unnecessary. If the secular government (and pagan priests) provided for the poor, then the need would not be so great for the Christians to do so. And if the Christians stopped fulfilling that need, they would not gain as many converts.

Emperor Julian's thinking was not far off. In our own day, we have access to studies that prove the merit of his reasoning. Anthony Gill and Erik Lundsgaarde, for instance, demonstrate based on cross-national data that there is a strong negative

---

[284] Hubner, Jamin. "How Private Generosity Embarrassed the Greatest Empire of the West." https://libertarianchristians.com/2018/05/30/how-private-generosity-embarrassed-empire/

[285] *The Works of Emperor Julian* (https://archive.org/stream/worksotemperorju02juliuoft/worksofemperorju02juliuoft_djvu.txt), 3.67-73

correlation between government welfare spending and religious participation. As welfare spending goes up, religious participation and affiliation go down.[286] Did this not prove true for Russia after the Soviet takeover? And has it not proven to be true for the rest of the European nations after the rise of their own welfare states? Has it not proven true for America over the last half century or so?

* * *

Policy Implications

Community is often overlooked in political discussions as more attention is focused on the balance between welfare and work. Certainly, it is important for able-bodied people to work because of the positive effects of work on self-esteem, health, and overall happiness. God designed human beings to work — to perform activities that steward the resources of creation effectively and add value to each others' lives. But work isn't everything. *Community* is another major part of a healthy, well-rounded life. Social isolation has negative effects on one's financial ability to get by, not to mention being literally detrimental to health. In the words of Dr. Dhruv Khullar of the Massachusetts General Hospital, who has witnessed countless cases of social isolation, "Human connection lies at the heart of human well-being."[287]

For Christians, there is a spiritual element to this as well, because we know that the Kingdom of God is meant to be lived out in community. "For where two or three are gathered in my name," says Jesus in Matthew 18:20, "there am I among them."

---

[286] Gill, Anthony and Lundsgaarde, Erik. "State Welfare Spending and Religiosity."
http://faculty.washington.edu/tgill/Gill%20Lundsgaarde%20Welfare%20Religion.pdf
[287] Khullar, Dhruv. "How Social Isolation is Killing Us."
https://www.nytimes.com/2016/12/22/upshot/how-social-isolation-is-killing-us.html

Therefore, we ought to seek out policies that will bolster, rather than erode, community. We have been using terms like social trust and social capital, but broadly speaking, these terms are simply substitutes for the word "community." When communities are strong, natural mechanisms of caring for each other are prevalent enough to make government involvement less necessary—perhaps even unnecessary.

One suggested way of addressing poverty while at the same time eliminating the negative effects on social capital caused by means-tested welfare is to implement a universal basic income (UBI). The idea is that, by eliminating means-tested programs and replacing them with a simple, unconditional, all-inclusive cash payout from the government that guarantees everyone a poverty-line income (or more), poverty can be alleviated while avoiding loss of social trust and community. Kumlin and Rothstein would certainly seem to favor this idea, since in their view, the problem is not welfare *per se* but welfare's lack of universality.

Much could be said about a universal basic income, both for and against, from economic, political, and sociological perspectives, but our primary task here is to evaluate it from a biblical perspective. Suffice it to say that, for at least four reasons, a universal basic income would scarcely be compatible with the abundant life of the Kingdom of God as described in Scripture.

First, while a UBI certainly would avoid some of the anti-family, anti-community effects of means-tested welfare, there remains no reason to view it as *pro*-family or *pro*-community. That is because the aid still comes from *outside* the family and the community rather than from within them. A UBI fails to comply with the Jethro Principle, then, because the cash payments would come from the furthest possible place—from *anyone and everyone who works to earn a living and pay taxes*. In short, the UBI would come from society itself, and when that happens, to whom can one be grateful? To whom can one return the favor? To what tangible community will one feel a greater sense of belonging? How is the "social fabric" of the nation strengthened in any way?

Second, we must recognize that, whether through universal cash payments or means-tested benefits, government provision for the poor renders the church a less important institution of aid for the needy in society. As Emperor Julian understood, when the church is less able or less necessary to serve as a social safety net, the faith is less attractive to outsiders and its growth is curbed accordingly. Macro data bears out this reasoning.

Third, a UBI distributes the same amount of cash to all citizens regardless of their level of wealth or income rather than on the basis of need, but the example of the early church in Acts 2 and 4 shows that aid ought to be distributed on the basis of *need*. Those making hundreds of thousands of dollars a year or more would still receive the same cash payment under a UBI, despite their lack of need. This makes little sense biblically or otherwise.

Fourth, just like other forms of welfare, a UBI would be funded through involuntary means. By necessity, it would not come from those who voluntarily and cheerfully give for the benefit of others. Perhaps some would happily give to support the UBI, but not everyone would. It's worth noting that those who like the idea of a UBI *could* get together to form their own version of it on a small scale, with a few dozen or hundred people. But it likely would not work that well because those who volunteer to participate would probably be roughly equal in their levels of income. They would need to recruit much wealthier people to make it feasible, but wealthier people would not likely be willing to join a group of strangers only to have their wealth extracted. Most wealthy people are not attracted to this form of philanthropy. Thus, a large-scale UBI could only operate by forcibly extracting wealth from those who have more of it and redistributing it to those with less. Such a system violates the Kingdom Principle of Voluntarism.

What is the solution, then? How do we undo so many

decades of government expansion and the accompanying social changes? How do we return to the self-help, mutual aid, and warmhearted yet discriminating charity system that dominated the 19th century without accepting the negative aspects of that generation — the social darwinism, the lower standard of living, the poor health?

First, we must recognize the importance of family and community in the provision of aid. We must refuse to accept the notion that these institutions were merely an imperfect stopgap measure to provide aid until the invention of the welfare state. There's a reason that human beings, in lieu of extraneous factors, naturally form these groups. It is because we thrive in community. We are not meant to be socially isolated but to do life *together*, as families, as networks of friends, as fellowships of believers.

So, again, the solution must be as radical as the problem. I use the word "radical" on purpose. It comes from the Latin *radix*, meaning "root." We must strike at the root of the problem. Tweaks here and there are not likely to solve such a big issue. The suggested solution, then, is very similar to that of the previous chapter: *Scrap the welfare state as it exists now.* Eliminate the food stamp program, section 8 and public housing, disability benefits, unemployment insurance, and all other federally funded and managed programs for alleviation of poverty. Do this not to protect the wealth and freedom of the rich, nor to punish the poor, but to create the need for churches, mutual aid associations, private charities, friend groups, neighborhoods, and other voluntary organizations to fill this gap. As Charles Murray puts it, "backed by powerful collateral evidence," we advocate this radical policy because "the lives of large numbers of poor people would be radically changed for the better."[288]

We must also communicate, loudly and clearly, that it is *not* a tragedy that such organizations have to step in to provide

---

[288] Murray, *Losing Ground*, 229

these social goods. Rather, it is *good* and *natural* that they should do so. They are the vital signs of American community showing vigor again.

Second, because there may be cracks in this system despite its overall superiority, we ought to support a public safety net that practices subsidiarity. Like the Swedish system, cities and municipalities ought to take up the bulk of publicly funded welfare, when and if aid is not being sufficiently provided privately. For example, the City of Los Angeles will know better how to remedy poverty on Skid Row, likely working in concert with multiple local charities already familiar with the problems, than will politicians in Sacramento or Washington D.C. Similarly, county officials in rural Texas will likely know better how to address poverty in their area than will bureaucrats that might live hundreds or thousands of miles away.

States may then follow, providing a support system and backstop to localities when needed. Federal involvement should be limited to providing tax benefits for charitable giving. Charitable giving for social services ought to be given more weight in our tax code than philanthropic giving that does not go toward the needy. If donations to one's local food pantry are 100% deductible, donations to an art museum or a university endowment fund should be less than 100% deductible—perhaps only 50%. Moreover, a way should be found to ensure that donors of any income level enjoy the same deductibility for the same giving, rather than having a relatively high standard deduction as in the Tax Cuts and Jobs Act of 2017, which effectively eliminates the tax incentive for small-dollar donors to give.[289]

Also, non-profit mutual aid associations, which are exempt from taxation under the Internal Revenue Code 501(c)(8) and

---

[289] Gleckman, Howard. "21 Million Taxpayers Will Stop Taking Charitable Deductions Under the New Tax Law." (https://www.forbes.com/sites/beltway/2018/01/11/21-million-taxpayers-will-stop-taking-charitable-deductions-under-the-new-tax-law/* * *e8b6db238f02)

501(c)(10), should keep their tax-favored status. Current rules concerning donations to benefit associations, which only allow tax-deductibility for philanthropic uses of the funds (spending for non-members), should be expanded to include tax deductibility for operating uses (spending for members).[290] The nation would be better off if organized mutual aid played even a fraction of the role it once did.

Such a major decentralization of power in this regard would, admittedly, require a fundamental shift in the nation's perspective from state- and bureaucracy-oriented solutions to community-oriented ones. We as a country must begin to see things differently. Personal relief should be preferred to impersonal, familial to non-familial, communal to bureaucratic, local or regional to national, informal to formal, and temporary to permanent.

Ultimately, we must remember that human beings cannot be reduced to their material needs. As said previously, we are more than mouths to feed and bodies to clothe and shelter. We are also social creatures who need affiliation both for our physical and psychological health *and* for financial security. "Government welfare programs need to be fought," writes Marvin Olasky, "not because they are too expensive—although, clearly, much money is wasted—but because they are inevitably too stingy in what is really important, treating people as people and not animals."[291]

At the same time, let us not make demands of others that we are not ourselves willing to practice. If we wish for the poor to have stronger families, let us pour ourselves wholeheartedly into our own families and set a good example. If we wish for the needy to find support from community, let us not allow ourselves to become socially isolated or cloistered in communities of only those who lack material needs. If we

---

[290] Internal Revenue Code, "Fraternal Benefit Societies and Fraternal Societies." (https://www.irs.gov/pub/irs-tege/eotopich80.pdf, https://www.irs.gov/pub/irs-tege/eotopic04.pdf)
[291] Olasky, 232-233

desire stronger social trust in our country, let us strive to be *trustworthy* to those in our social circles as well as those outside them. If we long for a world where people take care of each other of their own free will, let us demonstrate the feasibility of this beautiful vision.

This is, after all, what it means to be the "first fruits" of a new creation, a new way of life, a new Kingdom. We put on display in this world what many think could only be possible in a perfect world—in Heaven. By our lives, we prove that Heaven is a reality, that the Kingdom of God is not an impossible utopia but rather is within our grasp—if only we would reach out and grasp it.

* * *

"If you pour yourself out for the hungry and satisfy the desire of the afflicted then shall your light rise in the darkness and your gloom be as the noonday."
Isaiah 58:10

CHAPTER TEN

Abortion and Choice

Why begin our application of biblical principles to politics with such an extended study of marriage, family, and community breakdown? Why not first address abortion, which to many Christians is the most important issue in politics?

So often, political issues are addressed on an individual basis, as if they were small leaks in a dam that could be fixed simply by patching the exterior breach. Any structural engineer would tell you, though, that a leak nearly always signifies a larger, more fundamental problem. Even if you can patch that leak, leaving the more fundamental problem untouched ensures that another leak—perhaps multiple leaks—will appear elsewhere.

Abortion is not the fundamental problem. Abortion is the leak. The fundamental problem is the breakdown of marriage, family, and community. If marriage was more common, there would be less demand for abortion. If families were stronger, there would be less appeal to abortion. If communities were closer and more interdependent, there would be less need for abortion.

Abortion is probably never a desirable option for women, yet a great many women choose to have them. Why? Certain conditions exist which ultimately lead to that decision. And even if abortion could be eliminated as an option with the wave of a magic wand, the conditions which led to the abortion would still exist. Other outcomes would materialize instead, and many of those would likely be negative for the baby, for the mother, or for both.

Still, despite serious questions about the circumstances of the pregnant woman as well as the potential circumstances of mother and baby (if the pregnancy continues to birth), the moral status of the pre-born baby (or fetus) must not be ignored. When do personhood and human rights begin? Some are too comfortable with ignoring this question, and others are too quick to presume an answer to it. Likewise, too many Christians presume the Bible holds a certain view without digging into Scripture to confirm it. Or they claim total silence from Scripture on this issue and use that as a justification to hold onto their already-held beliefs.

We must avoid these errors. To do so, we'll explore biblical passages which suggest certain ways of thinking about and dealing with this difficult subject. Then we'll look at what thinkers and writers from church history have said about abortion. After that, we'll take a scientific and philosophical look at when life and personhood begin. Is life synonymous with personhood or do they mean something different? Does personhood begin at the same time as one's biological humanity begins, or does it develop later? Lastly, we'll discuss some practical ways that the church can be a force for good in this area, both in and out of the realm of politics.

But first, we need to address a vital issue about the rules of engagement.

* * *

Framing the Debate

Abortion as an issue is fraught with emotion. Conflicting viewpoints evoke passionate responses from the other side. That passion is understandable, as the debate is an attempt to parse a delicate and nuanced matter involving life and death, human rights for both woman and fetus, the dignity and self-determination of women, and government involvement or non-involvement.

Unfortunately, both sides of the debate often try to frame the terms of the debate in biased or one-sided terminology and rhetoric which is designed to tilt the debate in their favor. For instance, so far in this discussion I've referred to the prenatal life as both a "fetus" and an "pre-born baby." The term "fetus" is more distant and scientific. It's what we call the unborn offspring of all mammals, which tacitly reduces the unborn offspring of humans to the same level. A "fetus" feels less like a human being with the right to life, so it is more often used by pro-choicers. "Unborn" or "pre-born baby," on the other hand, suggests that the offspring holds the same moral status as a newborn baby and is thus used more often by pro-lifers.

The rhetorical framing only gets more one-sided from there. Pro-lifers say they are "pro-baby." Pro-choicers say they are "pro-woman." But isn't every normal person both pro-baby and pro-woman? Pro-lifers claim to stand for the "rights of the most vulnerable." Pro-choicers claim to stand for "reproductive rights." But again, don't we all stand for the rights of the vulnerable as well as the rights of each woman and couple to make their own reproductive choices? (What a clinical term to use about human beings—reproduction.) Even "pro-life" and "pro-choice" illustrate the marketing techniques of each side. How could anyone be *anti*-life? By the same token, how could anyone be against individual choice?

Participants in this debate often seem so intent on framing the terms of the debate—and by extension labeling their opponents as heartless or extremist that the substance of the debate is completely ignored. How does one weigh a woman's right to control her body with the moral status of the unborn [insert your preferred term here]? Sadly, to even ask this question in this emotionally wrought debate today is to evoke an angry, biased, alogical response.

* * *

The Bible on the Unborn

Surprisingly little in Scripture refers to the status of the unborn, but we can garner a few insights.

Perhaps the most often cited passage in relation to abortion is Psalm 139:13-15:

> For you formed my inward parts;
> you knitted me together in my mother's womb.
> I praise you, for I am fearfully and wonderfully made.
> Wonderful are your works;
> my soul knows it very well.
> My frame was not hidden from you,
> when I was being made in secret,
> intricately woven in the depths of the earth.

In this passage, David refers to himself in his unborn state in personal terms— "me" and "my." Furthermore, he speaks of this process of God crafting a growing child in his mother's womb in reverent terms. Twice the word "wonderful" is used about this act of creation, which is carried out "in secret" and "in the depths of the earth," both phrases which signify the unseen place in the womb. The Hebrew word for "earth" or "ground" is *adamah,* which is also strongly associated with "woman." Similar insights could be garnered from Job 31:15: "Did not he who made me in the womb make him? And did not one fashion us in the womb?" Being made or fashioned in the womb implies a process that is not completed instantly, but the fact that these adult writers equate their pre-born selves with their adult selves is meaningful. To them, it seems the unborn being in the womb *is* them, only in a different form and a different state.

Then again, we can't read too much into these passages as they are clearly not meant to define the beginning of human life or personhood in precise terms. These are poetic, not scientific, texts. Jeremiah 1:5 demonstrates the need to interpret statements about pre-born life cautiously:

Before I formed you in the womb I knew you,
and before you were born I consecrated you;
I appointed you a prophet to the nations.

How can one be said to have existed (in order to be known by God) even prior to conception, much less birth? Clearly, this passage is giving a poetic or theological truth, not a scientific one. "Such statements cannot be pressed as a way of making claims about the status of the fetus as a 'person,'" writes Richard Hays, "rather, they are confessions about God's divine foreknowledge and care. God knows and calls us not just from the time of conception but even *before* conception—even from the foundation of the world."[292]

Some theologians cite Psalm 51:5 as evidence that personhood begins at birth: "Behold, I was brought forth in iniquity, and in sin did my mother conceive me." The grammatical construction of the verse seems to imply that the sin in question here is that of his mother, not David— "in sin did *my mother* conceive me." She is the subject of this sentence, not him. But we know very little about David's mother from Scripture and cannot confirm whether her conception of him was under sinful circumstances. What's more, verse 5 falls in the middle of a passage of David confessing and lamenting *his own* sin. It would certainly be odd to suddenly refer to the sin of his mother, although perhaps he found it relevant to mention that even the circumstances of his physical creation were sinful, using it as a way to prove in this poetic text that he is sinful to his core. Another possible interpretation is that David considers it a sin that his mother conceived him not because the sexual act was itself sinful but because David, a dreadfully sinful person, resulted from it.

Wayne Grudem, however, does not see the sin in this passage as belonging to David's mother but to David himself. "He is saying that from the moment of conception he had a sinful nature. This means that *he thought of himself as a distinct*

---

[292] Hays, *Moral Vision of the New Testament*, 448

human being, a distinct person, from the moment of conception."[293] Many cite this verse as evidence that humans have a sinful nature that pre-exists any enculturation or choice to sin. A sin nature attributes moral accountability, one of the most important aspects of personhood, to the fetus and even the zygote from the moment of conception.

This view has some intuitive problems. Even if human beings have a sin nature in the sense that we do not naturally live and behave the way God designed us to in the beginning, fetuses and zygotes have no ability to live or behave in one way over another. While a newborn baby can behave in ways that do not conform to God's ideal will, whether by conscious choice or not, a zygote doesn't have even *that* ability. How would the nature of the zygote or fetus be any different in the womb of Eve prior to the Fall than it would be in the womb of a woman after the Fall? Furthermore, if even unborn babies are stricken with this sin nature, doesn't that mean that they would be eternally separated from God if they were to die in the womb?

With this in mind, it makes more sense to read Psalm 51:5 as poetic hyperbole, even if David is referring to his own sinful nature. In contrast to David's utterly corrupted essence presented in verse 5, God is presented in verse 6 as One who delights "in truth in the inward being" and teaches David "wisdom in the secret heart." David, in his penitent state, views himself as all bad, whereas God is all good and is alone responsible for any truth or wisdom David possesses. Notice that Psalm 51:5 is almost the antithesis of Psalm 139:13-15. Rather than being "fearfully and wonderfully made" by God, David here suggests that *even from conception* he was sinful. This indicates that these poetic lines are for exaggerative effect, not meant to express an anthropological or theological truth.

In short, the verse is not meant to be a comment about the moral status of the unborn generally but rather the moral status

---

[293] Grudem, *Politics According to the Bible*, 158

of David specifically.

Then again, there are at least two instances in Scripture of unborn babies acting in some way, which might lend credence to the notion that personhood exists prior to birth. One comes from Genesis 25:22-23, when Rebekah was pregnant with the twins Jacob and Esau. "The *children* struggled within her," the text says, which led her to inquire of the Lord who then explained her sons 'future division and conflict. The struggle, which Rebekah perhaps experienced as kicking from the unborn children, was a symbol of the future struggle between Jacob and Esau as well as the distinct peoples each would come to represent. This struggle is not necessarily a conscious one on the part of the unborn twins. It is likely a normal experience of a pregnant mother of twins which God used to illustrate her sons 'future.

What about the unborn twins being called "children?" They are not thought of as *potential* children but simply as children, as sons. This suggests that there is not a fundamental difference between humans in the womb and ones which have already been born.

Likewise, in Luke 1:41-44 it is written that Elizabeth's unborn baby (who would later be called John the Baptist) "leaped for joy" at the sound of Mary's greeting. The point of this passage, as Richard Hays points out, is not to draw attention to the status of the unborn John the Baptist but rather to symbolize John's future role as prophet announcing the coming of Jesus. He leaped for joy at the sound of Mary because Mary would give birth to Jesus. In this narrative, John was already bearing witness to the coming of Jesus. However, it would be a mistake to read a conclusion about the moral status of the unborn into a passage trying to make a Christological point. We should be cautious not to take it too literally. While it is true that babies in the womb can become familiar with the sound of family members 'voices, it would be a stretch to assume that the unborn John the Baptist was conscious of his future prophetic witness or that his Aunt Mary would mother his future cousin Jesus.

That brings us to one last passage, which proves the trickiest of all to interpret, and that is Exodus 21:22-25:

> When men strive together and hit a pregnant woman, so that her children come out, but there is no harm, the one who hit her shall surely be fined, as the woman's husband shall impose on him, and he shall pay as the judges determine. But if there is harm, then you shall pay life for life, eye for eye, tooth for tooth, hand for hand, foot for foot, burn for burn, wound for wound, stripe for stripe.

This passage proves to be a sort of Rorschach Test for believers 'preconceived views about abortion. Those who align with one position interpret it one way, while those who hold the opposite view interpret it another way.

A more pro-choice reading of the passage sees the scenario of the children coming out as referring to a miscarriage of the baby or babies but no significant harm to the pregnant woman. In this case, the only penalty is a fine. But if the woman is harmed, the punishment to the offender will accord with the law of retaliation: eye for an eye, tooth for a tooth, life for a life. By this reading, the life of the unborn is perhaps of some value, but does not possess the same legal protections as the mother. Harm to an unborn baby is not a crime high enough to merit the law of retaliation. However, even if this is the correct interpretation of the passage, there is scarcely any application to the contemporary issue of abortion. If the scenario presented here is akin to manslaughter because of the lack of intentionality, abortion is akin to murder because it is pursued intentionally. What would the penalty be for a man (or even the mother) who intentionally did something to cause a miscarriage but did no significant harm to the mother? Scripture does not say.

On the other hand, a more pro-life reading of the passage sees the children coming out as a premature birth but not one that results in any permanent harm to either mother or baby.

The fine is imposed on the offender for putting the mother and child's lives *at risk* of harm. But in the case where there is harm to either mother or baby, the law of retaliation applies.

Which interpretation is correct? Who is to say? Before one claims that one reading or the other is the "clear" meaning of the text, one's own bias should be acknowledged. The text simply is not clear.

What truths can be drawn from Scripture on this topic? Precious few, unfortunately. We know, first and foremost, that all life comes from God, "from whom are all things and for whom we exist" (1 Cor. 8:6). God is the creator and author of all life, as John makes clear in his gospel:

> All things came into being through him, and without him not one thing came into being. What has come into being in him was life, and the life was the light of all people. The light shines in darkness, and the darkness did not overcome it. (John 1:3-5)

Paradoxically, even in cases where sinful circumstances lead to pregnancy, somehow God is at work, crafting the body of a new human being and working to bring good out of all things. Human life certainly begins prior to birth—at conception—in the minds of the biblical authors, but whether those unborn lives have the same moral status and legal protections as an adult or newborn child is unclear. Despite the lack of biblical clarity on these questions, it *is* clear that unborn lives *are* of value to God and should be of value to His people as well. Even very early in the development of human life, God's handiwork is wonderful and ought to be acknowledged as such. And at least at some point during pregnancy, the unborn are considered "children"—not fundamentally different than an infant or a toddler or a teenager. They are sons and daughters, even before birth. It seems, then, that there would need to be a very good reason to overcome this attitude and conclude that, under certain circumstances, abortion is tragically necessary or justifiable.

* * *

Abortion in the Eyes of the Early Church

In ancient Hebrew culture, pregnancy was thought of as a blessing from God, as the primary roles of women in that culture were as wives and mothers. Hence we find Paul writing that women believers would be "saved" through childbearing "if they continue in faith and love and holiness, with self-control" (1 Tim. 2:15). While this refers to sanctification rather than justification, it paints motherhood as an important role for Christian women.

Greco-Roman culture did not share this reverence for all life and high view of motherhood. It was not uncommon to abandon infant children along roadsides either to die or to be taken by someone else. Typically, "exposed infants" who did not die of exposure were raised as slaves or prostitutes. Chemical abortions were also fairly common. Christians strongly rejected both practices, setting themselves apart through a witness of life, which included condemnation of abortion and infanticide as well as willingness to take and raise abandoned children. In this way, they inherited a pro-life position from the Jewish tradition. The *Sentences of Pseudo-Phocylides* (a collection of Jewish moral maxims composed sometime around the early first century), for example, takes a strong stance against abortion: "Do not let a woman destroy the unborn babe in her belly, nor after its birth throw it before the dogs and vultures as a prey."[294]

Christian writers continue this tradition seamlessly. We find a man named Barnabus, for instance, writing in the late first century or early second century, "You shall not murder a child by obtaining an abortion. Nor, again, shall you destroy him after he is born." Likewise, the Didache, a manual of church

---

[294] Bakke, Odd Magne. *When Children Became People: the birth of childhood in early Christianity* (Fortress Press: Minneapolis, 2005), 112

beliefs and practices dating to the first century, instructs, "You shall not murder a child by abortion nor kill one who has been born." [295]

Abortion was not fundamentally different in those days. Just as we now have both chemical and surgical forms of abortion, so also did they in the first few centuries of the church. Athenagoras denounced chemical abortions around the year 175 AD, writing:

> We say that those women who use drugs to bring on abortion commit murder. And we also say that they will have to give an account to God for the abortion. So on what basis could we commit murder? For it does not belong to the same person to regard the very fetus in the womb as a created being (and therefore an object of God's care)—yet, when he has passed into life, to kill him. We also teach that it is wrong to expose an infant. For those who expose them are guilty of child murder. [296]

Notice that there is no regard for what stage of the pregnancy the abortion takes place. Whenever it happens, it is considered murder. Marcus Minucius Felix, writing in the early third century, agreed with Athenagoras: "There are some women who, by drinking medical preparations, extinguish the source of the future man in their very bowels. So they commit murder before they bring forth [i.e. give birth]." Around 225 AD, Hippolytus also wrote about "reputed believers" who took these abortifacient drugs and "girded themselves around" in something like a diaper to catch the remains of the fetus as it was expelled from their bodies. To this Hippolytus exclaims, "See what a great impiety the lawless one has advanced! He teaches adultery and murder at the same time!"

Tertullian, writing sometime between Athenagoras and

---

[295] Bercot, *Dictionary of Early Christian Beliefs*, 2
[296] All quotations from the early church hereafter in this chapter come from Bercot, 2-3

Felix, took a similarly hard stance: "In our case, murder is once for all forbidden. Therefore, we may not destroy even the fetus in the womb. . . . To hinder a birth is merely a speedier way to kill a human. It does not matter whether you take away a life that has been born, or destroy one that is not yet born." In other words, the birthing process does not do anything to change the moral status of the fetus. In Tertullian's mind, intentionally taking the life of a fetus is no less immoral than intentionally taking the life of a newborn baby.

Tertullian also describes in grim detail how a surgical abortion was carried out in those days. Note that surgical abortions are not fundamentally different today, even if they are performed with contemporary tools.

> Among surgeons' tools there is a certain instrument that is formed with a nicely-adjusted flexible frame for first of all opening the uterus and then keeping it open. It also has a circular blade, by means of which the limbs within the womb are dissected with careful, but unflinching care. Its last appendage is a blunted or covered hook, by which the entire fetus is extracted by a violent delivery. There is also a copper needle or spike, by which the actual death is brought about in this treacherous robbery of life. From its infanticide function, they give it the name, "killer of the infant"— which infant, of course, had once been alive.

In other words, says Tertullian, the fact that this instrument bore the word "killer" in its name implies that the object being removed was once a living human.

Even as late as the turn of the fifth century, when Christianity had gained political power and intermixed with pagan Roman culture to a much greater extent than prior generations, church writings remained firmly against abortion. The *Apostolic Constitutions*, written around 390 AD, bears this unequivocal commandment:

> You shall not slay your child by causing abortion, nor kill the baby that is born. For "everything that is shaped

and has received a soul from God, if it is slain, shall be avenged, as being unjustly destroyed."

This statement forces us to ask the difficult question of *when* the fetus is "shaped" and when it has "received a soul from God." Should questions of ensoulment even play a part in the discussion of legal protection? Is there a time when a fetus has been "shaped" into human form whereas before it lacked human form? Does the resemblance of human form even matter? While unintentionally raising these questions, this instruction from the *Apostolic Constitutions* sidesteps them and issues a blanket condemnation of abortion.

* * *

What Does Science Tell Us About the Beginning of Life?

Let's set aside the Christian worldview for a moment and examine the abortion issue from a scientific angle. What must be acknowledged upfront is that questions about personhood, moral status, and legal protections are philosophical or theological, not scientific. Therefore, though science may be able to explain the process of life formation from a biological perspective, it cannot definitively tell us what the moral value of that life is or when it deserves the right to life. The purpose of invoking science here is to inform the philosophical and theological discussion about personhood.

In shedding our assumption of a Christian worldview, let us stipulate a few points before getting to the science. First, let's stipulate that there is no societal consensus on if such a thing as a soul exists or, if a soul *does* exist, when it inhabits the body. Let us also stipulate that there is no societal consensus on what it means to be a "person" or when personhood begins. With these stipulations in mind, it will be easier to approach science without using or expecting it to prove a certain philosophical or theological belief. Often relevant biological facts are oversimplified in order to serve a philosophical end. We must avoid that mistake.

One such example of biological facts being oversimplified relates to the "moment of conception." What does the "moment of conception" actually refer to? Conception, or fertilization, is tricky to precisely pin down. Is it the moment when sperm enters a woman's body? Is it when sperm hits the egg wall? Or up to an hour later when one successful sperm enters the egg? Or 12 hours later when the sperm DNA mixes with the egg's DNA? Or up to 24 hours later when the fertilized egg has become restructured with new chromosomes? The "moment" of conception isn't actually a moment. It can take two or three days to complete the process. By day four after fertilization, the zygote has divided itself into more and more cells until it has reached approximately 100 cells and would be called a blastocyst. Six days after fertilization, the blastocyst implants itself in the uterine wall, and it then becomes an embryo.

A zygote, once it has formed its own unique DNA, has the potential for up to two weeks to undergo the twinning process. This refers only to identical twins, as fraternal twins are the result of two distinct eggs becoming fertilized. Rather than the blastocyst remaining one group of cells, it may split into two, or sometimes, very rarely, three or four. When this happens early, each group of cells will develop independently (though sometimes sharing a placenta). When it happens late, the twinning process often fails to complete, resulting in conjoined ("Siamese") twins.

Biologically speaking, it is accurate to say that from the time the zygote has developed its own unique DNA, it is by nature human. In other words, it is a unique human being, not equivalent to a tumor or cyst or some other kind of growth. Further, it is motile, meaning it has the capacity to move around on its own — a distinguishing element of life. It is "living" in the sense that its DNA is active and that is is biologically "under construction" — in a growth mode that will characterize it for another 20 years or so.

It would be inaccurate to say that life begins when there is a discernible heartbeat, or that a heartbeat is a test of life, because a heartbeat does not begin until well after conception. Likewise, it would be inaccurate to say that life begins at viability—the age at which a fetus can survive with medical assistance outside the womb—because medical technology is constantly changing. While viability is now about 20 weeks, it was once much later than that. Because viability is determined by factors *external* to the fetus, it does not make sense to posit it as a test of life.

What about quickening, which doesn't take place until around week 15? Quickening is when the pregnant woman usually begins to feel the movement of the fetus and when the fetus can react to external stimuli. Reaction to external stimuli is another biological test for life, but it doesn't make sense to apply it to fetuses because they are not in the same position as other organisms with similar numbers of cells. Contrary to a tadpole, for instance, embryos and early fetuses are in a protected environment in which there is little need for the ability to react to external stimuli for self-preservation.

Medically, on the other hand, it is not accurate to say that the zygote, blastocyst, or embryo is yet a living human being—at least not in the usual meaning of the term concerning humans. What is often medically defined as life concerns the capacity for brain function and activity, which is the basis for all personality, thought, feeling, and emotion. Those are not yet possible in an embryo, which the unborn human is called until week 9, when it would then become a fetus. Active DNA does not necessarily equate to life in the medical sense, because DNA remains active in the body for some time after death. Brain death, or the cessation of electrical activity in the brain which leads to a shutdown of the other bodily systems, is what defines the *end* of life, so from a medical perspective it would make sense to say that the *beginning* of life has something to do with this electrical activity in the brain. Or at least the capacity for such activity.

Electrical activity in the brain, often called EEG activity

because it is measured by a machine called an electroencephalograph, does not appear until around the end of the second trimester or beginning of the third trimester. By week 20, the thalamus—part of the inner core of the cerebrum which forms the groundwork for all higher cortical and brain function—has become completely developed. Sustained EEG activity occurs in the fetus around week 24 or 25. Perhaps we could say, then, that in medical terms human life—or "brain life"—has definitively begun by the beginning of the third trimester.

Notice that neither a biological nor a medical definition of the beginning of life necessitates a certain moral stance on when personhood and legal protection begins. But they can inform the discussion.

* * *

Putting Science and Scripture Together

We know from Scripture that personhood—the part of a human being which identifies him or her as an individual—begins prior to birth. But when exactly *does* it begin? Does it begin at conception? While that might seem like the simplest answer, there are some complicating factors.

For one, while it is true that a zygote within the first few weeks is by nature human with its own unique DNA, there's still the possibility of twinning. In that case, the zygote splits and develops into two embryos, and then two fetuses, and ultimately two babies—two persons with identical DNA. So, prior to the split, was the zygote a person? Was it two people? Was it the *potential* for one person or two people? Until twinning occurs (or the single zygote becomes implanted in the uterine wall without twinning), it is unanswerable as to the number of persons contained in the zygote.

Some have suggested that, prior to twinning, a zygote is still an individual person, but it's one in the unique situation of bearing the potential to split into another genetically identical person. Sometimes the analogy is used that if you split a tapeworm in half, it becomes two tapeworms. The original tapeworm, they would say, was still an individual tapeworm, not a *potential* tapeworm or the *potential* for multiple tapeworms. But this analogy doesn't work. If a tapeworm is split in half, it may give the appearance that both sides are now individual tapeworms as both continue to wriggle around, but in reality, only the side with the head is capable of surviving longterm. It has the ability to regrow a tail, but the tail side will eventually die.

But even if a tapeworm could be split into two individual tapeworms at any time, this analogy still wouldn't work because it compares apples to oranges. Even if there is some adult creature that could be split into two identical yet individual creatures, it is not the same situation as a human zygote very early in pregnancy. The former involves an externally applied splitting, while the latter is an internal splitting—one that happens on its own.

Another analogy suggested by Catholic philosopher Christopher Kaczor is cloning. It's at least theoretically possible for humans to be cloned, meaning that one individual could become two individuals with identical genetics, so twinning doesn't necessarily exclude the pre-existing zygote from personhood. Again, though, this analogy doesn't work. Cloning involves an external catalyst, whereas twinning is internal, requiring no external catalyst. Cloning is an artificial process, while twinning is natural. And cloning does not necessarily involve a developing organism splitting in two but could be carried out with an already-developed organism. There's no such thing as spontaneous adult twinning in humans (or any other creature that I'm aware of).

A better analogy might be an organism that reproduces asexually, such as the hydra. The hydra is a sea creature that can grow to about a third of an inch long that reproduces by budding. One might argue that, prior to budding, a hydra is still an individual hydra, not two hydras or the potential for two hydras. Maybe so, but this analogy also doesn't work. Hydras lack any recognizable brain, they have only a simple nervous system, and they lack the capacity to develop either of these things. Human zygotes, on the other hand, will develop brains and advanced nervous systems in time. A hydra can never in its life be considered a "person," even if it is an individual hydra. But a human zygote, on the other hand, may be an individual human organism prior to twinning but is only *potentially* one or more persons.

Perhaps science will one day explain what causes identical twinning, but for now, the process is unexplained and seemingly random. However, lets assume that someday, scientific tests confirm that (to use a made-up example) a certain genetic abnormality in sperm causes twinning such that one could know immediately after conception whether the zygote would undergo twinning and become two embryos. Even in that case, prior to the twinning, how could it be said that the single zygote is either one person or two persons? Is there any other case (besides psychological disorders) in which two persons reside simultaneously in the same physical body? Conjoined twins share *part* of the same body, but not all of it. Wouldn't it be more accurate to say that the zygote *will become* two persons even though it is *currently* only one organism? If this is true, then it doesn't make sense to think of the zygote as a person, because it has not yet taken on the physical form, however small or primitive, that would identify it *as an individual person* for the rest of its life.

What do we call the zygote, then? Some have used the term "proto-human," indicating a primitive human or the precursor to a human, but this term isn't quite accurate because by genetics the zygote *is* human, not pre-human. I think the term "proto-person" works better, since it is the precursor to the physical form which will identify the person for the rest of his or her life.

When does personhood begin, if not at conception? Neither

Scripture nor science is unambiguously clear, which means we must be cautious before asserting a strong position on the subject. "The absence of explicit New Testament evidence," writes Hays, "suggests first of all that a certain humility about our claims and convictions concerning abortion is appropriate."[297]

One possibility for the origin of personhood is the beginning of electrical activity in the brain. This is when an unborn baby becomes able to feel things, to dream, to hear and recognize the voices of its parents. Brain function and activity is the basis for personality, character, emotion, and rationality—most (if not all) of the traits which make humans distinctive. Is this when personhood begins? Maybe. But even if it is, when exactly does this happen in the pregnancy? When the thalamus develops around week 20? Or when sustained EEG activity is detectable in the brain around week 24? It's difficult to pin down universally. Personhood what identifies one as an individual human being—develops gradually through a long process without a clear beginning or end.

However, it's also possible that thinking of *personhood* as the basis for legal protection of life is wrongheaded. Scripture tells us that *all* life comes from God. Human life in particular, even in the form of a zygote, should not be treated lightly. All life must be stewarded wisely and faithfully. That, after all, is the task God designated for humans from the beginning.

It should also be kept in mind that, though secular governments need to establish *some* point when the legal protection of life begins, talk of a "right to life," just as much as a "right to one's body," is the wrong way for Christians to approach this issue. As stated previously, human "rights" as a concept is foreign to Scripture. All life belongs to God and is a gift from Him, and stewardship of life on Earth is humanity's God-given job. Taking life, as in the case of animals slaughtered for sacrifice in the Old Testament era or merely for food in the

---

[297] Hays, 445

New Testament era, may sometimes be tragically necessary or justified, *but it should never be taken lightly*. Our presumption should always be to err on the side of life, of non-violence, of the nourishment of life rather than its extinction. Taking life, whether animal or human, ought to be a *last* resort and never a first one.

Whether the morning after pill is killing a human being or a person or merely a proto-person, it is still extinguishing the life of *something*. Whether a chemical abortion during the first trimester is killing a baby person or a non-person fetus, it is killing *something*. And, of course, when a surgical abortion is performed in the second or third trimester, it is definitely killing *something*. All of those *somethings* are lives, and every life has value.

But on the other hand, does killing a fetus carry the same moral weight as killing a 6-month old baby? Does killing a prenatal baby in the first trimester carry the same moral weight as killing one in the second? Does killing one in the second have the same moral weight as killing one in the third? It seems intuitively true that moral value gradually increases as more distinctly human traits develop during pregnancy.

Rather than definitively answer the question of when abortion ought to be prohibited, which neither Scripture nor science does, let's address a few prominent but faulty reasonings for abortion and how they could be addressed.

* * *

A Woman's Control Over Her Body

Probably the strongest argument for the pro-choice position was first articulated by moral philosopher Judith Jarvis Thomson and later by philosophy professor David Boonin. For their argument, they assume that the fetus (at whatever stage of development) *is* a person and has the right to life. But they also assume that every person, including women who might get pregnant, have a right to control their bodies. The right to control one's body entails the ability to decline to use one's body for the medical treatment or sustenance of another person's body.

Thomson gave this example. Imagine you wake up and are mortified to find that you are physically hooked up to a machine that is keeping another person alive. It is explained to you that for the next nine months, your body is needed to keep this other person alive, and at the end of the nine months, the process of detaching yourself from this person will be very unpleasant. You did not choose to be in this position, and for whatever reason (perhaps a myriad of reasons), you don't want to lend your body to this other person's survival for the next nine months. Should you be *forced* to remain attached to this other person and lend your body to them for the better part of a year?

David Boonin uses a real-world example of a man who needed a bone marrow transplant in order to live. Initially, the man's cousin agreed to donate his own bone marrow, but he later changed his mind and decided not to undergo the procedure of extracting and donating bone marrow. The man in need of a bone marrow transplant sued his cousin, attempting to force him to go through with the procedure that was initially agreed to. The courts, however, concluded that the state cannot *force* a person to donate part of their body, even to save another person's life.

Both Thomson and Boonin use these examples to arrive at the conclusion that, even if the prenatal life is a person with the right to life, that does not *obligate* the biological mother to let the fetus live in her uterus for the next nine months. The right to control one's body trumps the fetal human's right to life. In other words, a person with the right to life does not necessarily have the right to use another's body in order to live. Therefore, a woman should not be forced to incubate another human in her uterus for any amount of time.

It should be immediately apparent that this attitude stands

in stark contrast to the view we find in Scripture that all life is a gift from God, including the lives of the unborn. Consider, for instance, Psalm 127:3-5:

> Sons are indeed a heritage from the Lord,
> the fruit of the womb a reward.
> Like arrows in the hand of a warrior
> are the sons of one's youth.
> Happy is the man who has a quiver full of them.

But even on its own merits, the argument put forth by Thomson and Boonin is shaky. The flaw in the argument is easy to detect in Thomson's example, because in her example, the person wakes up attached to this machine seemingly through no fault or action of hers whatsoever. But pregnancies do not occur randomly. They are a potential consequence of sex. Unless the sexual act that led to the pregnancy wasn't voluntary, the pregnancy itself is a consequence of one's choices, not a random event that turns the subject into a victim.

In Boonin's example, the cousin *did* choose to donate part of his body and thus gave consent. But that initial choice, as the courts found, did not obligate him to go through with the procedure. In the same way, a woman who had sex, perhaps even with the intent of getting pregnant, is not obligated to let a fetal human use her body for the duration of the pregnancy. She has the right to change her mind, just as the cousin had a right to change his mind in Boonin's example.

But Boonin's argument has a flaw, too.

Actions have known risks and potential consequences. Riding a skateboard bears the risk of physical injury. Investing in the stock market bears the risk of losing money. Driving drunk bears the risk of harming others. When one knows that a certain action bears a certain risk, one tacitly gives permission to bear the consequences of that risk when one chooses to engage in the action. For instance, the person who injures themselves due to a skateboarding accident bears the responsibility for that injury. The person who loses money in the stock market bears responsibility for that lost money. The person who injures someone else while driving drunk bears responsibility for harming that other person. Likewise, if one knows that sex bears the risk of creating a new human, and that this human will inhabit one's uterus for nine months, then one has tacitly granted permission to live with this result through one's voluntary exposure to the risk.

But what if the woman claims she never intended to become pregnant? What if she even used contraceptives to prevent it from happening? That doesn't change the fact that she voluntarily engaged in an act that she knew would risk the creation of a new human life. It would be ridiculous for a skateboarder who injures himself to claim that it isn't his fault that he sustained this injury because he never wanted to be injured. Of course he didn't! Even if he wore knee pads and elbow pads in an attempt to prevent an injury and yet injured himself anyway, the injury still remains the consequence of his voluntary actions. Even if the stock market investor attempts to hedge and engage in various strategies to prevent losing money but loses money anyway, it is still the result of his voluntarily chosen actions. Even if the drunk driver claims that he never intended to hurt anyone, the fact that someone was hurt is still the result of his actions.

Why should the same not be said of a woman who voluntarily has sex in full knowledge of the potential consequences? Regardless whether she intended the pregnancy or attempted to avoid it, it's still the result of her actions, and she is responsible for it. And since pregnancy is the creation of a new human person with the right to life, the mother *is* responsible for that life. The father is also responsible, but it is the mother who must bear the physical consequences.

But there are two more reasons Boonin's example doesn't apply to the abortion issue. First, his example doesn't involve the *creation* of a new life but rather the decision to use one's body to sustain the life of another person. The man in need of a bone marrow transplant was not in that position *because of* his cousin. The cousin did not bring him into existence, nor did the cousin cause the bone marrow problem. In the case of a pregnancy, however, the prenatal life only exists because of the mother's (and father's) actions, and thus it would be accurate to say that she (along with the father) is responsible for it.

Second, Boonin's argument proves too much. If a pregnant woman is not obligated to keep her prenatal baby alive, why would she be obligated to keep her infant alive? Sure, adoption is possible after birth, but what if no adoptive parents can be found? What if the mother is stranded on an uninhabited island with her infant child, who could only survive through her breastmilk? (Let's say there is nothing on the island for the baby to eat.) Is she not obligated to at least do her best to keep the baby alive? If Boonin's argument is correct, then the mother has every right to let her baby die on the uninhabited island. But that seems intuitively wrong. If that scenario is wrong, then why would it be any less wrong to kill (which is more severe than passively letting die) her unborn baby?

* * *

Financial Inability to Care for a Child

Another argument in defense of abortion in certain situations pertains to poverty. How can it be right to force a woman to have a baby if she is financially incapable of caring for the child or giving it a decent life? Many women who get pregnant are in abusive relationships or live in poor neighborhoods with high crime rates. Wouldn't it be cruel to force women to try to raise children in such situations? Or would it push more children into the less-than-ideal foster home system?

This is a real quandary. Of course, it never seems justified to kill someone simply because they are all but certain to live a hard, underclass life. But if the life could be snuffed out while still in prenatal development, somehow that seems more justifiable. The pro-choice argument combines that sense of moral quandary with the statistic that low-income women, who are much less likely to use contraception, are five times more likely to have an abortion than middle- and upper-income women, concluding that abortion should be kept legal.[298] Since low-income women are mostly the ones who choose abortion, it should be kept legal to everyone for their sake. It would be too complicated and intrusive to force women to prove they are poor enough to obtain an abortion.

This may be a compelling argument, but it does not consider the moral value of the prenatal life. If there is good reason to think of the prenatal life as a person, and if our legal system is dedicated to protecting the lives of all persons, then the prenatal person's right to life trumps the mother's difficult circumstances, as hard as that may be to accept.

This problem, however, pertains more to poverty than it does to abortion. Rather than saying that abortion must remain legal because poverty persists, it would make more sense from a moral standpoint to address abortion and poverty simultaneously. One way to do this, as I suggested at the beginning of the chapter, would be to strengthen marriage. According to the National Abortion Federation (a pro-choice organization), the vast majority of women getting abortions are unmarried (83%). As of 2014, the CDC put the percentage at 85.5%.[299] Sixty-seven percent have never been married, and 16% are separated, divorced, or widowed. To quote the NAF, "Married women are significantly less likely than unmarried women to resolve unintended pregnancies through abortion."[300] The option of abortion, despite being most frequently and ardently defended by educated middle-class women, is mostly chosen by poor and unmarried women.

---

[298] Brookings Institute, https://www.brookings.edu/research/sex-contraception-or-abortion-explaining-class-gaps-in-unintended-childbearing/
[299] http://abort73.com/abortion_facts/us_abortion_statistics/
[300] National Abortion Federation, https://5aa1b2xfmfh2e2mkU3kk8rsx-wpengine.netdna-ssl.com/wp-content/uploads/women_who_have_abortions.pdf

If Christians want to effectively reduce abortion, then, the best change that could be made, short of a total ban, would be to alter the situation of poor, unmarried women for the better. But how would we go about this? As the previous chapters suggested, poverty would not be as severe a problem at the lowest end of the income spectrum if marriage was stronger, and marriage is weakened by the presence of the welfare alternative. Uprooting and fundamentally reorganizing social assistance to focus on community-oriented support and mutual aid would be a big step in the right direction.

What's more, there's some evidence to suggest that, in some cases, welfare paradoxically correlates with higher rates of abortion. According to the NAF, the abortion rate of women with Medicaid coverage is three times as high as that of other women.[301] But that may simply be a function of Medicaid being the healthcare provision of last resort for low-income people.

Laura S. Hussey from the University of Maryland uses data from the Fragile Families and Child Wellbeing study to demonstrate a partial correlation between women on welfare and rates of abortion. In predominantly pro-choice states where access to abortion is relatively easy, pregnant women on welfare choose abortion more often than women who are not on welfare. However, in predominantly pro-life states, where access to abortion is more difficult, pregnant women on welfare are *more likely* to have the baby than women who are not on welfare.[302]

Presumably, the women in pro-life states find it worthwhile to have the baby because (1) the threshold of effort required to obtain the abortion is high and (2) their babies will afford them increased benefits anyway. In pro-choice states, on the other hand, the threshold of effort required to have an

---

[301] http://abort73.com/abortion_facts/us_abortion_statistics/

[302] Hussey, Laura S., "Is Welfare Pro-life? Assistance Programs, Abortion, and the Moderating Role of States."
https://www.journals.uchicago.edu/doi/abs/10.1086/659227

abortion is lower but the welfare benefits of having the child are roughly the same. Women in these states tend to find abortion the better option than having the baby and collecting the benefits. But why would the women on welfare in pro-choice states be *more likely* than the average women to choose abortion? Probably because women on welfare are, by necessity, poorer than the average woman. They are also, by necessity, less likely to be married. And welfare has the unfortunate effect of incentivizing them to *remain* poor and unmarried.

Both of these scenarios present problems for the pro-life position. If abortion was totally banned but welfare remained more or less the same, Hussey's study suggests that there would be a significant rise in births to women on welfare. Moreover, having a child often precipitates a single woman going on welfare, and thus in this scenario where abortion is banned, the welfare rolls would expand significantly. How significantly? Very significantly. According to the NAF, almost half of all pregnancies are unintended. About half of those result in abortion.[303]

What would happen to those unplanned pregnancies in a world where abortion had been banned? Surely illegal abortions would still happen, but not to the same degree that legal abortions happen now. Perhaps women and couples would make greater attempts to prevent pregnancies, but of course, no prevention methods work 100% of the time. Simply put, if abortion was illegal but nothing else changed, there would be far more babies born in poverty, and more babies and mothers alike on welfare as a result. Already two-thirds of unplanned births are paid for by government programs such as Medicaid.[304] That reliance on state assistance would only

---

[303] https://5aa1b2xfmfh2e2mk03kk8rsx-wpengine.netdna-ssl.com/wp-content/uploads/women_who_have_abortions.pdf
[304] Sonfield, Adam and Kost, Kathryn. "Public Costs from Unintended Pregnancies..." https://www.guttmacher.org/report/public-costs-unintended-pregnancies-and-role-public-insurance-programs-paying-pregnancy

increase if abortion was banned without any corresponding change in the welfare system.

But the opposite scenario, in which state restrictions on abortion are removed, is equally troubling for the pro-lifer. When abortion is uninhibited, it naturally becomes more common, especially among women at the bottom of the income spectrum. Welfare dependence would likely be reduced, but only at the cost of many millions of abortions.

* * *

What is to Be Done?

It seems clear from Scripture that all life is a gift from God, that distinct humanity begins at conception, and that personhood begins sometime prior to birth. It's also noteworthy that the early church categorically denounced abortion. But that is not to say that the Bible, science, or the early church point to one moment in prenatal development when it would be murder to intentionally terminate the pregnancy. Unfortunately, they don't.

In the ages when the Bible was written, women found their identity predominantly in childbearing and motherhood. Today, however, the role of women in society has evolved to make childbearing and motherhood less necessary for many women to live fulfilling lives. As Richard Hays points out, "the canon—though it does not address abortion specifically— portrays a world in which abortion would be not so much immoral as unthinkable or unintelligible."[305]

Moreover, there is some evidence to suggest that the confluence of poverty, welfare, and sparsity of marriage contributes significantly to abortion. Without welfare, abortion would likely rise (at least temporarily). And without abortion, welfare dependence would likely rise. In a sinless world, there

---

[305] Hays, 449

would not be either either abortion or welfare. But sadly, we do not live in a sinless world.

How, then, can Christians be a light in the darkness on this issue? How can we live out the Kingdom of God in an imperfect world?

Theologians from the Anabaptist tradition like Richard Hays and Greg Boyd argue that the solution is not to enact certain government policies nor, indeed, does it have anything to do with politics. "The distinctly kingdom question is not, How should we *vote*?" writes Boyd. Rather,

> The distinctly kingdom question is, How should we *live*? How can we individually and collectively come under women struggling with unwanted pregnancies and come under the unborn babies who are unwanted? How can we who are worse sinners than any woman with an unwanted pregnancy—and thus have no right to stand over them in judgement—sacrifice our time, energy, and resources to ascribe unsurpassable worth to them and their unborn children? . . . How can we individually and collectively bleed for pregnant women and for unborn babies in a way that maximizes life and minimizes violence?[306]

For Boyd and other Anabaptists, political methods such as voting and picketing "costs us little," but the "kingdom approach costs us much." Political methods of stopping abortion like restrictions and bans exert power over others, but these are not the distinctly Christian approach, which emphasize bottom-up, voluntary, community-focused approaches. Hays agrees, writing of pregnant women in the church's midst that "the community must welcome her, bear her burden, and so fulfill the law of Christ (Gal. 6:1-2). If it were so, there would almost never be any need for a Christian woman to seek an abortion." And, echoing the Kingdom Community Principle, Hays concludes, "If this proposal

---

[306] Boyd, *Myth of a Christian Nation*, 143

sounds impractical, that is merely a measure of how far the church has drifted from its foundation in the New Testament."[307]

As an example of this community-focused, apolitical sentiment, Hays cites the Durham Declaration, a manifesto on abortion put out by a group of United Methodist pastors and theologians:

> We pledge, with God's help, to become a church that hospitably provides safe refuge for the so-called "unwanted child" and mother. We will joyfully welcome and generously support—with prayer, friendship, and material resources—both child and mother. This support includes strong encouragement for the biological father to be a father, in deed, to his child.[308]

Surely this kind of generosity, hospitality, and service ought to be second-nature to the church and to individual believers when it comes to helping pregnant mothers who are unmarried or financially incapable of caring for their child on their own. In some cases, it really does take a village to raise a child, and that village is the church body! This may mean considering adoption, or supporting adoption services and crisis pregnancy centers, or taking in and mentoring a young woman who is pregnant and feels alone. It involves *sacrifice*, either of time, money, or other resources. Surely this ought to be the *primary*, not the secondary or tertiary, way that the church combats the problem of abortion.

But the Anabaptist position also asserts that "we cannot coerce moral consensus in a post-Christian world" and thus the church "should not look to the state to compel women to complete, nor allow them to terminate, a pregnancy."[309] In other words, in the view of Boyd and Hays, Christians should

---

[307] Hays, *Moral Vision of the New Testament*, 453
[308] Ibid. 459
[309] Ibid. 457-458

remain completely apolitical on the issue of abortion—or, at least, it doesn't matter whether one is pro-life or pro-choice so long as believers are individually and collectively sacrificing for pregnant mothers and their prenatal babies.

But this argument isn't fully satisfying. Couldn't a Christian living in the mid-nineteenth century argue that slavery is wrong and should be avoided, *but* since it is impossible to coerce moral consensus, we ought to limit ourselves only to apolitical, sacrificial, voluntary methods of combating this societal problem? Wouldn't it be right to say that the government should ban the practice of forcing anyone into involuntary servitude? Likewise, if abortion *does* end an innocent person's life without their consent, then shouldn't it be banned by the government? Recall that the role of government is to punish and prevent harmful wrongs against others. Slavery is certainly a harmful wrong, and if abortion kills an innocent person, then it is also a harmful wrong. Therefore, it *would* be appropriate for Christians to encourage the government to prohibit abortion, just as it was appropriate for Christians to encourage the government to prohibit slavery.

Exactly when legal protection of life should begin is a question Christians can and should debate—both among ourselves and in the broader culture. But there is no question that it should begin before birth, and there is very good reason to believe it should begin before the third trimester, when brain activity has begun. A strong argument could even be made that abortion should be banned after the first few weeks of the second trimester, when prenatal babies can feel pain and react to external stimuli. By week 20, it's certain that the fetal life feels pain, perhaps just as much as a newborn. It gets more debatable during the first trimester, when the vast majority (roughly 90%) of abortions occur,[310] but it's a debate that Christians ought to have. We ought to wrestle, for instance, with questions about the morning-after pill. What kind of life has been terminated

---

[310] http://abort73.com/abortion_facts/us_abortion_statistics/

within the first few days after conception? Is it a tiny person or merely the precursor to a person? Is it morally wrong for Christians to use the morning-after pill as a form of contraception? Should it be illegal to use the morning-after pill or to use other chemicals to expel an embryo in later weeks of the first trimester? Christians need not have definite answers to these questions in order to make progress on abortion elsewhere.

So often the debate itself is framed in winner-take-all terms, but it doesn't need to be. Christians can work to chip away at abortion in ways that most people would agree on. Why not make our strongest appeal about the "low-hanging fruit" of this issue that is less morally ambiguous to most people rather than the more sweeping arguments on which agreement will be more difficult? Two examples of this low-hanging fruit are late-term abortions and public funding of abortion providers.

Images of late-term abortions are horrific and stomach-churning. Combine this with what we know about fetal development by the third trimester and the case against late-term abortions seems intuitive. Arguments about a woman's right to control her body gradually lose their instinctive appeal to most people the further a prenatal baby gets in its development. If the fetus feels the pain of the abortion, and if its brain has developed electrical activity like any other person, it just seems intuitively wrong to put it to death for the sake of the mother's convenience. If the pro-life movement articulated this argument, rather than emphasizing the argument that protection of life *must* begin at conception, progress would surely be made.

Likewise, progress could be made on the issue of public funding of abortion providers. Already, federal funds cannot be earmarked specifically for abortion procedures, but abortion providers such as Planned Parenthood are still subsidized with public funding. And according to the Guttmacher Institute, 14% of all abortions in the US are paid for by state-level public funding.[311] This, of course, helps to sustain their organization and continue to provide their abortion services. But why should it? Abortion is a contentious issue in America, and there are a range of opinions about when the protection of life should begin. How could it be right to force taxpayers to subsidize an organization that provides abortion services when there will inevitably be many who are morally opposed to such services? The argument made for the continued subsidies is that Planned Parenthood and other abortion providers also provide women's health services. But there are numerous other women's health organizations and clinics across the country, both religious and non-religious. The same level of subsidies could be shifted to those women's health organizations that *don't* provide abortion services. Doing this would arrive at the same desired result without forcing those with moral objections to abortion to provide subsidies for organizations that provide it.

Lastly, let us address the elephant in the room (no political pun intended). Before any political action prohibiting abortion after the first trimester, or any specific week during pregnancy, *Roe vs. Wade* would need to be overturned. The Supreme Court decision of 1973 ruled that every woman in America has a "right to privacy" that allows her to terminate her pregnancy (end the life of the fetus) at any point in her pregnancy. The *Planned Parenthood vs. Casey* ruling of 1992 allowed states to regulate abortion but also fundamentally upheld the right. This one-size-fits-all approach does not represent the diversity of opinions and beliefs about the beginning of personhood and legal rights. More importantly, it does not acknowledge in the slightest the moral value of the prenatal baby. Overturning the *Roe vs. Wade* ruling would return the full power to determine abortion policy to the states. At that point, individual states could design their own unique sets of laws surrounding the abortion issue, and Christians could argue for the protection of

---

[311] https://www.guttmacher.org/fact-sheet/induced-abortion-united-states

the unborn. In such an environment, nuanced approaches—rather than the black and white "pro-life vs. pro-choice" debate that plays out repeatedly—would become more common, as the United States would then have fifty individual sets of abortion laws, rather than one. (In a sense, there are already fifty sets of laws, but they are all limited by more extensive federal laws.)

Christians must remember, however, that even if *Roe vs. Wade* is overturned and abortion is prohibited or restricted, the need for the church to practice self-sacrificial love toward women experiencing unintended pregnancies will only rise. Indeed, it will rise dramatically. More time, money, and resources than ever will be required to care for the increase in scared, low-income mothers and their children.

Are we willing to make such sacrifices? Are we willing to give not only our money but also our time? Are we willing to house a single mother and her child in a spare room of our home? Are we willing to give her rides to job interviews and babysit her kids while she is at work? Are we willing to support or volunteer with organizations that provide her with counseling, childcare, or adoption services? Are we willing to bleed for her as Christ bled for us? Or, as is so often the case with poverty alleviation, do we merely want to outsource a difficult job to the government? Do we want to let the flawed foster care and welfare systems handle it for us?

The church *can be* a beacon of light, hope, and love in the midst of this complex issue, or we can be *merely* partisan. One thing is sure: there aren't any scared, poor, pregnant women who will find hope in a yard sign or bumper sticker. And a vote, on its own, shows no love to her or her baby. Only self-sacrificial love—something the government is incapable of providing—can lift her out of despair.

May we as the body of Christ resist the third temptation. May we resist the urge to use the levers of earthly power to escape from the harder, narrower path of self-sacrifice. May we always remember that what Christ did for us, we are called to do for others.

* * *

"But be doers of the word, and not hearers only, deceiving
yourselves."
James 1:22

CHAPTER ELEVEN

Culture Wars & Morality Issues

Twenty-first century Bible-believing Americans face a cultural impasse. Throughout the 20th century, we fought a prolonged, bitter culture war against the varied forces of secularism. The battlegrounds for this war were schools, universities, cinema, art, the workplace, sexual mores, and, woven through them all, the realm of politics. The courtroom proved the most significant battlefield.

And now, it can hardly be denied that evangelical Christians have definitively lost the culture war in America.

It may not be evident that evangelicals have lost the culture war until one steps back to look at the broad sweep of history. Battle after battle fought against the rising tide of secularism has ended in defeat. Perhaps one could point to a few victories here and there, but at best, they merely stemmed the tide for a short period. After each loss, aggrieved and aggravated evangelicals have organized to fight back, to restore order, to take our country back for God. Whether the subject is Darwinian evolution in schools or the legalization of gay marriage, we tell ourselves after each major political shift that we won't let this stand. We'll get the right people in office and judges on the courts to overturn these travesties and revive the Christian America that existed before the rise of secularism.

But, to our chagrin, we have found that even if we get the right people in office and the right judges on the courts, the steady advance of secularism does not stop. Evangelical

Christians thought that, perhaps, Ronald Reagan's administration would be the turning point in reversing the trend. When that didn't make much lasting change, we thought the turning point would come with George H. W. Bush's administration. When that bore no fruit, we thought it would come with George W. Bush's administration. But still the secularist trend continued unabated. Most recently, evangelical Christians rallied behind the person who perhaps least embodies Christian values and traditions in America—Donald Trump. Though many Christians did not initially support the egotistical philanderer-businessman, most eventually came around to voting for him. Part of the reasoning for this, as with Reagan and the two Bush presidencies, was the hope that Trump might blow some of the dust off of the old vision of Christian America. Even if Trump himself didn't exemplify that vision, maybe he could be persuaded by wise advisors to advance it.

American Christians have told themselves some variation of this story every fourth year for four decades. For at least half a century, evangelicals have wandered in an ever more secularist desert while the Promised Land seemed to grow further and further out of reach. The old Christian nation that once was is now only a dream, a pleasant memory in the minds of evangelicals. And the more time passes, the less likely it is that such a vision will ever be realized again. A cursory overview of history demonstrates this.

Though the Scopes Monkey Trial of 1926 officially ruled in the state's favor against substitute teacher John Thomas Scopes for teaching evolution, the highly publicized court battle opened America's eyes to the staying power of the theory of evolution. In 1968, *Epperson v. Arkansas* ruled that the teaching of evolution could not be prohibited. *McLean v. Arkansas Board of Education* ruled in 1982 that "creation-science" could not be taught alongside "evolution-science" in the classroom because the former was deemed a mix of science with the Christian religion. Christians fought the Darwinian advance for decades, but with every small step forward came several larger steps back.

Likewise, the *Engel v. Vitale* decision of 1962 rendered school prayer unconstitutional, and the following year, *School District of Abingdon Township v. Schempp* rendered mandatory Bible reading in schools unconstitutional. To this day, these two Supreme Court decisions have ranked among the least popular in American history, especially among Christians. Evangelical leader Jerry Falwell said, "When a group of nine 'idiots' can pass a ruling down that it is illegal to read the Bible in our public schools, they need to be called idiots."[312] But the laws remain, and their precedent has continued to expand. The *Santa Fe Ind. School District v. Doe* case of 2000 rendered even student-led prayer before a football game unconstitutional.

The same year the *Schempp* case was decided in court, Dr. Mary Calderone introduced sex education in schools, arguing that objective explanations about sex would have a greater dampening effect on teen and out-of-wedlock pregnancies than abstinence-only education. Here, again, evangelicals fought hard for decades to stamp out Calderone's method, arguing that it would only lead to more premarital sex. But sex education triumphed and remains dominant in public schools today.

In 2003, *Lawrence v. Texas* struck down all sodomy laws in Texas as well as thirteen other states, making gay sexual relations legal across the nation. And finally, in 2015, the most recent nail in the coffin of politically Christian America came in the form of the Supreme Court's decision in *Obergefell v. Hodges*, in which the right to marry was extended to same-sex couples in all fifty states.

Now American Christianity is conflicted about which direction to go, which path to pursue. Do we keep fighting this culture war that we've been consistently losing over the last century? Do we abandon the broader culture and retreat into

---

[312] Hartman, *War for the Soul of America*, 85

our Christian subculture? Do we embrace the cultural changes and simply try to explain them in Christian terms or nudge society toward Christian beliefs? Or is there some way out of the culture war? Is there a way to make peace in politics even if cultural and moral differences remain?

There are four main views on this issue in Christianity today, and those are **Social Conservatism**, the **Benedict Option, Compassion Politics**, and **Separationism**. Let's take a look at each of these views and compare them to each other.

* * *

Social Conservatism

A hundred years ago, there was scarcely the need for the term "social conservative" as a distinguishing characteristic of American political thought. In the early twentieth century, almost everyone agreed about most societal values, and those values were heavily influenced by Judeo-Christian thought and traditions because almost everyone was at least nominally Christian. In 1948, Gallup reported that 91% of Americans identified as Christian. Sixty-nine percent of those identified as Protestant and 22% as Catholic. Only 2% of Americans had no religious affiliation.

But the religious character of America changed in the mid-twentieth century as the effects of the Enlightenment matured into a strong secularist movement. In Gallup's 2016 survey, the percentage of self-identified Christian Americans had fallen to 71%. The losses are entirely accounted for by a shrinking number of Protestants, as Latino immigrants helped to keep the percentage of Catholics exactly the same — 22%. The biggest increase of religious affiliation from 1948 to 2016 were those claiming no religious affiliation, leaping from 2% to *18%*. The Millennial generation plays a large part of that increase, as more than a third of Millennials claim no religious affiliation.[313]

Early in the twentieth century, the teaching of evolution seemed instinctively objectionable to most people because it sounded like an assault on the foundations of the Judeo-Christian thought that undergirded society. The notion of jettisoning prayer from schools struck many the same way, along with sex education and eventually the legalization of gay sex and same-sex marriage. Over the course of the twentieth century, American society shifted away from its Christian influence to a posture of pluralism, social tolerance, and non-religiosity of state institutions.

Many evangelical Christians hope for a resurgence of Christian influence on society so that these trends can be halted or reversed. They would argue that a country's laws and social mores are a reflection of the morality of its people. Therefore, if we want to promote Christian morals and values in society, we must also seek to restore laws and social mores that conform to those morals and values. This is the view of **social conservatism.** It also carried the label "Moral Majority" in the 1980s and 1990s because, as the name suggests, believers persuaded by this view wanted to return America to a state where the majority of citizens adhered to Christian morality and shaped the nation's laws accordingly. Jerry Falwell, the founder of the Moral Majority movement, famously proclaimed: "This idea of 'religion and politics don't mix 'was invented by the devil to keep Christians from running their own country."[314]

Wayne Grudem calls his socially conservative stance "Significant Christian Influence" on government. "The 'significant influence 'view says that Christians *should* seek to influence civil government according to God's moral standards and God's purposes for government as revealed in the Bible

---

[313] Mike Hais, Doug Ross, and Morley Winograd. *Healing American Democracy: Going Local* (Blue Zephyr, 2018), 18
[314] Hartman, *War for the Soul of America*, 99

(when rightly understood)."[315] This sums up social conservatism in a nutshell. It's the view that a nation's laws ought to reflect biblical moral standards if believers in that nation are at all able to influence them.

To support this position, Grudem cites the Old Testament case of Daniel, who became an advisor to King Nebuchadnezzar and quite an influential political figure in Babylon. Consider, for instance, Daniel 4:27:

> Therefore, O king, let my counsel be acceptable to you: break off your sins by practicing righteousness, and your iniquities by showing mercy to the oppressed, that there may perhaps be a lengthening of your prosperity.

Grudem says that Daniel's exhortation to the king here "is the opposite of a modern multicultural approach" that would not presume to impose one's own moral standards on others. Rather than shying away from talk of morality, Daniel approached it head on with boldness and clarity: "*Break off your sins.*" Grudem surmises that, after this exhortation, Daniel likely went on to name "specific policies and actions of the king that were either good or evil in the eyes of God."[316]

Other examples of biblical figures who exercised a significant influence on secular governments include Joseph, who was the second highest authority in Egypt (Gen. 41:37-45, 42:6, 45:8-9); Moses, who stood before Pharaoh and relayed the message from God to "Let my people go" (Exod. 8:1); Nehemiah, who was cupbearer (an unofficial advisory role) to King Artaxerxes (Neh. 1:11); Mordecai, who "was second in rank to King Ahasuerus" of Persia (Esther 10:3); Esther, queen of Ahasuerus, who exercised significant influence on the king's decisions; and John the Baptist, who condemned Herod for taking his brother's wife "and for all the evil things that Herod had done" (Matt. 14:3-4, Lk. 3:18-20).[317]

---

[315] Grudem, *Politics According to the Bible*, 55
[316] Ibid. 58-59
[317] Ibid. 59-60

Grudem concludes that the church has "a *responsibility* before God to know what God expects of civil government and what kind of moral and legal standards he wants government to follow" and then to vote accordingly. In this way, Christians will act as the moral compass of their nation. "The simple fact is that if Christians do not speak publicly about what the Bible teaches regarding issues of right and wrong, there aren't many other good sources for finding any transcendent source of ethics, any source outside of ourselves and our own subjective feelings and consciences."[318]

Social conservatives argue that public speaking and teaching about morality *must* include political policies because, as Geisler and Turek assert, laws are inherently prescriptive. That is, they proclaim one behavior morally permissible and its opposite morally impermissible. Therefore, they say, "[w]e should legislate against what is objectively wrong regardless of whether or not it's difficult to enforce."[319] They would concede that laws can't change human hearts, but "even if laws can't make people *be* good morally, they can compel us to *do* good socially."[320]

Taken to its logical conclusion, then, social conservatism would call for many social laws to dramatically change. For instance, as Frank Turek has argued, no-fault divorce laws should be reversed, and divorce should only be legally allowable in cases of sexual infidelity.[321] Likewise, as Peter Sprigg, Senior Fellow at the Family Research Council, argued in a TV interview with Chris Matthews, gay sexual relations should be outlawed and the military should return to a "don't ask, don't tell" policy in which outed homosexuals are expelled

---

[318] Ibid. 69
[319] Geisler & Turek, *Legislating Morality*, 30
[320] Ibid. 35
[321] https://www.youtube.com/watch?v=_NXC4pD6l0w&t=2412s

from most military roles.[322]

Grudem quotes Jeremiah 29:7 in support of social conservatism: "Seek the welfare of the city where I have sent you into exile, and pray to the Lord on its behalf, for in its welfare you will find your welfare." Grudem says that in order to seek our city's (or nation's) welfare, we must seek "to bring good to its government (as Daniel did)." The only "true 'welfare 'of such a city will be advanced through governmental laws and policies that are consistent with God's teaching in the Bible, not by those that are contrary to the Bible's teachings."[323]

But, in my view, there are a few problems with Grudem's interpretation of Jeremiah 29:7, and with social conservatism's interpretation of other biblical texts. First, Jeremiah 29:7 is not directly referring to seeking the city's welfare through political means. As mentioned before, the Jews in exile typically commanded very little political power, so the original meaning of this likely had little to do with politics. And to whatever degree political means would be included in the instruction to seek the city's welfare, it's not clear that shaping secular state laws along the lines of Jewish morality is what is intended here. In fact, such an idea would probably strike the original audience as totally foreign to their thinking. God's moral law—the Torah—had been given to *one* people who had covenanted with God, and it was meant for *only* that people to follow. This is what made them holy—or "set apart"—from the other nations and tribes. Outsiders were brought into the covenant and under the Mosaic Law not through political dominance but through heartfelt conversion.

Rather than attempting to shape state laws along the lines of a distinctly Judeo-Christian ethic, Jeremiah 29:7's instruction for contemporary Christians is to seek the general welfare of one's fellow earthly citizens, promoting peace, prosperity, and

---

[322] http://www.nbcnews.com/id/35224225/ns/msnbc-hardball_with_chris_matthews/t/hardball-chris-matthews-tuesday-february-nd/%23.W7pJqhNKjR0* * *.W8PLmRNKjR0
[323] Grudem, 59

fair treatment for all. Sometimes that will involve politics in cases of oppression, such as slavery or systematic injustice against a certain class of society, but mostly, seeking the city's welfare will be non-political.

Similarly, Grudem makes the mistake of reading a political message into Daniel's admonition to King Nebuchadnezzar when he says, "break off your sins by practicing righteousness, and your iniquities by showing mercy to the oppressed." This, to Grudem, means that Daniel must have been advising the king to abandon the laws inspired by his own cultural mores in favor of adopting laws that conformed to Jewish morality. But there is no such indication in the text. Rather, we find that Daniel's message was directed specifically at Nebuchadnezzar's *personal pride*, and the only political implication for him was to "show mercy to the oppressed"—a policy that may be emphasized in Jewish moral teaching but is not exclusive to it.

What about John the Baptist's condemnation of Herod's actions? Again, we find no political implications of this in the text. John decried Herod's personal sins—taking his brother's wife and other evil things that he had done—not any political actions or policies. And Joseph, who held high political authority and stewarded it wisely, almost certainly did not attempt to impose distinctly Jewish morals onto a culture that would have been strongly opposed to many of them. At least, no evidence that he tried can be found in Scripture.

* * *

The Benedict Option

Some evangelicals despair at the current state of American culture and view social conservatism's efforts to mitigate or roll back secularist policies as a vain attempt to remain relevant as the political culture has moved on. They believe that the genie cannot be put back in the bottle. Now that it's out, it's going to stay out. The same rhetorical narrative that framed women's suffrage and desegregation as *progress* is now being used to frame LGBT rights, transgenderism, and radical feminism as causes of progress. Where Judeo-Christian culture once truly enjoyed a "moral majority" in America, that mantle of moral superiority has now shifted to the ideologues of the Left, known as "progressives." This ideology so pervades universities and media — from television to movies to music to cable news channels — that, by default, anyone who opposes it bears the onus to prove that they aren't a backwards-thinking "regressive."

Many evangelicals observe that, in the political realm, America is now more *post*-Christian than Christian. Law has been decoupled from religion. And, perhaps worst of all, the church is no longer widely viewed as a source of moral authority in society or political matters. What are Christians to do in such circumstances?

Some find an alternative in the life and teachings of Saint Benedict, a monk who lived in fifth century Italy. As the Roman Empire crumbled under the weight of decadence, corruption, and moral pluralism, Benedict fled the excesses of Rome to live simply in a rural area outside the city. Since Roman culture and politics had been so thoroughly degraded, Benedict found it impossible to inject Christian values into it. Such values would simply evaporate into the pluralistic cacophony. Instead, he founded an order of monks who focused on prayer, service, and rebuilding a distinctly Christian society. If the very big culture of Rome could not be mended, Benedict would start smaller, and those smaller enclaves of Christianity would be the salt and light that would draw in searching outsiders. These Christian communities served as wells of hope in the decades after the fall of Rome, and they helped the faith survive the loss of the Roman "Christian nation." This, according to Rod

Dreher, is the **Benedict Option**.[324]

The Benedict Option is predicated on the assumption that significant Christian influence on government was a good idea when Christians had a high probability of success — when the population identified more strongly as Christian and the culture was more Christianized. But now we are in a post-Christian culture in which the Moral Majority methods no longer work because we no longer *have* a "moral majority." Thus, as far as moral or social issues go, Christians should retreat from politics to focus on communities and institutions in which we can reinvigorate a distinctly Christian culture and from which we can reach out to affect the broader culture. These smaller communities and institutions include our church congregations, local communities, schools, and even city politics. In this way, we might actually be able to positively affect our culture. "Voting Republican, and expecting judges to save us, is over," says Dreher. "It's all about culture now."[325]

While the Benedict Option certainly acknowledges the steep uphill battle — if not impossibility — of turning back the clock and restoring America to its once strongly Christian orientation, its advocacy of full-scale cultural and political retreat is problematic. We may not be able to transform American culture wholesale, but does that absolve us from the responsibility to try? Likewise, trying to frame a legal system based on Christian morality for a society that largely bristles against those standards may be futile, but is futility the *only* reason we don't pursue this avenue?

* * *

---

[324] See Dreher, Rod. *The Benedict Option: A Strategy for Christians in a Post-Christian Nation*

[325] Dreher, Rod. "Benedict Option FAQ." https://www.theamericanconservative.com/dreher/benedict-option-faq/

Compassion Politics

Other Christians find both of these viewpoints wanting. A small but growing branch of Christians believes that the culture war is fundamentally misguided because of Christ's unique message of compassion. Unlike the moral code found in Jewish tradition that emphasized purity and cleanliness, expressed in the paradigm, "Be holy as God is holy," Christ shifted the focus of God's people to a new paradigm: "Be compassionate as God is compassionate." This radical shift of paradigm, argues theologian Marcus Borg, is all-encompassing. We have all sinned, and none of us can claim that our sin is better in God's sight than anyone else's sin. To say otherwise is to insert our own cultural biases into our theology. The fact that so much Christian energy has been poured into fighting a culture war and preserving laws about homosexuality, transgenderism, and the role of women demonstrates that Christians have forgotten the compassion paradigm of Christ and once again embraced the paradigm of the Old Testament.

"The dominant social vision [of the Israelites] was centered in holiness," writes Borg, "the alternative social vision of Jesus was centered in compassion." Many Christians, says Borg, have not fully comprehended what this means for their role in community and society. "To put it boldly: compassion for Jesus was political. He directly and repeatedly challenged the dominant sociopolitical paradigm of his social world and advocated instead what might be called a *politics of compassion*."[326]

In the Old Covenant, holiness—or "separation from everything unclean"—defined both moral and legal standards, as morality could not be decoupled from the Mosaic Law. Those who strayed from the Torah's instructions—including those who engaged in extramarital or same-sex relations—were

---

[326] Borg, Marcus. *Meeting Jesus Again for the First Time: The Historical Jesus & the Heart of Contemporary Faith* (HarperCollins: New York, 1995), 49

not only immoral but *lawbreakers*, worthy of punishment. Such violations of the cleanliness standards caused a person to become "unclean," which, unless reversed, would cause a person to be treated as an outcast. In that cultural context, though perhaps everyone sinned at some point in their life, the term "sinner" was reserved for those who had defiled themselves and become "unclean"—prostitutes, the diseased, the promiscuous. We see this mindset expressed by the Jews during Jesus's ministry, when they asked why Jesus would share a meal with "sinners."

Jesus, according to Borg, completely altered the paradigm for God's people—and in the process, refined our understanding of God Himself. Rather than a God who prioritizes holiness, separateness, cleanliness, and purity above all, Jesus portrays God as prioritizing mercy and compassion above all. Luke 6:36 is normally translated, "Be merciful, as your Father is merciful." But Borg believes "mercy" doesn't capture the full meaning of the original word, leaving out the element of heartfelt sympathy that is better captured by the term "compassion." Throughout his ministry, Jesus exemplified this focus on compassion over purity. Not only did he eat with those considered impure—an act that, in those days, signified mutual acceptance—he publicly *forgave* their sin! He accepted them as family, saying that those who followed him were his brothers and sisters and mother (Lk. 8:21). And he let even a promiscuous woman wash his feet in the presence of a pharisee (Lk. 7:36-50).

For Jesus, "purity is a matter not of external boundaries and observance but of the heart."[327] Pharisees are just as much sinners—if not more so—than those who carry the shameful label. The outwardly impure, according to Jesus, are no worse sinners than the inwardly impure. Therefore, no one has the right to treat anyone else as a worse sinner than themselves. We must insist on compassion rather than purity. And since this

---

[327] Ibid. 54

paradigm of compassion over purity is all-encompassing, meant to penetrate every area of life, our politics must also reflect an attitude of compassion rather than purity.

Borg says that much of the church — mainly those drawn to social conservatism — are tempted to fall back into a paradigm of purity rather than compassion. "In parts of the church there are groups that emphasize holiness and purity as the Christian way of life, and they draw their own sharp social boundaries between righteous and sinners." These Christians, according to Borg, have missed or ignored a significant element of Christ's teachings. "An interpretation of Scripture faithful to Jesus and the early Christian movement sees the Bible through the lens of compassion, not purity."[328]

For example, Borg argues that, "in addition to whatever nonreligious homophobic reasons may be involved," much of the church views homosexuality as a purity issue. "For these Christians, there's something 'dirty 'about it, boundaries are being crossed, things are being put together that do not belong together, and so forth." But this is the wrong way to view it, he says. "It seems to me that the shattering of purity boundaries by both Jesus and Paul should also apply to the purity code's perception of homosexuality."[329] Instead, operating under a paradigm of compassion, our goal both culturally and politically ought to be to reach out to LGBT individuals in an effort to make them feel loved and accepted.

The Supreme Court *Obergefell* ruling of 2015, then, should be celebrated as it broke down the last major barrier between gay and straight in the American political realm. It represented mutual acceptance no less than Jesus's sharing a meal with sinners. For Borg, just as there is no longer Jew or Greek, there is also no longer gay or straight. All should be treated equally under the law.

Unfortunately, Compassion Politics has one glaring

---

[328] Ibid. 59
[329] Ibid.

problem: it tries to purge the purity system from Christian morality *entirely*, which Jesus did not do. Notice, for instance, that when the promiscuous woman came to wash Jesus's feet and the pharisee objected, his response was not to insist on acceptance of her previous behavior or lifestyle. The woman didn't want that anyway. Rather, Jesus tells a parable of two debtors, one who owes more and another who owes less, both of whom are forgiven of their debts. Which one would be more grateful? The debtor who owed more, of course! Jesus uses this to illustrate that *both* the woman and the pharisee are sinners in need of forgiveness; only, one of them has acknowledged this while the other has not. "Therefore, I tell you," Jesus says, "her sins, which are many, are forgiven—for she loved much. But he who is forgiven little, loves little" (Lk. 7:47).

The view that Christians should push for the legality of any behavior that Scripture forbids is just as problematic as the view that Christians should push for the *illegality* of all behaviors that Scripture forbids.

Borg is certainly right that Christians ought to prioritize love and compassion for the LGBT community or anyone living in a way that is contrary to the lifestyle presented in the Bible. We are sinners no less than they are. But he and other progressive Christians go too far in jettisoning all social boundaries. God designed human beings a certain way, and we cannot simply discard elements of God's design if they create tension with our social vision of mutual acceptance. Nor should we push for the law to display moral standards that do not reflect a biblical worldview out of a desire to demonstrate mutual acceptance.

* * *

Separationism

Is there any hope of ending, or at least diminishing, the culture war so that the church can refocus its attention and energy on advancing the Kingdom of God? Recall from previous chapters the New Testament's vision of church-state relations. God designed church and state to function independently from each other, and that is how each works best. The church cannot fulfill the gospel by means of the sword, and the state cannot restrain and punish evil by means of the cross. Since our primary, God-given task on earth as the church is to spread the gospel and advance the Kingdom, we ought to abstain from government involvement in our task as much as possible. And since the government's sole, God-given task on earth is to punish and restrain evil, it ought to refrain from attempting to spread the gospel or advance the Kingdom as much as possible.

Christians, then, should stand for a strong separation of church and state, as the more the two mix, the less well each will be at fulfilling its God-given task. Hence the term **separationism.**

But can separationism actually have a positive effect on the culture war? Constitutional lawyer Douglas Kmiec thinks so (though he does not use the term "separationism"). He calls the idea that Christians can win the culture war through political means a "Fool's Game" that we ought to avoid.[330] Though good governance is necessary, "few of us seem to fully appreciate any longer that law cannot force moral consensus or instill virtue or character."[331] Therefore, "the more the law tries to impose or coerce virtue, the more likely it is to instill the opposite, raise false expectations, and worsen social tension."[332]

The real victories or losses in the culture war will not be—indeed, *cannot* be—in the political realm but in smaller social circles such as families, churches, and communities. As Kmiec puts it, "the primary agents in pursuit of cultural and individual virtue must be close at hand, part of what I call the smaller sovereigns—church, school, workplace, *and especially*

---

[330] Kmiec, Douglas. *Ceasefire on the Family: The End of the Culture War*. (Crisis Books, 1995), 5
[331] Ibid. 3
[332] Ibid. 2

the American family."[333] Politics is downstream from culture, as the saying goes. Political thought most often changes because cultural thought—and social mores—have already changed, or are in the process of changing. The *Obergefell* ruling, for instance, came after 36 states had already legalized same-sex marriage. Most of America had already come to accept the legitimacy of gay marriage, largely because the church no longer possessed moral authority to a sizable swath of Americans. Christians may blame the public school system, which may indeed deserve some of the blame for this development, but why not go further back and examine the responsibility due to parents themselves?

"The practice of virtue," says Kmiec, "comes from the observing of responsible parent and upright clergy, the family's closely applied discipline and encouragement of good behavior, and, ultimately, in the doing—of making right choices in sometimes difficult situations."[334] If children do not receive the discipline, training, and example of a virtuous life from their parents and role models, it is futile to expect teachers, employers, celebrities, or politicians to instill it later in life. Hence, "American families cannot afford to be distracted into playing a fool's game—the pursuit of truth and virtue principally, maybe even solely, through law and politics."[335]

Kmiec echoes our interpretation of Romans 13 that there is a limited function of law and political authority:

> The function of law is largely to keep the peace, to maintain order. In this, it is aimed most effectively at the control of conduct. The law is least effective when it tries to coerce belief. The law addresses external, not internal, man. While one hears the law described as a means of settling dispute, this is true to only a very limited extent. The law "settles" by employing a third party, usually a judge, to determine an outcome. If the

---

[333] Ibid.
[334] Ibid.
[335] Ibid. 5

> judge has faithfully employed relevant legal precedents (the law as announced in prior statute or cases), his opinion is said to be "well-reasoned," and the result is "settled" in the sense that no authority will listen to it further and the loser must comply under *force* of law. Odds are, however, the losing side retains the belief that it is right. The law has failed to persuade. It often does.[336]

This gets to the heart of the distinction between morality and legality. Morality comes from the heart and mind and is thus uncontrollable by external actors. It cannot be enforced by outside coercion. Legality is about behavior that citizens must—or must not—exhibit on pain of punishment. Observance of law can be enforced; moral conformity cannot. The church needs to recognize that "even if they can win the law to their side, it is impossible to compel the belief of another."[337]

While social conservative Wayne Grudem views the law as a legitimate means of teaching a citizenry right from wrong, Kmiec disagrees. "Neither law nor politics is up to the task of moral formation," he says. "Only the family, assisted by church, school, and workplace, can perform this function. Envisioning law and politics as primary moral educators merely aggravates cultural division." Indeed, if one could count the number of people who have been drawn to Christianity or had their faith strengthened as a result of the culture war, the number would likely be exceedingly few. The number who have left the church or had their faith weakened as a result of it are certainly many more. Statistics of religious identity—and Christianity's falling share of it—serve as evidence of this.

Again, though, we must confront the question, what *is* the function of law and politics? Contrary to the social conservatives' assertion that the law should forbid that which

---

[336] Ibid. 6
[337] Ibid. 10

is objectively wrong, Kmiec notes, "the mere fact that a law does not prohibit an activity does not mean that it is not wrongful or a vice." Excessive drinking or smoking, for example, may be morally wrong, but that doesn't mean we need laws to prohibit them. Disrespecting one's parents may be morally wrong, but it seems intuitively true that the government shouldn't be involved in prohibiting it. Rather, Kmiec quotes Thomas Aquinas, who argues that the law should forbid "only the more grievous vices, from which it is possible for the majority to abstain; and chiefly those that are injurious to others, without the prohibition of which human society could not be maintained."[338]

Aquinas' sentiment echoes that of Thomas Jefferson, which resonates with our interpretation of Romans 13 that criminal behavior — that which should be illegal — is any action for which retribution would be warranted. Such an action would be anything that causes or threatens to cause intentional, tangible, and undeserved harm to others. The separationist view holds that any behavior not warranting retribution falls outside the purview of law and government.

* * *

Specific Applications to the Culture War

Even if we fully accept the separationist view, there remain details to be worked out and issues to be wrestled with.

For example, whether or not it is wrong to smoke or consume marijuana, should it remain illegal? What evidence is there to show that it is any more dangerous or harmful than alcohol or cigarettes? We need to examine our hearts and ask if our arguments about the legal status of marijuana come from an earnest interest in the wellbeing of others or rather from a desire to moralize through the channels of state power. That is,

---

[338] Thomas Aquinas, *Summa Theologiae*, I-II, q. 95, a. 1, cited in Kmiec, 9

if we as the church advocate for the illegality of marijuana consumption, are we doing so out of a desire to use the levers of government as a means of moral instruction? If so, we need to acknowledge that we have given in to the Third Temptation; we are guilty of trying to use the government to carry out a task meant for the church. We have engaged in the futile exercise of attempting to change behavior before the heart has been changed.

With Paul, we must ask: What business is it of ours to judge those outside the church? Are we not to judge those inside it? (See 1 Cor. 5:12.) The "natural person" who has not yet accepted Christ "does not accept the things of the Spirit of God, for they are folly to him, and he is not able to understand them because they are spiritually discerned" (1 Cor. 2:14). Paul goes even further in Romans 8:7: "For the mind that is set on the flesh is hostile to God, for it does not submit to God's law; indeed, *it cannot.*" If this is true of non-believers, no human law administered by a secular government will ever be able to effectively teach or enforce God's moral standards.

As believers, we know that our bodies are temples to God through which we should glorify Him (1 Cor. 6:19-20), and thus our goal should not be to attain as much physical pleasure as possible but to be "filled with the Spirit" (Eph. 5:18). A strong argument could be made for Christians to avoid marijuana, then, unless there is some true medical use for it. But does this argument make sense to non-believers? Can it be translated into secular law? The answer to both is no.

What about other drugs? Surely if it's wrong for believers to consume marijuana, it's even worse to consume cocaine, ecstasy, heroine, crystal meth, and other hard drugs. Moreover, there's little evidence that any social good arises from the use of these drugs. But, when it comes to government policy, the question we as believers should ask is not whether it is morally wrong to use such drugs. We and most of society agree that it *is* wrong and harmful to the user. The two questions we should ask are (1) how would it be best to help the person who is addicted to these drugs, and (2) how can we diminish the chances of others becoming addicted?

Legitimate disagreements exist about how to answer these two questions, but we Christians need to ask ourselves if our current set of laws pertaining to illicit drugs are intended to moralize through punitive consequences for drug possession. A person caught with even a small amount of these drugs can be sent to prison for many years, if not decades. Is the motivation behind such laws the desire to rehabilitate or to punish? If the desire is to punish, we must ask ourselves if it fits with God's designated role for government to exact retribution on behavior that has not caused or threatened to cause intentional, tangible, or undeserved harm to anyone else. If the desire is to rehabilitate, we must ask if many years spent in prison is the best mechanism of achieving this. It is said that drugs are just as easy to come by — if not more so — in prisons than outside of them. Moreover, leaving prison with the scarlet letter of a felony on one's record often makes it more likely that a person will return to drugs (or worse crimes).

Of course, if one's drug use results in harm to an innocent person, state retribution is warranted. Besides that, however, we need to seriously question the efficacy of our current system. How much drug use has actually been prevented by the threat of punishment? Have drug users 'lives been bettered or worsened by passing through our justice and correctional systems? And most importantly, are we as the church guilty of giving in to the Third Temptation by trying to outsource to the government our role of administering the Kingdom's blessings? Rather than expecting the government to do something in our stead, should we not be asking what *we* can do to bring freedom from drugs to others? What programs, outreaches, or support groups can we facilitate in order to help each other and others achieve freedom from addiction?

Similar questions could be asked about gambling, pornography, prostitution, alcoholism, and other social ills. Do these behaviors violate biblical standards of conduct? Yes. Do they cause self-harm and moral degradation? Yes. But are they crimes worthy of retribution? In themselves, *no*. Is punishment or the threat of punishment the best way to prevent these social ills? In light of unredeemed humanity's sinful nature, again, our answer to that must be no.

One might object that Romans 13 makes clear the government is one of *God's* mechanisms for avenging sin in this age, and surely God will punish all sin that has not been covered by the blood of Christ. But the state is not necessarily God's mechanism for avenging *all* kinds of sin in this age. The kinds of sins that God avenges through the state are limited.

What about the issue of transgenderism? Scripture makes clear that God created humans to be male and female, two genders which correspond to each's biological sex (see Matt. 19:4-5). Transgenderism, the condition in which a person's gender identity does not correspond to their biological sex, does not fit into God's original design for humanity. A strong case could be made, then, that transgenderism is a psychological abnormality made possible only by the Fallen, sin-stained state of creation.

Christians ought to react to transgenderism in two ways. First, as a matter of practical evangelism, we need to recognize that *no identity of any kind is as important as one's identity in Christ.* That is, being cisgendered—where one's gender identity corresponds to their biological sex—should not be a prerequisite to entering into a relationship with God. Christ came to save *sinners*, a designation which in his day referred to those who lived outside of traditional norms and morality. If Christ came today, and the word "sinner" bore the same connotation that it did in the first century, then transgendered people would likely be called "sinners." Of course, many people, perhaps all of us, struggle with unchosen self-identity issues—whether it's body-image problems or egotism—that were not part of God's design or intent. So our priorities concerning transgendered people ought to be to introduce them to Christ *first*, and only after they have accepted Christ should we enter into a dialogue about their gender identity.

Second, in the political realm, Christians need to realize that no law will be able to dampen the trends of growing transgenderism. Nor will it be able to keep transgendered people out of public places, including public bathrooms. Support for laws against transgendered individuals using the bathrooms of their opposite biological sex creates a sense that Christians are *against* transgendered people, that we are singling them out with laws targeted against them. Such a strategy is a recipe for a heated culture war, as witnessed in North Carolina in 2016 when legislators passed a bill mandating individuals to use the bathroom of the sex assigned to them at birth. The bill triggered an impassioned reaction from a variety of groups ranging from the ACLU to the NBA.

When it comes to bathroom use, the Jethro Principle, also called the Principle of Localism, offers much wisdom. Property owners, school administrators, and local officials who know their customers or constituents should be allowed to set policy for their own domain of authority. What works in the suburbs of Houston may not work in urban San Francisco, and vice versa. What works at a retail store in one location may not work at a restaurant in another location. The various regions of the United States each have their own cultures, and the customers who frequent one store may be culturally different than the customers who frequent a different store. There need not be a one-size-fits-all solution to this unique and sensitive issue.

* * *

What About the Sanctity of Marriage?

American Christians fought for decades to keep "traditional marriage"—between one man and one woman— dominant over any alternative definitions of marriage. It was a well-intended struggle, meant to protect the Judeo-Christian character of marriage in American culture and government. But what is often lost on the Christians who fought in this area of the culture war is that the battle over the definition of marriage was just that—the clash over a *word*.

The government's definition of marriage had no effect whatsoever on the prevalence or suppression of sin in our society. Keeping a traditional definition of marriage did not prevent anyone from having same-sex relations, nor did it prevent same-sex couples from forming longterm relationships. It was a *symbolic* gesture showing the Judeo-Christian influence in American politics, but it did nothing in a practical sense to promote strong, godly marriages. Even as Christians fought to conserve this symbolic indication of our influence, the divorce rate among heterosexual couples (even self-identified Christian ones) crept up toward 50%.

To be fair, some social conservatives like Frank Turek call for ending no-fault divorce laws as well. To Turek, no-fault divorce is just as culpable for the breakdown of traditional marriage as the triumph of the "gay agenda." But blaming the degradation of marriage on no-fault divorce is like blaming symptoms for the disease. The symptoms are the result of the disease, not the other way around. Likewise, whether toxic marriages end in divorce, longterm separation, domestic abuse, or the suicide of a spouse, some marriages are ungodly and break down. Seeing the divorce rate rise due to a relaxation of legal divorce rules demonstrates that marriages weren't as strong as they should be to begin with.

Despite Turek's belief that no-fault divorce increased the divorce rate, studies have shown that divorce liberalization in the 1970s led only to a sharp, short-term spike in divorce rates that was reversed within a decade.[339] Stephanie Coontz demonstrates from her research that states adopting no-fault divorce laws experienced an 8-16% fall in wives 'suicide rates

---

[339] Wolfers, Justin. "Did Unilateral Divorce Laws Raise Divorce Rates? A Reconciliation and New Results."
http://users.nber.org/~jwolfers/papers/Divorce(AER).pdf

as well as a 30% drop in domestic violence occurrence.[340]

It should go without saying that, to the Christian, divorce is never a *good* thing. God hates divorce (Mal. 2:16), and His ideal is that the marital union should be permanent (Matt. 19:6). The only acceptable justification for divorce, according to Jesus, is sexual infidelity, because in that case the marriage covenant has already been broken (Matt. 19:9). The Mosaic Law allowed a man to divorce his wife "because your hearts were hard" — in other words, because of human sinfulness (v. 7-8). Believers, though, are held to a higher standard. God wants us to live the lives for which we were designed all along.

Does Turek want to restrict the legality of divorce to *only* cases of verifiable sexual infidelity? This would be a stricter standard than the previous divorce laws, which also allowed divorce in abusive situations. If not even the Israelites were held to the standard of God's ideal pertaining to divorce, how can the general public be reasonably held to that standard through a secular legal system?

Surely Turek is right to lament the rise in divorces due to unhappiness, abusiveness, or boredom. Surely he is right that the sanctity of marriage has been violated in a thousand ways in our generation. But our generation is not unique. We are not the first generation of sinful human beings who have violated the sanctity of marriage. Given that human sinfulness consistently produces toxic marriages, no-fault divorce might be the best policy for the *government* to follow. Of course, within our church congregations, we ought to teach and hold our fellow believers to a much higher standard.

What is the Third Temptation in this case? Remember that the essence of the Third Temptation is using earthly power and authority to carry out a task meant for the church. If marriage is a covenant relationship meant to symbolize the loving, faithful, and unending relationship between Christ and the

---

[340] Coontz, Stephanie. "Divorce, No-Fault Style."
https://www.stephaniecoontz.com/articles/article48.htm

church, who is capable of manifesting it? Only *believers*, empowered by the Spirit. That is why Jesus told his disciples, pertaining to his standards on divorce, "Not everyone can accept this word, but only to whom it has been given" (Matt. 19:11). Trying to impose these standards on those who have neither the Spirit nor any relationship with Christ is a futile endeavor.

What about gay marriage? Social conservatives argue that redefining marriage is a slippery slope: it may be same-sex couples today, but perhaps it will be polygamous marriages tomorrow. Perhaps even incestuous marriages or marriages between an adult and a child. Marriages of bestiality might even become in vogue!

Once again, we must remember the difference between morality and legality. Unredeemed humanity is and always has been depraved. Without heartfelt repentance and submission to Christ, no law could ever change that. And even after repentance and submission to Christ, believers are held to a law that is higher than whatever is contained in earthly legal systems.

Polyamorous and polygamous relationships have existed for a long, long time. Even David, a man after God's own heart, had at least seven wives (see 1 Chron. 3). Solomon had seven hundred (1 Kings 11:3). That doesn't mean polygamy is morally permissible, nor does it mean polygamy is likely to make a resurgence if made legal. Culture has changed and moved away from such relationships, except perhaps in fringe groups. But, in any case, is the law capable of preventing sexual perversions? Can it change what's in the heart? Can it produce, through force or the threat of force, godly marriages that symbolize the covenant between Christ and the church?

The answer is no. And that means that what the law allows for same-sex couples, polygamous groups, or any other perversion of God's design for marriage *does not matter to* Christians. It *cannot* hinder the implementation of true, biblical marriage. Only marriages between believers have the capability of demonstrating what God designed marriage to be.

All other relationships, even if deemed "marriages" by the government, are mere shades of this biblical covenant relationship. A toxic or abusive heterosexual marriage is no more a symbol of the covenant between Christ and the church than a same-sex marriage or a polygamous marriage. They all fall short of God's intent. To some degree, every marriage is flawed, but it is misguided to think that the law can fix this, or even mitigate it, by prohibiting gay marriage or restricting divorce. Only through the power of the Spirit can marriage between believers display this loving, faithful, and unending covenant.

* * *

Policy Implications

As Christians, we must recognize the distinction between the legal institution of marriage and the biblical covenant relationship of marriage. It is the covenant relationship that God designed and intended for us from the beginning. The legal institution is a man-made organization that developed many thousands of years later as the role of government expanded and penetrated more aspects of life.

This man-made organization confers special benefits in our legal system. For example, spouses don't pay estate taxes. Married couples can file jointly on their taxes, which may save quite a bit of money. Government benefits such as social security, Medicare, veterans stipends, and disability income can be transferred to spouses. Married couples can save money on health insurance by insuring together. Likewise, married couples can open joint bank accounts and jointly own property. They can also visit each other in the hospital without prior written permission.

Now that *Obergefell* has made gay marriage legal in all fifty states, have any of these lawfully granted benefits for gay couples threatened or impaired the biblical covenant relationship of marriage? Have they prevented any heterosexual couple who would like to enter into that covenant relationship from doing so? Simply put: no, they have not. The political war over the definition of marriage was about two different subcultures of America trying to dominate the other. The Moral Majority lost that battle, but biblical marriage didn't lose anything that it hadn't already lost.

That said, the current situation is not ideal either. Right now, the word "marriage" effectively has two meanings. It refers to both the legal institution of marriage, which includes gay couples, and the biblical covenant relationship, which (rightly understood) does not include gay couples. Though it would probably be too messy and complicated to completely extract marriage from government involvement, what the government calls marriage can feasibly be changed. *Obergefell* ruled that the legal institution of marriage cannot be restricted from gay couples, but no law or legal precedent (to my knowledge) demands that the legal institution be *called* marriage. It could be called a civil union, a domestic partnership, a familial unit, or anything that signifies the nature of the couple's legal status without conflating it with the biblical covenant relationship. And, importantly, the signature of an ordained minister should not be needed on the license. Why further conflate the two concepts by requiring clergy to sign a government document?

Effectively, this solution would change very little. Couples would still receive a license from the state in order to partake in the legal institution, but it could be obtained before or after the wedding ceremony since the officiant's signature is not required. And many who have such a license would continue to call themselves "married," even if they never partook in a wedding ceremony or religious ritual. But churches and religious institutions could then reclaim the word "marriage" and choose whom they are willing to marry and on what circumstances. Consequently, the meaning of marriage could be reclaimed by individual communities. Those that find "gay marriage" an oxymoron given the biblical definition of marriage would not have to sanction or conduct same-sex marriages. Congregations that approve of same-sex marriage would still criticize congregations that don't, and vice versa, but the two would not need to carry on the bitter tug-of-war battle in the realm of politics.

Our goal as Christians should not be to win the culture war through law or politics. That is a "fool's game." It is, in effect, giving in to the Third Temptation.

Rather, with Jeremiah 29:7 as our guiding principle, we ought to remember that we are citizens of a heavenly nation and are thus mere ambassadors to our earthly nation, not unlike the Israelites in exile. We are strangers in this land, a land that is under the influence of Satan the Deceiver. We must never forget that fact or be surprised and reactive when signs of Satan's influence appear. Rather, knowing this, we must aim for policies that seek the welfare of all our fellow citizens in this earthly land.

* * *

"Do not bring hastily to court, for what will you do in the end if your neighbor puts you to shame?"
Proverbs 25:8

CHAPTER TWELVE

Prosperity, Inequality, and Justice

"Inequality" is one of the buzziest of buzzwords in the Western world today, and not without good reason.

Income and wealth inequality are currently as high as they were in the Gilded Age of the Roaring Twenties, when the average man performed grueling manual labor for little pay while men like John Rockefeller and Andrew Carnegie swam in oceans of personal wealth the world had never before seen. Today's inequality, with billionaires like Jeff Bezos and Bill Gates claiming vast swathes of the world's wealth, rivals only the year 1929, just before the terrible stock market crash that precipitated the Great Depression.[341]

And the inequality is not limited to the United States. According to Oxfam, the world's richest one percent claimed 82% of the wealth created in 2017 while the poorest half of the world saw no net increase in wealth at all. In fact, the 42 richest people in the world hold the same wealth as the poorest half of the world combined (some 3.7 billion people). The wealth of billionaires has grown six times faster than the wages of average workers since 2010. According to Oxfam's report, it takes just four days for the CEO of a top fashion company to earn what a Bangladeshi garment factory worker will earn in a lifetime. US-specific inequality is a bit more mild: it takes a little

---

[341] See, for instance: Saez, Emmanuel and Zucman, Gabriel, "Wealth Inequality in the United States since 1913: Evidence from Capitalized Income Tax Data." (https://www.nber.org/papers/w20625)

over a day for American CEOs to make what it takes their average employee a year to make.[342]

Some, however, object to the way Oxfam calculates net wealth—subtracting liabilities from assets. "By Oxfam's measure, the poorest people in the world are recent Harvard graduates with student debt piles," says Ben Southwood of the Adam Smith Institute. "Having negative wealth may actually be a sign of prosperity, since only people with prospects can secure a loan."[343]

Others suggest that measuring wealth inequality by any one snapshot in time is misleading. More important is to look at patterns of income and wealth over time and whether individuals experience increases or decreases in their economic wellbeing. This is called "income mobility" in economics. Dr. Anne Bradley of the Institute for Faith, Work, and Economics uses data from a 2008 US Treasury Department report about income mobility. "Roughly half who started in the lowest quintile in 1996 moved into a higher quintile by 2005, in only nine years." What about the ultra-rich 1% of income earners? According to the data, they are more likely to slip downward in income from year to year than remain at that elevated level. Of those in the top 1% in 1996, 58% moved into a lower group by 2005. Forty-five percent of the top 5% moved lower in the same time period, and 39% of the top 10% likewise moved lower.[344]

It's also important to note that, as researchers from the Bank of England and the International Monetary Fund have shown, *global* wealth inequality has actually fallen in recent decades as the incomes of those in developing countries rise,

---

[342] https://www.oxfam.org/en/pressroom/pressreleases/2018-01-22/richest-1-percent-bagged-82-percent-wealth-created-last-year

[343] Farley, Harry. "Oxfam and inequality: The profound unfairness of the gospel." (https://www.christiantoday.com/article/oxfam-and-inequality-the-profound-unfairness-of-the-gospel/76966.htm)

[344] Bradley, Anne. "Does Hard Work Pay Off? Why Income Mobility Matters." (https://tifwe.org/does-hard-work-pay-off-why-income-mobility-matters/)

even if wealth disparities in certain countries continue to rise.[345]

* * *

What Caused the Rise in Inequality?

Before moving on to a moral and biblical discussion of inequality, it will be useful to cover some of the most commonly cited potential causes of the recent rise in income and wealth inequality.

A wide variety of plausible contributing factors have been suggested. Take, for example, assortative mating—the phenomenon that marriages tend to be between those in the same socioeconomic class and cultural background. If children of successful parents grow up and choose a spouse with similarly successful parents, and the same thing occurs with children of unsuccessful parents, over generations the successful will continue to get more successful, and the unsuccessful will remain unsuccessful.[346]

The decline of union membership has also been suggested as a contributing factor in inequality. This is certainly a plausible suggestion for those who belong to some of the more effective unions, though an argument can be made that those workers would have been successful without organized collective bargaining.

The decline in well-paid manufacturing jobs for the relatively low-skilled is another plausible culprit, as the disappearance of those jobs has pushed down the labor force participation rate in certain parts of America. Those who kept working often transitioned to lower-paying service jobs. Many of those that did not continue working transitioned to welfare dependence.

---

[345] Hellebrandt, Tomas and Mauro, Paolo. "The Future of Worldwide Income Distribution." (https://papers.ssrn.com/sol3/papers.cfm?abstract_id=2593894)

[346] Greenwood, Jeremy, et. al. "Marry Your Like: Assortative Mating and Income Inequality." (http://pareto.uab.es/nguner/ggksPandP-December2013.pdf)

Considering the correlation between single motherhood and crime, lower labor force participation, and other negative life outcomes, the disintegration of the family plausibly deserves some of the blame.

Anne Bradley of the Institute for Faith, Work, and Economics suggests a few additional contributing factors, citing previous work by author Frank Levy. Family structure is one. In households where both parents and sometimes a teenager or young adult work, the number of wage-earning workers might be multiples larger than households with only one worker. More workers living under the same roof means greater income and less expenses.

The evolution of technology is another factor. Robotics, automation, and artificial intelligence have replaced countless jobs and prevented many more from being created in the first place. The jobs that this evolution in technology *have* created are disproportionately high-skilled and high-paying jobs, thus widening inequality.

Growing markets have also paved the way for increased inequality. Globalization has opened markets across the world for the mature companies of developed countries to sell their products into. This makes an increasing amount of revenue flow upward to the owners and executives of those companies. Globalized markets have also created competition among low-skilled laborers of different countries who previously did not compete with one another. For instance, as the cost of living is cheaper in countries like China, India, Indonesia, and Mexico, workers command lower wages than American workers whose cost of living is much higher. Many manufacturing jobs have been outsourced in order to lower the cost of production and ultimately lower the prices of consumer products. The loss of jobs obviously promotes inequality, offset only somewhat by lower consumer prices.

Lastly, Dr. Bradley mentions the influx of primarily low-skilled immigrants who have competed for American jobs and driven down wages for low-skilled jobs.[347]

But there is one contributing factor in rising income inequality in the last few decades that has only recently been validated by substantial research. It is the idea that central bank monetary policies have disproportionately enriched the already wealthy while hurting the poor and middle class. How could something as arcane as monetary policy have an effect on the distribution of people's real income and wealth? The first thing to understand is that different groups benefit from higher and lower interest rates. Higher interest rates mostly benefit the lower and middle classes—those who tend to stash extra money in a savings account or certificate of deposit, or retirees who are living off the income from bonds. Low interest rates, on the other hand, mostly benefit wealthier people who borrow money to invest in businesses or other income-generating assets such as stocks and rental properties (real estate).

With this in mind, it's enlightening to compare a chart of the top 1% of income earners 'total share of US income with a chart showing the Federal Funds rate (the ultra-short term interest rate set by the Federal Reserve which affects all other interest rates in the market). Top income earners 'share of total US income—a convenient measure of inequality—fell from the stock market crash of 1929 to around 1980 or 1981, then the trend abruptly reversed and began its upward march again until arriving today at roughly the same level as the Gilded Age of the late 1920s (another time of historically low interest rates).[348] What happened to the Fed Funds rate during this time? It rose steadily from ultra-low rates in the middle of the century to peak in 1981, then fell steadily until hitting close to zero in December of 2008.[349] Is it a coincidence that the share of income garnered by top earners fell and rose in exactly the

---

[347] Bradley, Anne. *For the Least of These: A Biblical Answer to Poverty* (Zondervan: Grand Rapids, 2014), 156-158

[348] "Income Inequality in the United States." (https://inequality.org/facts/income-inequality/)

[349] "Effective Federal Funds Rate." (https://fred.stlouisfed.org/series/FEDFUNDS)

opposite pattern as that of interest rates? An increasing number of experts think not.

Banking policy researcher Karen Petrou is one of these experts. Noting that inequality has spiked even further since the Great Recession, she explains that

> the Fed's low-interest policy gave rise to yield-chasing. And what has the stock market done since 2010? Everybody who has money has seen their financial assets appreciate dramatically. Everybody who doesn't have money, which is the bottom 90%, what is their principal source of wealth? Houses? House-price appreciation for expensive houses is way up since 2012. But overall, real U.S. house prices are down 10%.[350]

She adds that Fed monetary policies have dropped "interest rates to very low levels, making savings a losing game even as the wealthy are motivated to buy more financial assets to maximize yield wherever they can."[351] Moreover, ultra-low interest rates also incentivize corporations to take on short-term debt in order to buy back their own shares, further lifting equity prices and benefiting equity holders (and corporate executives).

But dropping interest rates has only been one of the Fed's engines of inequality acceleration. The other has been quantitative easing (QE) — the practice of creating money out of thin air in order to purchase Treasuries and mortgage-backed securities from banks. The purpose of QE was to stimulate economic activity by injecting liquidity and the ability to continue lending to American banks. But QE did not accomplish that goal, as banks mostly kept the proceeds rather than reinvesting them.

---

[350] Nocera, Joe. "We Wanted Safer Banks. We Got More Inequality." (https://www.bloomberg.com/opinion/articles/2018-08-06/inequality-why-bank-rules-and-fed-rates-hurt-middle-class)

[351] Petrou, Karen. "The Fed's Unintended Impact on Income Inequality." (http://www.fedfin.com/blog/2126-karen-petrou-on-the-fed-s-unintended-impact-on-income-inequality)

What QE *did* accomplish was exacerbating wealth inequality. Petrou writes, "Of all the actions the Fed has taken since the crisis, its huge portfolio is the one that's done the most to make America far more unequal than it otherwise might be."[352] Prior to the coronavirus pandemic in 2020, this portfolio of debt assets purchased with fiat-created money stood at $4.5 trillion at its largest. That $4.5 trillion of debt assets, having been effectively removed from the market, lowered interest rates even more, further punishing savers and pushing investment capital into riskier assets such as stocks and real estate—assets already held by the wealthy.[353] This pushed up the values of desirable housing, leading to a fall in home affordability and a rise in the percentage of renters, "creating what is now referred to in Britain as 'generation rent.'"[354]

Data bears out this theory. First, the idea that the wealthy disproportionately own financial assets such as stocks and real estate is not just conjecture. NYU economist Edward N. Wolff shows that, as of 2016, the richest 10% of American households owned 84% of US stocks. This is up from the 77% owned by the top 10% in 2001. While only 27% of the middle class have "significant stock holdings" ($10,000 or more), 94% of the rich do.[355] And stocks have performed phenomenally well since the early 1980s.[356]

A study sponsored by the Federal Reserve Bank of

---

[352] Petrou, Karen. "Nice Talk, but Only Fed Action Will Reduce Inequality." (http://www.fedfin.com/blog/2810-karen-petrou-nice-talk-but-only-fed-action-will-reduce-inequality)

[353] See Bianchi, Giulio Alberto. "To Be Made Sick by Medicine: Quantitative Easing and Inequality After the Crisis." (https://digitalcommons.iwu.edu/uer/vol13/iss1/1/)

[354] Paul, Jean-Michel. "Easy Money of Stimulus Made Life Harder for Some." (https://www.bloomberg.com/opinion/articles/2018-04-10/qe-and-inequality-the-two-seem-to-go-together)

[355] "Richest 10% of Americans Now Own 84% of All Stocks." (http://time.com/money/5054009/stock-ownership-10-percent-richest/)

[356] "Dow Jones - 100 Year Historical Chart." (https://www.macrotrends.net/1319/dow-jones-100-year-historical-chart)

Minneapolis offers concurring data, concluding:

> Middle class portfolios are dominated by housing [primary residences], while rich households predominantly own equity. An important consequence is that the top and middle of the distribution are affected differentially by changes in equity and house prices. Housing booms lead to substantial wealth gains for leveraged middle-class households and tend to decrease wealth inequality, all else equal. Stock market booms primarily boost the wealth of households at the top of the distribution.[357]

When the housing market collapsed in 2007-2009, the middle class collapsed with it. While median household net worth stood at $102,200 in 2004 and $120,300 in 2007,[358] it had slumped to only $97,300 by 2016.[359] But due to Fed monetary policy, the wealthy soared out of the ashes of the crisis like the phoenix. An even more recent study published in the Journal of International Money and Finance uses a century of data to demonstrate that low interest rates have increased returns of stocks and real estate and thus have exacerbated income inequality.[360]

Researchers from the Brussels-based Bruegel Policy Contribution arrive at the same conclusion based on their study of European countries, giving the following summary:

> Low interest rates, asset purchases and other accommodative monetary policy measures tend to increase asset prices and thereby benefit the wealthier segments of society, at least in the short-term, given

---

[357] "Income and Wealth Inequality in America, 1949-2016."
(https://www.minneapolisfed.org/institute/working-papers-institute/iwp9.pdf)
[358] https://www.federalreserve.gov/econres/files/2007_scf09.pdf
[359] https://www.federalreserve.gov/publications/files/scf17.pdf
[360] "Income inequality equities, household debt, and interest rates: Evidence from a century of data."
(https://www.sciencedirect.com/science/article/pii/S0261560617301894)

that asset holdings are mainly concentrated among the richest households.[361]

A sharp steepening of inequality has been observed recently even in relatively egalitarian Denmark, where, according to a 2015 Danish Economic Council report, "larger incomes from equity investments and lower interest rate payments were partially responsible for the increase in inequality because they have increased the disposable income of people who own financial assets."[362]

This commonsense explanation of the rise in inequality has been embraced to some degree or another by economists on both the political Left, such as Joseph Stiglitz,[363] and the political Right, such as Kevin Warsh.[364]

* * *

Is Racial Equality a Myth?

Whatever the reason or reasons for the income gap, progressive Christians argue that the substantial gap between rich and poor signifies the existence of structural inequalities that make upward mobility much harder for certain kinds of people. For ethnic minorities and women (and some would add the LGBT community), they say, life is much more difficult because of the lasting ripple effects of historic oppression as

---

[361] Claeys, Darvas, Leandro, and Walsh. "The Effects of Ultra-Loose Monetary Policies on Inequality." (http://bruegel.org/2015/06/the-effects-of-ultra-loose-monetary-policies-on-inequality/)

[362] Nelson, Eshe. "Inequality is rising in Denmark, and negative interest rates are to blame." (https://qz.com/809970/inequality-is-rising-in-denmark-and-negative-interest-rates-are-to-blame/)

[363] Stiglitz, Joseph. "Fed's Zero-Rate Policy Boosts Inequality." (https://blogs.wsj.com/economics/2015/06/04/the-feds-zero-rate-policy-boosts-inequality-nobel-economist-joseph-stiglitz-says/)

[364] Wessel, David. "Kevin Warsh, Don Kohn on QE and Inequality." (https://www.brookings.edu/blog/up-front/2015/06/10/kevin-warsh-don-kohn-on-qe-and-inequality/)

well as subtler, less visible forms of oppression that persist today. In these cases, merely tending to the needs of the disadvantaged is not enough. "The Church is very good at feeding the poor, looking after the elderly, and seeing to the needs of the community," says one writer for Christianity Today, "but there are times when we have to change the system itself."[365]

Racial equality is one area in particular the church needs to improve upon, argues Ken Wytsma in his book, *The Myth of Equality*. The myth of racial equality, Wytsma says, is one that many white Christians are prone to believe nowadays because our laws no longer reflect the racism that once pervaded a broad swathe of our culture. Nevertheless, our culture and political system still bear some of the ripple effects of previous generations' racism, and Christians should play an active role in uprooting it.

Wytsma's line of reasoning begins with a bold assertion about the origins of racism: while we might be tempted to assume it has been around since the early days of humanity, racism is actually a relatively new thing. It originated in Europe during the era of exploration and colonialism, when white Europeans began interacting with other (typically less technologically advanced) ethnic groups around the globe. "Racism was appropriated as a handy way of justifying—in the name of conquest and even of religion—the robbery, subjugation, enslavement, and murder of entire people groups."[366] Viewing these ethnic groups as lesser than the white Europeans enabled white people to see themselves as the rightful stewards—or masters—of these lesser races. Hence the title of the famous Rudyard Kipling poem, "The White Man's Burden"—referring to the burden of empire.

---

[365] Davies, Louise. "Why Christians should care about massive inequality—and what we should do." (https://www.christiantoday.com/article/why-christians-should-care-about-massive-inequality-and-what-we-should-do/124417.htm)
[366] Wytsma, Ken. *The Myth of Equality* (InterVarsity Press: Downers Grove, 2017), 30

In short, Wytsma says, "the roots of the racism that continues to plague our culture today are to be found in the deliberate programs of 'Christian' Europeans near the end of the fifteenth century."[367]

But even after the end of slavery in the United States, systemic racism continued in the form of nearly a hundred years of segregation. And after the end of segregation, African Americans remained oppressed by other laws that targeted them, such as the drug war.

Data show that whites and blacks use drugs at similar rates, and more whites are dealers; yet while African Americans make up roughly 13 percent of the US population, they make up 31 percent of all those arrested for drug violations and nearly 40 percent of those incarcerated for drug-related convictions.[368]

Redlining was another method of systemic racism in the first half of the twentieth century. The term refers to the Federal Housing Administration's practice of mapping neighborhoods in order to determine which would be eligible for FHA mortgage loans. Neighborhoods could score an *A* through *D* score. *A* neighborhoods "lacked a single foreigner or negro" and were outlined in green, while *D* neighborhoods were those with black people living in them and were outlined in red — ineligible for FHA loans.[369] Wytsma asks,

> Have you ever wondered why America remains as segregated as it is, long after segregation in schools and public facilities was outlawed? The answer is simple: racial policies, to a large degree, directed, dictated, and determined the racial makeup of neighborhoods in America.[370]

These policies and their lasting effects have been less easy

---

[367] Ibid. 41-42
[368] Ibid. 62
[369] Ibid. 74
[370] Ibid. 75

to see for white Americans, according to Wytsma, because of the persistence of white supremacy in our thinking. He is not referring to the "hard" white supremacy marked by the "intentional building and maintaining of white power by those who did not or do not believe in equality." Rather, he is referring to the "soft" white supremacism that remained after "hard" white supremacy had been dismantled—the "white normative standard" against which all other races and cultures would be judged.[371]

This standard in America that whiteness and that which is associated with being white is "normal" and everything else is "abnormal" has tacitly granted white people a position of privilege in society not enjoyed by other races. However, "white privilege" is often misunderstood, says Wytsma. It doesn't mean that every white person is a rich aristocrat without problems. "White privilege doesn't mean your life isn't hard. It means that if you are a person of color, simply by virtue of that, your life might be harder." Therefore, "even if you're the unluckiest white person born in the United States, you were still born into a fortunate race."[372]

In Wytsma's view, justice is about transforming the world into the way it ought to be, what may broadly be called "restorative justice." "*Restorative justice* refers to all of the actions and efforts undertaken to make right the broken, bent, or perverted relationships in the world today."[373] As an example of restorative justice, Wytsma offers none other than Jesus Christ: "our salvation, wrought by Christ, is an act of restorative justice, baptizing us as new members in his body, into a shared missional reality."[374] By becoming human in the first place, Jesus was foregoing a position of infinite privilege ("equality with God") and humbling himself ("taking the form of a servant") so that humanity might come to know and

---

[371] Ibid. 20
[372] Ibid. 25-26
[373] Ibid. 109
[374] Ibid. 114

worship God (see Phil. 2:5-11). Followers of Jesus, likewise, should forego our various forms of privilege in order to better serve others.

While Wytsma gives some very helpful and insightful ways in which believers can carry out the ministry of reconciliation (2 Cor. 5:18) within the church, he also argues for the church to support a few controversial political movements—affirmative action and reparations. We'll get to these shortly, but first we need to assess the veracity of Wytsma's overarching line of reasoning.

Surely he is right about the egregious injustices forced upon black people and other minorities in the history of America and Western European countries. Support for slavery and segregation during their respective eras will forever be a stain on the church. Moreover, it is certainly true that, even after desegregation, African Americans have faced varied and widespread discrimination that has impeded their material success. As President Lyndon Johnson stated, "You do not take a man who, for years, has been hobbled by chains, liberate him, and bring him to the starting line of a race, saying, 'You are free to compete with all the others' and still justly believe you have been completely fair."[375]

However, Wytsma's reasoning also has some flaws. First, his view that racism as we know it today is an invention of colonialist Europeans is exceedingly Eurocentric and displays a narrow understanding of history. Elizabeth Culotta argues in Science Mag, based on a plethora of studies, that racism is merely a subset of a universal human trait: tribalism. Human brains are wired to associate with a tribe of similar people and to view those outside the tribe with suspicion. "The targets of outgroup prejudice vary from culture to culture and over time," says Culotta. Sometimes it's based on religious differences, other times geographical differences, and sometimes it's racial

---

[375] Sowell, Thomas. *The Quest for Cosmic Justice* (Touchstone: New York, 1999), 11-12

differences.[376] Perhaps it appears as though white European racism began in the fifteenth century simply because Europeans suddenly began interacting with racial groups of which they were previously unaware.

But another problem with Wytsma's view is that the sins of racism *and even slavery* were not exclusive to white Europeans. Many other races and cultures throughout history have looked down upon and enslaved members of other races. Take, for example, the lucrative Barbary slave trade that existed around roughly the same time period as the Trans-Atlantic Slave Trade. Robert Davis of Ohio State University estimates that, between 1530 and 1780, around 1-1.25 million Europeans were captured from coastal towns in Italy, Spain, Portugal, France, England, and even Iceland to be sold to Arabs in North Africa and Arabia.[377] Likewise, the Ottoman slave trade, which continued into the early 20th century, mostly trafficked in white Eastern Europeans and Circassians from the Caucasus region as well as black people from sub-Sahara Africa. This phenomenon led to the appearance of an article in the *New York Daily Times* in 1856 about the mass enslavement of white Circassians at the hands of the Ottoman Turks.[378]

The idea that racism is an inherently *human* problem—rather than one invented by white colonialist Europeans—is fairly easy to prove. For example, in recent years there have been a number of discriminatory incidents against black people in India, revealing racist attitudes against African

---

[376] Culotta, Elizabeth. "Roots of Racism."
(http://science.sciencemag.org/content/336/6083/825)
[377] "When Europeans Were Slaves: Research Suggests White Slavery Was Much More Common than Previously Believed." (https://news.osu.edu/when-europeans-were-slaves--research-suggests-white-slavery-was-much-more-common-than-previously-believed/)
[378] "Horrible Traffic in Circassian Women—Infanticide in Turkey." (https://lostmuseum.cuny.edu/archive/horrible-traffic-in-circassian)

immigrants.[379] Obviously, the Indians involved in these discriminatory acts are not white Europeans. Nor are they seeking intellectual justification to subjugate or enslave Africans. Rather, they simply view these members of a minority race as *different*—outside of their tribe. That doesn't excuse discrimination, but it does explain it in a narrative contradictory to that of Wytsma.

Likewise, in ancient China, there existed racism between the Chinese and Mongols, between the Chinese and Japanese, and on the part of the Chinese toward Westerners as well as minorities such as the Wusun people (an Indo-European nomadic group), who one Chinese writer of the seventh century referred to as "barbarians with green eyes and red whiskers, like the macaques [monkeys]."[380] Clearly, the racism of the Han Dynasty-era Chinese toward foreigners or ethnic minorities in no way fits the narrative of racism being either an invention of white Europeans or a justification for subjugation or enslavement.

One last piece of evidence to consider: preference for one's own racial group is detectable even in infancy, as 6-month old babies have been shown to demonstrate racial bias toward their own race, according to a study by University of Toronto researchers.[381] It's certainly difficult to think that infants are plotting the subjugation of each other! Rather, it's more likely that the human brain is wired to sympathize with familiar and similar people—those in our tribe—and distrust others.

This calls into question Wytsma's assertion that the problem of racism in America today is singularly about "soft" white supremacism in the form of a white normative standard

---

[379] Prabhu, Maya. "African victims of racism in India share their stories." (https://www.aljazeera.com/indepth/features/2017/04/african-victims-racism-india_share-stories-170423093250637.html)

[380] http://www.guoxue123.com/shibu/0101/01hsyz/111.htm [translated with Google Translate]

[381] "Infants show racial bias toward members of own race and against those of other races." (https://media.utoronto.ca/media-releases/infants-show-racial-bias-toward-members-of-own-race-and-against-those-of-other-races/)

against which other races and cultures are judged. If racism is an inherent human trait, then there are as many racial normative standards as there are races. That is because we associate the specific culture and traits of our tribe with the "normal." All else is suspect. There may be a white suburban normative standard, but there may also be a white working class normative standard, a black upper class normative standard, a Hispanic working class normative standard, etc.

The burden, of course, would fall on the majority race and socioeconomic class in any society to overcome their inherent bias and refrain from imposing it on others. White privilege, then, can basically be boiled down to the same privilege enjoyed by majority races and socioeconomic classes everywhere. A white person with a hard life, simply by virtue of her race, would have an even harder life living in a majority black society. A Hispanic person with a hard life, simply by virtue of her race, would have a harder life in a majority Asian society. And so on.

None of this is to diminish the plight of African Americans or other racial minorities in the Western World. It is simply to clarify the *reason* for their plight. It takes work to overcome one's innate prejudices, and that is a challenge *we all* must face, especially those in majority races and cultures.

As a final point, it must be acknowledged that American society—and likely other Western nations with similar racial makeups—have made great progress toward equal treatment of all races in society. Despite what a conflict-driven media would often have us believe, race relations are getting demonstrably *better* in this country, not worse. According to a 2016 Pew Research survey, 59% of blacks say that their race has *not* had a detrimental effect in their overall success.[382] Likewise, when it comes to blacks' views of the disparity with whites in jobs, income, and housing, the percentage of blacks who see the

---

[382] http://www.pewsocialtrends.org/2016/06/27/on-views-of-race-and-inequality-blacks-and-whites-are-worlds-apart/

disparity as due to discrimination has *fallen* from 44% in 1993 to 37% in 2013. Sixty percent of blacks viewed material disparity with whites as being attributable to factors *other than* discrimination in 2013.[383]

* * *

The Biblical View of Responsibility and Privilege

It's almost impossible to quickly summarize *the* biblical view of anything, but let's try to quickly summarize some key points underlying this subject before addressing the issues of reparations and affirmative action.

First, we must acknowledge God's ownership of everything in creation. "The earth is the Lord's and the fullness thereof, the world and those who dwell therein, for he has founded it upon the seas and established it upon the rivers" (Ps. 24:1-2). God is the rightful and ultimate owner of everything because He created it all.

And yet, there is a subordinate sense in which humans can claim ownership over pieces of creation, otherwise commandments such as "You shall not steal" (Exod. 20:15) and "You shall not covet your neighbor's house" (Exod. 20:17) would not make sense. Without such a concept as private property, what would make "stealing" a bad thing, or even meaningful at all? Quite simply, it wouldn't. Neither would there be anything wrong with coveting your neighbor's house because, without property rights, there is no way to explain why it rightfully belongs to him rather than you. Hence Peter asks Ananias and Sapphira after lying about the proceeds of the sale of their land, "While it remained unsold, *did it not remain your own*? And after it was sold, *was it not at your disposal?*" (Acts

---

[383] https://news.gallup.com/poll/163580/fewer-blacks-bias-jobs-income-housing.aspx?g_source=link_NEWSV9&g_medium=tile_4&g_campaign=item_163697&g_content=Fewer%2520Blacks%2520in%2520U.S.%2520See%2520Bias%2520in%2520Jobs%2c%2520Income%2c%2520and%2520Housing

5:4). Likewise, aren't property rights assumed by Jesus in the parable of the laborers in the vineyard who are paid equally by the master despite unequal work when the master asks, "Am I not allowed to do what I choose with what belongs to me?" (Matt. 20:15)?

But human ownership of property is not absolute and unconditional. In the Garden of Eden, God commanded humans to "fill the earth and subdue it and have dominion over the fish of the sea and over the birds of the heavens and over every living thing that moves on the earth" (Gen. 1:28). God also gave humans "every plant yielding seed that is on the face of all the earth, and every tree with seed in its fruit" (v. 29). We possess various pieces of this creation not for the sake of our own pleasure but for the sake of exercising godly, productive stewardship of it. Those who possess ownership of a larger share of creation possess a proportionately greater responsibility of stewardship. "Everyone to whom much was given, of him much will be required, and from him to whom they entrusted much, they will demand the more" (Lk. 12:48).

In our dealings and our laws, we should not be biased toward those with a relatively smaller or larger share of responsibility (ownership) over creation. "You must not pervert justice; you must not show partiality to the poor or favoritism to the rich; you are to judge your neighbor fairly" (Lev. 19:15). Notice that justice, as it is used in Scripture, refers only to fairness and lack of prejudice in the legal sphere. Unfairness and prejudice, either for or against the poor and disadvantaged, are a perversion of justice. "You shall not pervert the justice due to your poor in his lawsuit" (Exod. 23:6), but "nor shall you be partial to a poor man in his lawsuit" (Exod. 23:3). This principle of fairness applies also to foreigners and those outside the people of God—they deserve a fair hearing and judgement (Exod. 23:9, Deut. 1:16). Rather than lavishing attention and praise on the wealthy, God's people should not discriminate or give in to self-serving thoughts (Jam. 2:3-4). Nor would it be just to judge based on "outward appearances" such as skin color or socioeconomic class (John 7:24). Hence we find that, in God's people, racial distinctions such as that between Jew and Greek simply are not meaningful (Gal. 3:28).

And yet, even though we aren't to show partiality to the poor in our dealings or laws, God clearly has a special compassion for the poor and disadvantaged, and God's people ought to have the same attitude. "Whoever oppresses a poor man insults his Maker, but he who is generous to the needy honors him" (Prov. 14:31). Moreover, while it might be easy to ignore the plight of the poor and disadvantaged, God's people ought to be proactive in protecting their dignity. As King Lemuel's mother instructed him in Proverbs 31:8-9:

> Open your mouth for the mute,
> for the rights of all who are destitute.
> Open your mouth, judge righteously,
> defend the rights of the poor and needy.

Those who lack the power or ability to defend their own wellbeing still possess the innate value of being made in God's image, and God's people ought to promote their fair treatment and prevent others from taking advantage of them. We should speak for the vulnerable when no one else will. This includes the unborn, but it also includes the disadvantaged in society. For King Lemuel, a governing authority, fairness toward the poor and disadvantaged merely meant ensuring unbiased treatment and lack of exploitation. For God's people in the new covenant, however, the higher standard of Paul's Principle of Fairness also applies: Those who have the ability to provide for the material needs of others have the responsibility to do so. We must wonder, then, "if anyone has the world's goods and sees his brother in need, yet closes his heart against him, how does God's love abide in him?" (1 John 3:17).

Impartiality toward rich and poor also means that the rich or advantaged should not be judged by a different standard than those who are not. Wealth obtained by "unjust gain" is wrong regardless of one's income level (Prov. 1:19). "Better is a little with righteousness than great revenues with injustice," says Proverbs 16:8. Indeed, "Whoever oppresses the poor to increase his own wealth, or gives to the rich, will only come to poverty" (Prov. 22:16). However, wealth gained through hard work, faithful stewardship, and wisdom are a blessing (Prov. 8:12, 18, 20-21; 10:4; 14:24; 15:6). Some measure of inequality, then, is natural, as people have differing work ethics, skills, and abilities. And some are simply more fortunate than others.

Recall that whatever our level of wealth, we are called to steward it wisely and faithfully. Those with greater wealth have greater responsibility. Nowhere does Scripture indicate that unequal wealth or responsibilities are bad. But responsibility not properly stewarded is bad, because that is when responsibility becomes privilege. We may define "privilege" as a special right or advantage available only to a certain group of people that is used for the selfish gain of that group. It is to the privileged Jesus says in Luke 6:24: "But woe to you who are rich, for you have already received your comfort." The privileged are those who, rather than use their worldly advantages for the benefit of others, choose to relish in them selfishly.

The parable of the rich man and Lazarus illustrates this perfectly: "There was a rich man who was clothed in purple and fine linen and who feasted sumptuously every day. And at his gate was laid a poor man named Lazarus, covered with sores, who desired to be fed with what fell from the rich man's table" (Lk 16:19-21). The rich man passed by poor Lazarus every day but did nothing to help him, and when the rich man died, he found himself in a state of constant torment. He cried out for relief, but to this kind of person Jesus says, "you have already received your comfort." During his life, the rich man felt a sense of privilege and entitlement rather than responsibility. He confused his subordinate ownership of worldly wealth with the ultimate ownership that only God possesses. Being "conceited" and putting one's "hope in the uncertainty of wealth" conveys the attitude of privilege, but "to be generous and ready to share" conveys the attitude of responsibility (1 Tim 6:17-19).

The same distinction could be applied to racial issues. Majority races, cultures, and socioeconomic classes can and should be welcoming of minorities. It is not necessarily true that an attitude of superiority will pervade every member of the majority race. Many members of majority races strongly object to such an attitude, which is why some of the most impassioned debates about racial issues are carried out between members of the majority race. Similarly, though black activists played a significant role in the abolitionist movement, the debate over the abolition of slavery was mostly carried out between whites. While some bore an attitude of white privilege (and some still do), many others (such as William Wilberforce) realized that being in the majority race constituted a responsibility that should not be abused.

A "white normative standard" is indeed created and imposed by white supremacists, both hard and soft. But not every white person is either a hard or soft white supremacist. In today's America, most are neither. In fact, there are probably more white Americans who despise white supremacy—like Wytsma—than who could accurately be labeled as any form of white supremacist. Thus, the "white normative standard" which presumes whiteness and things associated with whiteness to be normal and all else abnormal is exaggerated.

That is not to say racism does not exist. Racism is a form of tribalism, a survival mechanism that humans developed in a Fallen, sinful world. It is a natural tendency in people of every race and ethnicity. Only through faith in Christ can we, like the Galatians, begin to undo the sinful effects of the Fall and see each other as equal children of God (Gal. 3:26-28).

* * *

Affirmative Action and Reparations

To be fair, Wytsma devotes only a small section of his book to a discussion of reparations and affirmative action. Nevertheless, he raises an interesting biblical example to argue for these policies.

Obviously, African Americans and other racial groups in America were severely mistreated in our history. In that sense, they are something like the Israelites after their enslavement in Egypt. Wytsma writes: "Exodus 12:35-36 tells us that the Israelites, upon leaving their Egyptian slavery, 'asked the Egyptians for jewelry of silver and gold, and for clothing, and the Lord had given the people favor in the sight of the Egyptians, so that they let them have what they asked. And so they plundered the Egyptians.'"[384] This is how the Israelites received the gold that would later be used to craft the golden calf. It's also akin to reparations, Wytsma implies, made by the Egyptians for the Israelites' enslavement.

There are problems, however, with the interpretation that this "plundering" of the Egyptians was akin to reparations payments. The first and most obvious problem is that this transfer of wealth from the Egyptians to the Israelites was not carried out through the channels of government and thus is not comparable to the sort of reparations policy that is being considered today. Second, the Egyptians did not offer these items out of a heartfelt desire to make amends for past wrongs but rather out of fear of Israel's God as well as an "urgent" desire "to send them out of the land in haste" (Exod. 12:33). More evidence of the lack of heartfelt sympathy for the Israelites is the fact that Pharaoh chased after them with his armies after they had left. The plundering, then, was probably more like a reluctant severance payment than reparations.

But let's assume that at least some of the Egyptians did feel a heartfelt sympathy for the Israelites and realized that they

---

[384] Wytsma, 179

had done Israel a great injustice. Even assuming that the Egyptians wanted to in some way make right the harm they had done, would this be equivalent to a reparations payment? Only in a very limited way. The difference between the case of the Egyptians and Israelites and white Americans (or Europeans) with African Americans today is that the recompense between Egyptians and Israelites was between the *actual* slavers and slaves. If reparations were enacted today between white Americans and African Americans, the recompense would be between the *possible descendants* of slavers and the *possible descendants* of slaves. Not every white American in today's world is a descendant of slave owners, and not every black American is a descendant of slaves. What if, for instance, a white person could directly trace their lineage to Abraham Lincoln or William Wilberforce? Similarly, what if a white person could trace their lineage to immigrants who came to America after the abolition of slavery from a country that never participated in the Trans-Atlantic slave trade? How would it be just for such a person to engage in (or be forced to engage in) reparations payments?

Let's assume that it was possible to determine with certainty which white Americans today are descendants of slavers. Would justice require those individuals to participate (voluntarily or otherwise) in reparations payments? From a Judeo-Christian perspective, the answer would still be no. Descendants of those who did heinous acts should not have to pay for the actions of anyone else, including their ancestors. "Fathers shall not be put to death because of their children," says Deuteronomy 24:16, "nor shall children be put to death because of their fathers. *Each one shall be put to death for his own sin.*" Morality and justice are judged on an *individual* basis. Every person is responsible for his or her own actions, not the actions of others. (See also Ezek 18:19-20, Jer. 31:29-34, and 2 Kings 14:6.)

What about the passages of Scripture which seem to indicate the opposite? Some verses explicitly state that God "visits the iniquity of the fathers on the children and the children's children, to the third and fourth generation" (Exod. 34:6-7, Deut. 5:8-10). If you read these passages carefully, however, you will notice that guilt for sin is still dependent on the sins of children and grandchildren. In Exodus 20:5, for instance, we find that God visits the "iniquity of the fathers on the children to the third and the fourth generation *of those who hate me*, but showing steadfast love to the thousands of those who love me and keep my commandments." Sins and sinful patterns in parents are not *destined* to be passed down and continued by their children, and therefore it would seem that children become guilty by *choosing* to participate in the same sins as their parents. As John Piper puts it, "The sins of the fathers are punished in the children *through becoming the sins of the children*."[385] God presents a choice to everyone, but at the same time it appears that there is some correlation between the choices we make and the choices made by our children: "Therefore choose life, *that you and your offspring may live*" (Deut. 30:19).

It is well-documented and intuitive that children take after their parents. Many habits and patterns of thinking are passed down from generation to generation, unless one makes a conscious effort to change this instinctive behavior. This is why God stresses the importance of passing down His laws and truths to one's children: "You shall teach [God's words] diligently to your children, and shall talk of them when you sit in your house, and when you walk by the way, and when you lie down, and when you rise" (Deut. 6:7). This is done so "that you may fear the Lord your God, you and your son and your son's son, by keeping all his statutes and commandments" (Deut. 6:2).

The principle of individual responsibility holds, then.

---

[385] Piper, John. "How God Visits Sins on the Third and Fourth Generation." (https://www.desiringgod.org/articles/how-god-visits-sins-on-the-third-and-fourth-generation)

Children should not be held accountable for the sins of their parents, and neither should descendants be held accountable for the sins of their ancestors. While voluntary reparations, in cases where the descendants of slave owners are able to find the descendants of their slaves, may be a meaningful and edifying act for both parties, any attempts at large-scale or structural reparations are sure to do more *injustice* than justice.

What about affirmative action? This is the policy of giving preferential treatment to minorities or members of historically disadvantaged groups in education, employment, or government appointments. Typically, the reasons given for implementing such policies are (1) to make the student body or employee base more representative of the general population and (2) to correct historic injustices against certain racial groups.

As for the first reason, we must point out that the degree to which affirmative action affects the outcome of student admission or job offers is the same degree to which meritocracy has been abandoned. When factors other than a person's abilities and skills are given weight in such decisions, merit can no longer be the primary deciding factor. And when merit is no longer the primary deciding factor, those who would otherwise be meritorious are excluded on the basis of race—a part of their identity they never chose. Such a process is inherently unfair and discriminatory toward those who are not in the favored groups. Thus, while those in favor of affirmative action may be motivated by the desire for equality of opportunity, the policy itself actually ensures the opposite.

Moreover, it's plausible that this unequal treatment of members of different racial groups engenders and perpetuates racial divisions and bitterness in society. It is only natural that those who do not get to enjoy an unfair advantage—whether that advantage is the result of affirmative action, nepotism, or any other form of partiality—will feel embittered toward those who do get to enjoy it.

If it is true that affirmative action is inherently unfair and discriminatory toward those who are not in the favored groups, then the second main reason for supporting the policy is also invalid because two wrongs do not make a right. Since there is a limited number of jobs to be filled and students to be admitted, increasing the number awarded to those in favored groups necessarily diminishes the number available to other groups. But it is impossible to correct a historic injustice by establishing an opposite injustice. Discrimination of the past cannot be corrected with reverse discrimination today. Justice is not served by forcing descendants to pay for the sins of their ancestors, nor is it served by paying recompense to the descendants of those who suffered oppression.

We all must accept the hard truth that we are responsible only for our own actions. We are not condemned to suffer the penalty due to our ancestors, nor are we entitled to the recompense due to our ancestors for any injustice they endured. We must be willing to acknowledge that, sadly, some innocent people have suffered great oppression, and some evil people have *inflicted* great oppression, without ever seeing proper justice carried out. We should take comfort, however, that everyone will stand before the Judgement Seat of God. Vengeance belongs to Him, and He *will* avenge those who never saw justice done in their lifetime.

* * *

Does Justice Require Equality?

What is the essence of justice? Despite its necessity for the operation of society, there is sharp disagreement about what constitutes justice.

Traditionally, justice has been closely tied with fairness — giving each person what is due to them and *refraining* from giving each person that which is *not* due to them. This traditional view assumes that every individual should be held to the same standards as everyone else. But then John Rawls' widely celebrated book, *A Theory of Justice*, proposed another layer to the meaning of justice. For Rawls, this traditional conception of justice does not cover the full range of the term. Rather, there is more to justice than impartial application of rules and standards, because "undeserved inequalities call for redress." And this redress aims to produce "genuine equality of opportunity." This is what Rawls calls "fair (as opposed to formal) equality of opportunity."[386] He seems to imply that true justice (fairness) requires ensuring that everyone has equal prospects for success in life. Undeserved inequalities, says Rawls, must be remedied for justice to be done. And the way to remedy undeserved inequalities is by counter-balancing their negative material effects with positive material benefits.

Many Christians—including Wytsma, it seems—are strongly influenced by Rawlsian thinking. Four of the five views represented in the book, *Christian Faith and Social Justice*[387], for instance, are either explicitly or implicitly shaped by Rawls' *Theory of Justice*. Contemporary academia in the Western world is likewise strongly influenced by Rawls. But does Scripture support his view that justice requires redistribution of material goods or unique treatment under the law so as to compensate for undeserved inequality?

To answer this question, it's insightful to look at the four vulnerable groups highlighted in the Bible as deserving of special attention: widows, orphans, the poor, and "sojourners"—a word which may refer to immigrants or to foreigners passing through a foreign land. Together, these four groups are sometimes called the "quartet of the vulnerable." They represent the neediest and most disadvantaged in society. Justice necessarily involves them, too, but in what way?

Deuteronomy 10:17-19 sheds light on this question:

---

[386] Cited in Sowell, *Quest for Cosmic Justice*, 12
[387] Ed. McCracken, Vic. *Christian Faith and Social Justice: Five Views* (Bloomsbury: New York, 2014)

> For the Lord your God. . . is not partial and takes no bribe. He executes justice for the fatherless and the widow, and loves the sojourner, giving him food and clothing. Love the sojourner, therefore, for you were sojourners in the land of Egypt.

Contrast this with the admonition in Leviticus 19:15 not to pervert justice by showing "partiality to the poor or favoritism to the rich." If it would be a perversion of justice to tilt the scales in favor of the poor, then what does it mean that God "executes justice for the fatherless and the widow"? And how does giving food and clothing to the sojourner not count as showing partiality?

The key point to notice in this verse is the subtle difference between justice and love. In verse 17, God is presented as just because He "is not partial and takes no bribe." Justice here falls into Rawls' category of "formal equality"—equal treatment under the law. The Israelites needed to remember the orphans, widows, the poor, and sojourners when judging cases concerning them because they were the most vulnerable and disadvantaged. They, along with the Levites, had no rightful claim to land in Hebrew society. Unlike most others in their culture, they had no ability to distort the judicial process, or defend themselves from distortion, because they were the most dependent on others. They were, therefore, the most easily oppressed and taken advantage of. God instructs Israel to prevent such a perversion of justice from happening.

Notice the shift in verbs when the instruction changes to caring for the sojourner with material goods—from executing justice to loving. God "*loves* the sojourner, giving him food and clothing," and God's people are commanded to do the same.

Why is this important? Because justice and love are two different concepts. To be sure, they must be paired with each other and applied equally, but they are not one and the same. Wherever we look in Scripture, we find that *justice* refers to the application of laws equally and fairly without tilting the scales toward one side or the other. Take, for instance, Deuteronomy

16:19-20:

> You shall not pervert justice. You shall not show partiality, and you shall not accept a bribe, for a bribe blinds the eyes of the wise and subverts the cause of the righteous. Justice, and only justice, you shall follow, that you may live and inherit the land that the Lord your God is giving you.

Justice would be granting everyone, including and especially the vulnerable, impartiality under the law and guarding against oppression. Injustice would be to deny others these rights or to take them away. Other examples of justice and injustice can be found in Exodus 22:21; Deuteronomy 24:14-15, 17; Job 24:3-4; Psalm 35:10, 72:4; Proverbs 23:10; Isaiah 1:17; Jeremiah 7:6, 21:12, 22:3; Ezekiel 45:9; and Zechariah 7:10. Notice that no instance when justice is mentioned in Scripture does it refer to remedying undeserved inequalities through redistribution of material goods. Unlike Rawls, justice has no concern for material equality or equality of opportunity. The Bible *does*, however, stress love for one's neighbor just as strongly as justice.

Love for one's neighbor includes a special care and concern for the most vulnerable, as is evidenced by Deuteronomy 24:19-21:

> When you reap your harvest in your field and forget a sheaf in the field, you shall not go back to get it. It shall be for the sojourner, the fatherless, and the widow, that the Lord your God may bless you in all the work of your hands. When you beat your olive trees, you shall not go over them again. It shall be for the sojourner, the fatherless, and the widow. When you gather the grapes of your vineyard, you shall not strip it afterward. It shall be for the sojourner, the fatherless, and the widow.

This compassionate concern for the neediest in society is not motivated by a desire for equality of opportunity or to redress undeserved inequalities. Rather, it is motivated merely by a brotherly love that sees one's own humanity in the other. Compassion—"suffering-with"—should be the driving factor behind such a redistribution of material goods. It comes not from a desire to be just *despite* the posture of one's heart, but rather from a sympathetic urge to help others *originating* in one's heart. Hence the motivating logic presented in the very next verse: "You shall remember that you were a slave in the land of Egypt; therefore, I command you to do this" (v. 22). The Israelites were to care for the most vulnerable in society because *they* were once the most vulnerable in society.

Justice does not care about one's feelings or motivation, but love is driven by sympathetic feelings and heartfelt motivation. Justice should be dispassionate. Love should be impassioned.

Justice and love are not the same, but both are necessary in a good society. It isn't enough to pursue one or the other. They must be intertwined. Justice without love can only keep the world from deteriorating into a worse state. Love builds upon a foundation of justice to better the world. But love without justice can accomplish very little. Justice compounds the effectiveness of love.

This partnership of justice and love is on display in Isaiah 58:6-7, when God says to His people:

> Is this not the fast that I choose:
> to loose the bonds of wickedness,
> to undo the straps of the yoke,
> to let the oppressed go free,
> and to break every yoke?
> Is it not to share your bread with the hungry
> and bring the homeless poor into your house;
> when you see the naked, to cover him,
> and not to hide yourself from your own flesh?

The "fast" (a symbol of purity and righteousness) that God desires of His people is a balanced pursuit of justice and love. Justice requires fighting against the forces that oppress and enslave the vulnerable (v. 6), and love requires heartfelt generosity and hospitality toward them (v. 7). *Both* should be core values of God's people.

* * *

The Problem of Inequality and the Policy Solutions

In this chapter, we have examined both material and racial inequality and found in Scripture a distinction between the way inequality ought to be seen in the private and public realms. Outside of government, we find no biblical condemnation of inequality *per se*, but poverty (especially undeserved poverty) is a great tragedy that must be remedied by and within God's people. In government laws and policies, however, everyone, including and especially the vulnerable, should be treated equally. For the church, advocacy of justice—equal application of rules and standards—should merge with a tangible, active love for everyone within our reach.

So should nothing be changed at the governmental level pertaining to inequality? Are there no problems associated with inequality that fall under the government's rightful purview? Not necessarily.

One major problem with inequality, as observed by researchers and academics in a variety of fields, is that it tends to give rise to populism—political movements that, in their view, divide "the people" on one side and the corrupt elites or outsiders on the other. Sometimes "the people" are a certain ethnicity or the native-born population as opposed to foreigners, and sometimes they are the workers and wage-earners as opposed to rich capitalists. As Martin Wolf explains in the *Financial Times*, populist leaders and political parties tend to gain popularity most strongly in countries that have experienced the most long-term economic changes such as "loss of manufacturing jobs, the globalization of supply chains, immigration. . . unemployment and [falling] labor force participation."[388] All of these factors depress wages for the lower half of the income spectrum even as the wealth of the upper echelons continues to rise with increased productivity and economic output (not to mention central bank interventions). This is why the wealthy capture far more of the gains in total wealth than the non-wealthy. Such a situation breeds in those who do not benefit a sense of distrust toward those who do. This distrust builds over time until divisive populist leaders arise who promise "the people" that they will fight on the people's behalf—and *only* their behalf.[389]

Herein lies the problem with populism. All populist movements form blanket groups of villains—immigrants, capitalists, certain races, or a certain gender—that must be uniformly suppressed in order to restore the rights of "the people" and correct perceived injustices that they have suffered. Dividing citizens into the virtuous and the corrupt may be cloaked in language of justice and fairness, but in reality it is an attempt to justify the restriction of the rights of some in favor of others. Take, as the most obvious and extreme example, Adolf Hitler, who rose to power by promising to rid "the people"—Aryan Germans—from the corrupt villains of society—Jews and other ethnic minorities. (In fact, the 1910s-1930s were a period of widespread populism in both Western Europe and America, and interest rates were quite low, dropping to zero after the market crash in 1929.)

But also look at a less obvious example like Malcolm X, the African American leader of the 1950s and 60s who advocated black supremacy and segregation and thus rejected the civil rights movement because of its emphasis on racial integration. In Malcolm X's worldview, white Americans were uniformly the villains, while his fellow black Americans were uniformly the virtuous "people." On the other end of the spectrum, the

---

[388] Wolf, Martin. "The economic origins of the populist surge." (https://www.ft.com/content/5557f806-5a75-11e7-9bc8-8055f264aa8b)
[389] See also Pastor, Lubos and Veronesi, Pietro. "Inequality Aversion, Populism, and the Backlash Against Globalism." (https://www.nber.org/papers/w24900)

equally indefensible Ku Klux Klan peddled white supremacy and painted African Americans as the villains.

Take, as a last example, the view expressed by some radical feminists that men (not just *some* men but men in general) are the reason that there is not material equality between the sexes. Hence Suzanna Danuta Walters writes:

> So men, if you really are with us and would like us to not hate you for all the millennia of woe you have produced and benefited from, start with this: Lean out so we can actually just stand up without being beaten down. Pledge to vote for feminist women only. Don't run for office. Don't be in charge of anything. Step away from the power. We got this. And please know that your crocodile tears won't be wiped away by us anymore. We have every right to hate you. You have done us wrong.[390]

In Walters' worldview, men are uniformly the corrupt villains who have rigged the system in their favor for millennia, and women are the uniformly virtuous "people" who must suppress the villainous men in order to achieve justice and equality.

In short, the problem with populism is its insistence on treating people not primarily as individuals but as members of a certain group. We know from Scripture that we are all responsible only for our own actions, not the actions of others, even if they are similar to us in some way. Perhaps some members of our group—whether that group is familial, racial, socioeconomic, occupational, or gender-based—are indeed corrupt and villainous. But we should not be punished for the sins of others in our group. Nor are we entitled to recompense for any injustice or oppression suffered by other members of our group. Populism of all varieties undermines the equal

---

[390] Walters, Suzanna Danuta. "Why can't we hate men?"
(https://www.washingtonpost.com/opinions/why-cant-we-hate-men/2018/06/08/f1a3a8e0-6451-11e8-a69c-b944de66d9e7_story.html?utm_term=.4431f3de58c8)

application of rules and standards in order to remedy some perceived oppression. In this way, it forsakes justice for the sake of addressing the grievance of a certain group.

If all of this is true, then for the sake of justice, Christians ought to push back against populism. We can do that through speaking out against it, which is important, but it is clear that the driving force behind populism — material inequality — must also be addressed if we hope to stem the populist surge. We must seek ways to address inequality as justly and fairly as possible without falling into the same trap as the populists who deny justice to some groups in favor of others. How do we do this?

First and foremost, we must prevent the government from tilting the scales of justice toward the rich and powerful at the expense of the poor and vulnerable. Secondly, we must seek out political ways to promote equality of opportunity that are applicable to everyone but will disproportionately help the most vulnerable in society. The following are three proposals for how to prevent tilting the scales of justice in favor of the rich as well as three proposals for how to justly and fairly promote equality of opportunity.

First, we should support the appointment of a Chairman of the Federal Reserve who will not continue the monetary regime that has been in place since the 1980s. Such monetary policies have been a boon to owners of financial assets and real estate — mainly the rich — but has harmed savers and retirees — mainly the working and middle classes. The "trickle-down" effect of low interest rates and quantitative easing has not worked as its proponents theorized it would. Working and middle class wages have risen at a crawling pace since around 1980, while the income of the wealthy has skyrocketed in that same period of time.[391] This is largely due to central bank policies that have been supportive of Wall Street and real estate. A term was

---

[391] Mishel, Gould, & Bivens. "Wage Stagnation in Nine Charts." (https://www.epi.org/publication/charting-wage-stagnation/)

coined during the tenure of Fed Chairman Alan Greenspan for this support—the "Greenspan put."[392] Every time financial markets fell significantly, the Fed would lower interest rates in order to encourage fund flows back into financial assets, thus supporting prices despite market weakness. This same term later became applied to Greenspan's successors, Ben Bernanke,[393] Janet Yellen,[394] and Jerome Powell.[395]

The role of a central bank should be to ensure stable currency value, to keep ultra-short term interest rates (which they control) in a historically normal range corresponding to market-determined rates, and to act as a clearing house for commercial banks. These three activities do not disproportionately benefit anyone at the expense of anyone else.

Second, we should support a law making federal-, state-, and city-provided subsidies, tax breaks, and bailouts for specific corporations—what's sometimes called "corporate welfare"—illegal. One example of such subsidies are those given (and others offered) by city governments to Amazon.com during their search for a second headquarters site. The two winning cities—Queens, New York, and Crystal City, Virginia—offered a combined $2 billion in public funds in order to ink a deal with the online retailer.[396] Such deals are made with corporations regularly. The argument of city officials in favor of these deals is that they will produce new jobs and will pay for themselves in the long run through

---

[392] "Greenspan Put." (https://www.investopedia.com/terms/g/greenspanput.asp)

[393] "Bernanke put." (https://moneyweek.com/glossary/bernanke-put/)

[394] Stone, Amey. "The 'Yellen Put' is for Bonds This Time." (https://www.barrons.com/articles/the-yellen-put-is-for-bonds-this-time 1429663683)

[395] Kawa, Luke. "Don't Count on the Fed to Save Stocks Again." (https://www.bloomberg.com/news/articles/2018-11-28/the-powell-put-saving-stocks-is-exercised-and-may-be-exhausted)

[396] Devereaux, James. "The Amazon Deal Shows Why We Must End Corporate Welfare." (https://fee.org/articles/the-amazon-deal-shows-why-we-must-end-corporate-welfare/)

increased economic activity in the city. The problem with this reasoning is that, as in most bidding wars, cities typically need to overpay in order to secure the deal. And because they overpay, they tend to justify the subsidies or tax breaks by overestimating the future benefits that will accrue to the city.

What's more, the corporation can always leave that city if offered a better deal by another city in the future, as was the case with the formerly St. Louis Rams. "As the St. Louis Rams became the Los Angeles Rams, a reasonable relocation for the franchise, they left their former city with $144 million in debt—a debt St. Louis owed in order to have an NFL team that is now halfway across the country," writes James Devereaux. Many cities bid high amounts for their sports teams. Thus, "[t]his NFL addiction has moved millions into the hands of the wealthy at the expense of local communities."[397]

This is not a small amount of money in question. A *New York Times* investigation estimated that state and local governments provide more than $80 billion *per year* in these subsidies and tax breaks. The percentage of potential tax revenue forgone by some states in order to retain corporations is staggering. "Oklahoma and West Virginia give up amounts equal to about one-third of their budgets," according to the Times study.[398] What return have these cities and states realized on their investment? In many cases, the answer is zero, or less than zero. The people of Ypsilanti Township, Michigan certainly did not see the return they expected when, in 2009, just two years after securing $200 million in taxpayer-funded incentives, General Motors closed down its plant in the city, along with plants in some fifty other cities that had offered similar incentives.[399] As of the time of this writing, Michigan, Ohio, and Maryland will likely see negative returns on their

---

[397] Ibid.

[398] Story, Louise. "As Companies Seek Tax Deals, Governments Pay High Price." (https://www.nytimes.com/2012/12/02/us/how-local-taxpayers-bankroll-corporations.html?_r=0)

[399] Ibid.

investment in GM as the auto manufacturer recently announced plans to close factories in each state in 2019.[400]

Even businesses that need to be in certain cities in order to sell their product, such as retailers and hotels, negotiate with local officials for subsidies. For Oliver Stone's 2010 film *Wall Street*, which obviously needed to do at least some shooting in New York City, Stone still secured $10 million in tax credits from the city.[401]

And none of these subsidies and tax breaks include the $100 billion in *federal* incentives awarded to corporations annually, leading companies to invest more time and money into lobbying efforts rather than jobs, capital expenditures, or product development.[402] Nor does it include the trillions of dollars spent by the federal government and Federal Reserve to bail out troubled banks and corporations during the financial crisis.[403]

These taxpayer-funded incentives to private companies exacerbate inequality by effectively transferring money from taxpayers to the owners of these companies. While competition between cities is a good thing in itself, spending tens of billions each year to poach companies from other American cities does little to help the average worker and much more to enrich the already wealthy, like Amazon's CEO, Jeff Bezos (currently the richest person in the world). Even if some cities do benefit (and that's a big "if"), the country as a whole suffers. This is an example, then, of the law showing partiality toward the rich. Therefore, Christians should support a law banning

---

[400] Bomey, Nathan. "GM poised to close plants in Michigan, Ohio, Maryland, will cut 15% of salaried workers."
(https://www.usatoday.com/story/money/cars/2018/11/26/gm-general-motors-plant-closures-job-cuts/2113275002/)
[401] Story, "Companies Seek Tax Deals."
[402] DeHaven, Ted. "Corporate Welfare in the Federal Budget."
(https://www.cato.org/publications/policy-analysis/corporate-welfare-federal-budget)
[403] See *The Atlantic Monthly*'s infographic
(http://cdn.theatlantic.com/static/coma/images/issues/200905/fed-map.gif)

governments at any level (city, state, or federal) from providing corporate welfare. Local governments can and should make their areas attractive to job-creating businesses through other means, but incentives to specific companies should not be allowed.

The third idea for how Christians can encourage state fairness toward rich and poor alike may be a bit more controversial, but it is really just a logical extension of the previous idea. *Christians should support a progressive tax on contributions to political campaigns, political action committees (PACs), and lobbying firms.* One might think that if corporate welfare was banned, there would be no need for a tax on political contributions and lobbying. One statistic should serve to disprove this reasoning: Over *seven thousand* lobbyists had a hand in crafting the Tax Cuts and Jobs Act of 2017. "Thirty-five separate industries dispatched at least 150 lobbyists each. Three industries—pharmaceuticals, insurance, and electronics—deployed more than 500 lobbyists each."[404] Lobbyists working on tax issues donated $9.7 million to members of Congress in just the first nine months of 2017.[405] That does not count other individuals, companies, or organizations that donated to politicians working on the tax legislation. Why would so much money and effort be spent trying to influence politicians toward a certain end if the donors did not expect to gain something from it?

Just how large of a return a financially capable group can expect from lobbying is difficult to quantify, but some scholars have tried. Karam Kang examines lobbying by the energy sector and concludes that returns from such lobbying expenditures average around 130%.[406] Economist Luigi

---

[404] Lincoln, Taylor. "Final Tally: More Than 7,000 Lobbyists Worked on Taxes in 2017." (https://citizenvox.org/2018/01/30/swamped-tax-revised/)

[405] West, Geoff. "Tax lobbyists donated millions to members of Congress." (https://www.opensecrets.org/news/2017/12/tax-lobbyists-contributions/)

[406] Kang, Karam. "Policy Influence and Private Returns Lobbying in the Energy Sector." (https://academic.oup.com/restud/article/83/1/269/2461194)

Zingales refers to the Troubled Asset Relief Program (TARP) as another example of the influence of lobbying, citing a study that controlled for ideology and "found that congressmen who received the greatest political contributions from the financial industry were the most likely to vote for TARP."[407]

This outsized influence often translates into longer, more complicated and byzantine legislation with myriad loopholes and carve-outs that benefit those with the most financial firepower. "The Glass-Steagall Act, which in 1933 separated investment banking from commercial banking, was just thirty-seven pages long," says Zingales. "The act that created the Federal Reserve in 1913 ran to thirty-one pages. Even the recent Sarbanes-Oxley Act, which was written in response to the Enron and WorldCom scandals, was only sixty-six pages long." What about the Dodd-Frank financial reform bill passed in 2010? It totaled a staggering 2,319 pages.[408] Who were the top donors to Barney Frank and Chris Dodd, the two men who spearheaded the legislation meant to regulate the financial industry and protect consumers? For Frank, the top two were FMR Corp (Fidelity Investments) and the American Bankers Association.[409] For Dodd, four of his top five contributors were in the financial services industry: Citigroup, Royal Bank of Scotland, JP Morgan Chase, and Hartford Financial Services.[410] Is it reasonable to believe that these donors expected nothing in return for their generous contributions or that they exerted no influence over the 2,319-page bill?

It is important to note that *political speech* is not the problem. Direct influence over individual politicians or pieces of legislation *is* a problem, because it rewards those with the most financial wherewithal. Corporations, unions, and wealthy

---

[407] Zingales, Luigi. *A Capitalism for the People* (Basic: New York, 2012), 187
[408] Ibid. 203
[409] https://www.opensecrets.org/members-of-congress/summary?cid=N00000275&cycle=Career
[410] https://www.opensecrets.org/members-of-congress/summary?cid=N00000581&cycle=Career

individuals are not tilting the scales of justice by spending money to influence *voters*. The scales of justice are tilted when the governing authorities are incentivized to cater to powerful donors rather than showing impartiality toward rich and poor alike.

A good way to realign the interests of authorities toward a posture of fairness to all, then, would be to install a steeply progressive tax on political contributions directed at specific politicians, whether such contributions take the form of lobbying or endorsements from political action committees (PACs). This would not hinder political speech for educational or informational purposes. Lobbying to inform politicians of a grievance in need of redress does not require donations. Nor would an organization devoted to spreading awareness about, say, environmental protection need to donate to specific politicians in order to advance their cause. Informing voters is a good thing and should not be taxed. But influencing politicians and legislation through financial remuneration is deleterious to justice and should be taxed.[411]

Such a tax should be structured so that 100% of small donors' contributions are shielded from any taxation, but beyond a modest threshold in probably the low thousands of dollars, larger donations should be taxed at a progressively higher rate. For those donating millions of dollars per year to specific politicians or to influence specific pieces of legislation, the tax should be prohibitively high. It should be so high that after-tax returns from lobbying for specific legislation or bankrolling specific candidates are slim to none. When corporations, unions, or wealthy individuals are doing a cost-benefit analysis of how to promote their interests, it should be far more worthwhile to spend money on influencing *the voter* through public awareness and educational efforts rather than going directly to legislators.

Without such an overpowering influence from moneyed

---

[411] See Zingales, 188-189, 223

special interests, laws will be simpler, fairer, and more intuitive. This should lessen inequality.

As for increasing equality of opportunity, the first thing to realize is that inequality arises even in fair societies because of differences in pay for work. Different jobs have differing levels of pay, but in any career, the further up the job ladder one goes, the higher the pay. And the longer one works in an industry, the more likely it is that one will rise up the ladder. Of paramount importance, then, is ensuring that everyone is incentivized to endure through the tough first few years of the career ladder ascension.

There is already a program in place to accomplish this goal. It's called the Earned Income Tax Credit (EITC). It is a refundable tax credit awarded to very low-income childless individuals and couples and also to moderately low-income individuals and couples with children. The government essentially matches one's pay up to a certain amount with a tax credit, and any additional dollars earned results in a gradually smaller credit. This gradual phaseout avoids the "welfare trap" of other programs that results in a drop in total income after earning a certain amount through one's job. Unlike other government aid programs that disincentivize work, marriage, or participation in community, the EITC actually *incentivizes* work and eventual self-reliance.

One study found that workers do indeed respond to this incentive. But the response has been to bring more workers into the workforce even more so than spurring a greater number of hours worked.[412] That means that the primary benefit of the EITC has been to encourage workers to begin their ascent up the career — and thus, the income — ladder. Perhaps this is why 62% of economists surveyed by the American Economic Association in 2011 were in favor of expanding the EITC.[413]

---

[412] Eissa, Nada and Hoynes, Hilary. "Behavioral Responses to Taxes: Lessons from the EITC and Labor Supply." (https://www.nber.org/papers/w11729)

[413] Fuller, Dan and Geide-Stevenson, Doris. "Consensus Among Economists— An Update." (https://www.tandfonline.com/doi/abs/10.1080/00220485.2014.889963)

The first step Christians should support taking toward equality of opportunity, then, is to modestly expand the EITC. While, currently, childless individuals and couples only qualify for the EITC with an income of under around $15,000 and $20,000, respectively, the income cap should be lifted so that entry-level workers can enjoy a few raises or promotions before the EITC support phases out. For couples with children, the current income cap is between $38,000 and $52,000, depending on the number of children. This may perhaps need to be lifted as well, but not to the point of incentivizing couples to have children before they are ready or to have more children than they are prepared for. It should not be a subsidy for poor family planning.

A second way to support equality of opportunity would be to introduce modified Universal Savings Accounts (USAs). These are tax-advantaged accounts that function much like Roth Individual Retirement Accounts (IRAs), except there is no restriction on when money can be taken out. A person would contribute to their USA from after-tax income, but once the money is in the account, all interest and dividend income as well as capital gains are tax-free.

You might be wondering why such accounts are needed, and how they would disproportionately benefit those most in need of help with saving. First, it should be noted that USAs would do the most good for lower- and middle-income individuals and families if combined with historically normal interest rates. During the early 1980s, when interest rates were quite high, the bottom 90% of income earners saved ten percent of their income, but by the mid-2000s, when interest rates had dropped considerably, their savings rate had fallen to *negative* ten percent.[414] Ultra-low interest rates (along with a political push for homeownership) had driven the non-wealthy to take

---

[414] Thompson, Derek. "Why Don't Americans Save More Money?" (https://www.theatlantic.com/business/archive/2016/04/why-dont-americans-save-money/478929/)

on home mortgage debt rather than saving. Similar drops in the savings rate can be observed in Canada, Germany, and Japan since the early 1980s as their interest rates have steadily fallen, taking away almost any rewards for saving.[415]

This low savings rate is a problem because, as a Federal Reserve survey from 2018 shows, about 40% of American adults report that they would not be able to cover an unexpected $400 expense without having to sell something or borrow money.[416] Clearly, the non-wealthy need to save more. One reason that many lower- and middle-income individuals don't save more is because the only tax-advantaged vehicles available require stashing money for events that are a long way off, such as retirement or a child's education. These vehicles are too inflexible. That's where the USA comes in. It is designed to be flexible, so that money can be taken out for any reason and at any time.

That said, there is a strong criticism of Universal Savings Accounts—namely, that they would disproportionately benefit those with the most money to save and would ultimately lower tax revenue.[417] This is a fair criticism and should be taken into account. Thus, any USA legislation that might be enacted in the future should mitigate this flaw by capping the total tax-free annual income or capital gains to a modest amount—perhaps only a few thousand dollars. Anyone with more than a few thousand dollars of annual investment income or capital gains likely does not need any additional help from the government. And yet, everyone would have access to the tax savings of a USA up to a certain amount, so the scales of justice would not be tilted toward either rich or poor.

---

[415] Garner, C. Alan. "Should the Decline in the Personal Saving Rate be a Cause for Concern?" (https://www.kansascityfed.org/publicat/econrev/pdf/2q06garn.pdf)
[416] O'Brien, Sarah. "Fed survey shows 40% of adults still can't cover a $400 emergency expense." (https://www.cnbc.com/2018/05/22/fed-survey-40-percent-of-adults-cant-cover-400-emergency expense.html)
[417] Wamhoff, Steve. "So-Called 'Universal Savings Accounts 'in Tax Cuts 2.0 Are a Giveaway to the Most Affluent Taxpayers." (https://itep.org/so-called-universal-savings-accounts-in-tax-cuts-2-0-are-a-giveaway-to-the-most-affluent-taxpayers/)

Workers would still have access to the 401(k), Traditional and Roth IRAs, Health Savings Accounts (HSAs), and 529 College Savings plans, which are all designed for longer term holding periods. The value of a USA would be to specifically increase short- to intermediate-term savings, not to replace those other vehicles.[418] This has been the experience of Canada and the United Kingdom, who have both instituted their own versions of USAs.[419] And although the most recent push for USAs in America came from congressional Republicans during Donald Trump's presidency, the previous three presidents—Barack Obama,[420] George W. Bush,[421] and Bill Clinton[422]—all proposed unique forms of Universal Savings Accounts as well. Christians should support a bipartisan variant of the USA that will accomplish increased savings without becoming a boon to the rich at the expense of taxpayers.

The final promising method of justly and fairly increasing equality of opportunity would be to require all high schools to teach a personal finance class to juniors or seniors (preferably seniors). As author and speaker Steve Siebold points out, wealthy parents already teach their kids how to make and handle money.[423] Children of non-wealthy parents are the ones most in need of guidance with personal finances. Since children learn how to handle money from the example of their parents, the many children whose parents have poor financial management skills could use help learning basic skills of how to budget, save, invest, and handle debt and credit cards.

---

[418] See Edwards, Chris. "Universal Savings Accounts Can Fix 401(k) Leakage." (https://www.cato.org/blog/universal-savings-accounts-can-fix-401k-leakage)

[419] Bourne, Ryan and Edwards, Chris. "Tax Reform and Savings: Lessons from Canada and the United Kingdom." (https://object.cato.org/sites/cato.org/files/pubs/pdf/tbb-77-update-2.pdf)

[420] https://obamawhitehouse.archives.gov/the-press-office/remarks-president-barack-obama-address-joint-session-congress

[421] https://money.cnn.com/2003/02/03/retirement/bushplan/

[422] https://clintonwhitehouse4.archives.gov/WH/New/html/19990414-3020.html

[423] Elkins, Kathleen. "Rich people teach their kids to be rich." (https://www.businessinsider.com/rich-people-teach-their-kids-to-be-rich-2015-9)

According to a study by Discover, many millennials who ramped up their saving in 2017 say that learning how to set up a budget was the key to their boost in savings.[424]

There is evidence that, unlike precalculus or chemistry, the information imparted from a high school personal finance course is not forgotten after the class is over. One study found that high school seniors who had taken a personal finance course were more likely to save money (93% versus 84% for students who hadn't taken the class), make a budget (60% versus 46%), and even invest (32% versus 17%).[425] And yet, despite these benefits, only one-third of US states currently require a high school personal finance class, according to the Council of Economic Education. This is up from the mere one state that required it in 1998, but there have been no additions since 2016.[426]

Thus, Christians should encourage their state to require a personal finance course for high schoolers, if their state doesn't require one already, as a way to equalize financial opportunity.

* * *

In closing, it's useful to remember that nothing in Scripture *requires* equality of opportunity, as odd as that may sound to 21st century Westerners. The previous six ideas for how to ease inequality and promote equality of opportunity are motivated by the desire to help the poor and disadvantaged as well as to stem the rising tide of populism. Inequality per se is not condemned in Scripture as it simply implies a greater responsibility of wise stewardship for some than others.

---

[424] https://www.discover.com/online-banking/banking-topics/savings-survey/

[425] Farzan, Antonia. "High schools are finally beginning to require personal finance courses." (https://www.businessinsider.com/high-schools-teaching-personal-finance-2015-4)

[426] Thompson, Daniel. "2018 Survey of the States Reveals Slow to No Growth in K-12 Personal Finance and Economic Education." (https://www.councilforeconed.org/2018/02/08/2018-survey-states-reveals-slow-no-growth-k-12-personal-finance-economic-education/)

Rather, by pursuing a less materially unequal society and providing more opportunities for the average person to succeed, we believers are seeking the welfare of our earthly country.

However, as it concerns wealth, race, gender, or anything else, Christians must always remember that justice requires *equal treatment* of everyone and for each person to be judged *individually*. If our earthly country puts these principles into practice, we believe that our society will be fairer, more just, more prosperous, and to some degree, more materially equal.

* * *

"The rich and the poor meet together; the Lord is the Maker of them all."
Proverbs 22:2

CHAPTER THIRTEEN

Silent Issues

To say Scripture is silent on any particular issue that we in the 21st century find important is not to say that Christians should take no position on it or ignore it. Undoubtedly, a book completed nearly two thousand years ago and intended for audiences of its respective ages will be silent about any number of issues that significantly affect life in today's world. This is true even of God's Word.

How should Christians think of automation, robotics, artificial intelligence, and all of the various social and economic impacts these technological advancements cause?

If humans are the primary cause of a warming atmosphere and climate change, how should we deal with the effects? Should we act to slow or reverse this atmospheric change in order to minimize the harm done from its effects?

In an age when education is increasingly important for success in the job market, what responsibilities do parents and societies have to younger generations to adequately prepare them? What role should government play in education? Should Christian parents choose only religious private schools if it's financially feasible?

What about global trade and immigration? Should governments act in the best interest of only their own citizens and legal residents or of everyone who might benefit from immigration and cross-border trade?

What is the best way to provide the highest possible quality healthcare to the most people? How should governments deal with financially inefficient or insolvent public pension programs like Social Security?

Should Christians support the right to own various kinds of weapons and firearms?

Does the Bible require a certain way of organizing the various powers and decision-making of government?

In my view, the Bible is silent on each of these issues. Let's consider the last question above first.

What kind of organization of government power does the Bible command? The answer is *none*. Remember, the *ideal* system of government is a theocracy. It's the Kingdom of God. Though this system has only arrived in part for now, it will someday be the governing structure of all humanity. Believers are primarily citizens of this heavenly government and only secondarily citizens of our earthly countries. As such, the question of how best to organize the distribution of power in this earthly government is secondary.

Moreover, the Bible never gives any specific indication of the best kind of government structure. I agree with Wayne Grudem when he writes, "The Bible does not explicitly command or directly teach that governments should be chosen by a democratic process, and in fact there are no commands telling how God wants governments to be chosen."[427] He goes on to argue, however, that some basic concepts from Scripture, put together, lend support to some kind of democracy. First, all humans are made equally in the image of God. Second, democracy promotes accountability of rulers to the people, which feeds into Grudem's third point that governments exist to serve for the benefit of the people (i.e. "God's servant for your good" from Rom. 13:4). Fourth, some instances in Scripture indicate that governments operate best with the consent of the people. Grudem cites the examples of Moses and the decentralized judge system (i.e. the Jethro Principle), the judge Samuel (1 Sam. 7:5-6), and Saul when he had been

---

[427] Grudem, *Politics According to the Bible*, 105

anointed as king (e.g. 1 Sam. 10:24).

There are several points to make in response to this line of reasoning. For one, being equally made in the image of God does not necessarily mean that the Bible endorses a universal or nearly universal franchise. In the age in which Scripture was written, men (the heads of households) were the ones who had the ability to voice their opinion in the election of judges or other local rulers. Women and servants were excluded. It's a stretch to compare that system to the near-universal franchise system we have today.

Likewise, Grudem's assertion that governments exist to serve the benefit of the people is too open-ended. As I've shown previously, Romans 13 and other passages suggest governments exist to serve a *certain* good for the people — namely, to punish and prevent harmful wrongs committed by evildoers against the innocent. This does not necessarily require a democratic form of government, which is why Paul did not mention anything about this.

Lastly, it's true that decentralized forms of governance that reflect the will of the people such as the judge system are treated favorably in Scripture, but it's difficult to derive any specific applications to our modern, secular context. For instance, the judge system had no central or top-down government, so does that mean that the Bible is against centralized governments? The "men of Judah came" to anoint David as king over the house of Judah, but women and servants probably were not consulted. Does that mean the Bible advocates a limited franchise? If so, how should it be limited?

It is much safer simply to state the obvious: the Bible does not take a position on the best type of government. Obviously, consent of the governed is good, and tyrannical or corrupt rulership is bad. But neither of these necessarily require a democratic form of government.

There are many persuasive arguments in favor of democratic government, such as those laid out by Natan Sharanksy (who spent nine years in a Soviet prison) in his book,

The Case for Democracy: The Power of Freedom to Overcome Tyranny and Terror. But it is important to acknowledge that these are extra-biblical arguments.

If climate change is real and primarily caused by human activity, what should we do about it? Here again, unfortunately, we find no direction from Scripture.

The whole idea behind man-made climate change is that human industry and technological advancement has led to massively increased greenhouse gas emissions into the atmosphere, which has trapped more heat in the air and begun to alter the landscape of the planet. It has led, for instance, to eroding ice caps at the poles and will, according to some climatologists, lead to increased severity of hurricanes and droughts, raised sea levels, coastal flooding, decreased snowfalls, and intensified heatwaves. For now, climatologists say, the changes we've witnessed in the climate are barely distinguishable from the normal swings that occur over long periods of time. But if carbon emissions growth continues unabated, while deforestation for industrial or agricultural uses persists (thus diminishing the earth's ability to absorb the increased carbon dioxide), many scientists warn that the earth will continue to heat and cause a host of problems around the globe.

Obviously, this is not an issue that was addressed in Scripture, as it was only made possible by the industrial revolution.

Now, you will not find a detailed explanation of climate science in this book. There are many sources of information one may consult on this subject, but here I will stick to what Scripture has to say (or, in this case, *doesn't* have to say).

Some argue that climate change is a hoax, a conspiracy, or an unproven idea that some politicians have clung onto as a way to increase their power. Certainly, politicians such as Al Gore, Bernie Sanders, and Alexandria Ocasio Cortez seem to fit the bill for this latter assertion. Many of the most alarmist voices on the subject of climate change support plans such as the

Green New Deal, which would not only seek to shift all energy provision to renewable, emissions-free sources in a very rapid period of time but would also enact a host of government programs unrelated to climate change. It would be natural to conclude that the politicians most conspicuously concerned about climate change view the issue primarily as a means by which to advance their political agenda.

Then again, on the other hand, one could also conclude that those most unwilling to acknowledge the potential threat of climate change are disingenuous as well, wishing to protect fossil fuel industries or prevent the political agendas associated with the Green New Deal from materializing. There have been numerous instances of scientists arguing against the veracity of the climate change theory being found to have taken funding from oil companies or other self-interested groups.

For now, let's simply assume that the majority of climate scientists who believe that global warming *is* occurring and *is* being caused primarily by human activity are correct. What then?

As believers, we must remember that all of the earth and everything in it belongs to God. That is, God owns all of creation, and we humans are stewards of the physical world and its resources. We are instructed to rule over it and subdue it, which refers to cultivation and care rather than exploitation and depletion. Remember: "ruling over" and "subduing" the fish, birds, and land animals originally did not include using them for food at all, as humans were only given plant foods to eat in the Garden of Eden. Rather, the gift of creation to humanity involved both *privilege* and *responsibility*. Therefore, regardless of how governments regulate environmental issues, Christians should of our own accord proactively steward earthly resources, including animals, land, oceans, and the atmosphere, with care and fidelity to God's ideals. We should be concerned with protecting the environment and seeking out alternative products to those of companies that abuse or pollute the planet.

On the other hand, Scripture makes clear that God's love is greater for humans than it is for animals or the environment. We alone are made in His image and meant to relate to Him in a special way. Care for the environment should not become a higher priority for believers than care for human wellbeing.

What to do about climate change, then? How best do we steward God's earthly resources and protect God's earthly environment while also seeking first the wellbeing of His human creatures? What should Christians encourage the government to do in this regard?

There are four basic options for dealing with climate change, according to science journalist and author Ronald Bailey.[428] One is to implement a carbon tax and distribute the proceeds to all citizens and legal permanent residents equally. The carbon tax would raise the costs of fossil fuels, which would encourage private enterprises to invent cheaper and cleaner alternatives, while the distributions from this tax would offset the heightened energy costs for everyday people. Bailey notes that this option is preferred by many economists.

A second option is to subsidize research and development of new technologies that would reduce emissions and/or sap existing carbon from the atmosphere. Various governments have already been doing this with subsidies for solar panels, wind turbines, all-electric cars, smart grid technologies, etc., and it appears to be working. That is, there's evidence to suggest that it has promoted greater private investment in clean and renewable energy technology than would have occurred otherwise.

Another option is to regulate the use of fossil fuels out of existence by making them too expensive or onerous to produce. The Green New Deal plan is one idea of how to do this, simultaneously eliminating emissions-producing fuels and

---

[428] Bailey, Ronald. "What Climate Science Tells Us About Temperature Trends" (https://reason.com/2019/11/21/what-climate-science-tells-us-about-temperature-trends/)

employing a mass of new renewable energy sources in a top-down, centralized way. The downside to this option is the high cost associated with it, the need to substantially raise taxes, and the massive disruption that it would require.

The fourth option is simply to ignore climate change at the government level and focus instead on policies that would continue economic growth. Bailey says that computer models "combining climate and economic components calculate that endeavoring now to slow warming would cost about the same as later efforts to adapt to a somewhat hotter world." He also cites the non-profit Climate Analytics Group, which contends that even if all countries in the Paris Agreement on Climate Change fulfilled all of their stated obligations, the average atmospheric temperature would still rise by 3 degrees Celsius by 2100. In other words, even if we expend scarce resources and forego economic growth now in order to cut carbon emissions, the earth will *still* be warmer eighty years from now, according to climate scientists. If, however, we did *nothing* now to curb global warming, says Bailey, "the *worst-case* scenario is that global GDP in 2100 would be 8.2 percent lower than it would otherwise be" due to the negative effects of higher sea levels, harsher hurricanes and droughts, etc.

In other words, whether we choose to spend money curbing emissions now or mitigating the effects of climate change later, the result in terms of dollars spent would be roughly the same. Therefore, says this option, we should focus more on economic growth so that we will have greater resources and technological capacities to deal with anything that comes our way in the future rather than stunting our ability to increase total wealth today.

Which option should Christians encourage their respective governments to pursue? The Bible gives us no guidance here, so believers will need to look at the evidence and decide for themselves what would work best.

Should it be legal for private citizens to own firearms? What kind of regulations around firearm ownership should

there be? Here, again, we find no answer in Scripture. Put aside all pragmatic or utilitarian arguments for now, as well as all the data factoids associated with the gun debate that float around the Internet. Focus only on what Scripture says and doesn't say.

Christian gun rights advocates argue that it is right to use violence, including with weapons such as firearms, to defend ourselves and others from physical attacks when we are able to do so. And since it's morally permissible to practice self-defense with firearms, it should also be legal to do so. Wayne Grudem falls into this camp. He cites Luke 22:36-38 to support his view. The passage reads:

> He [Jesus] said to them, "But now let the one who has a moneybag take it, and likewise a knapsack. And let the one who has no sword sell his cloak and buy one. For I tell you that this Scripture must be fulfilled in me: 'And he was numbered with the transgressors. 'For what is written about me has its fulfillment." And they said, "Look, Lord, here are two swords." And he said to them, "It is enough."

Gun rights advocates view the meaning of this verse as obvious: Jesus was instructing his disciples to arm themselves with enough swords to use for self-defense in the case of being attacked by robbers or those plotting against him. "The fact that Jesus was going to be crucified meant an increasing danger of people attacking the disciples as well," says Grudem.[429]

But if Jesus meant the swords to be used for self-defense, especially considering the knowledge of his impending arrest, it is certainly odd that he so sharply rebuked Peter when the disciple actually used the sword in defense of Jesus. Later in the same chapter of Luke (and perhaps even the same day), one of the disciples asked, "Lord, shall we strike with the sword?" (v. 49). It is a clear harkening back to the discourse of verses 36-38. After striking the servant of the high priest, Jesus exclaimed "No more of this!" and healed the servant (v. 50-51). In John's

---

[429] Grudem, *Politics*, 202

account, Jesus says, "Put your sword into its sheath; shall I not drink the cup that the Father has given me?" (John 18:11). This would seem to imply that self-defense generally may be permissible, but that Peter should stand down in this instance in order to let Jesus's mission play out. Jesus, says Grudem, "did not want his disciples to attempt to stop his crucifixion or to try to start a military uprising against Rome."[430]

Jesus's divinely ordained mission on earth is one important reason why He halted Peter from fighting in the Garden of Gethsemane. But Matthew adds one more reason, recording Jesus saying, "Put your sword back into its place. *For all who take the sword will perish by the sword*" (Matt. 26:52). This principle reads like a proverb, generally true but not absolutely or universally true. And notice that Jesus applies it to Peter's action, which was done in Jesus's defense. In other words, Peter used violence in defense of an innocent person, and yet Jesus criticized not only the act itself but also the spirit or motivation of the act.

When Grudem quotes the passage from Luke 22 in which Jesus instructs his disciples to carry swords, he conveniently leaves out the verse immediately preceding it. Here is the whole section together:

> And he [Jesus] said to them, "When I sent you out with no moneybag or knapsack or sandals, did you lack anything?" They said, "Nothing." He said to them, "But now let the one who has a moneybag take it, and likewise a knapsack. And let the one who has no sword sell his cloak and buy one. For I tell you that this Scripture must be fulfilled in me: 'And he was numbered with the transgressors.' For what is written about me has its fulfillment." And they said, "Look, Lord, here are two swords." And he said to them, "It is enough."

Just prior to this passage, Jesus foretells Peter's denial,

---

[430] Ibid. 203

saying "I have prayed for you that your faith may not fail" (v. 32). And then we find Jesus reminding the disciples that he had sent them out previously with no material provisions, and yet they lacked nothing. The disciples had faith, and the Lord provided for their needs. Does it make sense to say that Jesus turns around and in his very next breath recommends the disciples go back to relying on these material goods (swords) rather than leaning on faith?

And take note of the Scripture that Jesus says must be fulfilled in him: "And he was numbered with the transgressors." How exactly does his disciples' material preparation or carrying weapons for self-defense fulfill this passage?

The cited verse is Isaiah 53:12, though Jesus could be making reference to the whole chapter of Isaiah 53 here. The verse reads, "Therefore, I will divide him a portion with the many, and he shall divide the spoil with the strong, because he poured out his soul to death and *was numbered with the transgressors*; yet he bore the sin of many, and *makes intercession for the transgressors*." This refers to Jesus's impending crucifixion, but notice two things. Being "numbered with the transgressors" means that Jesus would be considered a rebel, a heretic, and an outlaw by the authorities. But who are the transgressors that Jesus is numbered among? It may be tempting to say that this refers to Jesus's eating with tax collectors and prostitutes previously in his ministry, but it wouldn't make sense to insert that in the Luke 22 passage, because it doesn't fit the context. Jesus mentions being numbered with the transgressors *in reference to* his disciples' material provisions and possession of swords. In this instance, then, the transgression is a reliance on material provision and swords rather than faith in God.

Notice also that the cited verse from Isaiah prophesies that Jesus "makes intercession for the transgressors." Indeed, we find that in the section of Luke 22 immediately preceding this passage, Jesus makes intercession for Peter "that your faith may not fail."

This entire passage, then, should be read as an extension of the foretelling of Peter's denial. Though Jesus's words are primarily directed at Peter, they apply more broadly to all his disciples, who would soon abandon him after his arrest. When Jesus says, "Satan demanded to have *you*, that he might sift *you* like wheat" (v. 31), both uses of "you" here are plural. But in the next verse, the "you" becomes singular. Though Peter insists that his faith is strong, proclaiming his willingness to go with Jesus to prison and death (v. 33), Jesus knows that his disciples' faith is not strong enough to hold up when He will be arrested, tried, tortured, and crucified. He knows they will abandon him. Thus, when the disciples miss Jesus's point about the material provisions and swords (as they so often do), holding up two swords, Jesus simply replies, "Enough" or "That's enough!" It's the same phrase used in Mark 14:41 when Jesus finds his disciples sleeping just before his arrest, proclaiming "Enough! The hour has come. The Son of Man is betrayed into the hands of sinners." The phrase implies exasperation.

In Luke 22:38, Jesus is not saying that two swords will be enough for the disciples to defend themselves from what is about to come. Clearly not, since Jesus never intended the weapons to be used for that purpose. He is rebuking their lack of understanding, saying "Enough!" It's as if the disciples unexpectedly proved his point by producing the swords, demonstrating their misunderstanding. Jesus was calling on them to have faith while not fearing the things of this world, but the disciples took Jesus literally and did not apprehend the true meaning of his words. The disciples were the transgressors among whom Jesus would be numbered, because Jesus knew that they would rely (and already were relying) on material possessions, such as swords, for their safety rather than faith in God.

The passage from Luke 22 does not lend support for the permissibility of self-defense or of gun rights. But then, neither does it necessarily lend support for pacifism or gun control. To try to squeeze an application to secular, democratic governments out of this passage is to take it far beyond its context or intention.

Since Jesus often healed sick or disabled people, does that mean Christians ought to support government involvement in healthcare so as to extend care to everyone? There is a slapdash argument often thrown together in haste by advocates of single-payer healthcare that goes like this: Jesus healed everyone equally without concern for money, and therefore his followers should be in favor of a healthcare system that does the same thing.

Like many disingenuous arguments in the political sphere, this one does not bother to consult the gospels to understand the context of Jesus's healings or to find out if there was an intended application in them to the modern provision of healthcare. It simply assumes, based on one's prior preference for a certain healthcare system, that the same Jesus who performed many healing miracles would also support their preference.

What we find in the New Testament is that God wants believers to care for others' needs, including the need for healthcare. Sometimes this comes through miraculous healing. Other times it comes through the provision of medical care. But *all* the time, it should come from a spirit of joy and voluntarism. If the costs or requirements of healthcare provision are greater than what the church (along with other private non-profit or for-profit organizations) in any given country is able to give, then government can play a valuable role in filling in the gaps. Perhaps those gaps will be massive, with the church only able to play a small role. Or, perhaps, those gaps will be relatively small.

There is room for debate among Christians what size and scope of a role the government should play in the provision of healthcare. But believers have abandoned their responsibilities as Kingdom citizens if they wish to outsource their own tasks in the provision of material wellbeing wholly to government.

No one can love their neighbor as themselves through government. Nor can anyone showcase the fruits of the Spirit, practice generosity, or impart the blessings of the Kingdom of God via the public purse.

How exactly believers interpret and apply this truth is an open-ended question.

What kind of immigration policy should Christians support?

Immigration policy is another issue in which believers often seek out Scripture to support their already-held beliefs and preferences.

Conservatives who favor a more restrictionist policy often cite the instruction to abide by the law of the land in Romans 13. They say that if a country has laws against crossing borders illegally, then it is good for believers to support and enforce those laws, and it is wrong for undocumented immigrants to break those laws. The law should be respected, because it comes from an authority that God has ordained.

But, as I covered in a previous chapter, this is a specious argument that could be used to justify *any* law. God has not ordained *every specific government* and *every specific law* but rather *governments generally* or *government as a concept*. God has instituted governments to keep the peace, prevent as much intentional harm to others as possible, and enact His vengeance against evildoers. If Romans 13 can be used to justify the status quo of immigration policy, why could it not also be used to justify the status quo policy toward Jews in Nazi Germany during the Holocaust? One could respond that laws directly opposed to biblical standards should obviously not be obeyed, but that simply pushes the debate back to the morality of immigration policy. What kind of immigration policy is most in line with biblical ethics? Before answering that question, we cannot answer whether it is right or wrong to abide by any given immigration policy.

Wayne Grudem also argues that Romans 13's injunction on governments to seek the good of their people suggests an immigration policy that prioritizes a nation's citizens and legal residents over those who want to migrate. But that is a matter of extra-biblical debate, as some economists and policy experts argue that immigrants do more to benefit a country's native-born population than to harm it.

A more sophisticated argument sometimes offered by conservatives is best articulated by James K. Hoffmeier in his book *The Immigration Crisis: Immigrants, Aliens, and the Bible*. Grudem also cites Hoffmeier's fundamental argument in his *Politics According to the Bible*. In this view, the Hebrew word for "sojourner" refers to what basically amounted to immigrants who had gained legal permission to settle in a new land and assimilated to the native culture and norms, while "foreigner" referred to migrants living in a land without the consent of its native population and thus not enjoying the same benefits or privileges as "sojourners." The instruction to welcome rather than oppress the "stranger" or "sojourner" (as in Leviticus 19:33) only applies when the immigrant has obtained the legal permission from the governing authority to live in the land.

But there are serious problems with this view. For one, the Hebrew word *ger* which is translated as "stranger" or "sojourner" does not definitionally refer to immigration, per se, but rather to one who submits to basic Jewish law. It is a *religious* concept rather than a *political* one. A *ger toshav* (or "resident alien") was a gentile who accepted the authority of the Torah and may have even also gone on to full conversion to Judaism. Ruth is one example of a *giyoret* (female form of *ger*), although, interestingly, she is never *called* by that term in Scripture. In this context it is easy to understand why the Mosaic Law would instruct the Jews to have the same policy toward both the "native" and the "sojourner" who "would keep the Passover to the Lord" when it comes to the Passover celebration (Num. 9:14). In other words, if a God-fearing gentile wants to participate in the Passover, the native Jews must let them participate on an equal basis. Hence, "You and the sojourner shall be alike before the Lord" (Num. 15:15).

There is no implication embedded in the meaning of the term of one who crosses a defined national border and obtains official legal permission to live in the land. There are some legal implications, such as being treated equally by judges in disputes (Deut. 1:16), but none related to immigration in itself. Neither does the word *zar* for "foreigner" or *oved zar* for "foreign worker." Rather than being related to immigration per se, these terms referred to gentiles living in the land who did not abide by the Torah or submit themselves to God. The way Jews often distinguished between *zar* and *ger* was that the former would work on the Sabbath, while the latter observed the Sabbath. Another word, *nekhar*, literally means "alien" or "foreigner," but that term also does not refer to illegal immigrants. It's rather a general term for a gentile. The Bible refers to Ruth, for instance, as a *nekhar* rather than a *ger*.

One cannot import a word used to describe a particular type of person in an ancient context to today's political environment. We find no Mosaic law banning or restricting immigration, and no border controls were in place in Israel that would have made such a policy possible anyway. Modern border controls, passport regimes, and immigration restrictions as we know them today are only about 100-150 years old. In the ancient Near East, every tribe and nation had what basically amounted to open borders, not because they wanted that policy or because God commanded it, but rather by default and necessity.

On the other end of the spectrum, liberals or progressives who are in favor of a more open borders policy (whether they call it that or not) often cite the numerous passages in the Old Testament that instruct a posture of fairness and compassion toward non-natives as evidence that God wants believers to be in favor of unlimited immigration. "You shall not wrong a sojourner or oppress him," says Exodus 22:21, "for you were sojourners in the land of Egypt." Indeed, "Cursed be anyone who perverts the justice due to the sojourner," says Deuteronomy 27:19. And Job, defending his personal righteousness to the Lord, shows this in part by saying that "the sojourner has not lodged in the street; I have opened my doors to the traveler" (Job 31:32). (See also Exodus 23:9; Leviticus 19:33; Deuteronomy 10:19, 27:19 for more passages along the same lines.)

But these passages command *God's people*, both individually and communally, to show compassion, warmth, and love to immigrants living in their land. It is a moral, apolitical instruction meant to guide the covenant community in their relations with outsiders. It is *not* a political or legal injunction. It does not reflect a certain policy stance on immigration. It does not specify, for example, whether *anyone and everyone* should be allowed by the governing authorities to immigrate into a nation, or merely *some* should be allowed to do so. And if only *some* should be allowed in, how should the law determine who is and is not?

These questions are not answered in Scripture. Admittedly, it would be difficult for believers to show love and compassion to immigrants if their nation had completely closed borders and allowed no immigration at all. But the fact that believers ought to be personally welcoming and compassionate to immigrants does not imply any given policy on how many immigrants ought to be allowed in or how those limited ones ought to be chosen for legal entry.

What is unequivocal in Scripture, however, is that those who do immigrate, legally or illegally, should be treated with as much kindness and gentleness as possible. Any form of cruelty as a method of deterring illegal immigration is antithetical to the fruits of the Spirit that believers ought to display, and it should not be encouraged or condoned. We ought to remember, as the ancient Israelites were instructed, that we too are sojourners in our own way. The Israelites were sojourners and foreigners in Egypt, and believers in the modern age are sojourners in this world.

"For the whole law is fulfilled in this one word: 'You shall love your neighbor as yourself.'" - Galatians 5:14

CONCLUSION

Live As Free People

As I write this, the United States is politically polarized like never before. Major news networks and online media sources (including social media) cater their presentation to individual preferences, which has fueled an increasing divide between conservatives and liberals. The ability to consume only the news sources that reinforce one's already held beliefs has created more distance between both ends of the political spectrum and led to an increasing inability to understand the way the other side thinks.

Those with more mixed, nuanced, or centrist views are overlooked in favor of the partisans, who offer a starker contrast and thus a sharper conflict between the opposing poles. In this divided environment, it has been natural for many people, including Christians, to develop an attitude that politics is an existential fight for the soul and character of the nation, a struggle between good and evil. Disdain for one's opponents and their starkly contrasting vision has become as much of a reason for voting a certain way as ideological alignment with a candidate.

If Christians are not careful, political disdain can easily lead them to compromise their values and even many of their policy views in favor of victory. Voting *against* a certain candidate or political party can become a higher priority than one's own morality or the morality of the candidate who has won one's favor and trust. This is a dangerous road to travel. It signifies that believers have largely given in to the Third Temptation.

They have allowed themselves to be seduced by the lure of political power such that moral purity, adherence to principles, the ability to be self-critical, and even the advancement of the Kingdom of God become less important than attaining or maintaining power.

The American church itself is sharply divided, mostly along demographic lines. In the 2016 presidential election, according to Pew Research, white evangelicals voted overwhelmingly (81% to 16%) in favor of Republican Donald Trump. Meanwhile, white Catholics were split and Hispanic Catholics voted mostly (67% to 26%) in favor Democrat Hillary Clinton.[431] An October, 2018, Public Religion Research Institute (PRRI) study found that while 71% of white evangelicals viewed President Trump favorably, 75% of black Protestants viewed the president unfavorably.[432]

As political polarization has settled into the American psyche, the association of white evangelicals as a demographic group with conservative politics or the Republican Party has become strong, and this has resulted in some negative consequences. "Politics can drive whether you identify with a faith, how strongly you identify with that faith, and how religious you are," says Michele Margolis, political scientist and author of *From Politics to the Pews: How Partisanship and the Political Environment Shape Religious Identity*. "And some people on the left are falling away from religion because they see it as so wrapped up with Republican politics."[433]

During the latter half of the 1970s and 1980s, largely in

---

[431] Martinez, Jessica and Gregory A. Smith. *Pew Research*, "How the faithful voted: A preliminary 2016 analysis." (https://www.pewresearch.org/fact-tank/2016/11/09/how-the-faithful-voted-a-preliminary-2016-analysis/)

[432] Vandermaas-Peeler, Alex, et al. *Public Religion Research Institute*, "Partisanship Trumps Gender." (https://www.prri.org/research/abortion-reproductive-health-midterms-trump-kavanaugh/)

[433] Thomson-Deveaux, Amelia and Daniel Cox. *Five Thirty Eight*, "The Christian Right Is Helping Drive Liberals Away From Religion." (https://fivethirtyeight.com/features/the-christian-right-is-helping-drive-liberals-away-from-religion/)

response to the *Roe vs. Wade* Supreme Court decision in 1973, Bible-believing Christians coalesced around the Moral Majority in order to fight back against a rising tide of secularism. But this rising tide of secularism from the 1950s to the 1970s did not necessarily translate into a swell of irreligiousness among the American population. In the early 1990s, a mere 7% of Americans claimed no religious affiliation, compared to nearly one in four today. Only 10% of liberals claimed no religion in the early 1990s, but as of 2018 that number had quadrupled to 40%. And since 1990, the share of liberals who never attend any religious services has tripled. Though conservatives and moderates have seen some uptick in irreligiousness among their ranks, the rise among liberals has been far sharper. They are the primary reason that those claiming no religion (23.1%) now outnumber both evangelicals (22.5%) and Catholics (23%) as a share of the total population, according to the 2018 General Social Survey.

What changed in the 1990s? Surely, multiple factors were at play, but one important factor is that the Moral Majority movement gained influence in the political sphere. White evangelicals became more visible and vocal in conservative politics, shaping the platform and rhetoric of the Republican Party like never before. Often, it is assumed that as individuals change their religious beliefs, they then gravitate toward politics that fit with their newfound religious identity. But social scientists Michael Hout and Claude Fischer demonstrated in an extended study following respondents over time that nearly the opposite is true.[434] They found that, over time, people's political views tended not to change, but their religious affiliation *did* shift in response to the rise of the Religious Right. Namely, liberals began leaving religion in

---

[434] Michael Hout & Claude Fischer. "Explaining Why More Americans Have No Religious Preference: Political Backlash and Generational Succession, 1987–2012." (https://www.sociologicalscience.com/download/volume%201/october/SocSci_v1_423to447.pdf)

droves over their disagreement with Christian political conservatism.

Now, religious affiliation does not equate to salvation or active participation in the church. But Hout and Fischer's research has found that liberals are increasingly resistant to religion and less likely to return to it later in life because of its strong association with Republican politics.

It is somewhat reminiscent of the situation in Europe. One of the most difficult mission fields in the world is the European continent, which is characterized by a largely post-Christian culture completely uninterested in religion or faith. Sadly, this tight association in the American psyche between Bible-believing Christianity and conservative politics seems likely to lead to a Europeanization of the United States in which ever larger swathes of people jettison faith with no interest in or openness to returning.

Likewise, polling data reveals that older evangelicals in the United States tend to view the nation as being on the decline, while younger evangelicals tend to take a more optimistic view.[435] For instance, older Christians, who have experienced more of life in a country with laws shaped by Christian morality (such as prayer in schools and traditional heterosexual marriage) than younger Christians, are more likely to be attracted to political slogans like "Make America Great Again." But, as we covered in previous chapters, it should come as no surprise to Christians when following Christ and standing for Christian values seem countercultural. In a world of constant spiritual battle, in which the governments of the world are under the influence of Satan, we should assume that the various nations of the world will look very different than the Kingdom of God. We should expect every culture to gradually slide away from Christian values, and we should *not* expect government

---

[435] Daniel Cox. *Five Thirty Eight*, "Could Trump Drive Young White Evangelicals Away From The GOP?" (https://fivethirtyeight.com/features/could-trump-drive-young-white-evangelicals-away-from-the-gop/)

laws or policies, on their own, to promote Christian morality or values. These come from heartfelt faith and the indwelling of the Holy Spirit, not from fear of the government "sword."

The way to change our culture for the better is not to retake political power in order to use the levers of government to enforce our vision. Rather, it is to set an example by living out the Kingdom community that we want to someday characterize the entire world. The role that Christians can play in politics is primarily to clear the way for this vision of the Kingdom of God to grow and flourish—to prevent the governing authorities from crowding out the church in its task of distributing the communal and material abundance of the Kingdom. Of course, merely clearing the way does not necessarily mean the church *will* fulfill its role as the hands and feet of Christ in this regard. That part of the equation requires far more sacrificial love, big-heartedness, and generosity than merely voting a certain way.

Moreover, we should not look to the state to teach or enforce morality and virtue, as that is simply not the role God has designated it to play. It is the mantle of the church to act as that shining city on a hill, that salt and light, demonstrating godliness and the fruits of the Spirit. Indeed, it is futile to expect non-believers, whose hearts have not been changed by submission to Christ or the indwelling of the Spirit, to be positively changed by laws or regulations. It is one thing to expect integrity and high moral character in our leaders, but it is quite another to think that those same leaders will be able to instill morality or virtue in the citizenry through the imposition of man-made and -administered statutes.

The church has a big role to play in society. It is not enough merely to preach the gospel and evangelize. And, likewise, it is not enough merely to love one's neighbor and do good to others. Believers are to spread the Kingdom through both the salvation of souls *and* social betterment. They are two sides of the same coin. The "abundant life" Jesus refers to in John 10:10 is neither wholly spiritual nor wholly material. It involves both.

The temptation for many believers is to cheapen grace

merely to a personal, private relationship with God that doesn't necessarily impact the way we interact with society and the world. It lets believers off the hook of taking responsibility for the plight of others. It gives the sense that the *only* thing important to God is our souls. But that isn't true. That *can't* be true. In the idyllic Garden of Eden, the Bible records the first humans' interactions with God as embodied ones, and on the New Earth, we will live with God in resurrected and perfected bodies once again. God cares for His creatures and wants them to live the prosperous, joyful life that He designed from the beginning.

Grace may be a free gift, but it's a gift with profound consequences for our lives and the world. Many Christians view evangelism and "saving souls" as our primary — perhaps even sole — purpose on Earth. Fixing the world's social problems can only be done by God, many believers say. Ironically, these are often the same Christians who have historically argued for the necessity of government involvement in social issues like marriage, sexuality, and the use of intoxicants. But the message of the gospel is that we need a personal relationship with God *in order to* change the way we interact with society and the world. Salvation is not the end of the story but the beginning. Faith without works of love, charity, generosity, and hospitality is empty and meaningless.

The Kingdom of God, a subject Jesus spent so much time on but that so easily escapes the conversation among evangelicals, concerns so much more than personal salvation. It's about the way humans were always intended to live with one another in creation. It may not be experienced in full until Christ returns to set all things right in the world, but we can and *should* seek the Kingdom as much as is possible in the present age. When Jesus prayed, "Your kingdom come on earth as it is in heaven," it was as much a call for human action as it was a supplication for divine action.

Sometimes, in extraordinary and miraculous moments, God works in a direct and powerful way to bring about spiritual, material, psychological, emotional, or social abundance. But most of the time, God wants His people, led by the inspiration of the Spirit and the example of Christ, to perform the everyday tasks of caring for the poor, feeding the hungry, sheltering the homeless, befriending the friendless, soothing the grief-stricken, casting out demons, and preaching the gospel. In all cases, we are called to display the first fruits of His coming Kingdom.

In 1 Peter 2, Peter refers to believers as both "a chosen race, a royal priesthood, a holy nation" (v. 9) and as "sojourners and exiles" in this world (v. 11). God's people truly are set apart, not just spiritually but also politically. When Peter instructs believers to be subject to the governing authorities in verses 13-14, the reasons he gives for this are not to be good citizens or to curry favor with state leaders. Rather, he writes in verse 15, "this is the will of God, that by doing good you should put to silence the ignorance of foolish people." Believers are to set an example with our behavior, "so that when [non-believers] speak against you as evildoers, they may see your good deeds and glorify God on the day of visitation" (v. 12). This is the same basic reason why servants are to be subject to their masters (v. 18-19) and wives to their husbands (3:1-2), even if they are cruel and unjust. It is not a temporary strategy to make peace until power can be gained over them. Rather, it is a way of demonstrating Christ to them in hopes that they would repent and be led to a saving knowledge of the truth.

Similarly, believers are subject to government authorities not because these authorities are virtuous or chosen specifically by God, nor because we ourselves want to assume the power that they hold, but rather because we want all people to see our honorable behavior and Christlike love and be drawn to it. Society improves not when the sword of government changes hands from non-believers to believers, or from the elected representatives of non-believers to those preferred by believers. It changes when believers publicly, unabashedly, and earnestly put Christ on display. It changes when non-believers not only *hear* the good news of Jesus Christ but *see* and *experience* it manifested in the church.

Satan knows this and ceaselessly tempts us to take a different path. The way of the Kingdom of God is hard. It involves self-sacrifice. It involves a mindset of stewardship that views nothing as ultimately one's own but rather as belonging to God, to be used according to God's will. It sometimes involves powerlessness in the face of an evil and demonically influenced world. It involves not just decency but *excellence*. Christ, after all, instructed his followers to be perfect as their Heavenly Father is perfect.

Satan, the Tempter, offers an easier path. This path involves no suffering, no self-denial, no sacrifice, no love, no high standards of behavior. What if believers could make non-believers subject to God's standards through the levers of government? What if believers could avoid the difficult path of self-sacrifice, generosity, and hospitality by using the institutions and programs of government to distribute the material blessings of God's Kingdom? What if God's name was honored and exalted through the means and mechanisms of the state?

This, I submit, is the Third Temptation, the same one faced by Christ in the wilderness. For Jesus, it was the option to achieve seemingly the same end while escaping the painful fate of the cross. For us, it is the offer of political power as a shortcut, a slight detour, on the path to fulfilling our assigned tasks on earth. For both, it involves a compromise of principles, a divergence from the harder path laid out before us by God — a deal with the Devil.

We are called neither to be servants of government, nor to bring it under servitude to us. We are called to freedom — from slavery to sin, from servitude to any political party or worldly identity, from the psychological turmoil of political polarization and disdain, from the compulsion to win and maintain political power. We are called not to use our freedom as an opportunity to serve our fleshly desires, including for authority. Rather, we are called to lovingly "serve one another" (Gal. 5:13).

"Live as people who are free," writes Peter in 1 Peter 2:16, "not using your freedom as a cover-up for evil, but living as servants of God." We are ultimately free from the political hierarchies of this world because we are citizens of a Heavenly Kingdom. We are free from the toils and snares of earthly politics because we are servants of a Higher Power. We are free to both fear God *and* honor the governing authorities, because we know that all authority comes from God and will return to Him someday.

Best of all, we live as a free people because we know we are not required to singlehandedly bring about or impose God's Kingdom in this world. We are called merely to be faithful, to do God's will, and to be Christ's hands and feet. In this way, Jesus's yoke truly is easy and his burden is light, giving rest to the weary (see Matt. 11:28-30). Neither perfect adherence to a set of rules nor the foisting of such rules upon others is necessary. All that is required is heartfelt faithfulness to God's plan and principles.

That is the narrow path — the less appealing path — leading to abundant life. Much, much wider is the way leading to something that *looks* like the abundant life but is instead a mirage, giving way to division, disdain, and despair. The Third Temptation is the wide path that seems harmless, at first, but eventually leads to moral erosion and self-destruction. It is the choice to evade the God-given duty of loving sacrificially and setting a moral example, which, in the process, forfeits the abundant life God desires for all humanity.

The duty of Christ could not — and the role of the church *cannot* — be carried out through the channels of the state, and the responsibilities of the state cannot be carried out through the methods of the church. In this age, the cross and the sword are complementary, but they cannot both be borne simultaneously. When Christians try to bear both, each is tainted, and the beauty of the cross is hidden behind the ugliness of the sword. When outsiders look at believers, just as they looked upon Christ, we want them to see our blood on the cross rather than others' blood on our swords.

Christ resisted the Third Temptation. Will we?